The Ultimate
Ninja Foodi UK

Cookbook for Beginners

1500-Day Tasty, Quick & Foolproof Ninja Foodi Recipes

for Your Friends and Family

Joshua Read

Contents

Introduction

So far, Ninja Foodi Multi-Cooker haven't been used as much as they could be in integrated cooking systems that work well. They are usually made of thick aluminum or stainless steel, which makes them heavier and more expensive than regular pots. They could also be hard to make in a lot of developing countries. Prices are rarely less than 17 GBP, and high-end items can easily cost more than 167 GBP. In places where Ninja Foodi Multi-Cooker aren't used very often, their relatively high prices make it hard for them to spread. People use Ninja Foodi Multi-Cooker more in cities, where fuel has to be paid for in cash, and in rural areas, where they can quickly cook local food. This is especially true in Asia (China, Nepal, and India).

Markets all over the world sell different models of pressure cookers. To find the best model, you must consider price, size, the primary type of stove used (electric, gas, or fire), durability, and maintenance.

This cookbook is the best way to learn how to use a Ninja Foodi Multi-Cooker and cook with it. This cookbook will help you get the variety of tasty recipes and instructions on how to clean it after use. In short, you will find precise information along with you need to know about your Ninja Foodi Multi-Cooker in this book.

Important Safeguards

Before using your Ninja Foodi Multi-Cooker for the first time, it is important to read all instructions and safeguards. This will help you understand how to safely use and care for your Ninja Foodi Multi-Cooker. Some important things to keep in mind when using your Ninja Foodi Multi-Cooker:
• Always use the cooker on a level surface
• Do not place the cooker on or near a hot gas or electric burner, or in a heated oven.
• Do not place the cooker on a cold or wet surface.
• Use only the Multi-Cooker accessories that came with your cooker. Other accessories may not fit properly and could be dangerous.
• Do not touch the hot surfaces of the cooker, such as the lid or body, while in use. Use oven mitts or pot holders when handling hot parts of the cooker.
• Always make sure the pressure release valve is in the correct position before operating the cooker.
• Always check the gasket and valve for damage before using the Multi-Cooker.
• Make sure the Multi-Cooker is properly ventilated.
• Do not overfill the Multi-Cooker.
• Do not use the Multi-Cooker for canning.
• Use only recipes that are specifically designed for Multi-Cooker.
• Follow the manufacturer's instructions for operating the Multi-Cooker.
• Do not use the Multi-Cooker if it is damaged or leaking.
• Do not attempt to repair the Multi-Cooker yourself.
• Always release the pressure from the Multi-Cooker before opening it.
• Be careful when removing items from the Multi-Cooker.

Parts and Accessories

Parts: Ninja Foodi Multi-Cooker is a versatile appliance that can be used as a pressure cooker, slow cooker, rice cooker, steamer, and more. It features an 8-Quart Removable Cooking Pot, a Deluxe Reversible Rack , and a steamer basket. The Multi-Cooker also has a browning function to sear meat or vegetables before cooking.
Deluxe Reversible Rack: Place the bottom layer of the Deluxe Reversible Rack in the lower position. Place ingredients on the bottom layer of the rack. Then slide the Deluxe layer through the bottom layer's handles. Place remaining ingredients on the Deluxe layer to increase cooking capacity.
Cook & Crisp Basket: To remove diffuser for cleaning, pull 2 diffuser fins off the groove on the basket, then pull diffuser down firmly. To assemble the Cook & Crisp Basket, place basket on top of diffuser and press down firmly.

Using the Control Panel

If you're like most people, you probably don't spend a lot of time thinking about your Ninja Foodi Multi-Cooker. But if you're trying to get the most out of your Ninja Foodi Multi-Cooker, it's worth taking a few minutes to familiarize yourself with the control panel. The control panel is located on the top of the Ninja Foodi Multi-Cooker. It has a digital display that shows the current pressure, time, and temperature.
Cooking Functions: As one of the most popular kitchen appliances on the market, the Ninja Foodi Multi-Cooker has a variety of functions that make it a versatile cooking tool. Whether you're looking to make a quick and easy meal or something more complicated, the Ninja Foodi Multi-Cooker can help you get the job done.
One of the most popular functions of the Ninja Foodi Multi-Cooker is

need to call a professional. Here's a step-by-step guide to cleaning or removing a clog from your Ninja Foodi Multi-Cooker. with a little time and effort, you can clear the clog and get your cooker working like new again.
1. Start by unplugging your cooker from the wall outlet.
2. Remove the pot from the cooker base.
3. Inspect the pot for any food or debris that may be causing the clog.
4. Use a soft-bristled brush to gently scrub away any debris.
5. Rinse the pot with warm water.
6. Reattach the pot to the cooker base.
7. Plug the cooker back into the wall outlet.
8. Turn the cooker on to the "steam" setting.
9. Allow the cooker to run for several minutes to clear the clog.
10. If the clog persists, repeat steps 1-9.

Using Your Ninja Foodi Multi-Cooker

There are so many things that you can do with your Ninja Foodi Multi-Cooker function! Here are just a few ideas to get you started:
1. Use it to steam veggies – perfect for a healthy and quick side dish.
2. Use it to steam fish or seafood – cooked to perfection in minutes.
3. Use it to make perfect rice – no more burnt or overcooked rice for you!
4. Use it to steam dumplings – a delicious and easy way to make a homemade meal.
5. Use it to steam eggs – a healthy and protein-packed breakfast option.
So, there you have it – 5 great ideas for using your Ninja Foodi Multi-Cooker function. Now get cooking!

Water Test: Get Started Pressure Cooking

If you're like me, you're always looking for ways to save time in the kitchen. The Ninja Foodi Multi-Cooker is a great way to do just that. With its 6-in-1 cooking capabilities, you can pressure cook, slow cook, air fry, bake, roast, and dehydrate all in one appliance. Plus, it comes with a built-in water test feature that takes the guesswork out of cooking times. Here's how it works:
1. Fill the Ninja Foodi Multi-Cooker with the amount of water specified in the user manual.
2. Place the food to be cooked in the cooking pot.
3. Close the lid and select the desired cooking function.
4. The water test feature will automatically start the cooking process and stop when the food is cooked.
5. Enjoy your perfectly cooked meal!

Pressure Steam Release

When it comes to pressure cookers, the Ninja Foodi Multi-Cooker is one of the best on the market. It's perfect for large families or those who like to cook in bulk. One of the best features of the Ninja Foodi Multi-Cooker is the pressure steam release. This allows you to release the pressure in the cooker without having to open the lid. This is perfect for when you're cooking something like chicken or beef and you don't want the meat to dry out. The pressure steam release is also great for when you're cooking something like rice or pasta and you don't want the water to boil over.

its ability to cook food quickly. This is thanks to the pressure cooking function, which uses steam to cook food faster than traditional methods. Whether you're looking to make a quick and easy meal or something more complicated, the Ninja Foodi Multi-Cooker can help you get the job done.

Another popular function of the Ninja Foodi Multi-Cooker is its ability to keep food warm. This is thanks to the slow cook function, which slowly cooks food over some time. This is perfect for those times when you want to make sure your food is cooked all the way.

Operating Buttons: There are many operating buttons on the Ninja Foodi Multi-Cooker. These include the power button, the pressure release valve, the cooking timer, and the warm button. Each of these buttons has a different function that helps you to cook your food more efficiently.
• The power button is located on the top of the Ninja Foodi Multi-Cooker. This button turns the cooker on and off.
• The pressure release valve is located on the side of the Multi-Cooker. This valve is used to release the pressure from the pot.
• The cooking timer is located on the front of the Multi-Cooker. This timer can be set for the desired cook time.
• The warm button is located on the front of the Multi-Cooker. This button keeps the food warm after it has been cooked.

Before First Use

If you've never used a pressure cooker before, the Ninja Foodi Multi-Cooker is a great option. Here are some things to keep in mind before you use it for the first time.
• Read the manual. This seems like a no-brainer, but it's important to familiarize yourself with the appliance and how it works. That way, you'll know what to expect and can avoid any potential mishaps.
• Inspect the pot. Make sure there are no cracks or chips in the pot. Also, check that the gasket and pressure release valve are in good condition.
• Choose the right size. The Ninja Foodi Multi-Cooker comes in two sizes, 6 quarts, and 8 quarts. Choose the size that best suits your needs.
• Add the ingredients. Once you've chosen your recipe, add the ingredients to the pot. Be sure to not fill it more than two-thirds full.

Removing and Installing the Condensation Collector

If you have a Ninja Foodi Multi-Cooker, you may need to remove and install the condensate collector at some point. This is a simple process that only requires a few tools. Here's how to do it:
1. First, disconnect the power to the Ninja Foodi Multi-Cooker.
2. Next, remove the screws that hold the condensate collector in place.
3. Lift the condensate collector out of the cooker.
4. To install the new condensate collector, simply reverse the steps above.
5. Reconnect the power to the Ninja Foodi Multi-Cooker and you're done!

Removing and Installing the Anti-Clog

If your Ninja Foodi Multi-Cooker is starting to experience clogs, it's time to clean it out. Depending on the severity of the clog, you may be able to clean it out yourself. However, if the clog is severe, you'll

Pressurizing

Pressurizing in the Ninja Foodi Multi-Cooker is easy. Simply add your food and liquid to the pot, seal the lid, and select the pressure cooking setting. The Ninja Foodi Multi-Cooker will do the rest, building up pressure and cooking your food to perfection. One thing to keep in mind when pressure cooking is that the food will cook faster than usual, so be sure to adjust your cook time accordingly. For example, if a recipe normally takes 30 minutes to cook, it will only take 10-15 minutes in the Ninja Foodi Multi-Cooker. Another thing to keep in mind is that the Ninja Foodi Multi-Cooker will release pressure automatically once the cooking time is up. So if you're still in the kitchen, be sure to move away from the pot to avoid getting hit with a blast of hot steam.

Using the Pressure Function

Pressure cooking is a method of cooking food in an enclosed environment where the pressure is increased to create a higher boiling point. This allows the food to cook faster than it would use other methods. The Ninja Foodi Multi-Cooker is a great option for those who want to try pressure cooking. It is a 6-quart Multi-Cooker that can be used to cook a variety of food items. One of the great things about the Ninja Foodi Multi-Cooker is that it has a pressure function. This function allows you to increase the pressure inside the cooker to cook the food faster. To use the pressure function, simply turn the knob to the pressure setting and then wait for the pressure to build up. Once the pressure has built up, the food will cook faster. Ninja Foodi Multi-Cooker is a great option for those who want to try pressure cooking. It is a 6-quart Multi-Cooker that can be used to cook a variety of food items.

Using the Steam Crisp Function

When it comes to cooking, there is nothing quite like a pressure cooker. And when it comes to pressure cookers, there is nothing quite like the Ninja Foodi Multi-Cooker. This incredible appliance is perfect for those who want to cook quickly and easily, without having to worry about overcooking or undercooking their food. With the Ninja Foodi Multi-Cooker, you can cook just about anything. Whether you want to make a quick and easy meal or you want to slow-cook a delicious stew, this Ninja Foodi Multi-Cooker can do it all. And because it is so easy to use, you'll be able to get the perfect results every time. If you're looking for a quick and easy meal, the Ninja Foodi Multi-Cooker is perfect for you. With its steam function, you can cook food in just minutes. And because it is so easy to use, you'll be able to get the perfect results every time.

Steam and Crisp

The Steam function is great for cooking things like fish, veggies, and rice. It's also great for steaming dumplings and buns. Anything that you would normally steam, you can now cook in your Ninja Foodi Multi-Cooker.
Here's how it works:
1. Add water to the pot. The amount of water you need will depend on the size of your pot and what you're cooking.
2. Place your food in the pot.
3. Set the timer for the desired cooking time.
4. When the timer goes off, open the pot and enjoy your perfectly cooked food.

Steam and Bake

As many home cooks know, the Ninja Foodi Multi-Cooker can also be used as an air fryer, slow cooker, and more. One of the lesser-known functions of the Ninja Foodi Multi-Cooker is the steam and bake function. This function is perfect for cooking delicate foods like fish and vegetables. To use the steam and bake function, simply add water to the Ninja Foodi Multi-Cooker and place your food on the steam rack. Then, select the steam and bake function and set the timer for the desired cook time. The Ninja Foodi Multi-Cooker will steam your food until it is cooked through. This function is perfect for those who want to cook healthy meals but don't have a lot of time. The steam and bake function can be used to cook a variety of foods, so get creative and experiment with different recipes.

Using the Air Fry/Stovetop Functions

Air Fry

The air fry function on the Ninja Foodi Multi-Cooker is amazing! I've used it to make chicken, fish, and even French fries, and they all come out perfectly cooked and crispy. The best part is that there's no need to preheat the air fryer, so it's super quick and easy to use.

Here's how to use the air fry function on the Ninja Foodi Multi-Cooker:
1. Place the food you want to air fry into the basket.
2. Set the air fryer temperature to 400 degrees F.
3. Set the cooking for the desired amount of time.
4. Press the start button.
5. When the cooking time is up, the air fryer will automatically shut off.

Broil

If you're looking for a quick and easy way to cook dinner, the broil function on your Ninja Foodi Multi-Cooker is a great option. Here's how to use it:
1. Preheat the broil function by pressing the power button, then selecting the broil setting.
2. Place your food in the pot and close the lid.
3. Cook for the desired time. The Ninja Foodi Multi-Cooker will automatically switch to the keep warm function when the timer expires.
4. When the timer goes off, open the lid and serve.
That's all there is to it! The broil function on the Ninja Foodi Multi-Cooker is a great way to cook up a quick and easy meal.

Bake/Roast

One of the great things about Multi-Cooker is that they can do so much more than just cooking food quickly. The Ninja Foodi Multi-Cooker has a bake function that allows you to bake cakes, cookies, and other desserts right in the cooker. The bake function works by using steam to cook the food, so it is important to make sure that you have enough water in the cooker to create the steam. The Ninja Foodi Multi-Cooker comes with a measuring cup so you can easily add the correct amount of water. Once you have the water in the cooker, you will need to add the cake mix or cookie dough to the baking pan that comes with the cooker. Make sure that the pan is properly lined with parchment paper or a silicone baking mat to prevent sticking. Once the cake mix or cookie dough is in the pan, you will need to put the lid on the Ninja Foodi Multi-Cooker and set it to the bake function.

Dehydrate

Not only can they cook food quickly and easily, but they can also be used to dehydrate foods. Dehydrating foods with a Multi-Cooker is a great way to preserve them for long-term storage, or to create your dehydrated snacks. To dehydrate foods in a Multi-Cooker, you'll need to use the dehydrate function. This function allows you to slowly cook foods at a low temperature, which is ideal for dehydrating. This is a great function to use if you want to make your own dried fruit, herbs, or even beef jerky! The process is pretty simple: First, you'll need to choose what you want to dehydrate. Cut fruit or vegetables into uniform pieces so they'll dry evenly. If you're making beef jerky, slice the meat against the grain into thin strips. Next, place the food onto the dehydrating racks that come with the Ninja cooking system. Make sure that the pieces are not touching each other so that air can circulate them. Then, set the Ninja cooking system to the dehydrate function and choose the appropriate time. For fruit, the time

will vary depending on how ripe the fruit is. For vegetables, the time will vary depending on how thick the pieces are. For beef jerky, the time will vary depending on how lean the meat is.

Proof

With its proof function, you can cook your food faster and more evenly. Here's how to use the proof function on your Ninja Foodi Multi-Cooker.
1. First, make sure that your Multi-Cooker is turned on and set to the correct settings.
2. Place your food in the Multi-Cooker pot.
3. Add water to the pot, ensuring that the water level is at least 1 inch 1. above the food.
4. Close the Multi-Cooker lid and turn the valve to the sealed position.
5. Set the timer for the desired cooking time. For most foods, the cooking time will be between 5 and 10 minutes.
6. Once the timer goes off, release the pressure from the cooker by turning the valve to the release position.
7. Carefully open the Multi-Cooker lid and remove your food.

Sear/Sauté

When you use the sear function on your Ninja Foodi Multi-Cooker, you can cook food at a higher temperature than usual. This is great for searing meat or making sauce. Here are some tips on how to use the sear function:
1. Place the food that you want to sear in the pot.
2. Set the Ninja Foodi Multi-Cooker to the sear function.
3. Set the timer for the desired cooking time.
4. When the timer goes off, open the pot and check the food.
5. If the food is not cooked to your liking, you can either sear it for longer or cook it on a lower setting.

Steam

One of the best features of the Ninja Foodi Multi-Cooker is the steam function. This is a great way to cook delicate items like fish or vegetables. The steam function can also be used to reheat food. Here is a step-by-step guide to using the steam function on your Ninja Foodi Multi-Cooker.
1. Fill the Ninja Foodi Multi-Cooker with water. The water should come up to the fill line on the inside of the pot.
2. Place the rack that comes with the cooker into the pot.
3. Place the food that you want to steam onto the rack. Make sure that the food is in a single layer and that it is not touching the sides of the pot.
4. Put the lid on the Ninja Foodi Multi-Cooker and turn the valve to the sealing position.
5. Press the steam button on the Ninja Foodi Multi-Cooker and set the time. The cook time will depend on what you are steaming.

Sous Vide

Sous vide is a cooking method that involves sealing food in a bag and then cooking it in water that is kept at a very consistent temperature. This method can be used to cook meats, fish, and vegetables. The Ninja Foodi Multi-Cooker has a sous vide function that can be used to cook food. To use the sous vide function, first, fill the Ninja Foodi Multi-Cooker with water and then set the temperature. Next, seal

the food in a bag and place it in the water. Make sure that the bag is completely submerged. Set the timer for the desired cooking time. Once the timer goes off, the food is cooked. The sous vide method is a great way to cook food because it results in food that is cooked evenly. This method is also great for retaining nutrients in food.

Slow Cook

One of the best features of the Ninja Foodi Multi-Cooker is the slow cook function. This is a great way to cook food for a longer period without having to worry about it burning or drying out. Here are some tips for using the slow cook function on your Ninja Foodi Multi-Cooker:
1. Choose the right recipe: Not all recipes are well suited for slow cooking. Look for recipes that specifically call for the slow cook function on your Ninja Foodi Multi-Cooker.
2. Preheat the cooker: Before you start cooking, be sure to preheat the cooker by pressing the slow cook button. This will help ensure that your food cooks evenly.

3. Use the right amount of liquid: When slow cooking, it's important to use the right amount of liquid. Too much liquid can cause your food to become waterlogged, while too little can cause it to dry out.
4. Don't open the lid: Once you've started cooking, resist the urge to open the lid.

Yogurt

One of the many functions of a Ninja Foodi Multi-Cooker is the ability to cook yogurt. Yogurt is a great source of probiotics, which are live bacteria that are good for gut health. You can make your yogurt at home using the Ninja Foodi Multi-Cooker, and it's quite simple. Here's what you'll need:
• -½ gallon of milk (whole milk works best, but you can also use skim, 2%, or even almond milk)
• -¼ cup of plain yogurt (make sure it has live and active cultures)
• -A Ninja Foodi Multi-Cooker
• -Measuring cups
• -Stirring spoon
• -Thermometer
• -Cheesecloth or coffee filter
• -Jar or container for storing the yogurt
To make the yogurt, simply combine the milk and yogurt in the cooker pot. Stir until the yogurt is fully incorporated.

Cleaning and Maintenance

Cleaning: Dishwasher & Hand-Washing

If your dishwasher is leaving spots on your dishes or not cleaning them as well as you'd like, there are a few things you can do to clean it and improve its performance. First, check the manual that came with your dishwasher to see if there are any special instructions for cleaning it. If not, start by cleaning the filters. Most dishwashers have a screen or filter at the bottom that can become clogged with food and grease. Cleaning this will help the dishwasher to run more efficiently. You can also clean the spray arm, which is the part of the dishwasher that sprays water onto the dishes. If it's clogged, the water won't be able to reach all of the dishes. Finally, run a cycle with just hot water and a cup of vinegar to help remove any lingering dirt and grime.

When it comes to hand washing your Ninja Foodi Multi-Cooker, it is best to use mild soap and warm water. Simply rinse the pot and lid with warm water and mild soap, then dry with a clean towel. If you have any stubborn stains, you can use a sponge or scrub brush to remove them. Be sure to rinse the pot and lid thoroughly to remove any soap residue.

Removing & Re-installing the Silicon Ring

If you need to remove the silicon ring from your Ninja Foodi Multi-Cooker, here's how:

1. Turn the Multi-Cooker off and unplug it from the power outlet.
2. Allow the Multi-Cooker to cool down completely.
3. Open the Multi-Cooker r lid and remove the inner pot.
4. Locate the silicon ring on the underside of the Multi-Cooker lid.
5. Use your fingers to twist and pull the silicon ring off the lid.
6. Wash the silicon ring in warm, soapy water.
7. Rinse the silicon ring well and allow it to air dry

It might be time to reinstall the silicon ring. Here's a quick guide on how to do it:

1. Remove the old silicon ring from the Ninja Foodi Multi-Cooker. You can do this by gently pulling it out or using a small knife to cut it away.
2. Clean the Ninja Foodi Multi-Cooker well, making sure to remove any food or grease residue that might be on the inside.
3. Place the new silicon ring into the Ninja Foodi Multi-Cooker, making sure that it's seated correctly.
4. Follow the instructions in your Ninja Foodi Multi-Cooker manual to ensure that the new silicon ring is installed correctly and that the Ninja Foodi Multi-Cooker is working properly.

Avoiding Cross Contamination & Cleaning the Lid

When cooking with a Ninja Foodi Multi-Cooker, it is important to avoid cross-contamination. This is when bacteria from one food item is transferred to another. Cross-contamination can occur when cooked food comes into contact with raw food, utensils, or surfaces. It can also happen if you use the same cutting board for both raw and cooked food. To avoid cross-contamination, always wash your hands thoroughly after handling raw food. Be sure to use separate cutting boards for raw and cooked food. And always cook food to the proper temperature. By following these simple tips, you can help keep your family safe from foodborne illness.

Troubleshooting Guide

If your Ninja Foodi Multi-Cooker is not working properly, there are a few things that you can do to troubleshoot the problem. First, make sure that the power cord is securely plugged into the outlet and that the Ninja Foodi Multi-Cooker is turned on. If the power cord is loose, it may need to be replaced. Next, check the gasket to make sure it is properly in place and not damaged. The gasket is what seals the Ninja Foodi Multi-Cooker and keeps the pressure inside. If the gasket is damaged, it will need to be replaced. If the Ninja Foodi Multi-Cooker is still not working, there may be an issue with the pressure regulator. The pressure regulator controls the amount of pressure inside the Ninja Foodi Multi-Cooker. If the pressure regulator is not working properly, it will need to be replaced. Finally, if the Ninja Foodi Multi-Cooker is still not working, you may need to contact a Ninja Foodi Multi-Cooker service center for assistance.

Helpful Tips

If you're like most people, you probably don't think much about your Ninja Foodi Multi-Cooker. But if you have one, or are thinking about purchasing one, there are a few things you should know. Here are some helpful tips for using a Ninja Foodi Multi-Cooker:

1. Read the manual! This may seem like a no-brainer, but you'd be surprised how many people don't do this. Every Multi-Cooker is different, so it's important to read the manual before using yours.
2. Don't overfill it. It's important not to overfill your Multi-Cooker, as this can lead to problems. Make sure you only fill it to the recommended level.
3. Don't open it until the pressure has been released. Once you've cooked your food, don't be tempted to open the Multi-Cooker straight away. Wait until the pressure has released first, otherwise, you could be in for a nasty surprise.
4. Be careful when using the pressure release valve.
5. Get to know your Multi-Cooker. Each pressure cooker is different, so it's important to understand how yours works before using it.
6. Use the correct amount of liquid. This is important for pressure cooking because it ensures that the food cooks properly.
7. Be careful when releasing the pressure. Always follow the instructions in your manual for releasing the pressure.
8. Know what not to cook in a Multi-Cooker. Some things, like pasta, just don't work well in a Ninja Foodi Multi-Cooker.
9. Use the right size Multi-Cooker for your needs. If you're cooking for a large group, make sure to use a large enough Multi-Cooker.

Replacement Parts

When it comes to cooking, few things are as versatile and convenient as a Multi-Cooker. But like any appliance, even the best Multi-Cooker need occasional maintenance and replacement parts. Here are a few things to keep in mind when shopping for replacement parts for your Ninja Foodi Multi-Cooker. First, make sure you know the model number of your Ninja Foodi Multi-Cooker. This will ensure that you get the correct parts for your machine. Second, check the Ninja website or contact customer service to see if they offer replacement parts for your specific model. Third, if you're comfortable doing so, you can also try shopping for parts on Amazon or eBay. Just be sure to do your research to make sure you're getting the correct parts for your cooker. Finally, remember that Ninja Foodi Multi-Cooker are designed to last for years, so don't be discouraged if you have to replace a few parts here and there. With proper care and maintenance, your Ninja Foodi Multi-Cooker will give you years.

Warranty

If you have a Ninja Foodi Multi-Cooker, you may be wondering about the warranty. The Ninja Foodi Multi-Cooker comes with a one-year limited warranty. This means that if your Multi-Cooker breaks down within the first year, Ninja will replace it for free. However, if it breaks down after the first year, you will have to pay for a replacement.

4 - Week Diet Plan

Week 1

Day 1:
Breakfast: Quiche with Kalamata Olives and No Crust
Lunch: Bok Choy with Sesame Seeds
Snack: Deviled Eggs
Dinner: Sweet Potato and Beef chili
Dessert: Cheesecake and Cookies

Day 2:
Breakfast: Yummy Gravy
Lunch: Delicious Cauliflower Queso
Snack: Sesame-Soy Frozen Pot Stickers
Dinner: Hungarian Chicken Stew
Dessert: Filled Apples

Day 3:
Breakfast: Hard bowl egg
Lunch: Honey Cayenne Carrots
Snack: Garlic White Bean Hummus
Dinner: Fresh Mixed Seafood Soup
Dessert: Crisp Pear and Cranberry

Day 4:
Breakfast: Granola Bars with Peanut Butter
Lunch: Butter Mashed Potatoes
Snack: Plant-Based Hummus
Dinner: Steamed Lemon Shrimp with Asparagus
Dessert: Yummy Pudding

Day 5:
Breakfast: Pecan and Apple Oatmeal
Lunch: Creamy Parmesan Polenta
Snack: Herbed Artichokes
Dinner: Homemade Beef Borscht Soup
Dessert: Pears in Buttery Caramel

Day 6:
Breakfast: Yummy Strawberry Jam
Lunch: Simple Zucchini Ratatouille
Snack: Fresh Tomato Chutney
Dinner: Tasty Satay Pork with Rice Noodles
Dessert: Baked Kugel

Day 7:
Breakfast: Cozy Fruit with Spice
Lunch: Delicious Scalloped Potatoes
Snack: Classic Black Beans
Dinner: Baby Back Pork Ribs
Dessert: Apple Maple Cake

Week 2

Day 1:
Breakfast: Squash Frittata Casserole
Lunch: Roasted Spaghetti Squash
Snack: Spicy Salsa
Dinner: Yummy meatballs
Dessert: Bread Pudding with Blueberries

Day 2:
Breakfast: Cozy Fruit with Spice
Lunch: Braised Eggplant
Snack: Greek Eggplant Dip
Dinner: Beef Stew
Dessert: Easy Maple-Sweetened Applesauce

Day 3:
Breakfast: Buckwheat Porridge
Lunch: Butter Potatoes Mash
Snack: Savory Cocktail Sausages
Dinner: Curry chicken with Honey
Dessert: Fresh Mango-Coconut Custard

Day 4:
Breakfast: Nutty Bread with Zucchini
Lunch: Butternut Squash and Parsnips
Snack: Lentil Balls
Dinner: Wraps with Carnitas Lettuce
Dessert: Chocolate Cheesecake with Coconut

Day 5:
Breakfast: Corn Muffins with Bananas
Lunch: Steamed Garlic Edamame
Snack: Cinnamon Almonds
Dinner: Biryani De Beef
Dessert: Creamy Rum Cheesecake

Day 6:
Breakfast: Frittata with Sausage and Cheese
Lunch: Parmesan Spaghetti Squash
Snack: Hearty Sausage Dip
Dinner: Spinach Fish Rice
Dessert: Traditional Apple Cake

Day 7:
Breakfast: Frittata with Leeks and Asparagus
Lunch: Savory Mushroom Polenta
Snack: Deviled Eggs with Jalapeno
Dinner: Mongolian beef
Dessert: Creamy Carrot Soufflé

Week 3

Day 1:
Breakfast: Yummy Gravy
Lunch: Green Beans with Tomatoes and Potatoes
Snack: Tasty Sun-Dried Tomato Cheesecake
Dinner: Mediterranean Fish Stew with Hot Sauce
Dessert: Glazed Doughnut and Apple Crisp

Day 2:
Breakfast: Yummy Shakshuka
Lunch: Gingered Sweet Potatoes
Snack: Lemony Shrimp with Cocktail Sauce
Dinner: Beef and Potato Stew
Dessert: Cake Made of Bananas

Day 3:
Breakfast: Berries Coconut Porridge with Chia Seeds
Lunch: Stuffed Acorn Squash
Snack: Smoky Roasted Red Pepper Hummus
Dinner: Delicious Chicken Noodle Soup
Dessert: Cake with Blueberries

Day 4:
Breakfast: Oatmeal Pumpkin Pie Bites
Lunch: Herbed Potato Salad
Snack: Luscious Baba Ghanoush
Dinner: Baked Fish with Parmesan
Dessert: Honey Stewed Dried Fruits

Day 5:
Breakfast: Boiled Eggs in Tomato Sauce
Lunch: Steamed Broccoli
Snack: Quinoa Energy Balls
Dinner: Greek-Shrimp with Feta Cheese
Dessert: Chocolate Pudding with Apricots

Day 6:
Breakfast: Maple Polenta with Nut
Lunch: Boiled Cabbage
Snack: Potato Pea Salad
Dinner: Sole Fillets with Vegetables
Dessert: Classical German Pancake

Day 7:
Breakfast: Creamy Oatmeal
Lunch: Saucy Brussels Sprouts and Carrots
Snack: Hot Cauliflower Bites
Dinner: Coconut Rice in Chicken Broth
Dessert: Spiced Apple Cider

Week 4

Day 1:
Breakfast: Bacon-Cheddar Egg Bites
Lunch: Ginger Broccoli and Carrots
Snack: Fresh Tomato Chutney
Dinner: Shrimp Scampi with Lemon Wedges
Dessert: Chai White Hot Chocolate

Day 2:
Breakfast: Brown Sugar Quinoa
Lunch: Garlic Green Beans
Snack: Refried Beans
Dinner: Halibut Steaks with Tomatoes
Dessert: Yummy Arroz Con Leche

Day 3:
Breakfast: Quinoa Greek Yogurt with Blueberries
Lunch: Maple Dill Carrots
Snack: Luscious Baba Ghanoush
Dinner: Drunken Chuck Roast
Dessert: Traditional Chewy Brownies

Day 4:
Breakfast: Maple Polenta with Nut
Lunch: Purple Cabbage Salad
Snack: Herbed Chickpea, Parsley, and Dill Dip
Dinner: Pork with Apple and Curry
Dessert: A Chocolate Cake without Flour

Day 5:
Breakfast: Baked Ham, Kale and Eggs
Lunch: Lemon Garlic Red Chard
Snack: Bacon-Chive Deviled Eggs
Dinner: Seamed Cod with Vegetables
Dessert: Crisp Pear and Cranberry

Day 6:
Breakfast: Feta Crustless Quiche with Spinach
Lunch: Eggplant Caponata
Snack: Plant-Based Hummus
Dinner: Butter dipped Lobster Tails
Dessert: Cake with Orange and Pecans

Day 7:
Breakfast: Oatmeal Diced Apple
Lunch: Burgundy Mushrooms
Snack: Black Bean Dip with Bacon
Dinner: Chicken Cajun with Rice
Dessert: Cups of Pumpkin Pie

Chapter 1 Breakfast Recipes

Fruit Compote

Prep time: 5 minutes | Cook time: 10 minutes | Serves: 2

1 pkg. (300g) fresh or frozen cranberries
130g packed brown sugar
60ml thawed orange juice concentrate

2 tablespoon raspberry vinegar
135g chopped dried apricots
70g golden raisins
60g chopped walnuts, toasted

1. In a Ninja Foodi XL Pressure Cooker Steam cooking pot, combine cranberries, brown sugar, orange juice concentrate and vinegar. 2. Lock lid; move slider towards PRESSURE. Adjust pressure release valve in the SEAL position. Close pressure-release valve. The cooking temperature will default to HIGH, which is accurate. Set minutes. Select START/STOP and start cooking. 3. When cooking is complete, let pressure release naturally for about 5 minutes, then quick-release any remaining pressure by turning it into VENT position. 4. Stir in apricots, raisins and walnuts. Refrigerate leftovers.
Per Serving: Calories 161; Fat 4g; Sodium 32mg; Carbs 32g; Fiber 3g; Sugar 28g; Protein 2g

Delicious Frittata Provencal

Prep time: 30 minutes | Cook time: 35 minutes | Serves: 6

1 teaspoon minced fresh thyme or
¼ teaspoon dried thyme
1 tablespoon olive oil
1 small onion, thinly sliced
½ teaspoon smoked paprika
240ml water
12 large eggs
1 teaspoon hot pepper sauce

½ teaspoon salt
¼ teaspoon pepper
1 log (100g) crumbled fresh goat cheese, divided
30g chopped sun-dried tomatoes (not packed in oil)
1 medium Yukon Gold potato, peeled, sliced

1. Move the slider towards "AIR FRY/STOVETOP" and set Ninja Foodi XL Pressure Cooker Steam Fryer with SmartLid to SEAR/SAUTÉ mode. Adjust the temperature to "Hi5" by using up arrow. Press START/STOP to begin cooking.; adjust for high heat. Then heat oil. Add potato and onion; cook and stir until potato is lightly browned, 5 to 7 minutes. Stir in paprika. Transfer potato mixture to a greased round baking dish. Pour in water. 2. In a large bowl, whisk next five ingredients; stir in 50g. cheese. Pour over potato mixture. Top with tomatoes and remaining goat cheese. Cover baking dish with foil; place on a deluxe reversible rack with handles. Lower into pot. 3. Lock lid; move slider towards PRESSURE. Adjust pressure release valve in the SEAL position. Close pressure-release valve. The cooking temperature will default to HIGH, which is accurate. Set the time for 35 minutes. Select START/STOP and start cooking. 4. When cooking is complete, let pressure release naturally for about 10 minutes, then quick-release any remaining pressure by turning it into VENT position. 5. Serve hot and enjoy.
Per Serving: Calories 245; Fat 14g; Sodium 12mg; Carbs 12g; Fiber 2g; Sugar 4g; Protein 15g

Omelet Frittata

Prep time: 25 minutes | Cook time: 35 minutes | Serves: 6

1 tablespoon olive oil
1 small onion, thinly sliced
240ml water
12 large eggs
1 teaspoon hot pepper sauce
½ teaspoon salt
¼ teaspoon pepper

200g. sliced deli ham, chopped
75g chopped green pepper
100g shredded cheddar cheese, divided
1 medium Yukon Gold potato, peeled, sliced

1. Move the slider towards "AIR FRY/STOVETOP" and set Ninja Foodi XL Pressure Cooker Steam Fryer with SmartLid to SEAR/SAUTÉ mode. Adjust the temperature to "Hi5" by using up arrow. Press START/STOP to begin cooking and adjust for high heat; then heat oil. Add potato and onion; cook and stir for 4 to 6 minutes or until potato is lightly browned. Transfer to a greased 1.5 L. (15- or 18-in.) soufflé dish. Wipe pressure cooker clean. Pour in water. 2. In a bowl, whisk the eggs, pepper sauce, salt, pepper; stir in ham, green pepper and the 50 g cheese. Pour on potato mixture. Top with the remaining cheese. Cover soufflé dish with foil and place on a deluxe reversible rack. 3. Lock lid; move slider towards PRESSURE. Adjust pressure release valve in the SEAL position. Close pressure-release valve. The cooking temperature will default to HIGH, which is accurate. Set the time for 10 minutes. Select START/STOP and start cooking. 4.

When cooking is complete, let pressure release naturally for about 10 minutes, then quick-release any remaining pressure by turning it into VENT position. 5. Serve hot and enjoy.
Per Serving: Calories 320; Fat 19g; Sodium 822mg; Carbs 12g; Fiber 1g; Sugar 3g; Protein 25g

Ham & Cheddar Casserole

Prep time: 20 minutes | Cook time: 35 minutes | Serves: 6

6 large eggs
120ml low-fat milk
½ teaspoon salt
¼ teaspoon pepper
375g frozen shredded hash brown

potatoes, thawed
270g cubed fully cooked ham
½ medium onion, chopped
200g shredded cheddar cheese
240ml water

1. Whisk together eggs, milk, salt and pepper. Combine the potatoes, ham, onion and cheese; transfer to a greased soufflé or round baking dish; pour egg mixture over top. 2. Pour water into a Ninja Foodi XL Pressure Cooker Steam Fryer cooking pot. 3. Cover baking dish with foil. Place on a Deluxe reversible; lower into pot. 4. Lock lid; move slider towards PRESSURE. Adjust pressure release valve in the SEAL position. Close pressure-release valve. The cooking temperature will default to HIGH, which is accurate. Set the time for 35 minutes. Select START/STOP and start cooking. 5. When cooking is complete, let pressure release naturally for about 10 minutes, then quickly release any remaining pressure by turning it into VENT position. 6. Let stand 10 minutes before serving.
Per Serving: Calories 324; Fat 19g; Sodium 17mg; Carbs 17g; Fiber 1g; Sugar 3g; Protein 22g

Sunday Brunch Egg Cups with Broccoli

Prep time: 10 minutes | Cook time: 15 minutes | Serves: 4

7 large eggs
36 g cream
3 tablespoons shredded Swiss cheese
2 teaspoons minced fresh parsley
1 teaspoon minced fresh basil

¼ teaspoon salt
⅛ teaspoon cayenne pepper
150g frozen broccoli florets, thawed
240ml water

1. Whisk three eggs with next six ingredients; pour into four greased 8-oz. ramekins. Divide broccoli among ramekins; top each with one remaining egg. 2. Add 240 ml water and Deluxe reversible rack to a Ninja Foodi XL Pressure Cooker Steam Fryer with SmartLid cooking pot. Place ramekins on Deluxe reversible rack, offset-stacking as needed, and covering loosely with foil. 3. Lock lid; move slider towards PRESSURE. Adjust pressure release valve in the SEAL position. Close pressure-release valve. The cooking temperature will default to HIGH, which is accurate. Set the time for 6 minutes. Select START/STOP and start cooking. 4. When cooking is complete, let pressure release quickly by turning it into VENT position. 5. Remove lid; using tongs, carefully remove the ramekins. 6. Let stand for 3 minutes before serving.
Per Serving: Calories 274; Fat 19g; Sodium 333mg; Carbs 5g; Fiber 1g; Sugar 4g; Protein 16g

Nutty Sweet Apple Butter

Prep time: 20 minutes | Cook time: 3 minutes | Serves: 5

1.8kg. (about 8) large apples, cored and quartered
150–200 g sugar
60ml water
3 teaspoon ground cinnamon

¼ teaspoon ground nutmeg
¼ teaspoon ground cloves
¼ teaspoon ground allspice
65g creamy peanut butter

1. In a Ninja Foodi XL Pressure Cooker Steam Fryer with SmartLid cooking pot, combine the first seven ingredients. 2. Lock lid; move slider towards PRESSURE. Adjust pressure release valve in the SEAL position. Close pressure-release valve. The cooking temperature will default to HIGH, which is accurate. Set the time for 3 minutes. Select START/STOP and start cooking. 3. When cooking is complete, let pressure release naturally for about 5 minutes, then quick-release any remaining pressure by turning it into VENT position. 4. Mash the apples with a potato masher or you can use an immersion blender until blended. Whisk in peanut butter until apple mixture is smooth. 5. Cool to room temperature. Store in airtight container in the refrigerator.
Per Serving: Calories 43; Fat 1g; Sodium 9mg; Carbs 9g; Fiber 1g; Sugar 8g; Protein 0g

Nutty Cherry Oatmeal

Prep time: 10 minutes | Cook time: 12 minutes | Serves: 6

96ml vanilla almond milk
80g steel-cut oats
120g dried cherries
65g packed brown sugar
½ teaspoon salt

½ teaspoon ground cinnamon
Cooking spray
Additional vanilla almond milk, optional

1. In a Ninja Foodi XL Pressure Cooker Steam Fryer with SmartLid cooking pot coated with cooking spray, combine first 6 ingredients. 2. Lock lid; move slider towards PRESSURE. Adjust pressure release valve in the SEAL position. Close pressure-release valve. The cooking temperature will default to HIGH, which is accurate. Set the time for 12 minutes. Select START/STOP and start cooking. 3. When cooking is complete, let pressure release naturally for about 10 minutes, then quick-release any remaining pressure by turning it into VENT position. 4. Serve with additional almond milk if desired.
Per Serving: Calories 276; Fat 4g; Sodium 57mg; Carbs 57g; Fiber 4g; Sugar 35g; Protein 5g

Baked Sausage & Waffle

Prep time: 20 minutes | Cook time: 20 minutes | Serves: 6

455g spicy breakfast pork sausage
1½ teaspoon rubbed sage
¼ teaspoon fennel seed
5 frozen waffles, cut into bite-sized pieces
240ml water
4 large eggs

160g cream
2 Tablespoon maple syrup
⅛ teaspoon salt
⅛ teaspoon pepper
100g shredded cheddar cheese
Additional maple syrup

1. Move the slider towards "AIR FRY/STOVETOP" and Set Ninja Foodi XL Pressure Cooker Steam Fryer with SmartLid to SEAR/SAUTÉ mode. Adjust the temperature to "Hi5" by using up arrow. Press START/STOP to begin cooking. and adjust for normal heat. Cook and crumble sausage; drain fat. Add sage and fennel. Place waffles in a greased 1.5L. soufflé or round (15 – 18 cm) baking dish; top with sausage. Wipe cooking pot clean; pour in 240 ml water. 2. In a bowl, mix eggs, cream, syrup and seasonings. Pour over sausage and waffles. Top with cheese. Cover baking dish with foil; place on a deluxe reversible rack with handles. Lower into pot. Lock lid; move slider towards PRESSURE. Adjust pressure release valve in the SEAL position. Close pressure-release valve. The cooking temperature will default to HIGH, which is accurate. Set the time to 20 minutes. Select START/STOP and start cooking. 3. When cooking is complete, let pressure release naturally for about 5 minutes, then quick-release any remaining pressure by turning it into VENT position. 4. Serve with additional maple syrup.
Per Serving: Calories 445; Fat 31g; Sodium 880mg; Carbs 20g; Fiber 1g; Sugar 7g; Protein 19g

Breakfast Hash Brown

Prep time: 15 minutes | Cook time: 15 minutes | Serves: 6

3 tablespoons butter
455g yellow potatoes, diced (no need to peel)
1 medium yellow onion, chopped
¼ teaspoon ground black pepper
1 teaspoon dried thyme
1 medium red pepper, stemmed, cored, and chopped
1 teaspoon dried sage

½ teaspoon celery seeds
¼ teaspoon table salt
1 medium green pepper, stemmed, cored, and chopped
455g smoked deli ham, any coating removed, the meat diced
360ml chicken stock
2 medium garlic cloves, peeled and minced (2 teaspoons)

1. Move the slider towards "AIR FRY/STOVETOP" and set Ninja Foodi XL Pressure Cooker Steam Fryer with SmartLid to SEAR/SAUTÉ mode. Adjust the temperature to "Hi5" by using up arrow. Press START/STOP to begin cooking. 2. Melt the butter in a cooking pot. Add the onion and both peppers. Then cook, stirring occasionally, until softened, about 4 minutes. Add the ham, salt, sage, celery seeds, garlic, thyme, and pepper. Then cook, stirring often, until fragrant, about 1 minute. 3. Turn off the SAUTÉ function. Stir in the potatoes and stock, scraping up any browned bits on the pot's bottom. 4. Lock lid; move slider towards PRESSURE. Adjust pressure release valve in the SEAL position. Close pressure-release valve. The cooking temperature will default to HIGH, which is accurate. Set time to 10 minutes. Select START/STOP and start cooking. 5. When cooking is complete, let pressure release quickly by turning it into VENT position. Unlatch the lid and open the Ninja Foodi cooking pot. Stir well. 6. Move the slider towards "AIR FRY/STOVETOP" and set Ninja Foodi XL Pressure Cooker Steam Fryer with SmartLid to SEAR/SAUTÉ mode. Adjust the temperature to "Hi5" by using up arrow. Press START/STOP to begin cooking. 7. Bring the mixture to a boil, stirring frequently. Continue without stirring until the liquid boils and stray bits that come in contact with the hot surface begin to turn brown, 3 to 4 minutes. 8. Stop cooking and remove the hot insert from the Ninja Foodi XL Pressure Cooker Steam Fryer. Some of potatoes may have fused to the surface. 9. Use a metal spatula to get them up. The point is to have some browned bits and some softer bits throughout the hash.
Per Serving: Calories 230; Fat 18.9g; Sodium 354mg; Carbs 1.3g; Fiber 0.3g; Sugar 0.2g; Protein 13.4g

Healthy Sweet Carrot Cake Oatmeal

Prep time: 10 minutes | Cook time: 10 minutes | Serves: 8

1L water
1 can (500g) crushed pineapple, undrained
200g shredded carrots
80g steel-cut oats

145g raisins
2 teaspoon ground cinnamon
1 teaspoon pumpkin pie spice
Brown sugar, optional

1. In a Ninja Foodi XL Pressure Cooker Steam Fryer with SmartLid cooking pot coated with cooking spray, combine the first seven ingredients. 2. Lock lid; move slider towards PRESSURE. Adjust pressure release valve in the SEAL position. Close pressure-release valve. The cooking temperature will default to HIGH, which is accurate. Set the time to 10 minutes. Select START/STOP and start cooking. 3. When cooking is complete, let pressure release naturally for about 10 minutes, then quick-release any remaining pressure by turning it into VENT position. 4. If desired, sprinkle with brown sugar.
Per Serving: Calories 197; Fat 2g; Sodium 46mg; Carbs 46g; Fiber 4g; Sugar 26g; Protein 4g

Spiced Pumpkin Oatmeal

Prep time: 6 minutes | Cook time: 15 minutes | Serves: 6

100g steel-cut oats
3 tablespoons brown sugar
1½ teaspoon pumpkin pie spice
1 teaspoon ground cinnamon
¾ teaspoon salt
920ml water

360ml low-fat milk
1 can (375g.) solid-pack pumpkin
Optional toppings: toasted chopped pecans, ground cinnamon, additional brown sugar and low-fat milk

1. Stir together first seven ingredients in a Ninja Foodi XL Pressure Cooker Steam Fryer cooking pot. 2. Lock lid; move slider towards PRESSURE. Adjust pressure release valve in the SEAL position. Close pressure-release valve. The cooking temperature will default to HIGH, which is accurate. Set the for time for 10 minutes. Select START/STOP and start cooking. 3. When cooking is complete, let pressure release naturally by for 10 minutes, then quick-release any remaining pressure by turning it into VENT position. 4. Stir in pumpkin; let stand 5 to 10 minutes to thicken. 5. Serve with toppings as desired.
Per Serving: Calories 208; Fat 4g; Sodium 329mg; Carbs 39g; Fiber 6g; Sugar 13g; Protein 7g

Oatmeal

Prep time: 10 minutes | Cook time: 25 minutes | Serves: 4

660ml liquid: 50/50 combo of water and canned evaporated milk.
80g steel-cut oats
1 tablespoon fat: choose butter,

coconut oil, or vegetable, corn, rapeseed, safflower, or any nut oil.
½ teaspoon table salt

1. Mix all the ingredients in a Ninja Foodi XL Pressure Cooker Steam Fryer with SmartLid cooking pot. 2. Lock lid; move slider towards PRESSURE. Adjust pressure release valve in the SEAL position. Close pressure-release valve. The cooking temperature will default to HIGH, which is accurate. Set the time to 3 minutes. Select START/STOP and start cooking. 3. When cooking is complete, let pressure release naturally. 4. Unlatch the lid and open the Ninja Foodi XL Pressure Cooker Steam Fryer. Stir well before serving.
Per Serving: Calories 232; Fat 12g; Sodium 578mg; Carbs 5g; Fiber 1g; Sugar 1g; Protein 7g

Toast Buttery Oatmeal

Prep time: 10 minutes | Cook time: 25 minutes | Serves: 4

3 tablespoons butter
80g steel-cut oats
660ml water
¼ teaspoon table salt

1. Move the slider towards "AIR FRY/STOVETOP" and Set Ninja Foodi XL Pressure Cooker Steam Fryer with SmartLid to SEAR/SAUTÉ mode. Adjust the temperature to "Hi5" by using up arrow. Press START/STOP to begin cooking. 2. Melt the butter in cooking pot. Add the oats and stir until they smell toasty, about 3 minutes. Turn off the SAUTÉ function; stir in the water and salt. 3. Lock lid; move slider towards PRESSURE. Adjust pressure release valve in the SEAL position. Close pressure-release valve. The cooking temperature will default to HIGH, which is accurate. Set the time to 3 minutes. Select START/STOP and start cooking. 4. When cooking is complete, let pressure release naturally for about 10 minutes, then quick-release any remaining pressure by turning it into VENT position. 5. Unlatch the lid and open the pot. Stir well before serving.
Per Serving: Calories 291; Fat 20.6g; Sodium 369mg; Carbs 2.7g; Fiber 1.3g; Sugar 1.5g; Protein 23.9g

Apple Oatmeal

Prep time: 10 minutes | Cook time: 22 minutes | Serves: 4

700ml water
120ml whole or low-fat evaporated milk (do not use fat-free)
80g steel-cut oats
45g chopped dried apples
2 tablespoons light or dark brown
sugar
2 tablespoons butter
½ teaspoon ground cinnamon
½ teaspoon table salt
2 tablespoons heavy cream

1. Mix the water, milk, oats, apples, brown sugar, butter, cinnamon, and salt in Ninja Foodi XL Pressure Cooker Steam Fryer with SmartLid cooking pot. 2. Lock lid; move slider towards PRESSURE. Adjust pressure release valve in the SEAL position. Close pressure-release valve. The cooking temperature will default to HIGH, which is accurate. Set time to 4 minutes. Select START/STOP and start cooking. 3. When cooking is complete, let pressure release naturally for 15 minutes, then quick-release any remaining pressure by turning it into VENT position. 4. Unlatch the lid and open the Ninja Foodi XL Pressure Cooker Steam Fryer. 5. Stir in the cream before serving.
Per Serving: Calories 240; Fat 14g; Sodium 256mg; Carbs 5g; Fiber 3g; Sugar 2g; Protein 8g

Banana Oatmeal

Prep time: 10 minutes | Cook time: 25 minutes | Serves: 4

3 tablespoons butter
55g packed dark brown sugar
2 very ripe bananas, peeled and thinly sliced
660ml water
80g steel-cut oats
2 teaspoons vanilla extract
½ teaspoon ground cinnamon
¼ teaspoon table salt
60g heavy cream

1. Move the slider towards "AIR FRY/STOVETOP" and Set Ninja Foodi XL Pressure Cooker Steam Fryer with SmartLid to SEAR/SAUTÉ mode. Adjust the temperature to "Hi5" by using up arrow. Press START/STOP to begin cooking. 2. Melt the butter in cooking pot. Add the brown sugar and stir until the sugar has dissolved and the mixture is bubbling. Stir in the bananas to coat them in the sugar syrup. Turn off the SAUTÉ function. Stir in the water, oats, vanilla, cinnamon, and salt. 3. Lock lid; move slider towards PRESSURE. Adjust pressure release valve in the SEAL position. Close pressure-release valve. The cooking temperature will default to HIGH, which is accurate. Set and time to 4 minutes. Select START/STOP and start cooking. 4. When cooking is complete, let pressure release naturally for about 20 minutes. 5. Unlatch the lid and open the Ninja Foodi XL Pressure Cooker Steam Fryer. Stir in the cream before serving.
Per Serving: Calories 102; Fat 7.9g; Sodium 456mg; Carbs 1.6g; Fiber 0.4g; Sugar 0.6g; Protein 4.3g

Tropical Porridge

Prep time: 15 minutes | Cook time: 45 minutes | Serves: 4 to 6

920ml water
95g pearl barley
40g steel-cut oats
35g unsweetened shredded
coconut
30g packed light brown sugar
1 tablespoon fresh lime juice
¼ teaspoon table salt
60ml coconut milk or coconut cream (do not use cream of coconut)

1. Mix the water, barley, oats, coconut, brown sugar, lime juice, and salt in Ninja Foodi XL Pressure Cooker Steam Fryer with SmartLid cooking pot. 2. Lock lid; move slider towards PRESSURE. Adjust pressure release valve in the SEAL position. Close pressure-release valve. The cooking temperature will default to HIGH, which is accurate. Set time to 15 minutes. Select START/STOP and start cooking. 3. When cooking is complete, let pressure release naturally. Unlatch the lid and open the Ninja Foodi XL Pressure Cooker Steam Fryer. 4. Stir in the coconut milk or coconut cream before serving.
Per Serving: Calories 190; Fat 7g; Sodium 423mg; Carbs 5g; Fiber 3g; Sugar 2g; Protein 3g

Bulger and Buckwheat Porridge

Prep time: 10 minutes | Cook time: 45 minutes | Serves: 6

1L water
95g bulgur wheat, preferably medium or coarse grind
95g raw buckwheat groats
50g packed raisins or dried cranberries, chopped
50g granulated white sugar
1 teaspoon vanilla extract
½ teaspoon ground cinnamon
¼ teaspoon table salt
120g heavy cream

1. Mix the water, bulgur, buckwheat, raisins, sugar, vanilla, cinnamon, and salt in Ninja Foodi XL Pressure Cooker Steam Fryer with SmartLid cooking pot. 2. Lock lid; move slider towards PRESSURE. Adjust pressure release valve in the SEAL position. Close pressure-release valve. The cooking temperature will default to HIGH, which is accurate. Set QUICK RELEASE and time to 16 minutes. Select START/STOP and start cooking. When cooking is complete, let pressure release quickly by turning it into VENT position. Unlatch the lid and open the Ninja Foodi XL Pressure Cooker Steam Fryer. 3. Move the slider towards "AIR FRY/STOVETOP" and set Ninja Foodi XL Pressure Cooker Steam Fryer with SmartLid to SEAR/SAUTÉ mode. Adjust the temperature to "Hi5" by using up arrow. Press START/STOP to begin cooking. 4. Stir often as the porridge comes to a bubble. Stir in the cream or half-and-half and continue stirring over the heat for 1 minute. 5. Serve warm.
Per Serving: Calories 101; Fat 5g; Sodium 236mg; Carbs 1.9g; Fiber 1g; Sugar g; Protein 12.4g

Creamy Rice Porridge

Prep time: 15 minutes | Cook time: 15 minutes | Serves: 6

1.4L water
25g raw long-grain white rice
3 tablespoons butter or a neutral-
flavoured oil like vegetable oil
½ teaspoon table salt

1. Mix all the ingredients in Ninja Foodi XL Pressure Cooker Steam Fryer with SmartLid cooking pot. 2. Lock lid; move slider towards PRESSURE. Adjust pressure release valve in the SEAL position. Close pressure-release valve. The cooking temperature will default to HIGH, which is accurate. Set time to 35 minutes. Select START/STOP and start cooking. 3. When cooking is complete, let pressure release naturally. 4. Unlatch the lid and open the Ninja Foodi XL Pressure Cooker Steam Fryer. 5. Stir well before serving.
Per Serving: Calories 242; Fat 12g; Sodium 366mg; Carbs 5g; Fiber 3g; Sugar 2g; Protein 9g

Shell Eggs

Prep time: 15 minutes | Cook time: 15 minutes | Serves: 12

240ml water
1 to 12 large eggs, cold

1. Place the Cook & Crisp Basket in Ninja Foodi XL Pressure Cooker Steam Fryer with SmartLid cooking pot and pour in the water. Pile as many eggs as you like onto Basket. 2. Lock lid; move slider towards PRESSURE. Adjust pressure release valve in the SEAL position. Close pressure-release valve. The cooking temperature will default to HIGH, which is accurate. Set QUICK RELEASE and time to 12 minutes. Select START/STOP and start cooking. 3. When cooking is complete, let pressure release quickly by turning it into VENT position. 4. Unlatch the lid and open the Ninja Foodi XL Pressure Cooker Steam Fryer. 5. Transfer the eggs to a bowl or wire rack. Peel as soon as you can handle them.
Per Serving: Calories 537; Fat 39.4g; Sodium 745mg; Carbs 1.4g; Fiber 0.1g; Sugar 0g; Protein 42.7g

Delicious Coddled Eggs

Prep time: 15 minutes | Cook time: 15 minutes | Serves: 6

240ml water
Butter or vegetable, corn, canola, or olive oil for greasing the ramekins

1 to 6 large eggs
1 to 6 teaspoons heavy cream
Table salt and ground black pepper for garnishing

1. Place a Deluxe Reversible Rack in Ninja Foodi XL Pressure Cooker Steam Fryer with SmartLid cooking pot. Pour in the water. Butter or oil the inside of one to six heat- and pressure-safe 1-cup ramekins. Crack an egg into each, spoon 1 teaspoon cream on top, and season with salt and pepper to taste. 2. Place the ramekins on the Deluxe reversible rack, making sure that no one ramekin completely covers another. 3. Lock lid; move slider towards PRESSURE. Adjust pressure release valve in the SEAL position. Close pressure-release valve. The cooking temperature will default to HIGH, which is accurate. Set time to 2 minutes. Select START/STOP and start cooking. 4. When cooking is complete, let pressure release quickly by turning it into VENT position. 5. Unlatch the lid and open the Ninja Foodi XL Pressure Cooker Steam Fryer. 6. Transfer the hot ramekins to heat-safe serving plates and dig in.
Per Serving: Calories 214; Fat 14g; Sodium 332mg; Carbs 4g; Fiber 2g; Sugar 4g; Protein 9g

Cheesy Potato Frittata

Prep time: 15 minutes | Cook time: 30 minutes | Serves: 4

1 tablespoon rapeseed oil
225g refrigerated diced potatoes with onion
240ml water
8 large egg whites
4 large eggs

120ml fat-free milk
2 green onions, chopped
2 teaspoon minced fresh parsley
¼ teaspoon salt
¼ teaspoon pepper
50g shredded cheddar cheese

1. In a large frying pan, heat oil over medium-high heat. Add potatoes; cook and stir until lightly browned, 4-6 minutes. Transfer to a greased 1.5 L -2.5 L soufflé or round baking dish. Add 240 ml water and deluxe reversible rack in Ninja Foodi XL Pressure Cooker Steam Fryer with SmartLid cooking pot. 2. Whisk next seven ingredients; stir in shredded cheese. Pour egg mixture over potatoes. Loosely cover baking dish with aluminum foil. 3. Lock lid; move slider towards PRESSURE. Adjust pressure release valve in the SEAL position. Close pressure-release valve. The cooking temperature will default to HIGH, which is accurate. Set QUICK RELEASE and time to 30 minutes. Select START/STOP and start cooking. 4. When cooking is complete, let pressure release quickly by turning it into VENT position. 5. Remove baking dish. Let stand for 10 minutes.
Per Serving: Calories 241; Fat 13g; Sodium 555mg; Carbs 11g; Fiber 1g; Sugar 2g; Protein 19g

Ninja Foodi XL Pressure Cooker Steam Fryer Frittata

Prep time: 15 minutes | Cook time: 15 minutes | Serves:4 to 6

360ml water
9 large eggs
6 tablespoons creamy liquid: Choose whole milk, low-fat milk, light cream, heavy cream, hemp
1½ cups filling:
Choose one or several from chopped baby spinach; chopped, jarred roasted red pepper; cooked onions, shallots, or spring onions; cored, seeded, and finely chopped pepper; cooked sliced mushrooms; cooked diced and

milk, soy milk, coconut milk, cashew milk, or any nut milk.
½ teaspoon table salt
Up to 1 teaspoon ground black pepper

peeled potatoes; shredded semi-firm or hard cheese like Swiss, Cheddar, mozzarella, pecorino, or Parmigiano-Reggiano; sliced sun-dried tomatoes; thawed, frozen broccoli or cauliflower florets.

1. Pour the water into Ninja Foodi XL Pressure Cooker Steam Fryer with SmartLid cooking pot. Set Deluxe reversible rack in the pot. Butter or grease the inside of a 2-litre, high-sided, round soufflé dish. Make an aluminum foil sling and set the baking dish in the middle of it. 2. Whisk the eggs, creamy liquid, salt, and pepper in a large bowl until smooth and uniform, about 2 minutes. Stir in the filling mixture. Pour and scrape every drop of this mixture into the prepared baking dish. Cover it tightly with foil, then use the sling to pick it up and lower it onto the Deluxe reversible rack. 3. Lock lid; move slider towards PRESSURE. Adjust pressure release valve in the SEAL position. Close pressure-release valve. The cooking temperature will default to HIGH, which is accurate. Set time to 25 minutes. Select START/STOP and start cooking. 4. When cooking is complete, let pressure release quickly by turning it into VENT position. 5. Unlatch the lid and open the Ninja Foodi XL Pressure Cooker Steam Fryer. 6. Use the sling to transfer the baking dish to the wire rack. Uncover the baking dish and cool the frittata for 5 minutes. 7. Run a flatware knife around the interior perimeter of the baking dish. 8. Set a large plate or a serving platter over the top, then invert the hot baking dish and plate so that the frittata comes free. Cut into quarters or smaller wedges to serve.
Per Serving: Calories 157; Fat 12.2g; Sodium 695mg; Carbs 1.5g; Fiber 0g; Sugar 0g; Protein 10.7g

No-Crust Quiche

Prep time: 15 minutes | Cook time: 15 minutes | Serves: 4

360ml water
250g frozen chopped spinach, thawed and squeezed dry by the handful
100g smoked ham, any coatings removed, the meat diced
½ teaspoon dried oregano

½ teaspoon ground black pepper
¼ teaspoon table salt
75g shredded Swiss or Monterey Jack cheese
4 large eggs
120ml whole milk
2 tablespoons plain flour

1. Generously coat or butter the inside of the Cook & Crisp Basket. Pour the water into Ninja Foodi XL Pressure Cooker Steam Fryer with SmartLid cooking pot. Set a Deluxe reversible rack inside the pot. Make an aluminum foil sling and set the Cook & Crisp Basket in the middle of it. 2. Mix the spinach, ham, oregano, pepper, and salt in a medium bowl and smooth it into an even layer in the Cook & Crisp Basket. Sprinkle the cheese evenly over this mixture. 3. Whisk the eggs, milk, and flour in that same bowl until smooth, about 2 minutes. Gently pour this mixture over the ingredients in the Cook & Crisp Basket. Cover the basket tightly with foil. Use the sling to pick it up and lower it onto the Deluxe reversible rack in the pot. 4. Lock lid; move slider towards PRESSURE. Adjust pressure release valve in the SEAL position. Close pressure-release valve. The cooking temperature will default to HIGH, which is accurate. Set time to 25 minutes. Press START/STOP to cooking. 5. When cooking is complete, let pressure release quickly by turning it into VENT position. 6. Unlatch the lid and open the Ninja Foodi XL Pressure Cooker Steam Fryer. Use the sling to transfer the Cook & Crisp Basket to a wire rack. 7. Uncover and cool for 10 minutes. Run a flatware knife around the inside perimeter of the basket. Unlatch the sides and remove the ring. Slice the quiche into quarters to serve.
Per Serving: Calories 207; Fat 14g; Sodium 411mg; Carbs 4g; Fiber 3g; Sugar 1g; Protein 8g

Gouda Egg Casserole with Bacon

Prep time: 12 minutes | Cook time: 30 minutes | Serves: 4

Nonstick cooking spray
1 slice whole grain bread, toasted
50g shredded smoked Gouda cheese
3 slices bacon, chopped
6 large eggs

60ml milk
¼ teaspoon salt
¼ teaspoon freshly ground black pepper
¼ teaspoon dry mustard

1. Spray a 15 cm cake pan with cooking spray, or if the pan is nonstick, skip this step. If you don't have a 15 cm cake pan, any bowl or pan that fits inside your pressure cooker should work. 2. Crumble the toast into the bottom of the pan. Sprinkle with the cheese and bacon. 3. In a medium bowl, whisk together the eggs, half-and-half, salt, pepper, and dry mustard. 4. Pour the egg mixture into the pan. Loosely cover the pan with aluminum foil. 5. Pour 360 ml water into the Ninja Foodi XL Pressure Cooker Steam Fryer with SmartLid cooking pot and insert a Deluxe reversible rack. Place the covered pan on top of the rack. 6. Lock lid; move slider towards PRESSURE. Adjust pressure release valve in the SEAL position. Close pressure-release valve. The cooking temperature will default to HIGH, which is accurate. Set time to 20 minutes. Select START/STOP and start cooking. 7. When cooking is complete, let pressure release quickly by turning it into VENT position. 8. Carefully transfer the pan from the pressure cooker to a cooling rack and let it sit for 5 minutes. 9. Cut into 4 wedges and serve.
Per Serving: Calories 82; Fat 4.5g; Sodium 231mg; Carbs 4.9g; Fiber 0.8g; Sugar 0.6g; Protein 6.2g

Bundt Bread

Prep time: 15 minutes | Cook time: 15 minutes | Serves: 8

360ml water	120g regular, low-fat, or fat-free plain yogurt
Flour-and-fat baking spray	2 tablespoons fresh lemon juice
100g granulated white sugar	1 teaspoon vanilla extract
2 large eggs	185g plain flour
3 tablespoons butter, at room temperature	1½ teaspoons baking soda
2 very ripe medium bananas, peeled	¼ teaspoon table salt
	60g walnuts

1. Pour the water into Ninja Foodi XL Pressure Cooker Steam Fryer with SmartLid cooking pot. Set a Deluxe reversible rack into the pot. Generously spray the inside of the Cook & Crisp Basket with baking spray, making sure the flour and fat mixture gets into all the crevices. Make an aluminum foil sling and set the pan in the middle of it. 2. Put the sugar, eggs, butter, and bananas in a food processor. Cover and process until smooth, stopping the machine once to scrape down the canister. Add the yogurt, lemon juice, and vanilla. Cover and process until smooth. Stop the machine and scrape down the inside. 3. Add the flour, baking soda, and salt. Cover and pulse until a uniform batter forms. Add the nuts and pulse to chop a bit and blend them in. 4. Pour, dollop, and scrape the batter into the Cook & Crisp Basket. Use a rubber spatula to smooth the top of the batter. Use the sling to pick up the Cook & Crisp Basket and set it on the Deluxe reversible rack in the pot. Fold down the ends of the sling so they fit into the pot without touching the batter. Lay a large paper towel over the top of the cake to cover it without touching the batter below. 5. Lock lid; move slider towards PRESSURE. Adjust pressure release valve in the SEAL position. Close pressure-release valve. The cooking temperature will default to HIGH, which is accurate. Set time to 18 minutes. Select START/STOP and start cooking. 6. When cooking is complete, let pressure release naturally. Unlatch the lid and open the Ninja Foodi XL Pressure Cooker Steam Fryer. 7. Remove the paper towel, then use the sling to lift the Bundt pan out of the cooker and onto a wire cooling rack. Cool for 5 minutes, then invert the pan onto a plate and shake gently to release the cake onto a cutting board. 8. Slip the cake back onto the wire rack and continue to cool for at least 20 minutes before slicing into wedges.
Per Serving: Calories 179; Fat 14.3g; Sodium 311mg; Carbs 1.9g; Fiber 0.5g; Sugar 0.3g; Protein 11.6g

Chicken Hash

Prep Time: 10 minutes | Cook Time: 14 minutes | Serves: 3

150g of cauliflower, chopped	½ yellow onion, diced
175g chicken fillet	1 teaspoon black pepper
1 tablespoon water	3 tablespoons butter
1 green pepper, chopped	1 tablespoon cream

1. Place the Cook & Crisp Basket in your Pressure Cooker Steam Fryer. 2. Chop the cauliflower and place in the blender and blend it until you get cauliflower rice. Chop the chicken fillet into small pieces. Sprinkle the chicken fillet with black pepper and stir. In a suitable mixing bowl, mix the ingredients, then add mixture to Cook & Crisp Basket. 3. Put on the Smart Lid on top of the Ninja Foodi Steam Fryer. 4. Move the Lid Slider to the "Air Fry/Stovetop". Select the "Air Fry" mode for cooking. 5. Cook at 195°C for 14 minutes. Then serve chicken hash warm!
Per Serving: Calories: 312; Fat: 7.9g; Sodium: 704mg; Carbs: 6g; Fiber: 3.6g; Sugar 6g; Protein 18g

Nutty Bread Pudding

Prep time: 15 minutes | Cook time: 15 minutes | Serves: 6

360ml water	80g maple syrup
Butter for greasing the baking dish	2 tablespoons light brown sugar
2 large eggs, at room temperature	2 teaspoons vanilla extract
180ml whole or low-fat milk	200g white bread, preferably country-style bread, cut into 2.5 cm squares (do not remove the crusts)
120g heavy cream	
130g creamy natural-style peanut butter	

1. Pour the water into Ninja Foodi XL Pressure Cooker Steam Fryer with SmartLid cooking pot. Set a Deluxe reversible rack in the pot. 2. Generously butter the inside of a 2 liter, high-sided, round soufflé dish. Make an aluminum foil sling and set the baking dish in the center of it. 3. Whisk the eggs, milk, or cream, peanut butter, maple syrup, brown

sugar, and vanilla in a large bowl until the peanut butter dissolves and the mixture is uniform, about 2 minutes. Add the bread cubes and toss well to soak up the egg mixture. 4. Pile the bread cubes into the prepared baking dish in a fairly even layer, pouring any additional liquid in the bowl over them. Cover the baking dish tightly with foil, then use the sling to pick up and lower the baking dish onto the Deluxe reversible rack. 5. Lock lid; move slider towards PRESSURE. Adjust pressure release valve in the SEAL position. Close pressure-release valve. The cooking temperature will default to HIGH, which is accurate. Set time to 10 minutes. Select START/STOP and start cooking. 6. When cooking is complete, let pressure release quickly by turning it into VENT position. Unlatch the lid and open the Ninja Foodi XL Pressure Cooker Steam Fryer. 7. Use the sling to transfer the hot baking dish to a wire rack. Uncover and cool for 5 minutes before serving by the big spoonful.
Per Serving: Calories 240; Fat 14g; Sodium 288mg; Carbs 5g; Fiber 2g; Sugar 1g; Protein 11g

Bagel Bread Pudding with Cinnamon-Raisin

Prep time: 15 minutes | Cook time: 15 minutes | Serves: 4 to 6

360ml water	½ teaspoon vanilla extract
Cooking spray or butter use for greasing the baking dish	¼ teaspoon table salt
4 large eggs, at room temperature	3 large cinnamon-raisin bagels, halved as if to toast them, then the halves cut into 2.5 cm pieces
480ml whole milk	
2 tablespoons light brown sugar	

1. Pour the water into Ninja Foodi XL Pressure Cooker Steam Fryer with SmartLid cooking pot. Set Deluxe reversible rack in the pot. 2. Generously coat or butter the inside of a 2 liter, high-sided, round soufflé dish. Make an aluminum foil sling and set the baking dish in the center of it. 3. Whisk the eggs, brown sugar, vanilla, milk, brown sugar, vanilla, and salt in a large bowl until uniform, about 1 minute. Add the bagel pieces, toss well, and set aside for 10 minutes to soak up more of the egg mixture. 4. Stir the bagel mixture again, then pile the pieces into the prepared baking dish, pouring any additional liquid over them. Drape the baking dish tightly with foil, then use the sling to pick up and lower the baking dish onto the Deluxe reversible rack. Fold down the ends of the sling so they fit in the pot. 5. Lock lid; move slider towards PRESSURE. Adjust pressure release valve in the SEAL position. Close pressure-release valve. The cooking temperature will default to HIGH, which is accurate. Set time to 10 minutes. Select START/STOP and start cooking. 6. When cooking is complete, let pressure release naturally for 10 minutes, then quick-release any remaining pressure by turning it into VENT position. 7. Unlatch the lid and open the Ninja Foodi XL Pressure Cooker Steam Fryer. Use the sling to transfer the hot baking dish to a wire rack. 8. Uncover and cool for 10 minutes before serving by the big spoonful.
Per Serving: Calories 81; Fat 4.4g; Sodium 269mg; Carbs 5.7g; Fiber 0.4g; Sugar 0.3g; Protein 4.9g

Parmesan Omelet

Prep Time: 10 minutes | Cook Time: 10 minutes | Serves: 4

1 green pepper	1 teaspoon oregano, dried
5 eggs	1 teaspoon coriander, dried
½ yellow onion, diced	1 teaspoon olive oil
75g Parmesan cheese, shredded	3 tablespoons cream cheese, softened
1 teaspoon butter	

1. Place the Cook & Crisp Basket in your Pressure Cooker Steam Fryer. 2. In a suitable bowl, add the eggs and mix them. Sprinkle the coriander, oregano, and cream cheese into the eggs. Add the shredded parmesan and mix the egg mixture well. Pour the egg mixture into the Cook & Crisp Basket and place it into the Pressure Cooker Steam Fryer. Put on the Smart Lid on top of the Ninja Foodi Steam Fryer. 3. Move the Lid Slider to the "Air Fry/Stovetop". Select the "Air Fry" mode for cooking. 4. Cook the omelet at 180°C for around 10 minutes. Meanwhile, chop the green pepper and dice the onion. Pour olive oil into a suitable frying pan. preheat well over medium heat. 5. Add the chopped green pepper and onion to frying pan and cook for around 8 minutes. Stir veggies often. 6. Remove the omelet from "cook & crisp basket" and place it on a serving plate. Add the roasted vegetables and serve warm.
Per Serving: Calories: 214; Fat: 10.9g; Sodium: 454mg; Carbs: 10g; Fiber: 3.1g; Sugar 5.2g; Protein 10g

Savory Sausage Pudding

Prep time: 15 minutes	Cook time: 15 minutes	Serves: 4

1 tablespoon butter, plus more for greasing the baking dish
340g smoked sausage diced
360ml water
3 large eggs, at room temperature
360ml whole, low-fat, or fat-free milk
200g white bread, preferably country-style bread, cut into 2.5 cm squares
15g Parmigiano-Reggiano, finely grated
1 teaspoon dried thyme
½ teaspoon ground black pepper

1. Move the slider towards "AIR FRY/STOVETOP" and set Ninja Foodi XL Pressure Cooker Steam Fryer with SmartLid to SEAR/SAUTÉ mode. Adjust the temperature to "Hi5" by using up arrow. Press START/STOP to begin cooking. 2. Melt the butter, then add the sausage. Cook, stirring often, until lightly browned, for about 3 minutes. Turn off the SAUTÉ function. Scrape the contents of the pot. Set aside to cool for 15 minutes. Wipe out the pot. 3. Pour the water into the cooking pot. Set Deluxe reversible rack in the pot. Generously butter the inside of a 2 liter, high-sided, round soufflé dish. Make an aluminum foil sling and set the baking dish in the center of it. 4. Whisk the eggs and milk in a second large bowl until uniform, about 2 minutes. Add the cooled sausage, the bread cubes, cheese, thyme, and pepper. Stir well until the bread is thoroughly coated in the egg mixture. 5. Pile the bread cubes into an even layer in the prepared baking dish, pouring any additional liquid over them. Cover the baking dish tightly with foil, then use the sling to pick up and lower the baking dish onto the Deluxe reversible rack. Fold down the ends of the sling so they fit in the pot. 6. Lock lid; move slider towards PRESSURE. Adjust pressure release valve in the SEAL position. Close pressure-release valve. The cooking temperature will default to HIGH, which is accurate. Set time to 3 minutes. Select START/STOP and start cooking. 7. When cooking is complete, let pressure release naturally for about 10 minutes, then quick-release any remaining pressure by turning it into VENT position. 8. Unlatch the lid and open the Ninja Foodi XL Pressure Cooker Steam Fryer. Use the sling to transfer the hot baking dish to a wire rack. 9. Uncover and cool for 10 minutes before serving by the big spoonful.
Per Serving: Calories 240; Fat 13g; Sodium 147mg; Carbs 6g; Fiber 4g; Sugar 2g; Protein 9g

Applesauce

Prep time: 15 minutes	Cook time: 15 minutes	Serves: 8

1.3kg tart apples, such as Granny Smith, peeled, cored, and chopped
240ml unsweetened apple juice
Up to 55g packed light brown sugar
1 tablespoon fresh lemon juice
½ teaspoon ground cinnamon
¼ teaspoon grated nutmeg
¼ teaspoon table salt

1. Stir all the ingredients in a Ninja Foodi XL Pressure Cooker Steam Fryer with SmartLid cooking pot until the brown sugar dissolves. 2. Lock lid; move slider towards PRESSURE. Adjust pressure release valve in the SEAL position. Close pressure-release valve. The cooking temperature will default to HIGH, which is accurate. Set time to 4 minutes. Select START/STOP and start cooking. 3. When cooking is complete, let pressure release naturally. 4. Unlatch the lid and open the Ninja Foodi XL Pressure Cooker Steam Fryer. Use a potato masher to pulverize the apples into sauce right in the cooker. 5. Serve warm or pack into two liter-sized containers, seal, and store in the fridge for up to 4 days, or in the freezer for up to 3 months.
Per Serving: Calories 126; Fat 8.g; Sodium 477g; Carbs 0.7g; Fiber 0g; Sugar 0g; Protein 11.1g

Nutty Dried Fruit Compote

Prep time: 15 minutes	Cook time: 15 minutes	Serves: 6

240ml water
240ml unsweetened apple juice
105g packed light brown sugar
1 tablespoon fresh lemon juice
¼ teaspoon table salt
One 10 cm cinnamon stick
455g mixed dried fruit, such as pitted prunes, apricots, quartered pear halves, and/or quartered nectarines or peaches

1. Mix all the ingredients in Ninja Foodi XL Pressure Cooker Steam Fryer with SmartLid cooking pot until the brown sugar dissolves. 2. Lock lid; move slider towards PRESSURE. Adjust pressure release valve in the SEAL position. Close pressure-release valve. The cooking temperature will default to HIGH, which is accurate. Set the time to 4 minutes. Select START/STOP and start cooking. When cooking

is complete, let pressure release naturally for about 15 minutes. 3. Unlatch the lid and open the Ninja Foodi XL Pressure Cooker Steam Fryer. Find and discard the cinnamon stick. Stir well before serving. 4. If desired, store in a sealed container or covered bowl in the fridge for up to 3 days.
Per Serving: Calories 200; Fat 4g; Sodium 411mg; Carbs 4g; Fiber 2g; Sugar 1g; Protein 4g

Walnut Vanilla Pancake

Prep Time: 5 minutes	Cook Time: 20 minutes	Serves: 4

3 tablespoons butter into thirds
125g flour
1½ teaspoons baking powder
¼ teaspoon salt
2 tablespoons sugar
180 ml milk
1 egg, beaten
1 teaspoon pure vanilla extract
60g walnuts, chopped
Maple syrup, for serving

1. Place the Cook & Crisp Basket in your Pressure Cooker Steam Fryer. 2. Place 1 tablespoon of the butter in the Cook & Crisp Basket. Put on the Smart Lid on top of the Ninja Foodi Steam Fryer. Move the Lid Slider to the "Air Fry/Stovetop". Select the "Air Fry" mode for cooking. Air Fry at 165°C for around 3 minutes to melt. 3. In a suitable dish or pan, melt the remaining 2 tablespoons of butter either in the microwave or on the stove. 4. In a suitable bowl, stir the flour, baking powder, salt, and sugar. Add milk, beaten egg, the 2 tablespoons of melted butter, and vanilla. Stir until mixed but do not beat. Batter may be lumpy. 5. Pour batter over the melted butter in the Cook & Crisp Basket. Sprinkle nuts evenly over top. 6. Put on the Smart Lid on top of the Ninja Foodi Steam Fryer. 7. Move the Lid Slider to the "Air Fry/Stovetop". Select the "Air Fry" mode for cooking. 8. Cook at 165°C for around 20 minutes or cook until toothpick inserted in center comes out clean. Let pancake rest for around 2 minutes. 9. Remove pancake from pan, slice, and serve with syrup or fresh fruit.
Per Serving: Calories: 351; Fat: 7.9g; Sodium: 704mg; Carbs: 6g; Fiber: 3.6g; Sugar 6g; Protein 18g

Egg Scramble

Prep Time: 10 minutes	Cook Time: 17 minutes	Serves: 4

4 eggs
4 tablespoons butter
1 teaspoon salt

1. Place the Cook & Crisp Basket in your Pressure Cooker Steam Fryer. 2. Cover the Ninja Foodi Pressure Steam Fryer basket with foil and place the eggs there. Transfer the basket into the Pressure Cooker Steam Fryer. 3. Put on the Smart Lid on top of the Ninja Foodi Steam Fryer. Move the Lid Slider to the "Air Fry/Stovetop". Select the "Air Fry" mode for cooking. Cook for the eggs for around 17 minutes at 160°C. 4. When the time is over, remove the eggs from the "cook & crisp basket" and put them in cold water to chill them. After this, peel the eggs and chop them up finely. 5. Mix the chopped eggs with butter and add salt. Mix it until you get the spread texture. 6. Serve the egg butter with the keto almond bread.
Per Serving: Calories: 284; Fat: 9g; Sodium: 441mg; Carbs: 7g; Fiber: 4.6g; Sugar 5g; Protein 19g

Western Cheese Omelet

Prep Time: 5 minutes	Cook Time: 22 minutes	Serves: 2

40g chopped onion
35g chopped pepper, green or red
35g diced ham
1 teaspoon butter
4 large eggs
2 tablespoons milk
⅛ teaspoon salt
75g grated sharp Cheddar cheese

1. Place the Cook & Crisp Basket in your Pressure Cooker Steam Fryer.2. Place onion, pepper, ham, and butter in the Cook & Crisp Basket. 3. Put on the Smart Lid on top of the Ninja Foodi Steam Fryer. 4. Move the Lid Slider to the "Air Fry/Stovetop". Select the "Air Fry" mode for cooking. 5. Air Fry omelet at 200°C for 1 minute and stir. Continue cooking 4 to 5 minutes, until vegetables are tender. 6. Beat eggs, milk, and salt. Pour over vegetables and ham in the Cook & Crisp Basket. Put on the Smart Lid on top of the Ninja Foodi Steam Fryer. Move the Lid Slider to the "Air Fry/Stovetop". Select the "Air Fry" mode for cooking. Air Fry at 180°C for around 13 to 15 minutes or until eggs set and top has browned slightly. 7. Sprinkle grated cheese on top of omelet. Cook 1 minute or just long enough to melt the cheese.
Per Serving: Calories: 221; Fat: 7.9g; Sodium: 704mg; Carbs: 6g; Fiber: 3.6g; Sugar 6g; Protein 18g

Almond Egg Bread

Prep Time: 10 minutes | Cook Time: 25 minutes | Serves: 19

95g almond flour	55g butter
¼ sea salt	3 eggs
1 teaspoon baking powder	

1. Place the Cook & Crisp Basket in your Pressure Cooker Steam Fryer. 2. Crack the eggs into a suitable bowl then using a hand blender mix them up. Melt the butter at room temperature. Take the melted butter and add it to the egg mixture. 3. Add the salt, baking powder and almond flour to egg mixture and knead the prepared dough. Cover the prepared dough with a towel for around 10 minutes to rest. 4. Place the prepared dough in the Cook & Crisp Basket. Put on the Smart Lid on top of the Ninja Foodi Steam Fryer. 5. Move the Lid Slider to the "Air Fry/Stovetop". Select the "Air Fry" mode for cooking. Cook the bread at 180°C for around 10 minutes. 6. Then reduce its heat to 175°C. Cook the bread for an additional 15 minutes. You can use a toothpick to check to make sure the bread is cooked. 7. Transfer the bread to a wooden board to allow it to chill. Once the bread has chilled, then slice and serve it.
Per Serving: Calories: 82; Fat: 7.9g; Sodium: 704mg; Carbs: 6g; Fiber: 3.6g; Sugar 6g; Protein 18g

Sesame Flax Meal Porridge

Prep Time: 10 minutes | Cook Time: 8 minutes | Serves: 4

2 tablespoons sesame seeds	3 tablespoons flax meal
½ teaspoon vanilla extract	240ml almond milk
1 tablespoon butter	4 tablespoons chia seeds
1 tablespoon liquid Stevia	

1. Place the Cook & Crisp Basket in your Pressure Cooker Steam Fryer. 2. Put the sesame seeds, chia seeds, almond milk, flax meal, liquid Stevia and butter into the Ninja Foodi Pressure Steam Fryer basket tray. Add the vanilla extract. 3. Put on the Smart Lid on top of the Ninja Foodi Steam Fryer. Move the Lid Slider to the "Air Fry/ Stovetop". Select the "Air Fry" mode for cooking. Adjust the cooking temperature to 190°C. 4. Cook porridge at 190°C for around 8 minutes. When porridge is cooked stir it carefully then allows it to rest for around 5 minutes before serving.
Per Serving: Calories: 289; Fat: 14g; Sodium: 791mg; Carbs: 8.9g; Fiber: 4.6g; Sugar 8g; Protein 16g

Kale Fritters

Prep Time: 10 minutes | Cook Time: 8 minutes | Serves: 8

300g kale, chopped	2 tablespoons almond flour
1 teaspoon oil	1 egg
1 tablespoon cream	1 tablespoon butter
1 teaspoon paprika	½ yellow onion, diced
½ teaspoon sea salt	

1. Place the Cook & Crisp Basket in your Pressure Cooker Steam Fryer. 2. Wash and chop the kale. Add the chopped kale to blender and blend it until smooth. Dice up the yellow onion. 3. Beat the egg and mix it in a suitable mixing bowl. Add the almond flour, paprika, cream and salt into bowl with whisked egg and stir. Add the diced onion and blended kale to mixing bowl and mix until you get fritter dough. 4. Grease the inside of the Ninja Foodi Pressure Steam Fryer basket with olive oil. Make medium-sized fritters with prepared mixture and place them into "cook & crisp basket". 5. Put on the Smart Lid on top of the Ninja Foodi Steam Fryer. Move the Lid Slider to the "Air Fry/ Stovetop". Select the "Air Fry" mode for cooking. 6. Cook the kale fritters on each side at 180°C for 4 minutes. 7. Once they are cooked, allow them to chill then serve.
Per Serving: Calories: 219; Fat: 10g; Sodium: 891mg; Carbs: 22.9g; Fiber: 4g; Sugar 4g; Protein 13g

Breakfast Eggs with Cream

Prep Time: 10 minutes | Cook Time: 17 minutes | Serves: 2

4 eggs	1 tablespoon chives, chopped
1 teaspoon oregano	1 tablespoon cream
1 teaspoon parsley, dried	1 teaspoon paprika
½ teaspoon sea salt	

1. Place the Cook & Crisp Basket in your Pressure Cooker Steam

Fryer. 2. Place the eggs in the Ninja Foodi Pressure Steam Fryer basket. 3. Put on the Smart Lid on top of the Ninja Foodi Steam Fryer. 4. Move the Lid Slider to the "Air Fry/Stovetop". Select the "Air Fry" mode for cooking. 5. Cook them for around 17 minutes at 160°C. Meanwhile, mix the parsley, oregano, cream, parpkia, and salt in shallow bowl. Chop the chives and add them to cream mixture. 6. When the eggs are cooked, place them in cold water and allow them to chill. After this, peel the eggs and cut them into halves. 7. Remove the egg yolks and add yolks to cream mixture and mash to blend well with a fork. 8. Then fill the egg whites with the cream-egg yolk mixture. Serve immediately.
Per Serving: Calories: 219; Fat: 10g; Sodium: 891mg; Carbs: 22.9g; Fiber: 4g; Sugar 4g; Protein 13g

Creamy Seed Porridge

Prep Time: 10 minutes | Cook Time: 12 minutes | Serves: 3

1 tablespoon butter	¼ teaspoon salt
¼ teaspoon nutmeg	3 tablespoons sesame seeds
80g heavy cream	3 tablespoons chia seeds
1 egg	

1. Place the Cook & Crisp Basket in your Pressure Cooker Steam Fryer. 2. Place the butter in the Cook & Crisp Basket. Add the chia seeds, sesame seeds, heavy cream, nutmeg, and salt. Stir gently. Beat the egg in a cup and mix it with a fork. 3. Add the whisked egg to cook & crisp basket. Stir the mixture with a wooden spatula. 4. Place the Cook & Crisp Basket into Pressure Cooker Steam Fryer. Put on the Smart Lid on top of the Ninja Foodi Steam Fryer. Move the Lid Slider to the "Air Fry/Stovetop". Select the "Air Fry" mode for cooking. 5. Cook the porridge at 190°C for around 12 minutes. Stir it about 3 times during the cooking process. 6. Remove the porridge from cook & crisp Basket immediately and serve hot!
Per Serving: Calories: 382; Fat: 10.9g; Sodium: 354mg; Carbs: 20.5g; Fiber: 4.1g; Sugar 8.2g; Protein 06g

Breakfast Chicken Sandwich

Prep Time: 10 minutes | Cook Time: 10 minutes | Serves: 2

150g chicken	½ teaspoon sea salt
2 slices of cheddar cheese	1 egg
2 lettuce leaves	1 teaspoon cayenne pepper
1 tablespoon dill, dried	1 teaspoon tomato puree

1. Place the Cook & Crisp Basket in your Pressure Cooker Steam Fryer. 2. Mix the chicken with the pepper and sea salt. Add the dried dill and stir. Beat the egg into the chicken mixture. Make 2 medium-sized burgers from the chicken mixture. Grease the Ninja Foodi Pressure Steam Fryer basket with olive oil and place the chicken burgers inside of it. 3. Put on the Smart Lid on top of the Ninja Foodi Steam Fryer. Move the Lid Slider to the "Air Fry/Stovetop". Select the "Air Fry" mode for cooking. 4. Adjust the cooking temperature to 195°C. 5. Cook the chicken burgers at 195°C for around 10 minutes. 6. Flip the burgers. Cook for 6minutes. 7. When the burgers are cooked, transfer them to the lettuce leaves. Sprinkle the top of them with tomato puree and with a slice of cheddar cheese. 8. Serve immediately!
Per Serving: Calories: 251; Fat: 19g; Sodium: 354mg; Carbs: 15g; Fiber: 5.1g; Sugar 8.2g; Protein 12g

Coconut Porridge

Prep Time: 10 minutes | Cook Time: 7 minutes | Serves: 4

240ml coconut milk	1 teaspoon cinnamon
3 tablespoons blackberries	5 tablespoons chia seeds
2 tablespoons walnuts	3 tablespoons coconut flakes
1 teaspoon butter	¼ teaspoon salt

1. Place the Cook & Crisp Basket in your Pressure Cooker Steam Fryer. 2. Pour the coconut milk into the "cook & crisp basket". Add the coconut, salt, chia seeds, cinnamon, and butter. Up the walnuts and add them to the "cook & crisp basket". 3. Sprinkle the mixture with salt. Mash the blackberries with a fork and add them also to the Ninja Foodi Pressure Steam Fryer basket. 4. Put on the Smart Lid on top of the Ninja Foodi Steam Fryer. Move the Lid Slider to the "Air Fry/Stovetop". Select the "Air Fry" mode for cooking. 5. Cook the porridge at 190°C for around 7 minutes. Stir porridge with a wooden spoon and serve warm.
Per Serving: Calories: 282; Fat: 7.9g; Sodium: 704mg; Carbs: 6g; Fiber: 3.6g; Sugar 6g; Protein 18g

Spinach Cheddar Quiche

Prep Time: 10 minutes | Cook Time: 21 minutes | Serves: 6

150g cheddar cheese, shredded
1 teaspoon olive oil
3 eggs
1 teaspoon black pepper
½ yellow onion, diced

60g cream cheese
30g spinach
1 teaspoon sea salt
4 tablespoons water, boiled
45g almond flour

1. Place the Cook & Crisp Basket in your Pressure Cooker Steam Fryer. 2. Mix the almond flour, water, and salt. Mix and knead the prepared dough. Grease inside of the fryer basket with olive oil. Roll the prepared dough and place it in your Ninja Foodi Pressure Steam Fryer basket tray in the shape of the crust. Place "cook & crisp basket" in your Pressure Cooker Steam Fryer. 3. Put on the Smart Lid on top of the Ninja Foodi Steam Fryer. 4. Move the Lid Slider to the "Air Fry/Stovetop". Select the "Air Fry" mode for cooking. 5. Cook at 190°C for around 5 minutes. Chop the spinach leaves and mix it with the cream cheese and black pepper. Dice the yellow onion and add it to the spinach mixture and stir. Mix eggs in a suitable bowl. 6. When the quiche crust is cooked—transfer the spinach filling. Sprinkle the filling top with shredded cheese and pour the whisked eggs over the top. 7. Put on the Smart Lid on top of the Ninja Foodi Steam Fryer. Move the Lid Slider to the "Air Fry/Stovetop". Select the "Air Fry" mode for cooking. Cook the quiche at 175°C for around 7 minutes. 8. Reduce its heat to 150°C Cook for the quiche for an additional 9 minutes. Allow the quiche to chill and then cut it into pieces for serving.
Per Serving: Calories: 284; Fat: 9g; Sodium: 441mg; Carbs: 7g; Fiber: 4.6g; Sugar 5g; Protein 19g

Pancake Hash

Prep Time: 10 minutes | Cook Time: 9 minutes | Serves: 7

1 egg
60g heavy cream
5 tablespoons butter
95g coconut flour

1 teaspoon ginger
1 teaspoon salt
1 tablespoon apple cider vinegar
1 teaspoon baking soda

1. Place the Cook & Crisp Basket in your Pressure Cooker Steam Fryer. 2. Mix the salt, baking soda, ginger and flour in a suitable mixing bowl. 3. In a separate bowl crack, the egg into it. Add butter and heavy cream. Mix well using a hand mixer. Mix the liquid and dry mixtures and stir until smooth. 4. Pour the pancake mixture into the Ninja Foodi Pressure Steam Fryer basket. Put on the Smart Lid on top of the Ninja Foodi Steam Fryer. 5. Move the Lid Slider to the "Air Fry/Stovetop". Select the "Air Fry" mode for cooking. Cook the pancake hash at 200°C for around 4 minutes. 6. After this, scramble the pancake hash well and continue to cook for another 5 minutes more. 7. When dish is cooked, transfer it to serving plates, and serve hot!
Per Serving: Calories: 224; Fat: 7.9g; Sodium: 704mg; Carbs: 6g; Fiber: 3.6g; Sugar 6g; Protein 18g

Spinach Parsley Omelet

Prep Time: 10 minutes | Cook Time: 10 minutes | Serves: 1

1 teaspoon olive oil
3 eggs
3 tablespoons ricotta cheese

1 tablespoon parsley, chopped
10g spinach, chopped
Black pepper and salt to taste

1. Place the Cook & Crisp Basket in your Pressure Cooker Steam Fryer. 2. Pour olive oil on the Cook & Crisp Basket. 3. Mix eggs adding black pepper and salt as seasoning. Stir in the ricotta, spinach, and parsley with eggs. Pour the egg mixture into the Cook & Crisp Basket. 4. Put on the Smart Lid on top of the Ninja Foodi Steam Fryer. Move the Lid Slider to the "Air Fry/Stovetop". Select the "Air Fry" mode for cooking. Adjust the cooking temperature to 165°C. 5. Cook for around 10 minutes. Serve warm.
Per Serving: Calories: 219; Fat: 10g; Sodium: 891mg; Carbs: 22.9g; Fiber: 4g; Sugar 4g; Protein 13g

Bacon Egg Cups

Prep Time: 10 minutes | Cook Time: 12 minutes | Serves: 2

2 eggs
1 tablespoon chives, fresh, chopped
½ teaspoon paprika
½ teaspoon cayenne pepper

75g cheddar cheese, shredded
½ teaspoon butter
¼ teaspoon salt
100g bacon, cut into tiny pieces

1. Place the Cook & Crisp Basket in your Pressure Cooker Steam Fryer. 2. Sprinkle the bacon with cayenne pepper, salt, and paprika. Mix the chopped bacon. Spread butter in bottom of ramekin dishes and beat the eggs there. 3. Add the chives and shredded cheese. Add the chopped bacon over egg mixture in ramekin dishes. 4. Place the ramekins in your Ninja Foodi Pressure Steam Fryer basket. Place the Cook & Crisp Basket in your Ninja Foodi Pressure Steam Fryer. 5. Put on the Smart Lid on top of the Ninja Foodi Steam Fryer. Move the Lid Slider to the "Air Fry/Stovetop". Select the "Air Fry" mode for cooking. 6. Cook at 180°C for around 12 minutes. Serve.
Per Serving: Calories: 334; Fat: 7.9g; Sodium: 704mg; Carbs: 6g; Fiber: 3.6g; Sugar 6g; Protein 18g

Courgette Hash

Prep Time: 10 minutes | Cook Time: 8 minutes | Serves: 4

175g bacon, cooked
1 courgette, cubed into small pieces
100g cheddar cheese, shredded
2 tablespoons butter

1 teaspoon thyme
1 teaspoon coriander
1 teaspoon paprika
1 teaspoon black pepper
1 teaspoon salt

1. Place the Cook & Crisp Basket in your Pressure Cooker Steam Fryer. 2. Chop the courgette into small cubes and sprinkle with black pepper, salt, paprika, coriander and thyme. Add butter to the Cook & Crisp Basket. Melt the butter and add the courgette cubes. 2. Put on the Smart Lid on top of the Ninja Foodi Steam Fryer. Move the Lid Slider to the "Air Fry/Stovetop". Select the "Air Fry" mode for cooking. Cook the courgette cubes at 200°C for around 5 minutes. 3. Meanwhile, shred the cheddar cheese. Add the bacon to the courgette cubes. Sprinkle the courgette mixture with shredded cheese. Cook for around 3 minutes more. 4. When cooking is completed, transfer the breakfast hash into serving bowls.
Per Serving: Calories: 372; Fat: 20g; Sodium: 891mg; Carbs: 29g; Fiber: 3g; Sugar 8g; Protein 7g

Garlic Toast

Prep Time: 10 minutes | Cook Time: 10 minutes | Serves: 2

1 vegan bread loaf, large
2 teaspoons chives
2 tablespoons nutritional yeast

2 tablespoons garlic puree
2 tablespoons olive oil
Black pepper and salt to taste

1. Place the Cook & Crisp Basket in your Pressure Cooker Steam Fryer. 2. Slice the bread loaf (not all the way through). In a suitable bowl, mix the garlic puree, olive oil, and nutritional yeast. 3. Add this mixture on top of the bread loaf. Sprinkle loaf with chives and season with black pepper and salt. Place loaf inside of the Cook & Crisp Basket. 4. Put on the Smart Lid on top of the Ninja Foodi Steam Fryer. Move the Lid Slider to the "Air Fry/Stovetop". Select the "Air Fry" mode for cooking. Adjust the cooking temperature to 190°C. 5. Cook for around 10 minutes.
Per Serving: Calories: 234; Fat: 12.9g; Sodium: 414mg; Carbs: 11g; Fiber: 5g; Sugar 9g; Protein 11g

Morning Sausages

Prep Time: 10 minutes | Cook Time: 12 minutes | Serves: 6

175g chicken
175g pork
1 teaspoon coriander
1 teaspoon basil, dried
½ teaspoon nutmeg
1 teaspoon olive oil

1 teaspoon minced garlic
1 tablespoon coconut flour
1 egg
1 teaspoon soy sauce
1 teaspoon sea salt
½ teaspoon black pepper

1. Place the Cook & Crisp Basket in your Pressure Cooker Steam Fryer. 2. Mix the pork, chicken, soy sauce, black pepper, garlic, basil, coriander, nutmeg, sea salt, and egg. 3. Add the coconut flour and mix the mixture well to mix. Make medium-sized sausages with the meat mixture. 4. Grease the inside of the Ninja Foodi Pressure Steam Fryer basket with the olive oil. Place prepared sausages into the "cook & crisp basket" and place inside of Pressure Cooker Steam Fryer. 5. Put on the Smart Lid on top of the Ninja Foodi Steam Fryer. Move the Lid Slider to the "Air Fry/Stovetop". Select the "Air Fry" mode for cooking. 6. Cook the sausages at 180°C for around 6 minutes. Turn the sausages over. Cook for around 6 minutes more. 7. Serve warm.
Per Serving: Calories: 184; Fat: 5g; Sodium: 441mg; Carbs: 17g; Fiber: 4.6g; Sugar 5g; Protein 9g

Liver Pate

Prep Time: 10 minutes | Cook Time: 10 minutes | Serves: 7

455g chicken liver
1 teaspoon salt
½ teaspoon coriander, dried
1 yellow onion, diced

1 teaspoon black pepper
240ml water
4 tablespoons butter

1. Place the Cook & Crisp Basket in your Pressure Cooker Steam Fryer. 2. Chop the chicken liver and place it in the Cook & Crisp Basket. Add water and diced onion. Put on the Smart Lid on top of the Ninja Foodi Steam Fryer. Move the Lid Slider to the "Air Fry/Stovetop". Select the "Air Fry" mode for cooking. 3. Cook the chicken liver at 180°C for around 10 minutes. When it is finished cooking, drain the chicken liver. 4. Transfer the chicken liver to blender, add butter, black pepper and dried coriander and blend. 5. Once you get a pate texture, transfer to liver pate bowl and serve immediately or keep in the fridge for later.
Per Serving: Calories: 221; Fat: 7.9g; Sodium: 704mg; Carbs: 6g; Fiber: 3.6g; Sugar 6g; Protein 18g

Meatloaf Slices

Prep Time: 10 minutes | Cook Time: 20 minutes | Serves: 6

200g pork
175g beef
1 teaspoon olive oil
1 teaspoon butter
1 tablespoon oregano, dried
1 teaspoon cayenne pepper

1 teaspoon salt
1 tablespoon chives
1 tablespoon almond flour
1 egg
1 onion, diced

1. Place the Cook & Crisp Basket in your Pressure Cooker Steam Fryer. 2. Beat egg in a suitable bowl. Add the beef and pork. Add the chives, almond flour, cayenne pepper, salt, dried oregano, and butter. Add diced onion to beef mixture. 3. Use hands to shape a meatloaf mixture. Grease the inside of the "cook & crisp basket" with olive oil and place the meatloaf inside it. 4. Put on the Smart Lid on top of the Ninja Foodi Steam Fryer. Move the Lid Slider to the "Air Fry/Stovetop". Select the "Air Fry" mode for cooking. 5. Cook the meatloaf at 175°C for around 20 minutes. When the meatloaf has cooked, allow it to chill for a bit. Slice and serve it.
Per Serving: Calories: 312; Fat: 12.9g; Sodium: 414mg; Carbs: 11g; Fiber: 5g; Sugar 9g; Protein 11g

Bacon Burger

Prep Time: 10 minutes | Cook Time: 8 minutes | Serves: 2

200g beef
50g lettuce leaves
½ teaspoon minced garlic
1 teaspoon olive oil
½ teaspoon sea salt
1 teaspoon black pepper

1 teaspoon butter
100g bacon, cooked
1 egg
½ yellow onion, diced
½ cucumber, slice finely
½ tomato, slice finely

1. Place the Cook & Crisp Basket in your Pressure Cooker Steam Fryer. 2. Begin by whisking the egg in a suitable bowl, then add the beef and mix well. Add cooked, chopped bacon to the beef mixture. Add butter, black pepper, minced garlic, and salt. Mix and make burgers. 3. Grease the Ninja Foodi Pressure Steam Fryer basket with olive oil and place the burgers inside of it. Put on the Smart Lid on top of the Ninja Foodi Steam Fryer. 4. Move the Lid Slider to the "Air Fry/Stovetop". Select the "Air Fry" mode for cooking. Adjust the cooking temperature to 185°C. Cook the burgers for around 8-minutes on each side. 5. Meanwhile, slice the cucumber, onion, and tomato finely. Place the tomato, onion, and cucumber onto the lettuce leaves. 6. When the burgers are cooked, allow them to chill at room temperature, and place them over the vegetables and serve.
Per Serving: Calories: 282; Fat: 10.9g; Sodium: 354mg; Carbs: 20.5g; Fiber: 4.1g; Sugar 8.2g; Protein 06g

Minced Beef Sandwich

Prep Time: 10 minutes | Cook Time: 16 minutes | Serves: 2

150g minced beef
4 lettuce leaves
1 teaspoon flax seeds
1 teaspoon olive oil
Salt, to taste

½ teaspoon black pepper
½ teaspoon chili flakes
½ tomato, sliced
½ avocado, pitted, sliced

1. Place the Cook & Crisp Basket in your Pressure Cooker Steam Fryer. 2. Mix the chili flakes with the minced beef and salt. Add the flax seeds and stir the meat mixture using a fork. 2. Pour the olive oil into the Ninja Foodi Pressure Steam Fryer basket. Make 2 burgers from the beef mixture and place them in the "cook & crisp basket". 3. Put on the Smart Lid on top of the Ninja Foodi Steam Fryer. Move the Lid Slider to the "Air Fry/Stovetop". Select the "Air Fry" mode for cooking. 4. Adjust the cooking temperature to 185°C Cook the burgers for around 8 minutes on each side. 5. Meanwhile, slice the avocado and tomato. Place the avocado and tomato onto 2 lettuce leaves. 6. Add the cooked minced beef burgers and serve them hot!
Per Serving: Calories: 289; Fat: 14g; Sodium: 791mg; Carbs: 8.9g; Fiber: 4.6g; Sugar 8g; Protein 6g

Beef Chili

Prep Time: 10 minutes | Cook Time: 10 minutes | Serves: 4

200g beef
½ yellow onion, diced
1 teaspoon tomato puree
150g cheddar cheese, shredded
1 teaspoon parsley, dried

1 teaspoon coriander, dried
1 teaspoon oregano, dried
1 tablespoon dill weed
1 teaspoon mustard
1 tablespoon butter

1. Place the Cook & Crisp Basket in your Pressure Cooker Steam Fryer. 2. Mix beef with diced onion in a suitable bowl. Sprinkle the mixture with tomato puree, coriander, parsley, oregano and dried dill. Then add the butter and mustard and mix well. Add beef mixture to "cook & crisp basket". 3. Put on the Smart Lid on top of the Ninja Foodi Steam Fryer. Move the Lid Slider to the "Air Fry/Stovetop". Select the "Air Fry" mode for cooking. 4. Adjust the cooking temperature to 190°C. Cook for the chili for around 9 minutes. After about 6 minutes of cooking stir the chili. 5. When the chili is cooked, sprinkle the top with shredded cheddar cheese and stir carefully. 6. Transfer chili mixture into serving bowls. Serve warm.
Per Serving: Calories: 334; Fat: 7.9g; Sodium: 704mg; Carbs: 6g; Fiber: 3.6g; Sugar 6g; Protein 18g

Eggs and Sausage Muffins

Prep Time: 10 minutes | Cook Time: 20 minutes | Serves: 2

3 eggs
60g cream
2 sausages, boiled
Chopped fresh herbs

Sea salt to taste
4 tablespoons cheese, grated
1 piece of bread, sliced lengthwise

1. Place the Cook & Crisp Basket in your Pressure Cooker Steam Fryer. 2. Break the eggs in a suitable bowl, add cream, and scramble. Grease 3 muffin cups with cooking spray. Add equal amounts of egg mixture into each. 3. Arrange sliced sausages and bread slices into muffin cups, sinking into egg mixture. Sprinkle the tops with cheese, and salt to taste. 4. Put on the Smart Lid on top of the Ninja Foodi Steam Fryer. Move the Lid Slider to the "Air Fry/Stovetop". Select the "Air Fry" mode for cooking. 5. Adjust the cooking temperature to 180°C. Cook the muffins for around 20 minutes. Season with fresh herbs and serve warm.
Per Serving: Calories: 361; Fat: 7.9g; Sodium: 704mg; Carbs: 6g; Fiber: 3.6g; Sugar 6g; Protein 18g

Italian Frittata

Prep Time: 10 minutes | Cook Time: 10 minutes | Serves: 2

4 cherry tomatoes, sliced into halves
½ Italian sausage, sliced
½ teaspoon Italian seasoning

3 eggs
1 tablespoon parsley, chopped
Black pepper and salt to taste

1. Place the Cook & Crisp Basket in your Pressure Cooker Steam Fryer. Put the sausage and cherry tomatoes into the Cook & Crisp Basket. 2. Put on the Smart Lid on top of the Ninja Foodi Steam Fryer. Move the Lid Slider to the "Air Fry/Stovetop". Select the "Air Fry" mode for cooking. Adjust the cooking temperature to 180°C. 3. Cook for around 5 minutes. Crack eggs into small bowl, add parsley, Italian seasoning and mix well by whisking. 4. Pour egg mixture over sausage and cherry tomatoes and place back into Pressure Cooker Steam Fryer and cook for an additional 5 minutes. 5. Serve warm.
Per Serving: Calories: 372; Fat: 20g; Sodium: 891mg; Carbs: 29g; Fiber: 3g; Sugar 8g; Protein 7g

English Bacon Breakfast

Prep Time: 10 minutes | Cook Time: 20 minutes | Serves: 4

8 medium sausages	2 tomatoes, sliced, sauté
8 slices of back bacon	50g mushrooms, finely sliced,
4 eggs	sauté
8 slices of toast	1 tablespoon olive oil
1 can baked beans	

1. Place the Cook & Crisp Basket in your Pressure Cooker Steam Fryer. 2. Heat olive oil in suitable saucepan over medium-high heat. Add mushrooms to pan and sauté for a few minutes. 3. Remove mushrooms from pan and set aside, add tomatoes to pan and sauté for a few minutes then set aside. Place your sausages and bacon into the Cook & Crisp Basket. 4. Put on the Smart Lid on top of the Ninja Foodi Steam Fryer. Move the Lid Slider to the "Air Fry/Stovetop". Select the "Air Fry" mode for cooking. Adjust the cooking temperature to 160°C. Cook for around 10 minutes. 5. Place the baked beans into a ramekin and your eggs in another ramekin. Transfer to the Cook & Crisp Basket. 6. Put on the Smart Lid on top of the Ninja Foodi Steam Fryer. Move the Lid Slider to the "Air Fry/Stovetop". Select the "Air Fry" mode for cooking. Cook for an additional 10 minutes at 200°C. 7. Serve warm.
Per Serving: Calories: 234; Fat: 19g; Sodium: 354mg; Carbs: 15g; Fiber: 5.1g; Sugar 8.2g; Protein 12g

Veggies on Toast

Prep Time: 10 minutes | Cook Time: 11 minutes | Serves: 4

1 tablespoon olive oil	2 green onions, sliced
180g soft goat cheese	1 small yellow squash, sliced
2 tablespoons softened butter	100g button mushrooms, sliced
4 slices French bread	1 red pepper, cut into strips

1. Place the Cook & Crisp Basket in your Pressure Cooker Steam Fryer. 2. Sprinkle the Cook & Crisp Basket with olive oil. Mix the red peppers, squash, mushrooms and green onions. 3. Put on the Smart Lid on top of the Ninja Foodi Steam Fryer. Move the Lid Slider to the "Air Fry/Stovetop". Select the "Air Fry" mode for cooking. 4. Cook them at 175°C for around 7 minutes. Place vegetables on a plate and set aside. 5. Spread the bread slices with butter and place into the Cook & Crisp Basket, with butter side up. 6. Put on the Smart Lid on top of the Ninja Foodi Steam Fryer. Move the Lid Slider to the "Air Fry/Stovetop". Select the "Air Fry" mode for cooking. Adjust the cooking temperature to 175°C. 7. Toast for around 4 minutes. Spread the cheese on toasted bread and top with veggies. 8. Serve warm.
Per Serving: Calories: 184; Fat: 5g; Sodium: 441mg; Carbs: 17g; Fiber: 4.6g; Sugar 5g; Protein 9g

Rice Paper Breakfast

Prep Time: 10 minutes | Cook Time: 30 minutes | Serves: 4

4 pieces white rice paper, cut into	2 tablespoons liquid smoke
2.5 cm thick strips	2 tablespoons cashew butter
2 tablespoons water	3 tablespoons soy sauce or tamari

1. Place the Cook & Crisp Basket in your Pressure Cooker Steam Fryer. 2. In a suitable mixing bowl, add soy sauce, cashew butter, liquid smoke, and water, mix well. Soak the rice paper in this mixture for around 5 minutes. Place the rice paper the Cook & Crisp Basket and do not overlap pieces. 3. Put on the Smart Lid on top of the Ninja Foodi Steam Fryer. Move the Lid Slider to the "Air Fry/Stovetop". Select the "Air Fry" mode for cooking. Adjust the cooking temperature to 175°C. 4. Air Fry for around 15 minutes or until crispy. Serve with steamed vegetables!
Per Serving: Calories: 382; Fat: 10.9g; Sodium: 354mg; Carbs: 20.5g; Fiber: 4.1g; Sugar 8.2g; Protein 06g

Broccoli Tofu Scramble

Prep Time: 10 minutes | Cook Time: 30 minutes | Serves: 3

350g broccoli florets	1 teaspoon turmeric powder
1 block tofu, chopped finely	½ teaspoon garlic powder
350g red potatoes, chopped	½ teaspoon onion powder
2 tablespoons olive oil	80g onion, chopped
2 tablespoons tamari	

1. Place the Cook & Crisp Basket in your Pressure Cooker Steam Fryer. 2. Mix the potatoes in a suitable bowl with half of the olive oil. Place the potatoes into the Cook & Crisp Basket. 3. Put on the Smart Lid on top of the Ninja Foodi Steam Fryer. Move the Lid Slider to the "Air Fry/Stovetop". Select the "Air Fry" mode for cooking. Adjust the cooking temperature to 200°C. Cook for them for around 15 minutes. 4. Mix the remaining olive oil, tofu, tamari, turmeric, garlic powder and onion powder. Stir in the chopped onions. Add the broccoli florets. Pour this mixture on top of the air-fried potatoes. 5. Put on the Smart Lid on top of the Ninja Foodi Steam Fryer. Move the Lid Slider to the "Air Fry/Stovetop". Select the "Air Fry" mode for cooking. Cook for an additional 15 minutes. 6. Serve warm.
Per Serving: Calories: 282; Fat: 7.9g; Sodium: 704mg; Carbs: 6g; Fiber: 3.6g; Sugar 6g; Protein 18g

Chapter 2 Vegetable and Sides Recipes

Creamy Polenta

Prep time: 20 minutes | Cook time: 40 minutes | Serves: 4

2 tablespoons butter	80g polenta
½ sweet onion, chopped	¼ teaspoon sea salt, or more to
1 shallot, minced	taste
240ml chicken stock	225g mozzarella cheese, shredded
240ml milk	25g parmesan cheese, shaved

1. Add butter, onion, and shallot to cooking pot. 2. Move the slider towards "AIR FRY/STOVETOP" and set Ninja Foodi XL Pressure Cooker Steam Fryer with SmartLid to SEAR/SAUTÉ mode. Adjust the temperature to "Hi5" by using up arrow. Press START/STOP to begin cooking. Cook until onion is soft and translucent, stirring occasionally, for 10 to 15 minutes. 3. Add chicken stock, milk, polenta, and sea salt. Lock lid; move slider towards AIR FRY/STOVETOP. Select STEAM. Set time to 20 minutes. Press START/STOP to begin cooking. Cook until polenta has absorbed the liquid; stir occasionally. Fold in the cheese and stir until melted. 4. Serve hot and enjoy!
Per Serving: Calories 267; Fat 11g; Sodium 247mg; Carbs 6g; Fiber 4g; Sugar 2g; Protein 16g

Refreshing Steamed Artichokes

Prep time: 15 minutes | Cook time: 30 minutes | Serves: 2

2 whole artichokes	Olive oil, for drizzling
2 lemons, cut into wedges	Sea salt, to serve

1. Cut a third of the top off an artichoke. Trim the stem off, as well as any thorny tips from the outer leaves. 2. Rub lemon wedges over the cut edges to prevent browning. 3. Add 180 ml of water to the cooking pot. 4. Add the artichoke to the Cook & Crisp Basket. 5. Lock lid; move slider towards AIR FRY/STOVETOP. Select STEAM. Set time to 30 minutes. Press START/STOP to begin cooking. Cook until leaves pull off easily. 6. Remove from pot, drizzle with olive oil and a dash of sea salt to serve.
Per Serving: Calories 337; Fat 16.7g; Sodium 245mg; Carbs 13.1g; Fiber 7.1g; Sugar 2g; Protein 31.6g

Garlicky Mashed Potatoes

Prep time: 15 minutes | Cook time: 30 minutes | Serves: 8

455g russet potatoes, peeled and cut into 5 cm chunks	115g butter, salted
2 garlic cloves, peeled and cut in half	1 teaspoon sea salt
240g sour cream	1 teaspoon black pepper
	120ml milk

1. Add 360 ml water to the Ninja Foodi XL Pressure Cooker Steam Fryer with SmartLid cooking pot and place the potatoes and garlic in the Cook & Crisp Basket. 2. Lock lid; move slider to AIR FRY/STOVETOP. Select STEAM, and set time to 25 minutes until very tender. Press START/STOP to begin cooking. 3. Meanwhile, combine the cream, 185 g of the butter; and the salt in a medium saucepan, heat until the cream simmers and the butter melts. 4. When the potatoes are tender, mash them with a hand masher or in a food processer or blender. 5. Transfer potatoes and garlic to a large mixing bowl. Add butter, sour cream, salt, pepper, and half the milk. Mash until butter starts to dissolve. 6. Add the other half of the milk and continue to mash until smooth. 7. If potatoes are still lumpy add an additional tablespoon of sour cream until they blend smooth. 8. Return to the Ninja Foodi XL Pressure Cooker Steam Fryer cooking pot and Keep Warm until ready to serve.
Per Serving: Calories 285; Fat 12g; Sodium 647mg; Carbs 7g; Fiber 4g; Sugar 2g; Protein 15g

Sweet Potato Salad

Prep time: 15 minutes | Cook time: 35 minutes | Serves: 6

6 russet potatoes, peeled and cubed	1 teaspoon yellow mustard
240ml water	⅛ teaspoon Worcestershire sauce
3 eggs	⅛ teaspoon sugar
40g sweet onion, chopped	2 tablespoons finely chopped celery
150g red pepper, diced	1 tablespoon dill pickle juice
240g sour cream	Sea salt, for serving
60g mayonnaise	Black pepper, for serving

1. Add the water to the cooking pot. Add potatoes and the eggs to the Cook & Crisp Basket. 2. Lock lid; move slider to AIR FRY/STOVETOP. Select STEAM. Set time to 25 minutes. Press START/STOP to begin cooking. Remove eggs and place them in an ice bath to cool. Return potatoes to Steam for another 10 to 15 minutes or until tender, but not falling apart. 3. Combine onion, pepper, sour cream, mayo, yellow mustard, Worcestershire sauce, sugar, celery and pickle juice in a large mixing bowl. 4. Gently fold potatoes into the sour cream mixture. 5. Peel and chop the cooled eggs. Gently fold them into the potato salad. Add sea salt and black pepper to taste. 6. Place in the refrigerator and chill at least one hour before serving.
Per Serving: Calories 149; Fat 5.5g; Sodium 362mg; Carbs 0.3g; Fiber 0.1g; Sugar 0g; Protein 19.3g

Delicious Sweet Potatoes

Prep time: 5 minutes | Cook time: 40 minutes | Serves: 6

4 sweet potatoes, cut in half	Cinnamon, for garnish
480ml water	Sea salt, for garnish
Butter, for garnish	Black pepper, for garnish

1. Add 480ml of water to the Ninja Foodi XL Pressure Cooker Steam Fryer with SmartLid cooking pot. 2. Add sweet potatoes to the Deluxe Reversible Rack, and place inside the pot. 3. Lock lid; move slider to AIR FRY/STOVETOP. Select STEAM. Set time to 30 minutes. Press START/STOP to begin cooking. Cook 5 minutes more. Garnish with butter, cinnamon, sea salt and black pepper.
Per Serving: Calories 280; Fat 13g; Sodium 3mg; Carbs 6g; Fiber 3g; Sugar 6g; Protein 14g

Jacket Potatoes

Prep time: 5 minutes | Cook time: 21 minutes | Serves: 4

4 medium baking potatoes	Sour cream, for serving
240ml water	Additional toppings as desired:
Butter, for serving	Crumbled bacon, black beans,
Sea salt, for serving	tuna, baby spinach
Black pepper, for serving	

1. Fill the Ninja Foodi XL Pressure Cooker Steam Fryer with SmartLid cooking pot, add 240 ml of water. 2. Prick the potatoes, all over, with a fork. Place them in the Cook & Crisp Basket. 3. Lock lid; move slider to AIR FRY/STOVETOP. Select STEAM, and set time to 20 minutes. Press START/STOP to begin cooking. 4. Serve with sea salt, black pepper, butter and sour cream. Add any additional toppings to create a fancier
Per Serving: Calories 265; Fat 23.9g; Sodium 189mg; Carbs 0.1g; Fiber 0.1g; Sugar 0g; Protein 11.6g

Sweet Potatoes with nuts

Prep time: 5 minutes | Cook time: 25 minutes | Serves: 6

105g brown sugar	sliced
1 tablespoon lemon zest	55g butter
½ teaspoon sea salt	80g maple syrup
160ml water	1 tablespoon corn flour
4 large sweet potatoes, peeled and	110g pecans, chopped

1. In the Ninja Foodi XL Pressure Cooker Steam Fryer with SmartLid cooking pot, combine the sugar, lemon zest, salt and water. Stir well. 2. Add the potatoes to the pot. Close and lock the lid. 3. Lock lid; move slider towards PRESSURE. Adjust pressure release valve in the SEAL position. Close pressure-release valve. The cooking temperature will default to HIGH, which is accurate. Set time to 15 minutes. Select START/STOP and start cooking. 4. When cooking is complete, let pressure release quickly by turning it into VENT position. 5. Carefully unlock the lid. Transfer the potatoes to a serving bowl. 6. Move the slider towards "AIR FRY/STOVETOP" and set Ninja Foodi XL Pressure Cooker Steam Fryer with SmartLid to SEAR/SAUTÉ mode. Adjust the temperature to "Hi5" by using up arrow. Press START/STOP to begin cooking, add the butter and melt it. Add the maple syrup, corn flour, and chopped pecans. Stir to combine and sauté the sauce for 2 minutes. 7. Serve the potatoes with sauce and whole pecans.
Per Serving: Calories 247; Fat 11.9g; Sodium 112mg; Carbs 0g; Fiber 0g; Sugar 0g; Protein 32.8g

Spanish Paella

Prep time: 15 minutes | Cook time: 40 minutes | Serves: 6

2 tablespoons olive oil, divided
1 yellow onion, diced
1 red pepper, diced
1 green pepper, diced
2 cloves garlic, minced
2 teaspoons smoked paprika
2 teaspoons dried oregano
1 pinch saffron
¾ teaspoon sea salt
½ teaspoon crushed red pepper flakes
Coarse ground black pepper
1 bay leaf
1 (375g) can diced tomatoes

720ml low-sodium vegetable or chicken stock
185g brown rice
3 boneless skinless chicken thighs, cut into 2.5 cm pieces
12 large prawns or tiger prawns, deveined and peeled
35g chorizo
70g frozen peas, defrosted
35g sliced black olives
Hot sauce, for garnish
Freshly chopped parsley, for garnish

1. Move the slider towards "AIR FRY/STOVETOP" and set Ninja Foodi XL Pressure Cooker Steam Fryer with SmartLid to SEAR/SAUTÉ mode. Adjust the temperature to "Hi5" by using up arrow. Press START/STOP to begin cooking. 2. Heat 1 tablespoon olive oil in the cooking pot for 3 minutes. Add onion and peppers. Cook until soft, about 7 minutes. Add garlic to cooker and sauté for 1 minute or until fragrant. 3. Add the stock, then fold in smoked paprika, oregano, sea salt, crushed red pepper, black pepper, bay leaf, diced tomatoes, and rice. 4. Lock lid; move slider to AIR FRY/STOVETOP. Select STEAM, set time to 10 minutes. Press START/STOP to begin cooking. 5. Heat remaining olive oil in a frying pan over medium-high heat. Add chicken thighs and chorizo. 6. Cook until browned and no pink shows in the chicken; about 10 to 12 minutes. 7. Fold cooked chicken and sausage into the rice. Add saffron, peas, and black olives to the pot. Steam for 5 minutes to combine flavours. 8. Serve garnished with hot sauce and chopped parsley.
Per Serving: Calories 250; Fat 12g; Sodium 178mg; Carbs 6g; Fiber 4g; Sugar 1g; Protein 14g

Refreshing Quinoa and Pomegranate Salad

Prep time: 10 minutes | Cook time: 45 minutes | Serves: 8

340g quinoa, rinsed
960ml water
Pinch of sea salt
½ lemon, juiced
2 teaspoons olive oil
⅛ teaspoon coarse ground black pepper

1 teaspoon honey
1 teaspoon balsamic vinegar
150g pomegranate seeds
15g chopped fresh mint
Manchego cheese, chopped, optional garnish

1. Add quinoa, water, and a pinch of salt to the Ninja Foodi XL Pressure Cooker Steam Fryer with SmartLid cooking pot. 2. Lock lid; move slider to AIR FRY/STOVETOP. Select STEAM, set time to 20 minutes. Press START/STOP to begin cooking. 3. Open the lid and transfer quinoa to a large mixing bowl. Add everything except mint and cheese; stir well to combine. 4. Gently fold in mint and cheese and enjoy!
Per Serving: Calories 214; Fat 9g; Sodium 123mg; Carbs 0.6g; Fiber 0.2g; Sugar 0g; Protein 30.9g

Colourful Vegetable Buddha Bowl

Prep time: 8 minutes | Cook time: 40 minutes | Serves: 4

4 tablespoons extra-virgin olive oil, divided
1 large sweet potato, peeled and cut into 2.5 cm pieces
170g quinoa, rinsed and drained
1 large clove garlic, minced
½ teaspoon sea salt
2 small carrots, peeled and cut in half

1 stalk Chinese broccoli
80g chopped kale
240g water
1 tablespoon lime juice
1 (375g) can chickpeas, drained and rinsed for garnish
Unsalted pistachios, for garnish
1 whole avocado, sliced for garnish

1. Heat 2 tablespoons of olive oil over medium heat in a large frying pan. Add sweet potato, broccoli, carrots, quinoa, garlic and sea salt. Cook, while stirring, until the garlic is fragrant; about 3 minutes. 2. Add the quinoa mixture to the Ninja Foodi XL Pressure Cooker Steam Fryer with SmartLid cooking pot. Stir in kale and water. 3. Lock lid; move slider to AIR FRY/STOVETOP. Select STEAM. Press START/STOP to begin cooking. 4. Remove the lid and let stand for 5 minutes. Combine the remaining 2 tablespoons of olive oil, and lime juice in a small mixing bowl. 5. Divide the quinoa mixture among 2 to 4 bowls. 6. Top each portion with vegetables, chickpeas, pistachios and sliced avocado. Drizzle with the lime dressing and serve!
Per Serving: Calories 254; Fat 14g; Sodium 129mg; Carbs 6g; Fiber 4g; Sugar 1g; Protein 15g

Creamy Mashed Sweet Potatoes

Prep time: 5 minutes | Cook time: 25 minutes | Serves: 6

240ml water
455g sweet potatoes, peeled and cubed
2 cloves garlic
¼ teaspoon dried thyme
¼ teaspoon dried sage
¼ teaspoon dried rosemary

½ teaspoon dried parsley
60ml milk
2 tablespoon butter
25g parmesan cheese, grated
Salt and ground black pepper to taste

1. Pour the water into the Ninja Foodi XL Pressure Cooker Steam Fryer with SmartLid cooking pot and insert a Cook & Crisp Basket. 2. Put the sweet potatoes and garlic in the basket. 3. Lock lid; move slider towards PRESSURE. Adjust pressure release valve in the SEAL position. Close pressure-release valve. The cooking temperature will default to HIGH, which is accurate. Set time to 15 minutes. Select START/STOP and start cooking. 4. When cooking is complete, let pressure release quickly by turning it into VENT position. Carefully unlock the lid. Transfer the potatoes to a serving bowl. 5. Add the thyme, sage, rosemary, and parsley. Stir well. 6. Using a potato masher or electric beater, slowly blend milk and butter into potatoes until smooth and creamy. 7. Add cheese and season with salt and pepper, stir well. Serve.
Per Serving: Calories 271; Fat 12g; Sodium 510mg; Carbs 6g; Fiber 4g; Sugar 1g; Protein 13g

Spicy Potato Wedges

Prep time: 5 minutes | Cook time: 20 minutes | Serves: 4

3 large sweet potatoes, peeled
240ml water
2 tablespoon vegetable oil

½ teaspoon salt
1 teaspoon paprika
1 tablespoon dry mango powder

1. Cut the potatoes into medium-sized wedges. Prepare the Ninja Foodi XL Pressure Cooker Steam Fryer with SmartLid cooking pot by adding the water to the pot and placing the Deluxe Reversible Rack in it. 2. Place the sweet potatoes on the rack. 3. Lock lid; move slider towards PRESSURE. Adjust pressure release valve in the SEAL position. Close pressure-release valve. The cooking temperature will default to HIGH, which is accurate. Set time to 15 minutes. Select START/STOP and start cooking. When cooking is complete, let pressure release quickly by turning it into VENT position. 4. Carefully unlock the lid. Drain the liquid from the pot and remove the rack as well. Add the potatoes to cooking pot. 5. Move the slider towards "AIR FRY/STOVETOP" and set Ninja Foodi XL Pressure Cooker Steam Fryer with SmartLid to SEAR/SAUTÉ mode. Adjust the temperature to "Hi5" by using up arrow. Press START/STOP to begin cooking. 6. Add and heat the oil. Add the cooked sweet potatoes and sauté the wedges for 3-5 minutes, until they turn brown. 7. Season with salt, paprika, and mango powder. Stir well. Serve.
Per Serving: Calories 200; Fat 9.7g; Sodium 321mg; Carbs 0.5g; Fiber 0.3g; Sugar 0.2g; Protein 26.4g

Colourful Steamed Vegetables

Prep time: 5 minutes | Cook time: 10 minutes | Serves: 4

240ml water
3 small courgettes, sliced (2.5 cm thick)
2 peppers, sliced (2.5 cm thick)

70g garlic, peeled and minced
1 tablespoon Italian herb mix
Salt to taste
2 tablespoons olive oil

1. Prepare the Ninja Foodi`XL Pressure Cooker Steam Fryer with SmartLid cooking pot by adding the water to the pot and placing the Deluxe Reversible Rack in it. 2. In a large bowl, combine the courgettes, peppers, and garlic. Season the veggies with Italian herb mix, salt and oil. Stir well. Place the vegetables on the rack. 3. Lock lid; move slider to AIR FRY/STOVETOP. Select STEAM. Press START/STOP to begin cooking. Set time to 7 minutes. 4. Carefully unlock the lid. Serve.
Per Serving: Calories 230; Fat 13g; Sodium 456mg; Carbs 6g; Fiber 4g; Sugar 2g; Protein 16g

Refresh Steamed Broccoli

Prep time: 10 minutes | Cook time: 0 minutes | Serves: 2

60ml water
265g broccoli florets
Bowl with iced water

Salt and ground black pepper to taste

1. Prepare the Ninja Foodi XL Pressure Cooker Steam Fryer with SmartLid cooking pot by adding the water to the pot and placing the Cook & Crisp Basket in it. 2. Put the broccoli in the basket. 3. Lock lid; move slider towards PRESSURE. Adjust pressure release valve in the SEAL position. Close pressure-release valve. The cooking temperature will default to HIGH, which is accurate. Cook at HIGH pressure for 0 minutes. Press START/STOP to begin cooking. 4. Prepare the bowl with very cold water. When cooking is complete, let pressure release quickly by turning it into VENT position. 5. Carefully open the lid. Immediately transfer the broccoli to the bowl with cold water to keep bright green color. 6. Season the chilled broccoli with salt and pepper and serve.
Per Serving: Calories 105; Fat 6.9g; Sodium 147mg; Carbs 0.8g; Fiber 0.2g; Sugar 0.1g; Protein 9.2g

Broccoli with Mushrooms

Prep time: 5 minutes | Cook time: 15 minutes | Serves: 2

2 tablespoon coconut oil
70g mushrooms, sliced
1 tablespoon soy sauce

175g broccoli florets
240ml vegetable stock

1. Move the slider towards "AIR FRY/STOVETOP" and set Ninja Foodi XL Pressure Cooker Steam Fryer with SmartLid to SEAR/SAUTÉ mode. Adjust the temperature to "Hi5" by using up arrow. Press START/STOP to begin cooking. 2. Once hot, add the coconut oil to the pot. Add the mushrooms and sauté for 5 minutes. 3. Add the soy sauce and broccoli and cook for another 1 minute. 4. Pour in the stock and stir. Press the START/STOP button to reset the cooking program. 5. Lock lid; move slider towards PRESSURE. Adjust pressure release valve in the SEAL position. Close pressure-release valve. The cooking temperature will default to HIGH, which is accurate. Set time to 2 minutes. Select START/STOP and start cooking. 6. When cooking is complete, let pressure release quickly by turning it into VENT position. 7. Carefully unlock the lid. Let it cool a few minutes before serving.
Per Serving: Calories 89; Fat 3.6g; Sodium 411mg; Carbs 0.7g; Fiber 0.1g; Sugar 0.1g; Protein 12.8g

Coconut Cauliflower Curry

Prep time: 5 minutes | Cook time: 5 minutes | Serves: 4

1150g. cauliflower florets
1 can full-fat coconut milk
6 teaspoon garam masala

480ml water
Salt and ground black pepper to taste

1. In the Ninja Foodi XL Pressure Cooker Steam Fryer with SmartLid cooking pot, combine the cauliflower, coconut milk, garam masala, and water. 2. Season with salt and pepper, stir well. 3. Lock lid; move slider towards PRESSURE. Adjust pressure release valve in the SEAL position. Close pressure-release valve. The cooking temperature will default to HIGH, which is accurate. Set time to 4 minutes. Select START/STOP and start cooking. 4. When cooking is complete, let pressure release quickly by turning it into VENT position. Carefully open the lid. 5. Serve.
Per Serving: Calories 227; Fat 20.4g; Sodium 365mg; Carbs 1.8g; Fiber 0.5g; Sugar 0g; Protein 9.9g

Pomegranate Brussels Sprouts

Prep time: 5 minutes | Cook time: 15 minutes | Serves: 2

240ml water
455g Brussels sprouts, trimmed and cut into half
Salt and ground black pepper to

taste
35g pine nuts, toasted
1 pomegranate, seeds separated
1 teaspoon olive oil

1. Pour the water into the Ninja Foodi XL Pressure Cooker Steam Fryer with SmartLid cooking pot and insert a Cook & Crisp Basket. 2. Place the Brussels sprouts in the basket. 3. Lock lid; move slider towards PRESSURE. Adjust pressure release valve in the SEAL position. Close pressure-release valve. The cooking temperature will default to HIGH, which is accurate. Set time to 4 minutes. Select START/STOP and start cooking. 4. When cooking is complete, let pressure release quickly by turning it into VENT position. Carefully unlock the lid. 5. Transfer the sprouts to a serving plate. 6. Season with salt, pepper and pine nuts. Add the pomegranate seeds and stir. 7. Drizzle with oil and stir well. Serve.
Per Serving: Calories 189; Fat 8g; Sodium 489mg; Carbs 1.1g; Fiber 0.6g; Sugar 0g; Protein 26.7g

Traditional Ratatouille

Prep time: 15 minutes | Cook time: 15 minutes | Serves: 6

1 tablespoon olive oil
1 medium onion, sliced
2 cloves garlic, chopped
2 small aubergines, peeled and sliced thin
4 small courgettes, sliced thin

1 jar (150g) roasted red peppers, drained and sliced
1 can (220g) tomatoes, chopped
120ml water
1 teaspoon salt

1. Move the slider towards "AIR FRY/STOVETOP" and set Ninja Foodi XL Pressure Cooker Steam Fryer with SmartLid to SEAR/SAUTÉ mode. Adjust the temperature to "Hi5" by using up arrow. Press START/STOP to begin cooking and heat the oil. 2. Add the onion, garlic, aubergine, courgette, and peppers. Sauté for 3-4 minutes until softened. 3. Add the tomatoes and water and sprinkle with salt, stir well. Press the START/STOP button to stop the SAUTE function. 4. Lock lid; move slider towards PRESSURE. Adjust pressure release valve in the SEAL position. Close pressure-release valve. The cooking temperature will default to HIGH, which is accurate. Set time to 4 minutes. Select START/STOP and start cooking. 5. When cooking is complete, let pressure release quickly by turning it into VENT position. 6. Carefully unlock the lid. Serve warm or chilled.
Per Serving: Calories 284; Fat 14g; Sodium 477mg; Carbs 6g; Fiber 2g; Sugar 2g; Protein 20g

Crispy Brussels Sprouts

Prep time: 5 minutes | Cook time: 5 minutes | Serves: 2

455g Brussels sprouts
240ml water
Salt and ground black pepper to

taste
1 teaspoon extra virgin olive oil
35g pine nuts

1. Wash the Brussels sprouts and remove the outer leaves, then cut into halves. 2. Prepare the Ninja Foodi XL Pressure Cooker Steam Fryer with SmartLid cooking pot by adding the water to the pot and placing the Cook & Crisp Basket in it. 3. Place the Brussels sprouts in the basket. 4. Lock lid; move slider towards PRESSURE. Adjust pressure release valve in the SEAL position. Close pressure-release valve. The cooking temperature will default to HIGH, which is accurate. Set time to 4 minutes. Select START/STOP and start cooking. 5. When cooking is complete, let pressure release quickly by turning it into VENT position. Carefully unlock the lid. 6. Transfer the Brussels sprouts to a serving bowl. 7. Season with salt, pepper and drizzle with oil. Top with the pine nuts and serve.
Per Serving: Calories 219; Fat 8.5g; Sodium 548mg; Carbs 0.7g; Fiber 0.2g; Sugar 0g; Protein 32.9g

Potatoes and Brussels Sprouts

Prep time: 5 minutes | Cook time: 15 minutes | Serves: 4

675g Brussels sprouts
150g new potatoes cut into 2.5 cm cubes
120ml chicken stock

Salt and ground black pepper to taste
1½ tablespoon butter
1½ tablespoon bread crumbs

1. Wash the Brussels sprouts and remove the outer leaves, then cut into halves. 2. In the Ninja Foodi XL Pressure Cooker Steam Fryer with SmartLid cooking pot, combine the potatoes, sprouts, stock, salt and pepper. 3. Lock lid; move slider towards PRESSURE. Adjust pressure release valve in the SEAL position. Close pressure-release valve. The cooking temperature will default to HIGH, which is accurate. Set time to 5 minutes. Select START/STOP and start cooking. 4. When cooking is complete, let pressure release quickly by turning it into VENT position. Carefully open the lid. 5. Move the slider towards "AIR FRY/STOVETOP" and set Ninja Foodi XL Pressure Cooker Steam Fryer with SmartLid to SEAR/SAUTÉ mode. Adjust the temperature to "Hi5" by using up arrow. Press START/STOP to begin cooking, add the butter and bread crumbs to the pot. 6. Mix well and serve.
Per Serving: Calories 236; Fat 12g; Sodium 321mg; Carbs 6g; Fiber 4g; Sugar 2g; Protein 15g

Refreshing Vegetable Dish

Prep time: 5 minutes | Cook time: 20 minutes | Serves: 4

1 tablespoon extra-virgin olive oil
1 red onion, sliced
2 red peppers, sliced thinly
2 green pepper, sliced thinly
1 yellow peppers, sliced thinly

2 tomatoes, chopped
Salt and ground black pepper to taste
2 cloves garlic, chopped
1 bunch parsley, finely chopped

1. Move the slider towards "AIR FRY/STOVETOP" and set Ninja Foodi XL Pressure Cooker Steam Fryer with SmartLid to SEAR/SAUTÉ mode. Adjust the temperature to "Hi5" by using up arrow. Press START/STOP to begin cooking and heat the oil. 2. Add the onion and sauté for 3 minutes. 3. Add the peppers, stir and sauté for another 5 minutes. 4. Add the tomatoes and sprinkle with salt and pepper. Mix well. Close and lock the lid. Press the STOP button to reset the cooking program. 5. Lock lid; move slider towards PRESSURE. Adjust pressure release valve in the SEAL position. Close pressure-release valve. The cooking temperature will default to HIGH, which is accurate. Set time to 6 minutes. Select START/STOP and start cooking. 6. When cooking is complete, let pressure release quickly by turning it into VENT position. 7. Carefully unlock the lid. Transfer the veggies to a serving bowl and add the garlic and parsley. Stir well. Serve.
Per Serving: Calories 437; Fat 30.8g; Sodium 698mg; Carbs 1.2g; Fiber 0.1g; Sugar 0g; Protein 36.5g

Cauliflower Mash

Prep time: 5 minutes | Cook time: 15 minutes | Serves: 4

360ml water
1 cauliflower, florets separated
Salt and ground black pepper to taste

1 tablespoon butter
½ teaspoon turmeric
2 chives, finely chopped

1. Prepare the Ninja Foodi XL Pressure Cooker Steam Fryer with SmartLid cooking pot by adding the water to the pot and placing the Cook & Crisp Basket in it. 2. Put the cauliflower in the basket. 3. Lock lid; move slider towards PRESSURE. Adjust pressure release valve in the SEAL position. Close pressure-release valve. The cooking temperature will default to HIGH, which is accurate. Set time to 6 minutes. Select START/STOP and start cooking. 4. When cooking is complete, let pressure release naturally for 5 minutes by turning it into VENT position, then quick-release any remaining pressure. Uncover the pot. 5. Using a potato masher or fork, mash the cauliflower. 6. Season with salt and pepper. Add in the butter and turmeric and mix well. 7. Top with chopped chives and serve.
Per Serving: Calories 240; Fat 12g; Sodium 268mg; Carbs 6g; Fiber 4g; Sugar 2g; Protein 15g

Easy Cauliflower Patties

Prep time: 15 minutes | Cook time: 15 minutes | Serves: 4

360ml water
1 cauliflower head, chopped
95g ground almonds
100g vegan cheese, shredded

Salt and ground black pepper to taste
2 tablespoons olive oil

1. Pour the water into the Ninja Foodi XL Pressure Cooker Steam Fryer with SmartLid cooking pot and insert a Cook & Crisp Basket. 2. Put the cauliflower in to the basket. 3. Lock lid; move slider towards PRESSURE. Adjust pressure release valve in the SEAL position. Close pressure-release valve. The cooking temperature will default to HIGH, which is accurate. Set time to 5 minutes. Select START/STOP and start cooking. 4. When cooking is complete, let pressure release quickly by turning it into VENT position. Carefully unlock the lid. 5. Place the cauliflower in a food processor and ground it. 6. Add the almonds and cheese. Season with salt and pepper. Mix well. 7. Shape the mixture into oval patties 1 cm thick. 8. Carefully pour the water out of the pot and completely dry the pot before replacing it. 9. Move the slider towards "AIR FRY/STOVETOP" and set Ninja Foodi XL Pressure Cooker Steam Fryer with SmartLid to SEAR/SAUTÉ mode. Adjust the temperature to "Hi5" by using up arrow. Press START/STOP to begin cooking and heat the oil. 10. Add the patties and cook on both sides until golden. You may have to do it in two batches. Serve.
Per Serving: Calories 283; Fat 12g; Sodium 322mg; Carbs 5g; Fiber 3g; Sugar 1g; Protein 15g

Creamy Garlicky Artichoke, Courgette

Prep time: 5 minutes | Cook time: 20 minutes | Serves: 8

2 tablespoons olive oil
8 cloves garlic, minced
2 medium courgettes, sliced thin
1 large artichoke hearts, cleaned and sliced

120g whipping cream
120ml vegetable stock
Salt and ground black pepper to taste

1. Move the slider towards "AIR FRY/STOVETOP" and set Ninja Foodi XL Pressure Cooker Steam Fryer with SmartLid to SEAR/SAUTÉ mode. Adjust the temperature to "Hi5" by using up arrow. Press START/STOP to begin cooking and heat the oil. 2. Add the garlic and sauté for 2 minutes, until fragrant. 3. Add the courgettes, artichoke hearts, stock, and cream. Season with salt and pepper. Stir well. Close and lock the lid. 4. Press the START/STOP button to stop the SAUTE function. 5. Lock lid; move slider towards PRESSURE. Adjust pressure release valve in the SEAL position. Close pressure-release valve. The cooking temperature will default to HIGH, which is accurate. Set time to 10 minutes. Select START/STOP and start cooking. 6. When cooking is complete, let pressure release quickly by turning it into VENT position. 7. Carefully unlock the lid. Serve.
Per Serving: Calories 95; Fat 4.4g; Sodium 430mg; Carbs 0.3g; Fiber 0.2g; Sugar 0g; Protein 12.7g

Cheesy Asparagus

Prep time: 5 minutes | Cook time: 15 minutes | Serves: 4

240ml water
455g asparagus, trimmed (2.5 cm of the bottom)
3 tablespoons butter
2 cloves garlic, chopped

Salt and ground black pepper to taste
3 tablespoons parmesan cheese, grated

1. Pour the water into the Ninja Foodi XL Pressure Cooker Steam Fryer with SmartLid cooking pot and set a Deluxe Reversible Rack in the pot. 2. Place the asparagus on a tin foil, add butter and garlic. Sprinkle with salt and pepper. 3. Fold over the foil and seal the asparagus inside so the foil doesn't come open. 4. Put the asparagus on the rack. 5. Lock lid; move slider towards PRESSURE. Adjust pressure release valve in the SEAL position. Close pressure-release valve. The cooking temperature will default to HIGH, which is accurate. Set time to 8 minutes. Select START/STOP and start cooking. 6. When cooking is complete, let pressure release quickly by turning it into VENT position. Carefully unlock the lid. 7. Unwrap the foil packet and transfer the asparagus to a serving plate. Sprinkle with cheese and serve.
Per Serving: Calories 274; Fat 12g; Sodium 402mg; Carbs 5g; Fiber 3g; Sugar 1g; Protein 14g

Traditional Broccoli Salad

Prep time: 5 minutes | Cook time: 20 minutes | Serves: 2

120ml chicken stock
455g broccoli florets
1 onion, sliced
1 tablespoon lemon juice
1 teaspoon oregano
1 teaspoon garlic powder

3 tablespoon raisins
2 tablespoon walnuts, crushed
1 teaspoon olive oil
1 tablespoon salt
Bowl with iced water

1. Pour the stock into the Ninja Foodi XL Pressure Cooker Steam Fryer with SmartLid cooking pot and insert a Cook & Crisp Basket. 2. Put the broccoli in the basket. 3. Lock lid; move slider towards PRESSURE. Adjust pressure release valve in the SEAL position. Close pressure-release valve. The cooking temperature will default to HIGH, which is accurate. Cook at HIGH pressure for 0 minutes. Select START/STOP and start cooking. 4. When cooking is complete, let pressure release quickly by turning it into VENT position. 5. Carefully unlock the lid. Immediately transfer the broccoli to the bowl with cold water to keep bright green color. 6. Transfer the chilled broccoli to a serving bowl. 7. Add the onion, raisins, crushed walnuts and season with lemon juice, oregano, garlic powder, salt and oil. Gently stir to combine. 8. Serve.
Per Serving: Calories 250; Fat 12g; Sodium 663mg; Carbs 6g; Fiber 4g; Sugar 1g; Protein 15g

Tasty Steamed Asparagus

Prep time: 5 minutes | Cook time: 15 minutes | Serves: 4

455g asparagus
240ml water
Salt and fresh ground pepper to taste
4 teaspoons olive oil
1 tablespoon onion, chopped

1. Wash asparagus and trim off bottom of stems by about 4 cm. 2. Prepare the Ninja Foodi XL Pressure Cooker Steam Fryer with SmartLid cooking pot by adding the water to the pot and placing the Deluxe Reversible Rack in it. 3. Place the asparagus on the Rack. Brush the asparagus with the olive oil. 4.Sprinkle with the onion. 5. Lock lid; move slider to AIR FRY/STOVETOP then select STEAM, set time to 2 minutes. Press START/STOP to begin cooking. 6. Carefully unlock the lid. 7. Season with salt and pepper and serve.
Per Serving: Calories 171; Fat 8.8g; Sodium 336mg; Carbs 1.8g; Fiber 0.8g; Sugar 0g; Protein 20.8g

Delicious Prosciutto Wrapped Asparagus

Prep time: 5 minutes | Cook time: 10 minutes | Serves: 4

360ml water
455g asparagus
250g. prosciutto, sliced

1. Wash asparagus and trim off bottom of stems by about 2.5 cm. 2. Prepare the Ninja Foodi XL Pressure Cooker Steam Fryer with SmartLid cooking pot by adding the water to the pot and placing the Deluxe Reversible Rack in it. 3. Wrap the prosciutto slices around the asparagus spears. 4. Place the un-wrapped asparagus on the rack, and then place the prosciutto-wrapped spears on top. 5. Lock lid; move slider towards PRESSURE. Adjust pressure release valve in the SEAL position. Close pressure-release valve. The cooking temperature will default to HIGH, which is accurate. Set time to 3 minutes. Select START/STOP and start cooking. 6. When cooking is complete, let pressure release naturally for 5 minutes, then quick-release any remaining pressure by turning it into VENT position. 7. Open the lid. Serve.
Per Serving: Calories 293; Fat 15.4g; Sodium 222mg; Carbs 0.4g; Fiber 0.1g; Sugar 0.1g; Protein 36.4g

Corn Cob

Prep time: 5 minutes | Cook time: 9 minutes | Serves: 6

6 ears corn
240ml water
6 tablespoon butter
Salt to taste

1. Shuck the corn husks and rinse off the corn. Cut off the pointy ends. 2. Add the water to the Ninja Foodi XL Pressure Cooker Steam Fryer with SmartLid cooking pot. 3. Arrange the corn vertically, with the larger end in the water. If the ear is too tall break it in half. 4. Lock lid; move slider towards PRESSURE. Adjust pressure release valve in the SEAL position. Close pressure-release valve. The cooking temperature will default to HIGH, which is accurate. Set QUICK RELEASE and time to 3 minutes. Select START/STOP and start cooking. 5. When cooking is complete, let pressure release quickly by turning it into VENT position. 6. Carefully unlock the lid. Transfer the corn to a serving bowl. 7. Serve with butter and salt.
Per Serving: Calories 257; Fat 12g; Sodium 620mg; Carbs 5g; Fiber 4g; Sugar 1g; Protein 14g

Orange Pumpkin Puree

Prep time: 5 minutes | Cook time: 25 minutes | Serves: 6

900g small-sized sugar pumpkin, halved and seeds scooped out
300ml water
Salt to taste, optional

1. Prepare the Ninja Foodi XL Pressure Cooker Steam Fryer with SmartLid cooking pot by adding 240ml water to the pot and placing the Deluxe Reversible Rack in it. 2. Place the pumpkin halves on the rack. 3. Lock lid; move slider towards PRESSURE. Adjust pressure release valve in the SEAL position. Close pressure-release valve. The cooking temperature will default to HIGH, which is accurate. Set time to 14 minutes. Select START/STOP and start cooking. 4. When cooking is complete, let pressure release quickly by turning it into VENT position. Carefully open the lid. 5. Transfer the pumpkin to a plate and let it cool. Then scoop out the flesh into a bowl. 6. Add 60ml water. Using an immersion blender or food processor, blend until puree. 7. Season with salt and serve.

Per Serving: Calories 130; Fat 8.3g; Sodium 130mg; Carbs 1g; Fiber 0.1g; Sugar 0g; Protein 12.2g

Buffalo Cauliflower

Prep Time: 5 minutes | Cook Time: 13 minutes | Serves: 4

4 tablespoons unsalted butter, melted
60ml buffalo wing sauce
430g cauliflower florets
110g panko bread crumbs
Olive oil

1. Place the Cook & Crisp Basket in your Pressure Cooker Steam Fryer. 2. Grease the Ninja Foodi Pressure Steam Fryer basket with olive oil. 3. In a suitable bowl, mix the melted butter with the buffalo wing sauce. 4. Put the panko bread crumbs in a separate small bowl. 5. Dip the cauliflower in the sauce, making sure to coat the top of the cauliflower, then dip the cauliflower in the panko. 6. Place the cauliflower into the greased "cook & crisp basket", being careful not to overcrowd them. Grease the cauliflower generously with olive oil. 7. Put on the Smart Lid on top of the Ninja Foodi Steam Fryer. 8. Move the Lid Slider to the "Air Fry/Stovetop". Select the "Air Fry" mode for cooking. 9. Adjust the Ninja Foodi Pressure Steam Fryer temperature to 175°C. Set the timer and cook for around 7 minutes. 10. Using tongs, flip the cauliflower. Spray generously with olive oil. 11. Reset the timer and cook for another 6 minutes.
Per Serving: Calories: 212; Fat: 10.9g; Sodium: 454mg; Carbs: 10g; Fiber: 3.1g; Sugar 5.2g; Protein 10g

Bacon Brussels Sprouts with Orange Zest

Prep time: 5 minutes | 8 Cook time: minutes | Serves: 4

1 tablespoon avocado oil
2 slices bacon, diced
120ml freshly squeezed orange juice
120ml water
455g Brussels sprouts, trimmed and halved
2 teaspoons orange zest

1. Move the slider towards "AIR FRY/STOVETOP" and set Ninja Foodi XL Pressure Cooker Steam Fryer with SmartLid to SEAR/SAUTÉ mode. Adjust the temperature to "Hi5" by using up arrow. Press START/STOP to begin cooking. And heat avocado oil. Add bacon. Stir-fry 3–5 minutes or until bacon is almost crisp and the fat is rendered. Add the orange juice and water and deglaze the pot by scraping the bits from the sides and bottom. 2. Add Brussels sprouts. 3. Lock lid; move slider towards PRESSURE. Adjust pressure release valve in the SEAL position. Close pressure-release valve. The cooking temperature will default to HIGH, which is accurate. Set time to 3 minutes. Select START/STOP and start cooking. When cooking is complete, let pressure release quickly by turning it into VENT position. Unlock lid. 4. Using a slotted spoon, transfer Brussels sprouts to a serving dish. Garnish with orange zest and serve warm.
Per Serving: Calories 195; Fat 18.3g; Sodium 278mg; Carbs 5.4g; Fiber 1g; Sugar 2g; Protein 5.8g

Mustard Bacon Brussels Sprouts

Prep time: 5 minutes | Cook time: 10 minutes | Serves: 4

455g Brussels sprouts, trimmed and cut into halves
55g bacon, chopped
1 tablespoon mustard
240ml chicken stock
Salt and ground black pepper to taste
1 tablespoon butter
2 tablespoon dill, chopped

1. Move the slider towards "AIR FRY/STOVETOP" and set Ninja Foodi XL Pressure Cooker Steam Fryer with SmartLid to SEAR/SAUTÉ mode. Adjust the temperature to "Hi5" by using up arrow. Press START/STOP to begin cooking. And add the bacon. Sauté until it is crispy. 2. Add the Brussels sprouts and cook, stirring occasionally, for 2 minutes more. 3. Add the mustard and stock. Season with salt and pepper, stir. 4. Press the START/STOP key to stop the SAUTÉ function. 5. Lock lid; move slider towards PRESSURE. Adjust pressure release valve in the SEAL position. Close pressure-release valve. The cooking temperature will default to HIGH, which is accurate. Set time to 4 minutes. Select START/STOP and start cooking. 6. When cooking is complete, let pressure release quickly by turning it into VENT position. 7. Carefully unlock the lid. Add the butter and sprinkle with dill, stir. 8. Select SAUTÉ again and cook for 1 minute more. Serve.
Per Serving: Calories 236; Fat 12g; Sodium 297mg; Carbs 6g; Fiber 4g; Sugar 3g; Protein 13g

Lemony Steamed Artichokes

Prep time: 10 minutes | Cook time: 30 minutes | Serves: 4

2 medium whole artichokes (about 150g each)

1 lemon wedge
240ml water

1. Wash the artichokes and remove any damaged outer leaves. 2. Trim off the stem and top edge. Rub the top with lemon wedge. 3. Prepare the Ninja Foodi XL Pressure Cooker Steam Fryer with SmartLid cooking pot by adding the water to the pot and placing the Cook & Crisp Basket in it. 4. Lock lid; move slider towards PRESSURE. Adjust pressure release valve in the SEAL position. Close pressure-release valve. The cooking temperature will default to HIGH, which is accurate. Set time to 20 minutes. Select START/STOP and start cooking. 5. When cooking is complete, let pressure release naturally for 10 minutes, then quick-release any remaining pressure by turning it into VENT position. 6. Uncover the pot. Transfer the artichokes to a serving plate and serve warm with your favorite sauce.
Per Serving: Calories 284; Fat 13g; Sodium 423mg; Carbs 5g; Fiber 3g; Sugar 2g; Protein 15g

Parmesan Courgette Gratin

Prep Time: 10 minutes | Cook Time: 15 minutes | Serves: 2

125g parmesan cheese, shredded
1 tablespoon coconut flour
1 tablespoon dried parsley

2 courgettes
1 teaspoon butter, melted

1. Place the Cook & Crisp Basket in your Pressure Cooker Steam Fryer. 2. Mix the parmesan and coconut flour in a suitable bowl, seasoning with parsley to taste. 3. Cut the courgette in half lengthwise and chop the halves into four slices. 4. Pour the melted butter over the courgette and then dip the courgette into the parmesan-flour mixture, coating it all over. 5. Put on the Smart Lid on top of the Ninja Foodi Steam Fryer. 6. Move the Lid Slider to the "Air Fry/Stovetop". Select the "Air Fry" mode for cooking. 7. Adjust the cooking temperature to 200°C. 8. Cook the courgette for 13 minutes.
Per Serving: Calories: 382; Fat: 10.9g; Sodium: 354mg; Carbs: 20.5g; Fiber: 4.1g; Sugar 8.2g; Protein 06g

Parmesan Kale

Prep Time: 10 minutes | Cook Time: 15 minutes | Serves: 2

455g kale
200g parmesan cheese, shredded
1 onion, diced

1 teaspoon butter
240g heavy cream

1. Place the deluxe reversible rack in your Pressure Cooker Steam Fryer. 2. Dice up the kale, discarding any hard stems. In a suitable baking dish small enough to fit inside the Pressure Cooker Steam Fryer, mix the kale with the parmesan, onion, butter and cream. 3. Put the baking dish on the rack. Put on the Smart Lid on top of the Ninja Foodi Steam Fryer. Move the Lid Slider to the "Air Fry/Stovetop". Select the "Air Fry" mode for cooking. Adjust the cooking temperature to 120°C. 4. Cook for 12 minutes. Make sure to give it a good stir before serving.
Per Serving: Calories: 372; Fat: 20g; Sodium: 891mg; Carbs: 29g; Fiber: 3g; Sugar 8g; Protein 7g

Roasted Garlic Asparagus

Prep Time: 5 minutes | Cook Time: 10 minutes | Serves: 4

455g asparagus
2 tablespoons olive oil
1 tablespoon balsamic vinegar

2 teaspoons minced garlic
Salt
Black pepper

1. Place the Cook & Crisp Basket in your Pressure Cooker Steam Fryer. 2. Cut or snap off the white end of the asparagus. 3. In a suitable bowl, mix the asparagus, olive oil, vinegar, garlic, salt, and pepper. 4. Using your hands, gently mix all the recipe ingredients together, making sure that the asparagus is coated. 5. Lay out the asparagus in the Ninja Foodi Pressure Steam Fryer basket. 6. Put on the Smart Lid on top of the Ninja Foodi Steam Fryer. 7. Move the Lid Slider to the "Air Fry/Stovetop". Select the "Air Fry" mode for cooking. 8. Adjust the air fryer temperature to 200°C. Set the timer and cook for around 5 minutes. 9. Using tongs, flip the asparagus. 10. Reset the timer and cook for around 5 minutes more.
Per Serving: Calories: 172; Fat: 20g; Sodium: 191mg; Carbs: 9g; Fiber: 3g; Sugar 8g; Protein 7g

Broccoli with Parmesan

Prep Time: 5 minutes | Cook Time: 4 minutes | Serves: 4

455g broccoli florets
2 teaspoons minced garlic
2 tablespoons olive oil

25g grated or shaved Parmesan cheese

1. Place the Cook & Crisp Basket in your Pressure Cooker Steam Fryer. 2. In a suitable mixing bowl, mix the broccoli florets, garlic, olive oil, and Parmesan cheese. 3. Place the broccoli in the Ninja Foodi Pressure Steam Fryer basket in a single layer. 4. Put on the Smart Lid on top of the Ninja Foodi Steam Fryer. 5. Move the Lid Slider to the "Air Fry/Stovetop". Select the "Air Fry" mode for cooking. 6. Adjust the cooking temperature to 180°C. 7. Set the timer and steam for around 4 minutes.
Per Serving: Calories: 219; Fat: 10g; Sodium: 891mg; Carbs: 22.9g; Fiber: 4g; Sugar 4g; Protein 13g

Roasted Corn

Prep Time: 5 minutes | Cook Time: 10 minutes | Serves: 4

1 tablespoon vegetable oil
4 ears of corn, husks and silk removed

Unsalted butter, for topping
Salt, for topping
Black pepper, for topping

1. Place the Cook & Crisp Basket in your Pressure Cooker Steam Fryer. 2. Rub the vegetable oil onto the corn, coating it thoroughly. 3. Adjust the Ninja Foodi Pressure Steam Fryer temperature to 200°C. Set the timer. Put on the Smart Lid on top of the Ninja Foodi Steam Fryer. Move the Lid Slider to the "Air Fry/Stovetop". Select the "Air Fry" mode for cooking. Cook the corn at 200°C for around 5 minutes. 4. Using tongs, flip or rotate the corn. 5. Reset the timer. Air Fry for around 5 minutes more. 6. Serve with a pat of butter and a generous sprinkle of black pepper and salt.
Per Serving: Calories: 282; Fat: 12.9g; Sodium: 414mg; Carbs: 11g; Fiber: 5g; Sugar 9g; Protein 11g

Honey Carrots

Prep Time: 5 minutes | Cook Time: 12 minutes | Serves: 4

365g baby carrots
1 tablespoon extra-virgin olive oil
1 tablespoon honey

Salt
Black pepper
Fresh dill

1. Place the Cook & Crisp Basket in your Pressure Cooker Steam Fryer. 2. In a suitable bowl, mix the carrots, olive oil, honey, salt, and pepper. Make sure that the carrots are coated with oil. 3. Place the carrots in the Ninja Foodi Pressure Steam Fryer basket. 4. Put on the Smart Lid on top of the Ninja Foodi Steam Fryer. 5. Move the Lid Slider to the "Air Fry/Stovetop". Select the "Air Fry" mode for cooking. 6. Adjust the Ninja Foodi Pressure Steam Fryer temperature to 200°C. Set the timer and cook for around 12 minutes, or until fork-tender. 7. Pour the carrots into a suitable bowl, sprinkle with dill, if desired, and serve.
Per Serving: Calories: 80; Fat: 14g; Sodium: 101mg; Carbs: 8.9g; Fiber: 4.6g; Sugar 8g; Protein 6g

Fried Cabbage

Prep Time: 5 minutes | Cook Time: 7 minutes | Serves: 4

1 head cabbage, sliced in 2.5 cm-thick ribbons
1 tablespoon olive oil
1 teaspoon salt

1 teaspoon black pepper
1 teaspoon garlic powder
1 teaspoon red pepper flakes

1. Place the Cook & Crisp Basket in your Pressure Cooker Steam Fryer. 2. In a suitable bowl, mix the cabbage, olive oil, salt, pepper, garlic powder, and red pepper flakes. Make sure that the cabbage is coated with oil. 3. Place the cabbage in the Ninja Foodi Pressure Steam Fryer basket. 4. Put on the Smart Lid on top of the Ninja Foodi Steam Fryer. 5. Move the Lid Slider to the "Air Fry/Stovetop". Select the "Air Fry" mode for cooking. 6. Adjust the Ninja Foodi Pressure Steam Fryer temperature to 175°C. Set the timer and cook for around 4 minutes. 7. Using tongs, flip the cabbage. 8. Reset the timer and cook for around 3 minutes more. 9. Serve with additional salt, pepper, or red pepper flakes, if desired.
Per Serving: Calories: 78; Fat: 7.9g; Sodium: 704mg; Carbs: 6g; Fiber: 3.6g; Sugar 6g; Protein 8g

Sweet Potato Fries

Prep Time: 5 minutes | Cook Time: 20 to 22 minutes | Serves: 4

2 sweet potatoes	½ teaspoon black pepper
1 teaspoon salt	2 teaspoons olive oil

1. Place the Cook & Crisp Basket in your Pressure Cooker Steam Fryer. 2. Cut the sweet potatoes lengthwise into 1 cm-thick slices. Then cut each slice into 1 cm-thick fries. 3. In a suitable mixing bowl, toss the sweet potato with the salt, pepper, and olive oil, making sure that all the potatoes are coated with oil. Add more oil as needed. 4. Place the potatoes in the Ninja Foodi Pressure Steam Fryer basket. 5. Put on the Smart Lid on top of the Ninja Foodi Steam Fryer. 6. Move the Lid Slider to the "Air Fry/Stovetop". Select the "Air Fry" mode for cooking. 7. Adjust the cooking temperature to 195°C. 8. Set the timer and cook for around 20 minutes. Shake the basket several times during cooking so that the fries will be evenly cooked and crisp. 9. Pour the potatoes into a serving bowl and toss with additional black pepper and salt, if desired.
Per Serving: Calories: 221; Fat: 7.9g; Sodium: 704mg; Carbs: 6g; Fiber: 3.6g; Sugar 6g; Protein 18g

Delicious Pumpkin Stew

Prep time: 5 minutes | Cook time: 20 minutes | Serves: 4

350g pumpkin, peeled and cubed (2.5cm thick)	105g mixed greens
1 large can diced tomatoes	Salt and ground black pepper to taste
1.2L vegetable stock	

1. Combine all of the ingredients in the Ninja Foodi XL Pressure Cooker Steam Fryer with SmartLid cooking pot and stir to mix. 2. Lock lid; move slider towards PRESSURE. Adjust pressure release valve in the SEAL position. Close pressure-release valve. The cooking temperature will default to HIGH, which is accurate. Set time to 10 minutes. Select START/STOP and start cooking. 3. When cooking is complete, let pressure release quickly by turning it into VENT position. 4. Carefully unlock the lid. Taste for seasoning and add more salt if needed. Serve.
Per Serving: Calories 267; Fat 13g; Sodium 520mg; Carbs 6g; Fiber 4g; Sugar 2g; Protein 16g

Roasted Sweet Potatoes

Prep Time: 10 minutes | Cook Time: 45 minutes | Serves: 4

4 sweet potatoes	2 teaspoons salt
60ml olive oil	½ teaspoon black pepper

1. Place the Cook & Crisp Basket in your Pressure Cooker Steam Fryer. 2. Use any fork to poke a few holes in each of the sweet potatoes. 3. Rub the skins of the sweet potatoes with olive oil, salt, and pepper. 4. Place the coated sweet potatoes in the Ninja Foodi Pressure Steam Fryer basket. 5. Put on the Smart Lid on top of the Ninja Foodi Steam Fryer. 6. Move the Lid Slider to the "Air Fry/Stovetop". Select the "Air Fry" mode for cooking. 7. Adjust the Ninja Foodi Pressure Steam Fryer temperature to 200°C. Set the timer and cook for around 15 minutes. 8. Using tongs, flip or rotate the potatoes. 9. Reset the timer and cook for another 15 minutes. Check to see if the sweet potatoes are fork-tender. If not, add up to 15 minutes more.
Per Serving: Calories: 289; Fat: 14g; Sodium: 791mg; Carbs: 18.9g; Fiber: 4.6g; Sugar 8g; Protein 6g

Hassel back Potatoes

Prep Time: 10 minutes | Cook Time: 35 minutes | Serves: 4

4 russet potatoes	½ teaspoon black pepper
2 tablespoons olive oil	25g grated Parmesan cheese
1 teaspoon salt	

1. Place the Cook & Crisp Basket in your Pressure Cooker Steam Fryer. 2. Without slicing all the way through the bottom of the potato (so the slices stay connected), cut each potato into 1 cm-wide horizontal slices. 3. Brush the potatoes with olive oil, being careful to brush in between all the slices. Season with black pepper and salt. 4. Place the potatoes in the Ninja Foodi Pressure Steam Fryer basket. 5. Put on the Smart Lid on top of the Ninja Foodi Steam Fryer. 6. Move the Lid Slider to the "Air Fry/Stovetop". Select the "Air Fry" mode for cooking. 7. Adjust the Ninja Foodi Pressure Steam Fryer temperature

to 175°C. Set the timer. Air Fry for around 20 minutes. 8. Brush more olive oil onto the potatoes. 9. Reset the timer. Air Fry for around 15 minutes more. Remove the potatoes when they are fork-tender. 10. Sprinkle the cooked potatoes with salt, pepper, and Parmesan cheese.
Per Serving: Calories: 220; Fat: 10.9g; Sodium: 354mg; Carbs: 20.5g; Fiber: 4.1g; Sugar 8.2g; Protein 06g

Rosemary Potatoes

Prep Time: 5 minutes | Cook Time: 22 minutes | Serves: 4

675g small red potatoes, cut into 2.5cm cubes	½ teaspoon black pepper
2 tablespoons olive oil	1 tablespoon minced garlic
1 teaspoon salt	2 tablespoons minced fresh rosemary

1. Place the Cook & Crisp Basket in your Pressure Cooker Steam Fryer. 2. In a suitable mixing bowl, mix the diced potatoes, olive oil, salt, pepper, minced garlic, and rosemary and mix well, so the potatoes are coated with olive oil. 3. Place the potatoes into the Ninja Foodi Pressure Steam Fryer basket in a single layer. 4. Put on the Smart Lid on top of the Ninja Foodi Steam Fryer. 5. Move the Lid Slider to the "Air Fry/Stovetop". Select the "Air Fry" mode for cooking. 6. Adjust the cooking temperature to 200°C. 7. Set the timer and cook for around 20 to 22 minutes. Every 5 minutes, shake the basket, so the potatoes redistribute in the basket for even cooking. 8. Pour the potatoes into a suitable serving bowl, toss with additional black pepper and salt, and serve.
Per Serving: Calories: 282; Fat: 12.9g; Sodium: 414mg; Carbs: 11g; Fiber: 5g; Sugar 9g; Protein 11g

Honey Bread

Prep Time: 10 minutes | Cook Time: 20 minutes | Serves: 4

125g plain flour	1 large egg
160g polenta	240ml milk
100g sugar	80ml vegetable oil
1 teaspoon salt	85g honey
2 teaspoons baking powder	

1. Place the Cook & Crisp Basket in your Pressure Cooker Steam Fryer. 2. Spray the Cook & Crisp Basket with oil or cooking spray. 3. In a suitable mixing bowl, mix the flour, polenta, sugar, salt, baking powder, egg, milk, oil, and honey and mix lightly. 4. Pour the bread batter into the basket. 5. Put on the Smart Lid on top of the Ninja Foodi Steam Fryer. Move the Lid Slider to the "Air Fry/Stovetop". Select the "Air Fry" mode for cooking. Adjust the Ninja Foodi Pressure Steam Fryer temperature to 180°C. Set the timer. Air Fry for around 20 minutes. 6. Insert a toothpick into the center of bread to make sure the middle is cooked; if not, air fry for another 3 to 4 minutes. 7. Using silicone oven mitts, remove the basket from the Ninja Foodi Pressure Steam Fryer and let cool slightly. Serve warm.
Per Serving: Calories: 302; Fat: 19g; Sodium: 354mg; Carbs: 15g; Fiber: 5.1g; Sugar 8.2g; Protein 12g

Mexican Corn

Prep Time: 10 minutes | Cook Time: 7 minutes | Serves: 4

4 medium ears corn, husked	¼ teaspoon salt
Olive oil spray	50g crumbled feta cheese
2 tablespoons mayonnaise	2 tablespoons chopped fresh coriander
1 tablespoon fresh lime juice	
½ teaspoon ancho chili powder	

1. Place the Cook & Crisp Basket in your Pressure Cooker Steam Fryer. 2. Spritz the corn with olive oil. Working in batches, arrange the ears of corn in the Ninja Foodi Pressure Steam Fryer basket in a single layer. 3. Put on the Smart Lid on top of the Ninja Foodi Steam Fryer. 4. Move the Lid Slider to the "Air Fry/Stovetop". Select the "Air Fry" mode for cooking. 5. Adjust the cooking temperature to 190°C. 6. Cook for about 7 minutes, flipping halfway, until the kernels are tender when pierced with a paring knife. When cool enough to handle, cut the corn kernels off the cob. 7. In a suitable bowl, mix mayonnaise, lime juice, ancho powder, and salt. Add the corn kernels and mix to mix. Transfer this mixture to a serving dish and top with the Cotija and coriander. Serve immediately.
Per Serving: Calories: 361; Fat: 7.9g; Sodium: 704mg; Carbs: 6g; Fiber: 3.6g; Sugar 6g; Protein 18g

Feta Stuffed Portobellos

Prep Time: 10 minutes | Cook Time: 12 minutes | Serves: 4

4 large portobello mushroom caps (about 75g each)
Olive oil spray
Salt
2 medium plum tomatoes, chopped
30g baby spinach, chopped
185g crumbled feta cheese
1 shallot, chopped
1 large garlic clove, minced
10g chopped fresh basil

2 tablespoons panko bread crumbs, regular or gluten-free
1 tablespoon chopped fresh oregano
1 tablespoon freshly grated Parmesan cheese
⅛ teaspoon black pepper
1 tablespoon olive oil
Balsamic glaze, for drizzling (Optional)

1. Place the Cook & Crisp Basket in your Pressure Cooker Steam Fryer. 2. Use a suitable metal spoon to carefully scrape the black gills out of each mushroom cap. Grease both sides of the mushrooms with olive oil and season with a dash of salt. 3. In a suitable bowl, mix the tomatoes, spinach, feta, shallot, garlic, basil, panko, oregano, Parmesan, ¼ teaspoon salt, pepper, and olive oil and mix well. Carefully fill the inside of each mushroom cap with the mixture. 4. Spread a single layer of the stuffed mushrooms in the Ninja Foodi Pressure Steam Fryer basket. Put on the Smart Lid on top of the Ninja Foodi Steam Fryer. Move the Lid Slider to the "Air Fry/Stovetop". Select the "Air Fry" mode for cooking. Adjust the cooking temperature to 185°C. 5. Air Fry mushrooms for around 10 to 12 minutes, until mushrooms become tender and the top is golden. 6. Use a flexible spatula to carefully remove the mushrooms from the basket and transfer to a serving dish. Drizzle the balsamic glaze (if using) over the mushrooms and serve.
Per Serving: Calories: 334; Fat: 7.9g; Sodium: 704mg; Carbs: 6g; Fiber: 3.6g; Sugar 6g; Protein 18g

Teriyaki Tofu Steaks

Prep Time: 10 minutes | Cook Time: 10 minutes | Serves: 2

Tofu
175g tofu (about ½ block), sliced
2 tablespoons soy sauce
1 teaspoon toasted sesame oil
1 teaspoon unseasoned rice vinegar
1 teaspoon light brown sugar
Sriracha mayo
4 teaspoons mayonnaise
1 teaspoon Sriracha sauce

1 garlic clove, grated
½ teaspoon grated fresh ginger
45g white and black sesame seeds
1 large egg
Olive oil spray

1 spring onion, chopped, for garnish

1. Place the Cook & Crisp Basket in your Pressure Cooker Steam Fryer. 2. For the tofu: Put the tofu slices on a kitchen towel. Place another towel on top and press to remove the water from the tofu. Transfer to a shallow bowl or baking dish big enough for tofu to lie in a single layer. 3. In a suitable bowl, mix the sesame oil, ginger, brown sugar, vinegar, garlic, and soy sauce. Put half of the marinade over the tofu, and gently flip and drizzle the rest on the other side. Place in refrigerator for at least an hour, or up to overnight. 4. Place the sesame seeds on a suitable plate or pie dish. In another small dish or bowl, beat the egg. 5. Remove the tofu from marinade, let the excess drip off, and dip it in the egg. Dip a fork into the sesame seeds, coating each side. Transfer to a work surface. Spray one side with olive oil, then gently flip and coat the other side with oil. Spread a single layer of the tofu in the Ninja Foodi Pressure Steam Fryer basket. Put on the Smart Lid on top of the Ninja Foodi Steam Fryer. Move the Lid Slider to the "Air Fry/Stovetop". Select the "Air Fry" mode for cooking. 6. Adjust the cooking temperature to 200°C. 7. Air Fry tofu for about 10 minutes, flip it halfway, until toasted and crisp. 8. Meanwhile, for the Sriracha mayo: In a suitable bowl, mix the mayonnaise and Sriracha. 9. To serve, top each tofu "steak" with the Sriracha mayo and some spring onion (if using).
Per Serving: Calories: 184; Fat: 5g; Sodium: 441mg; Carbs: 17g; Fiber: 4.6g; Sugar 5g; Protein 9g

Cauliflower Nuggets

Prep Time: 10 minutes | Cook Time: 9 minutes | Serves: 4

3 large eggs, beaten
60g plain flour
28 bite-size (about 11 cm) cauliflower florets (400g)
Olive oil spray
6 tablespoons Frank's Red-hot sauce

1 tablespoon unsalted butter, melted
Blue cheese dip, homemade or store-bought (optional)
Carrot sticks and celery sticks, for serving (optional)

1. Place the Cook & Crisp Basket in your Pressure Cooker Steam Fryer. 2. Place the eggs in a suitable bowl. Place the flour in a separate bowl. 3. Dip the cauliflower in the egg, then in the flour to coat, shaking off the excess. Place on a work surface and spray both sides with olive oil. 4. Working in batches, spread a single layer of the cauliflower in the Ninja Foodi Pressure Steam Fryer basket. Put on the Smart Lid on top of the Ninja Foodi Steam Fryer. 5. Move the Lid Slider to the "Air Fry/Stovetop". Select the "Air Fry" mode for cooking. 6. Adjust the cooking temperature to 195°C. 7. Cook for around 7 to 8 minutes. When all the batches are done, return all the cauliflower to the air fryer. Cook for around 1 minute to heat through. 8. Transfer to a suitable bowl and toss with the hot sauce and melted butter. Serve.
Per Serving: Calories: 382; Fat: 7.9g; Sodium: 704mg; Carbs: 6g; Fiber: 3.6g; Sugar 6g; Protein 18g

Spicy Acorn Squash

Prep Time: 10 minutes | Cook Time: 15 minutes | Serves: 2

1 teaspoon coconut oil
1 medium acorn squash, halved crosswise and seeded

1 teaspoon light brown sugar
Few dashes of nutmeg
Few dashes of cinnamon

1. Place the Cook & Crisp Basket in your Pressure Cooker Steam Fryer. 2. Rub the coconut oil on the cut sides of the squash. Sprinkle with the brown sugar, nutmeg, and cinnamon. 3. Place the squash halves, cut sides up, in the Ninja Foodi Pressure Steam Fryer basket. 4. Put on the Smart Lid on top of the Ninja Foodi Steam Fryer. 5. Move the Lid Slider to the "Air Fry/Stovetop". Select the "Air Fry" mode for cooking. 6. Adjust the cooking temperature to 160°C. 7. Cook for around 15 minutes, until soft in the center when pierced with a paring knife. Serve immediately.
Per Serving: Calories: 212; Fat: 7.9g; Sodium: 704mg; Carbs: 6g; Fiber: 3.6g; Sugar 6g; Protein 18g

Bacon Brussels Sprouts

Prep Time: 10 minutes | Cook Time: 25 minutes | Serves: 4

3 slices center-cut bacon, halved
455g Brussels sprouts, trimmed and halved
1½ tablespoons extra-virgin olive

oil
¼ teaspoon salt
¼ teaspoon dried thyme

1. Place the Cook & Crisp Basket in your Pressure Cooker Steam Fryer. 2. Spread the bacon in a single layer in the basket. 3. Put on the Smart Lid on top of the Ninja Foodi Steam Fryer. 4. Move the Lid Slider to the "Air Fry/Stovetop". Select the "Air Fry" mode for cooking. 5. Adjust the cooking temperature to 175°C. 6. Air fry them for 10 minutes until crispy then transfer to a bowl. 7. Toss Brussel sprouts with oil, salt and thyme then add to the Ninja Foodi Pressure Steam Fryer. 8. Put on the Smart Lid on top of the Ninja Foodi Steam Fryer. 9. Move the Lid Slider to the "Air Fry/Stovetop". Select the "Air Fry" mode for cooking. 10. Adjust the cooking temperature to 175°C. Air fry the sprouts for 15 minutes until crispy. 11. Add the sprouts to the bacon and mix well. 12. Serve.
Per Serving: Calories: 221; Fat: 7.9g; Sodium: 704mg; Carbs: 6g; Fiber: 3.6g; Sugar 6g; Protein 6g

Sesame Green Beans

Prep Time: 10 minutes | Cook Time: 8 minutes | Serves: 4

1 tablespoon soy sauce or tamari
½ tablespoon Sriracha sauce
4 teaspoons toasted sesame oil

150g trimmed green beans
½ tablespoon toasted sesame seeds

1. Place the Cook & Crisp Basket in your Pressure Cooker Steam Fryer. 2. In a suitable bowl, mix well the soy sauce, Sriracha, and 1 teaspoon of the sesame oil. 3. In a suitable bowl, mix the green beans with the remaining 3 teaspoons sesame oil and toss to coat. 4. Working in batches, spread a single layer of the green beans in the Ninja Foodi Pressure Steam Fryer basket. Put on the Smart Lid on top of the Ninja Foodi Steam Fryer. Move the Lid Slider to the "Air Fry/Stovetop". Select the "Air Fry" mode for cooking. 5. Adjust the cooking temperature to 190°C. 6. Air Fry for about 8 minutes, shaking the basket halfway, until charred and tender. Transfer to a serving dish. Toss with the sauce and sesame seeds and serve.
Per Serving: Calories: 77; Fat: 14g; Sodium: 791mg; Carbs: 8.9g; Fiber: 4.6g; Sugar 1g; Protein 2g

Bacon-Wrapped Asparagus

Prep Time: 10 minutes | Cook Time: 10 minutes | Serves: 4

20 asparagus spears (300g), tough ends trimmed
Olive oil spray
½ teaspoon grated lemon zest
⅛ teaspoon salt
Black pepper
4 slices center-cut bacon

1. Place the Cook & Crisp Basket in your Pressure Cooker Steam Fryer. 2. Place the asparagus on a suitable sheet pan and spritz with olive oil. Season with the lemon zest, salt, and pepper to taste, tossing to coat. Group the asparagus into 4 bundles of 5 spears and wrap the center of each bundle with a slice of bacon. 3. Working in batches, place the asparagus bundles in the "cook & crisp basket". Put on the Smart Lid on top of the Ninja Foodi Steam Fryer. Move the Lid Slider to the "Air Fry/Stovetop". Select the "Air Fry" mode for cooking. 4. Adjust the cooking temperature to 200°C. 5. Air Fry until the bacon is browned and the asparagus is charred on the edges, 8 to 10 minutes, depending on the thickness of the spears. Serve immediately.
Per Serving: Calories: 226; Fat: 10.9g; Sodium: 354mg; Carbs: 20.5g; Fiber: 4.1g; Sugar 8.2g; Protein 06g

Potatoes Fries

Prep Time: 10 minutes | Cook Time: 15 minutes | Serves: 2

2 (150g) Yukon Gold or russet potatoes, washed and dried
2 teaspoons olive oil
¼ teaspoon salt
¼ teaspoon garlic powder
Black pepper

1. Place the Cook & Crisp Basket in your Pressure Cooker Steam Fryer. 2. Slice the potatoes lengthwise into ½ cm-thick slices, then cut each slice into ½ cm-thick fries. 3. In a suitable bowl, toss the potatoes with the oil. Season with the salt, garlic powder, and pepper to taste, tossing to coat. 4. Working in batches, arrange a single layer (no overlapping) of the potatoes in the Ninja Foodi Pressure Steam Fryer basket. 5. Put on the Smart Lid on top of the Ninja Foodi Steam Fryer. 6. Move the Lid Slider to the "Air Fry/Stovetop". Select the "Air Fry" mode for cooking. 7. Adjust the cooking temperature to 195°C. 8. Cook for around 12 to 15 minutes, flipping halfway, until the potatoes are golden and crisp. Serve immediately.
Per Serving: Calories: 226; Fat: 10.9g; Sodium: 354mg; Carbs: 20.5g; Fiber: 4.1g; Sugar 8.2g; Protein 06g

Broccoli Gratin

Prep Time: 10 minutes | Cook Time: 14 minutes | Serves: 2

Olive oil spray
½ tablespoon olive oil
1 tablespoon flour
80ml fat-free milk
½ teaspoon sage
¼ teaspoon salt
⅛ teaspoon black pepper
125g broccoli florets, chopped
6 tablespoons (35g) shredded extra-sharp cheddar cheese
2 tablespoons panko bread crumbs, regular or gluten-free
1 tablespoon freshly grated Parmesan cheese

1. Place the Cook & Crisp Basket in your Pressure Cooker Steam Fryer. 2. Spray the Cook & Crisp Basket with oil. 3. In a suitable bowl, mix the olive oil, flour, milk, sage, salt, and pepper. Add the broccoli, cheddar, panko, and Parmesan and mix well. 4. Place the mixture in the Ninja Foodi Pressure Steam Fryer basket. 5. Put on the Smart Lid on top of the Ninja Foodi Steam Fryer. 6. Move the Lid Slider to the "Air Fry/Stovetop". Select the "Air Fry" mode for cooking. 7. Adjust the cooking temperature to 165°C. 8. Cook for around 12 to 14 minutes, until the broccoli is crisp-tender and the cheese is golden brown on top. Serve immediately.
Per Serving: Calories: 184; Fat: 5g; Sodium: 441mg; Carbs: 17g; Fiber: 4.6g; Sugar 5g; Protein 9g

Onion Rings

Prep Time: 10 minutes | Cook Time: 10 minutes | Serves: 4

1 medium Vidalia onion (225g)
35g cornflakes
50g seasoned bread crumbs
½ teaspoon sweet paprika
120ml buttermilk
1 large egg
30g plain flour
½ teaspoon salt
Olive oil spray

1. Place the Cook & Crisp Basket in your Pressure Cooker Steam Fryer. 2. Trim the ends off the onion, then quarter the onion crosswise (about 1 cm-thick slices) and separate into rings. 3. In a food processor, pulse the cornflakes until fine. Transfer to a suitable bowl and stir in the bread crumbs and paprika. In another medium bowl, mix the buttermilk, egg, flour, and ½ teaspoon salt until mixed. 4. Dip the onion rings in the buttermilk batter, then into the cornflake mixture to coat. Set aside on a work surface and spray both sides with oil. 5. Working in batches, spread a single layer of the onion rings in the Ninja Foodi Steam Fryer basket. Put on the Smart Lid on top of the Ninja Foodi Steam Fryer. Move the Lid Slider to the "Air Fry/Stovetop". Select the "Air Fry" mode for cooking. Adjust the cooking temperature to 170°C. 6. Air Fry the rings for about 10 minutes, flipping halfway, until golden brown. Serve immediately.
Per Serving: Calories: 219; Fat: 10g; Sodium: 891mg; Carbs: 22.9g; Fiber: 4g; Sugar 4g; Protein 13g

Baked Potatoes with Yogurt

Prep Time: 10 minutes | Cook Time: 35 minutes | Serves: 4

4 (175g) russet potatoes, washed and dried
Olive oil spray
½ teaspoon salt
120g low fat Greek yogurt
10g minced fresh chives
Black pepper

1. Place the Cook & Crisp Basket in your Pressure Cooker Steam Fryer. 2. Using any fork, pierce the potatoes all over. Spray each potato with a few spritzes of oil. Season the potatoes with ¼ teaspoon of the salt. 3. Place the potatoes in the Ninja Foodi Pressure Steam Fryer basket. 4. Put on the Smart Lid on top of the Ninja Foodi Steam Fryer. 5. Move the Lid Slider to the "Air Fry/Stovetop". Select the "Air Fry" mode for cooking. 6. Adjust the cooking temperature to 200°C. 7. Cook for about 35 minutes, flipping halfway through, until a knife can easily be inserted into the center of each potato. 8. Split open the potatoes and serve topped with the yogurt, chives, the remaining ¼ teaspoon salt, and pepper to taste.
Per Serving: Calories: 120; Fat: 19g; Sodium: 354mg; Carbs: 15g; Fiber: 5.1g; Sugar 8.2g; Protein 12g

Garlic Sweet Potato Fries

Prep Time: 10 minutes | Cook Time: 8 minutes | Serves: 2

2 (150g) sweet potatoes, peeled
2 teaspoons olive oil
½ teaspoon salt
½ teaspoon garlic powder
¼ teaspoon sweet paprika
Black pepper

1. Place the Cook & Crisp Basket in your Pressure Cooker Steam Fryer. 2. Slice the potatoes lengthwise into ½ cm-thick slices, then cut each slice into ½ cm-thick fries. Transfer to a suitable bowl and toss with the oil, salt, garlic powder, paprika, and pepper to taste. 3. Working in batches, spread a single layer of the fries in the Ninja Foodi Pressure Steam Fryer basket. 4. Put on the Smart Lid on top of the Ninja Foodi Steam Fryer. 5. Move the Lid Slider to the "Air Fry/Stovetop". Select the "Air Fry" mode for cooking. 6. Adjust the cooking temperature to 200°C. Cook for about 8 minutes. 7. Serve immediately.
Per Serving: Calories: 334; Fat: 7.9g; Sodium: 104mg; Carbs: 3g; Fiber: 3.6g; Sugar 6g; Protein 3g

Tostones with Green Sauce

Prep Time: 10 minutes | Cook Time: 24 minutes | Serves: 2

1 large green plantain, peeled and sliced
Salt
¾ teaspoon garlic powder
Olive oil spray
Peruvian Green Sauce, for serving

1. Place the Cook & Crisp Basket in your Pressure Cooker Steam Fryer. 2. In a suitable bowl, mix 240 ml water with 1 teaspoon salt and the garlic powder. 3. Spritz the plantain all over with olive oil and transfer to the Ninja Foodi Pressure Steam Fryer basket. 4. Put on the Smart Lid on top of the Ninja Foodi Steam Fryer. 5. Move the Lid Slider to the "Air Fry/Stovetop". Select the "Air Fry" mode for cooking. 6. Cook at 200°C for around 6 minutes, shaking halfway, until soft. Immediately transfer to a work surface. 7. Dip each piece, one at a time, in the seasoned water, then transfer to the work surface. Generously spray both sides of the plantain with oil. 8. Working in batches, spread in a single layer of the plantain in the "cook & crisp basket". Put on the Smart Lid on top of the Ninja Foodi Steam Fryer. 9. Move the Lid Slider to the "Air Fry/Stovetop". Select the "Air Fry" mode for cooking. 10. Cook at 200°C for about 10 minutes, turning halfway, until golden and crisp. Transfer to a serving dish. While still hot, spray with olive oil and season with ⅛ teaspoon salt. 11. Serve immediately with the green sauce on the side.
Per Serving: Calories: 349; Fat: 2.9g; Sodium: 511mg; Carbs: 12g; Fiber: 3g; Sugar 8g; Protein 7g

Fried Aubergine

Prep Time: 10 minutes | Cook Time: 24 minutes | Serves: 8

1 large aubergine (about 675g)
¾ teaspoon salt
Black pepper
3 large eggs

165g seasoned bread crumbs,
whole wheat or gluten-free
Olive oil spray
Marinara sauce, for dipping

1. Place the Cook & Crisp Basket in your Pressure Cooker Steam Fryer. 2. Slice the ends off the aubergine and cut into ½ cm-thick rounds, 40 to 42 slices. Season both sides with the black pepper and salt to taste. 3. On a shallow plate, beat the eggs with 1 teaspoon water. Place the bread crumbs on another plate. Dip the aubergine slice in the egg, then in the bread crumbs, pressing gently to adhere. Remove the excess bread crumbs and place on a work surface. Generously spray both sides of the aubergine with oil. 4. Air frying in batches, arrange a single layer of the aubergine in the Ninja Foodi Pressure Steam Fryer basket. 5. Put on the Smart Lid on top of the Ninja Foodi Steam Fryer. Move the Lid Slider to the "Air Fry/Stovetop". Select the "Air Fry" mode for cooking. 6. Adjust the cooking temperature to 195°C. 7. Air Fry for about 8 minutes, flipping halfway, until crisp, golden, and cooked through in the center. Serve.
Per Serving: Calories: 116; Fat: 1.9g; Sodium: 224mg; Carbs: 18g; Fiber: 3.6g; Sugar 3g; Protein 2g

Chapter 3 Poultry Mains Recipes

Vietnamese-Style Chicken and Noodle Soup

Prep time: 15 minutes | Cook time: 25 minutes | Serves: 4

1-star anise pod
2 large shallots, root end intact, halved
2.5 cm piece fresh ginger, peeled and thinly sliced
5 dried shiitake mushrooms (about 12g)
1 bunch fresh coriander, stems and leaves reserved separately

2 boneless, skinless chicken breasts (250g)
1.7L low-sodium chicken stock
Salt and ground black pepper
100g glass noodles
1 tablespoon fish sauce, plus more if needed
Lime wedges, to serve

1. In a Ninja Foodi XL Pressure Cooker Steam Fryer with SmartLid cooking pot, combine the star anise, shallots, ginger, mushrooms, coriander stems, chicken breasts, stock and 1 teaspoon each salt and pepper. 2. Lock lid; move slider towards PRESSURE. Adjust pressure release valve in the SEAL position. Close pressure-release valve. The cooking temperature will default to HIGH, which is accurate. Set time to 5 minutes. Select START/STOP and start cooking. 3. When cooking is complete, let pressure release naturally for 5 minutes, then quick-release any remaining pressure by turning it into VENT position. 4. Press START/STOP, then carefully open the pot. 5. Using tongs, transfer the chicken and mushrooms to a plate and set aside. Using a slotted spoon, scoop out and discard the remaining solids in the stock. 6. Thinly slice the mushrooms, discarding any tough stems. Using two forks, shred the chicken into bite-size pieces. 7. Move the slider towards "AIR FRY/ STOVETOP" and Set Ninja Foodi XL Pressure Cooker Steam Fryer with SmartLid to SEAR/SAUTÉ mode. Adjust the temperature to "Hi5" by using up arrow. Press START/STOP to begin cooking and bring the stock to a boil. 8. Stir in the noodles and fish sauce, then cook, stirring occasionally, until tender, 3 to 6 minutes. Press START/STOP to turn off the pot. 9. Using kitchen shears, snip the noodles a few times directly in the pot to cut them into shorter lengths. Stir in the sliced mushrooms and chicken, then taste and season with additional fish sauce, if needed, and pepper. 10. Serve sprinkled with additional pepper and coriander leaves and serve with lime wedges on the side.

Per Serving: Calories 195; Fat 4.9g; Sodium 110mg; Carbs 1.7g; Fiber 1g; Sugar 0.7g; Protein 33.4g

Chicken, Chickpea Soup with Toasted Orzo

Prep time: 10 minutes | Cook time: 40 minutes | Serves: 6

2 tablespoons salted butter, cut into 3 pieces
120g orzo
1 medium leek, white and light green parts halved, thinly sliced, rinsed and dried
Salt and ground black pepper
3 medium garlic cloves, finely chopped
1¼ teaspoons red pepper flakes

2 bone-in, skin-on chicken breasts (250–300g), skin removed
390g can chickpeas, rinsed and drained
35g lightly packed baby spinach, chopped
180g plain whole-milk yogurt
5g chopped fresh dill, plus more to serve

1. Move the slider towards "AIR FRY/STOVETOP" and set Ninja Foodi XL Pressure Cooker Steam Fryer with SmartLid to SEAR/SAUTÉ mode. Adjust the temperature to "Hi5" by using up arrow. Press START/STOP to begin cooking. 2. Add the butter and orzo, then cook, stirring often, until golden brown, 6 to 8 minutes. 3. Using a slotted spoon, transfer to a small bowl and set aside. Add the leek, 1½ teaspoons salt and ¼ teaspoon black pepper to the fat remaining in the pot. 4. Cook, stirring occasionally, until the leek is softened, about 6 minutes. 5. Add the garlic and pepper flakes, then cook, stirring, until fragrant, about 1 minute. 6. Pour in 2 liters water and place the chicken breasts in the pot in an even layer. 7. Lock lid; move slider towards PRESSURE. Adjust pressure release valve in the SEAL position. Close pressure-release valve. The cooking temperature will default to HIGH, which is accurate. Set time to 12 minutes. Select START/STOP and start cooking. 8. When cooking is complete, let pressure release naturally for 10 minutes, then quick-release any remaining pressure by turning it into VENT position. 9. Carefully open the pot. Using tongs, transfer the chicken to a plate. 10. Select Sauté again and bring the stock to a boil. Stir in the toasted orzo and cook, stirring occasionally, until al dente, 10 to 12 minutes. 11. Meanwhile, using 2 forks, shred the chicken into bite-size pieces, discarding the bones. Press START/STOP to turn off the pot. 12. Stir in the shredded chicken, the chickpeas and spinach. Using potholders, carefully remove the insert from the housing. 13. Let cool for about 2 minutes, then stir in the yogurt and dill. Taste and season with salt and pepper. Serve sprinkled with additional dill and black pepper.

Per Serving: Calories 285; Fat 12g; Sodium 541mg; Carbs 6g; Fiber 3g; Sugar 2g; Protein 16g

Gingery Chicken Soup with Bok Choy

Prep time: 10 minutes | Cook time: 30 minutes | Serves: 6

1 tablespoon grapeseed or other neutral oil
10 cm piece fresh ginger (about 75g), peeled and cut into 4 pieces
5 medium garlic cloves, smashed and peeled
120ml dry sherry
2 teaspoons white peppercorns
Salt and ground white pepper
900g bone-in, skin-on chicken

thighs, skin removed
455g baby bok choy, trimmed and cut crosswise into 1.5 cm pieces
Salt and ground white pepper
4 spring onions, thinly sliced
30g chopped fresh coriander
2 tablespoons unseasoned rice vinegar
Chili oil or toasted sesame oil, to serve

1. Move the slider towards "AIR FRY/STOVETOP" and set Ninja Foodi XL Pressure Cooker Steam Fryer with SmartLid to SEAR/SAUTÉ mode. Adjust the temperature to "Hi5" by using up arrow. Press START/STOP to begin cooking. 2. Add the oil and heat until shimmering. Add the ginger and garlic and cook, stirring, until fragrant, about 30 seconds. 3. Pour in the sherry and bring to a boil. Stir in 1.4 L water, the peppercorns and 2 teaspoons salt. Add the chicken thighs, arranging them in an even layer. 4. Lock lid; move slider towards PRESSURE. Adjust pressure release valve in the SEAL position. Close pressure-release valve. The cooking temperature will default to HIGH, which is accurate. Set time to 20 minutes. Select START/STOP and start cooking. 5. When cooking is complete, let pressure release naturally for 15 minutes, then quick-release any remaining pressure by turning it into VENT position. 6. Carefully open the pot. Using a slotted spoon, transfer the chicken to a plate and set aside. Pour the stock through a fine mesh strainer set over a large bowl; discard the solids in the strainer. 7. Let the stock settle for about 5 minutes, then, using a large spoon, skim off and discard the fat from the surface. Return the stock to the pot. Remove and discard any bones from the chicken and shred or chop the meat into bite-size pieces. 8. Select Sauté again and bring the stock to a simmer. Stir in the bok choy and cook, stirring occasionally, until the stems are tender, about 3 minutes. 9. Press START/STOP to turn off the pot. Stir in the chicken, spring onions, coriander and vinegar. Taste and season with salt and ground white pepper. 10. Serve drizzled with chili oil or sesame oil.

Per Serving: Calories 208; Fat 12g; Sodium 145mg; Carbs 6.8g; Fiber 3.7g; Sugar 0.6g; Protein 17.5g

Herby Georgian-style Chicken Stew with Tomatoes

Prep time: 15 minutes | Cook time: 30 minutes | Serves: 4

2 tablespoons extra-virgin olive oil
8 medium garlic cloves, finely chopped
1 medium yellow onion, chopped
1½ teaspoons fennel seeds
Salt and ground black pepper
340g grape or cherry tomatoes, halved
120ml dry white wine

2 teaspoons dry mustard
1½ teaspoons ground coriander
900g boneless, skinless chicken thighs, trimmed
15g lightly packed fresh coriander, chopped
15g lightly packed fresh dill, chopped

1. Move the slider towards "AIR FRY/STOVETOP" and Set Ninja Foodi XL Pressure Cooker Steam Fryer with SmartLid to SEAR/SAUTÉ mode. Adjust the temperature to "Hi5" by using up arrow. Press START/STOP to begin cooking. 2. Add the oil and garlic, then cook, stirring, until golden brown, about 4 minutes. Add the onion, fennel seeds and 2 teaspoons salt. Cook, stirring often, until the onion begins to soften, about 4 minutes. 3. Stir in the tomatoes, wine, mustard and coriander, then bring to a simmer. Cook, stirring occasionally, until the liquid has thickened and the tomatoes begin to stick to the bottom of the pot, about 8 minutes. 4. Nestle the chicken in an even layer, slightly overlapping the pieces, if needed. 5. Lock lid; move slider towards PRESSURE. Adjust pressure release valve in the SEAL position. Close pressure-release valve. The cooking temperature will default to HIGH, which is accurate. Set time to 8 minutes. Select START/STOP and start cooking. 6. When cooking is complete, let pressure release naturally for 15 minutes, then quick-release any remaining pressure by turning it into VENT position. 7. Carefully open the pot. Stir in the coriander and dill, then taste and season with salt and pepper.

Per Serving: Calories 112; Fat 2g; Sodium 12mg; Carbs 8g; Fiber 1g; Sugar 6g; Protein 0g

Indian Chicken Stew

Prep time: 15 minutes | Cook time: 30 minutes | Serves: 4

50g lightly packed fresh coriander leaves and tender stems, roughly chopped, plus coriander leaves, to serve
5 cm piece fresh ginger, peeled and cut into 4 pieces
6 medium garlic cloves, smashed and peeled
2 jalapeño chilies, stemmed, halved and seeded
3 spring onions, roughly chopped
1 teaspoon ground coriander
Salt and ground black pepper
900g boneless, skinless chicken thighs, trimmed
2 tablespoons packed brown sugar
240ml coconut milk
1 tablespoons lime juice, plus lime wedges to serve

1. In a blender, combine the coriander, ginger, garlic, jalapeños, spring onions, coriander, 1 teaspoon salt, ½ teaspoon pepper and 120 ml water. Blend until smooth, about 30 seconds. 2. Add the chicken and half the puree to a Ninja Foodi XL Pressure Cooker Steam Fryer with SmartLid cooking pot. 3. Toss to coat, then let stand for 15 minutes. Meanwhile, transfer the remaining puree to a small bowl; set aside at room temperature if pressure cooking or cover and refrigerate if slow cooking. Stir another 120 ml water and the sugar into the chicken mixture, then distribute in an even layer. 4. Lock lid; move slider towards PRESSURE. Adjust pressure release valve in the SEAL position. Close pressure-release valve. The cooking temperature will default to HIGH, which is accurate. Set time to 4 minutes. Select START/STOP and start cooking. 5. When cooking is complete, let pressure release naturally for 10 minutes, then quick-release any remaining pressure by turning it into VENT position. Carefully open the pot. 6. Using a slotted spoon, transfer the chicken to a medium bowl and let cool for about 5 minutes. Using two forks, shred the meat. Return the chicken to the pot and stir in the coconut milk. 7. Move the slider towards "AIR FRY/STOVETOP" and set Ninja Foodi XL Pressure Cooker Steam Fryer with SmartLid to SEAR/SAUTÉ mode. Adjust the temperature to "Hi5" by using up arrow. Press START/STOP to begin cooking and bring to a simmer, then press START/STOP to turn off the pot. 8. Stir in the remaining puree and the lime juice. Taste and season with salt and pepper. 9. Serve sprinkled with coriander leaves, additional black pepper and lime wedges on the side.
Per Serving: Calories 311; Fat 6g; Sodium 112mg; Carbs 15g; Fiber 6g; Sugar 12g; Protein 2g

Chicken in Green

Prep time: 15 minutes | Cook time: 40 minutes | Serves: 4

4 medium tomatillos, husked and halved
1 small white onion, peeled, root end intact, quartered lengthwise
100g can chopped green chilies
1 bunch coriander, stems roughly chopped and leaves chopped, reserved separately
20g lightly packed fresh mint, chopped
1½ teaspoons fennel seeds
Salt and ground black pepper
Five 15 cm corn tortillas, torn into quarters
900g boneless, skinless chicken thighs, trimmed and halved crosswise
1 medium yellow summer squash, quartered lengthwise and thinly sliced

1. Move the slider towards "AIR FRY/STOVETOP" and set Ninja Foodi XL Pressure Cooker Steam Fryer with SmartLid to SEAR/SAUTÉ mode. Adjust the temperature to "Hi5" by using up arrow. Press START/STOP to begin cooking. 2. Add the tomatillos and onion, then cook, turning occasionally, until the vegetables are charred all over, 5 to 7 minutes. Press START/STOP to turn off the pot. 3. Transfer the vegetables to a blender and let cool slightly, about 5 minutes. 4. To the blender, add the green chilies with their liquid, the coriander stems, half the mint, the fennel seeds and 120 ml water. Blend on high until smooth, about 1 minute. Pour the puree into the pot. 5. Select Sauté again and bring to a simmer, scraping up any browned bits. Stir in 600 ml water, the tortillas, 2 teaspoons salt and ½ teaspoon pepper. Add the chicken, stir to combine and distribute in an even layer. 6. Lock lid; move slider towards PRESSURE. Adjust pressure release valve in the SEAL position. Close pressure-release valve. The cooking temperature will default to HIGH, which is accurate. Set time to 8 minutes. Select START/STOP and start cooking. 7. When cooking is complete, let pressure release naturally for 20 minutes, then quick-release any remaining pressure by turning it into VENT position. Carefully open the pot. 8. Move the slider towards "AIR FRY/STOVETOP" and set Ninja Foodi XL Pressure Cooker Steam Fryer with SmartLid to SEAR/SAUTÉ mode. Adjust the temperature to "Hi5" by using up arrow. Press START/STOP to begin cooking and bring the mixture to a simmer. 9. Add the squash and cook, stirring often, until the stock is slightly thickened and the squash is tender, 5 to 8 minutes. Press START/STOP to turn off the pot, then taste and season with salt and pepper. 10. Stir in the coriander leaves and the remaining mint.
Per Serving: Calories 429; Fat 32.4g; Sodium 325mg; Carbs 5g; Fiber 1g; Sugar 3g; Protein 28g

Miso and Bourbon Chicken

Prep time: 5 minutes | Cook time: 35 minutes | Serves: 4

3 tablespoons soy sauce
2 tablespoons white miso
120ml orange juice
2 tablespoons rapeseed oil
2 medium yellow onions, halved and thinly sliced
200g shiitake mushrooms, stemmed, caps thinly sliced
5 medium garlic cloves, finely chopped
180ml bourbon
1.3kg bone-in, skin-on chicken thighs, skin removed and discarded
2 tablespoons corn flour
2 tablespoons tahini
Salt and ground black pepper
1 spring onions, thinly sliced on the diagonal

1. In a small bowl, whisk the soy sauce and miso until smooth, then whisk in the orange juice; set aside. Move the slider towards "AIR FRY/STOVETOP" and set Ninja Foodi XL Pressure Cooker Steam Fryer with SmartLid to SEAR/SAUTÉ mode. Adjust the temperature to "Hi5" by using up arrow. Press START/STOP to begin cooking. 2. Add the oil and heat until shimmering. Add the onions and cook, stirring occasionally, until softened, 5 to 8 minutes. Add the mushrooms and garlic, then continue to cook, stirring occasionally, until the vegetables are lightly browned, about 5 minutes. Add the bourbon and cook, scraping up any browned bits, until most of the liquid has evaporated, 1 to 2 minutes. Stir in the miso mixture and 240 ml water, then nestle the chicken, skin side down, in an even layer, slightly overlapping the pieces if needed. 3. Lock lid; move slider towards PRESSURE. Adjust pressure release valve in the SEAL position. Close pressure-release valve. The cooking temperature will default to HIGH, which is accurate. Set time to 15 minutes. Select START/STOP and start cooking. 4. When cooking is complete, let pressure release naturally for 10 minutes, then quick-release any remaining pressure by turning it into VENT position. Carefully open the pot. 5. Using tongs, transfer the chicken to a serving dish and tent with foil. In a small bowl, whisk the corn flour and about 80 ml of the cooking liquid until smooth, then stir the mixture into the pot. 6. Select Sauté again and bring to a simmer, stirring constantly, then cook until the sauce is thickened, 2 to 3 minutes. Press START/STOP to turn off the pot. 7. Using potholders, carefully remove the insert from the housing. Stir in the tahini, if using. 8. Taste and season with salt and pepper. Pour the sauce over the chicken and top with the spring onions.
Per Serving: Calories 173; Fat 13.6g; Sodium 281mg; Carbs 3g; Fiber 1g; Sugar 1g; Protein 10g

Mustard Chicken Thighs

Prep Time: 10 minutes | Cook Time: 15 minutes | Serves: 6

1 large egg, well whisked
2 tablespoon whole-grain Dijon
60g of chili sauce
½ teaspoon sugar
1 teaspoon fine sea salt
½ teaspoon black pepper, or more to taste
mustard
60g of mayonnaise
½ teaspoon turmeric powder
10 chicken thighs
140g crushed crackers

1. Place the Cook & Crisp Basket in your Pressure Cooker Steam Fryer. 2. In a suitable bowl, mix the egg, mustard, mayonnaise, chili sauce, sugar, salt, pepper, and turmeric, incorporating everything well. 3. Coat the chicken thighs with the mixture. Place a layer of aluminum foil over the bowl, transfer it to the refrigerator and allow the chicken to marinate for at least 5 hours or overnight. 4. Separate the chicken from the marinade. 5. Put the crushed crackers into a shallow dish and use them to coat the chicken. 6. Place the chicken in the basket. Put on the Smart Lid on top of the Ninja Foodi Steam Fryer. Move the Lid Slider to the "Air Fry/Stovetop". Select the "Air Fry" mode for cooking. Adjust the cooking temperature to 180°C. 7. Cook for around 15 minutes, ensuring the thighs are cooked through. 8. Serve with the rest of the marinade as a sauce.
Per Serving: Calories 471; Fat: 7.9g; Sodium: 704mg; Carbs: 6g; Fiber: 3.6g; Sugar 6g; Protein 18g

Delicious Chicken Paprikash

Prep time: 15 minutes | Cook time: 25 minutes | Serves: 4

2 tablespoons salted butter
1 large yellow onion, finely chopped
Salt and ground black pepper
2 tablespoons sweet paprika
1 tablespoon tomato paste

1.3kg bone-in, skin-on chicken thighs, skin removed and discarded
240ml sour cream
1 tablespoon corn flour
1 tablespoons chopped fresh dill, divided

1. Move the slider towards "AIR FRY/STOVETOP" and set Ninja Foodi XL Pressure Cooker Steam Fryer with SmartLid to SEAR/SAUTÉ mode. Adjust the temperature to "Hi5" by using up arrow. Press START/STOP to begin cooking. 2. Add the butter and let melt. Add the onion, ½ teaspoon salt and ¼ teaspoon pepper, then cook, stirring occasionally, until the onion is golden brown, about 6 minutes. Add the paprika and tomato paste and cook, stirring, until fragrant, about 1 minute. Stir in 120ml water, scraping up the browned bits. Nestle the chicken in an even layer, skin side down, slightly overlapping the pieces if needed. 3. Lock lid; move slider towards PRESSURE. Adjust pressure release valve in the SEAL position. Close pressure-release valve. The cooking temperature will default to HIGH, which is accurate. Set time to 10 minutes. Select START/STOP and start cooking. 4. When cooking is complete, let pressure release naturally for 10 minutes, then quick-release any remaining pressure by turning it into VENT position. Carefully open the pot. 5. Using tongs, transfer the chicken to a dish and tent with foil. In a small bowl, whisk together the sour cream and corn flour. 6. Whisk the mixture into the pot, then move the slider towards "AIR FRY/STOVETOP" and set Ninja Foodi XL Pressure Cooker Steam Fryer with SmartLid to SEAR/SAUTÉ mode. Adjust the temperature to "Hi5" by using up arrow. Press START/STOP to begin cooking, whisking constantly, until the sauce begins to simmer and is lightly thickened. Press START/STOP to turn off the pot, then taste and season with salt and pepper. 7. Stir in 2 tablespoons of dill. Using potholders, carefully remove the insert from the housing and pour the sauce over the chicken. 8. Sprinkle with the remaining 2 tablespoons dill.
Per Serving: Calories 152; Fat 50g; Sodium 438mg; Carbs 7g; Fiber 0g; Sugar 7g; Protein 132g

Rogan Josh

Prep time: 15 minutes | Cook time: 40 minutes | Serves: 4

2 tablespoons salted butter
2 medium yellow onions, finely chopped
4 medium garlic cloves, smashed and peeled
6 whole cardamom pods, lightly crushed
2 cinnamon sticks
2 tablespoons finely grated fresh ginger

2 tablespoons tomato paste
1½ teaspoons cumin seeds
1 teaspoon sweet paprika
¼ teaspoon ground allspice
¼ teaspoon cayenne pepper
Salt and ground black pepper
1.3kg bone-in, skin-on chicken thighs, skin removed and discarded
120g whole-milk Greek yogurt
Chopped fresh coriander, to serve

1. Move the slider towards "AIR FRY/STOVETOP" and set Ninja Foodi XL Pressure Cooker Steam Fryer with SmartLid to SEAR/SAUTÉ mode. Adjust the temperature to "Hi5" by using up arrow. Press START/STOP to begin cooking. 2. Add the butter and let melt, then add the onions, garlic, cardamom, cinnamon and ½ teaspoon salt. Cook, stirring often, until the onions have softened, about 5 minutes. Add the ginger, tomato paste, cumin, paprika, allspice, cayenne, and 1 teaspoon each salt and black pepper, then cook, stirring, until fragrant, about 30 seconds. Stir in 240 ml water, scraping up any browned bits. Nestle the chicken in an even layer, slightly overlapping the pieces if needed. 3. Lock lid; move slider towards PRESSURE. Adjust pressure release valve in the SEAL position. Close pressure-release valve. The cooking temperature will default to HIGH, which is accurate. Set time to 10 minutes. Select START/STOP and start cooking. 4. When cooking is complete, let pressure release naturally for 15 minutes, then quick-release any remaining pressure by turning it into VENT position. Carefully open the pot. 5. Remove and discard the cinnamon and cardamom pods. Using a slotted spoon, transfer the chicken to a serving dish and tent with foil. 6. Move the slider towards "AIR FRY/STOVETOP" and set Ninja Foodi XL Pressure Cooker Steam Fryer with SmartLid to SEAR/SAUTÉ mode. Adjust the temperature to "Hi5" by using up arrow. Press START/STOP to begin cooking. 7. Bring the cooking liquid to a boil and cook, stirring occasionally, until a spatula drawn though the mixture leaves a very brief trail, about 15 minutes. 8. Press START/STOP to turn off the pot, then whisk

in the yogurt. Taste and season with salt and black pepper. 9. Using potholders, carefully remove the insert from the housing and pour the sauce over the chicken and sprinkle with coriander.
Per Serving: Calories 134; Fat 9.8g; Sodium 394mg; Carbs 2g; Fiber 0g; Sugar 1g; Protein 9g

Chicken Tagine with Squash and Spinach

Prep time: 15 minutes | Cook time: 35 minutes | Serves: 4

4 tablespoons extra-virgin olive oil, divided
Salt and ground black pepper
2 teaspoons ground cinnamon
2 teaspoons ground cumin
2 teaspoons sweet paprika
1 teaspoon ground coriander
675g boneless, skinless chicken thighs, trimmed and cut into 4 cm pieces
1 large yellow onion, thinly sliced

lengthwise
4 medium garlic cloves, peeled and smashed
4 teaspoons finely grated fresh ginger
360g can diced tomatoes
200g peeled butternut squash, cut into 1.5 cm cubes
125g container baby spinach
2 teaspoons grated lemon zest, plus 3 tablespoons lemon juice

1. In a small bowl, stir together 2 tablespoons of oil, 2½ teaspoons salt, ½ teaspoon pepper, the cinnamon, cumin, paprika and coriander. In a medium bowl, toss the chicken with 1 tablespoon of the spice paste. 2. Move the slider towards "AIR FRY/STOVETOP" and set Ninja Foodi XL Pressure Cooker Steam Fryer with SmartLid to SEAR/SAUTÉ mode. Adjust the temperature to "Hi5" by using up arrow. Press START/STOP to begin cooking. 3. Add the remaining 2 tablespoons oil and heat until shimmering. Add the onion and 1 teaspoon salt, then cook, stirring occasionally, until softened, about 6 minutes. Add the garlic, ginger and the remaining spice paste. Cook, stirring constantly, until fragrant, 30 to 60 seconds. Stir in 600 ml water, scraping up any browned bits. Add the tomatoes with their juices, the squash and chicken; stir to combine, then distribute the ingredients in an even layer. 4. Lock lid; move slider towards PRESSURE. Adjust pressure release valve in the SEAL position. Close pressure-release valve. The cooking temperature will default to HIGH, which is accurate. Set time to 3 minutes. Select START/STOP and start cooking. 5. When cooking is complete, let pressure release naturally for 10 minutes, then quick-release any remaining pressure by turning it into VENT position. 6. Carefully open the pot. Stir in the spinach, then re-cover the pot without locking the lid in place. Let stand until the spinach wilts, about 3 minutes. 7. Stir in the lemon zest and juice, then taste and season with salt and pepper.
Per Serving: Calories 227; Fat 9.8g; Sodium 525mg; Carbs 7g; Fiber 2g; Sugar 4g; Protein 28g

Spicy Korean Braised Chicken with Vegetables

Prep time: 10 minutes | Cook time: 55 minutes | Serves: 4

3 tablespoons gochujang
2 tablespoons unseasoned rice vinegar
2 tablespoons soy sauce
1 tablespoon packed brown sugar
1 tablespoon toasted sesame oil, plus more to serve
5 cm piece fresh ginger (35g), peeled, cut into 3 pieces and smashed
5 medium garlic cloves, finely

chopped
1 bunch spring onions, whites chopped, greens cut into 2.5 cm lengths, reserved separately
900g boneless, skinless chicken thighs, trimmed and halved
250g Yukon Gold potatoes, peeled and cut into 2.5 cm chunks
2 medium carrots, peeled and cut into 2.5 cm pieces
Sesame seeds, toasted, to serve

1. In a Ninja Foodi XL Pressure Cooker Steam Fryer with SmartLid cooking pot, whisk together the gochujang, vinegar, soy sauce, sugar, sesame oil, ginger, garlic and scallion whites. 2. Add the chicken and toss to coat. Let stand for 15 minutes. Stir in the potatoes, carrots and 120 ml water, then distribute in an even layer. 3. Lock lid; move slider towards PRESSURE. Adjust pressure release valve in the SEAL position. Close pressure-release valve. The cooking temperature will default to HIGH, which is accurate. Set time to 8 minutes. Select START/STOP and start cooking. 4. When cooking is complete, let pressure release naturally for 10 minutes by turning it into VENT position, then quick-release any remaining pressure. 5. Remove and discard the ginger, then stir in the scallion greens. 6. Transfer to a serving bowl, drizzle with additional sesame oil and sprinkle with sesame seeds.
Per Serving: Calories 293; Fat 13.8g; Sodium 855mg; Carbs 28g; Fiber 8g; Sugar 11g; Protein 19g

Tropical Spicy Braised Chicken

Prep time: 15 minutes | Cook time: 35 minutes | Serves: 4

3 tablespoons grapeseed or other neutral oil	80ml coconut milk
1 medium yellow onion, halved and thinly sliced	85g roasted cashews, finely chopped
Salt	2 habanero chilies
2 tablespoons tomato paste	1.3kg bone-in, skin-on chicken thighs, skin removed and discarded
1 tablespoon ground ginger	
2 teaspoons ground turmeric	Chopped fresh coriander or flat-leaf parsley, to serve
360g can diced tomatoes	Lime wedges, to serve

1. Move the slider towards "AIR FRY/STOVETOP" and set Ninja Foodi XL Pressure Cooker Steam Fryer with SmartLid to SEAR/SAUTÉ mode. Adjust the temperature to "Hi5" by using up arrow. Press START/STOP to begin cooking. 2. Add the oil and heat until shimmering. Add the onion and 1½ teaspoons salt, then cook, stirring occasionally, until lightly browned, 7 to 10 minutes. Add the tomato paste, ginger and turmeric, then cook, stirring, until fragrant, about 30 seconds. 3. Press START/STOP, then stir in the tomatoes with their juices, the coconut milk, cashews, habanero chilies and 80 ml water, scraping up any browned bits. Nestle the chicken in an even layer, skin side down, slightly overlapping the pieces if needed. 4. Lock lid; move slider towards PRESSURE. Adjust pressure release valve in the SEAL position. Close pressure-release valve. The cooking temperature will default to HIGH, which is accurate. Set time to 10 minutes. Select START/STOP and start cooking. 5. When cooking is complete, let pressure release quickly by turning it into VENT position. Press START/STOP, then carefully open the pot. 6. Using tongs, transfer the chicken to a serving dish and tent with foil. Remove and discard the chilies. 7. Move the slider towards "AIR FRY/STOVETOP" and set Ninja Foodi XL Pressure Cooker Steam Fryer with SmartLid to SEAR/SAUTÉ mode. Adjust the temperature to "Hi5" by using up arrow. Press START/STOP to begin cooking. 8. Bring the cooking liquid to a simmer and cook, stirring often to prevent scorching, until the sauce is thick and creamy, about 15 minutes. Press START/STOP to turn off the pot. Taste and season with salt. 9. Using potholders, carefully remove the insert from the housing and pour the sauce over the chicken. Sprinkle with coriander and serve with lime wedges.

Per Serving: Calories 248; Fat 21.1g; Sodium 429mg; Carbs 2g; Fiber 0g; Sugar 1g; Protein 12g

Braised Chicken

Prep time: 15 minutes | Cook time: 20 minutes | Serves: 4

1 tablespoon grapeseed or other neutral oil	thighs, skin removed and discarded, trimmed
5 medium garlic cloves, finely chopped	1 tablespoon corn flour
8 cm piece fresh ginger (about 50g), peeled and sliced into thin coins	5 spring onions, thinly sliced on the diagonal, white and green parts reserved separately
4 teaspoons fish sauce	1 Fresno or serrano chili, halved, seeded and thinly sliced
120ml sake	1 teaspoon unseasoned rice vinegar
1.3kg bone-in, skin-on chicken	

1. Move the slider towards "AIR FRY/STOVETOP" and set Ninja Foodi XL Pressure Cooker Steam Fryer with SmartLid to SEAR/SAUTÉ mode. Adjust the temperature to "Hi5" by using up arrow. Press START/STOP to begin cooking. 2. Add the oil and heat until shimmering. Add the garlic and ginger, then cook, stirring, until fragrant, about 30 seconds. Add the fish sauce and sake, then bring to a gentle simmer. Nestle the chicken in an even layer, slightly overlapping the pieces, if needed. 3. Lock lid; move slider towards PRESSURE. Adjust pressure release valve in the SEAL position. Close pressure-release valve. The cooking temperature will default to HIGH, which is accurate. Set time to 10 minutes. Select START/STOP and start cooking. 4. When cooking is complete, let pressure release naturally, then quick-release any remaining pressure by turning it into VENT position. 5. Carefully open the pot. Using tongs, transfer the chicken to a serving dish and tent with foil. In a small bowl, whisk together the corn flour and 60 ml of the cooking liquid until combined, then stir the mixture into the pot along with the scallion whites and half of the scallion greens. 6. Move the slider towards "AIR FRY/STOVETOP" and set Ninja Foodi XL Pressure Cooker Steam Fryer with SmartLid to SEAR/SAUTÉ mode. Adjust the temperature to "Hi5" by using up arrow. Press START/STOP to begin cooking. 7. Bring to a simmer and cook, stirring constantly, until the sauce

is lightly thickened, about 1 minute. Stir in the chilies and vinegar. Press START/STOP to turn off the pot. 8. Using potholders, carefully remove the insert from the housing and pour the sauce over the chicken, then sprinkle with the remaining spring onion greens.

Per Serving: Calories 509; Fat 40.6g; Sodium 525mg; Carbs 8g; Fiber 2g; Sugar 5g; Protein 28g

Senegalese Braised Chicken

Prep time: 15 minutes | Cook time: 35 minutes | Serves: 4

2 tablespoons grated lime zest, plus 60 ml lime juice	2 medium yellow onions, halved and thinly sliced
1 habanero chili, stemmed, seeded and minced	1.3kg bone-in, skin on chicken thighs, skin removed and discarded
3 tablespoons grapeseed or other neutral oil, divided	1 tablespoon corn flour
Salt and ground black pepper	Chopped fresh chives, to serve

1. In a small bowl, mix together the lime zest, habanero, 1 tablespoon oil, 1 tablespoon salt and 1 teaspoon pepper. Measure out 1 tablespoon of the mixture into another small bowl and set aside. 2. Move the slider towards "AIR FRY/STOVETOP" and set Ninja Foodi XL Pressure Cooker Steam Fryer with SmartLid to SEAR/SAUTÉ mode. Adjust the temperature to "Hi5" by using up arrow. Press START/STOP to begin cooking. Heat the remaining 2 tablespoons oil until shimmering. Add the onions and cook without stirring until golden brown on the bottom, about 7 minutes. Stir and continue to cook, stirring only occasionally, until the onions are evenly golden brown, another 7 to 10 minutes. Press START/STOP. 3. Add the lime juice, 2 tablespoons water and remaining zest-habanero mixture, scraping up any browned bits. Nestle the chicken in an even layer, skin side down, slightly overlapping the pieces if needed. 4. Lock lid; move slider towards PRESSURE. Adjust pressure release valve in the SEAL position. Close pressure-release valve. The cooking temperature will default to HIGH, which is accurate. Set time to 10 minutes. Select START/STOP and start cooking. 5. When cooking is complete, let pressure release naturally for 15 minutes by turning it into VENT position, then quick-release any remaining pressure. Carefully open the pot. Using tongs, transfer the chicken to a serving dish and tent with foil. In a small bowl, whisk together the corn flour and 60 ml of the cooking liquid until combined, then stir into the pot. 6. Move the slider towards "AIR FRY/STOVETOP" and set Ninja Foodi XL Pressure Cooker Steam Fryer with SmartLid to SEAR/SAUTÉ mode. Adjust the temperature to "Hi5" by using up arrow. Press START/STOP to begin cooking. 7. And bring to a simmer, stirring constantly, then cook until lightly thickened, about 1 minute. Stir in the reserved zest-habanero mixture, then taste and season with salt and pepper. 8. Using potholders, carefully remove the insert from the housing and pour the sauce over the chicken, then sprinkle with chives.

Per Serving: Calories 288; Fat 23.3g; Sodium 308mg; Carbs 6g; Fiber 1g; Sugar 5g; Protein 14g

Turkey Sliders

Prep Time: 10 minutes | Cook Time: 15 minutes | Serves: 6

For the Turkey Sliders:

340g turkey mince	coriander
20g pickled jalapeno, chopped	2 tablespoon chopped spring onions
1 tablespoon oyster sauce	
1–2 cloves garlic, minced	Sea salt and black pepper to taste
1 tablespoon chopped fresh	

For the Chive Mayo:

240g mayonnaise	1 teaspoon salt
1 tablespoon chives	Zest of 1 lime

1. Place the Cook & Crisp Basket in your Pressure Cooker Steam Fryer. 2. In a bowl, mix all of the recipe ingredients for the turkey sliders. Use your hands to shape 6 equal amounts of the mixture into slider patties. 3. Transfer the patties to the Ninja Foodi Pressure Steam Fryer. 4. Put on the Smart Lid on top of the Ninja Foodi Steam Fryer. 5. Move the Lid Slider to the "Air Fry/Stovetop". Select the "Air Fry" mode for cooking. 6. fry them at 185°C for around 15 minutes. 7. In the meantime, prepare the Chive Mayo by combining the rest of the ingredients. 8. Make sandwiches by placing each patty between two burger buns and serve with the mayo.

Per Serving: Calories 343; Fat: 20.1g; Sodium 903mg; Carbs: 0.2g; Fiber: 0.1g; Sugars 0.2g; Protein 37.1g

Vermouth-Braised Chicken with potatoes Fennel

Prep time: 15 minutes | Cook time: 15 minutes | Serves: 4

120ml white vermouth
6 medium garlic cloves, smashed and peeled
1 tablespoon fennel seeds
Salt and ground black pepper
900g boneless, skinless chicken thighs, trimmed
200g small Yukon Gold potatoes
(2.5 cm–3 cm in diameter), halved
1 medium fennel bulb, trimmed, halved, cored and thinly sliced
1 tablespoon plain flour
25g lightly packed baby rocket, roughly chopped
1 tablespoon lemon juice

1. In the Ninja Foodi XL Pressure Cooker Steam Fryer with SmartLid cooking pot, stir together the vermouth, garlic, fennel seeds, 1 teaspoon salt and ¼ teaspoon pepper. Add the chicken, potatoes and fennel; stir to combine, then distribute in an even layer. 2. Lock lid; move slider towards PRESSURE. Adjust pressure release valve in the SEAL position. Close pressure-release valve. The cooking temperature will default to HIGH, which is accurate. Set time to 8 minutes. Select START/STOP and start cooking. 3. When cooking is complete, let pressure release naturally, then quick-release any remaining pressure by turning it into VENT position. 4. Carefully open the pot. Using a slotted spoon, transfer the chicken and potatoes to a serving dish, then tent with foil. In a small bowl, whisk the flour with 2 tablespoons of the cooking liquid until smooth, then stir into the pot. 5. Move the slider towards "AIR FRY/STOVETOP" and Set Ninja Foodi XL Pressure Cooker Steam Fryer with SmartLid to SEAR/SAUTÉ mode. 6. Adjust the temperature to "Hi5" by using up arrow. Press START/STOP to begin cooking and bring the liquid to a simmer. Cook, stirring often, until lightly thickened, 2 to 5 minutes. 7. Off heat, stir in the rocket and lemon juice, then taste and season with salt and pepper. 8. Using potholders, carefully remove the insert from the housing and pour the sauce over the chicken and potatoes.
Per Serving: Calories 138; Fat 10.6g; Sodium 102mg; Carbs 1g; Fiber 0g; Sugar 1g; Protein 9g

Turkey Meatballs in Chipotle Sauce

Prep time: 15 minutes | Cook time: 30 minutes | Serves: 4

75g fine dry breadcrumbs
4 teaspoons ground cumin
15g finely chopped fresh coriander, divided
2 or 3 chipotle chilies in adobo, minced, plus 1 tablespoon adobo sauce
100g pepper jack cheese, 50g finely shredded, 50g shredded
Salt and ground black pepper
455g turkey mince (preferably dark meat)
2 tablespoons salted butter
700g can crushed tomatoes
360g can diced tomatoes
Finely chopped white onion, to serve
Lime wedges, to serve

1. In a large bowl, stir together the breadcrumbs, cumin, 5g of coriander, the adobo sauce, the finely shredded cheese, 1½ teaspoons salt and 120ml water until well combined. Add the turkey and mix with your hands until homogenous. Divide into 10 portions (about ⅓ cup each), then form into balls about 5 cm in diameter and place on a large plate. Refrigerate uncovered for 15 minutes. 2. Move the slider towards "AIR FRY/STOVETOP" and set Ninja Foodi XL Pressure Cooker Steam Fryer with SmartLid to SEAR/SAUTÉ mode. Adjust the temperature to "Hi5" by using up arrow. Press START/STOP to begin cooking. 3. Add the butter and let melt. Add the crushed tomatoes, diced tomatoes with juices and minced chipotle chilies, then bring to a simmer, stirring occasionally. Place the chilled meatballs in an even layer in the tomato mixture, gently pressing to submerge them. 4. Lock lid; move slider towards PRESSURE. Adjust pressure release valve in the SEAL position. Close pressure-release valve. The cooking temperature will default to HIGH, which is accurate. Set time to 10 minutes. Select START/STOP and start cooking. 5. When cooking is complete, let pressure release naturally for about 10 minutes, then quickly release any remaining pressure by turning it into VENT position. Carefully open the pot. 6. Using a slotted spoon, place the meatballs to a serving dish. Sprinkle with the shredded cheese, dividing it evenly, then tent with foil. 7. Move the slider towards "AIR FRY/STOVETOP" and set Ninja Foodi XL Pressure Cooker Steam Fryer with SmartLid to SEAR/SAUTÉ mode. Adjust the temperature to "Hi5" by using up arrow. Press START/STOP to begin cooking. 8. Bring the tomato mixture to a simmer and cook, stirring frequently, until the sauce has thickened, about 10 minutes. Press START/STOP to turn off the pot. Taste and season with salt and pepper. Stir in the remaining 5g coriander, then spoon about half of the sauce over the meatballs. 9. Sprinkle with chopped onion and serve with the remaining sauce and lime wedges on the side.
Per Serving: Calories 196; Fat 15.3g; Sodium 423mg; Carbs 1.6g; Fiber 0.1g; Sugar 0.3g; Protein 12.9g

Buttery Chicken

Prep time: 15 minutes | Cook time: 25 minutes | Serves: 6

700g can whole peeled tomatoes
130g roasted salted cashews
20g garam masala
5 teaspoons ground cumin
2 tablespoons finely grated fresh ginger
Salt and ground black pepper
1.1kg boneless, skinless chicken thighs, cut into 4 cm pieces
2 tablespoons salted butter, cut into 2 pieces
1 medium yellow onion, chopped
6 medium garlic cloves, finely chopped
4 tablespoons finely chopped fresh coriander, divided
2 tablespoons lime juice
2 tablespoons honey

1. Use a blender, puree tomatoes with their juices until smooth, for about 1 minute; place to a medium bowl and set aside. Put the cashews and 180ml water in the blender, then puree until smooth, for about 1 minute; set aside if pressure cooking or transfer to a small bowl, cover and refrigerate if slow cooking. 2. In a large bowl, whisk together the garam masala, ginger, cumin and 2 teaspoons salt. Then add the chicken and toss to coat; set aside. 3. Move the slider towards "AIR FRY/STOVETOP" and set Ninja Foodi XL Pressure Cooker Steam Fryer with SmartLid to SEAR/SAUTÉ mode. Adjust the temperature to "Hi5" by using up arrow. Press START/STOP to begin cooking. Add the butter and let it melt. 4. Add the onion and cook, stirring occasionally, until softened, for 3 to 5 minutes. Add the garlic and cook, stirring, until fragrant, for about 30 seconds. Stir in the chicken and tomatoes and spread evenly. 5. Lock lid; move slider towards PRESSURE. Adjust pressure release valve in the SEAL position. Close pressure-release valve. The cooking temperature will default to HIGH, which is accurate. Set time to 10 minutes. Select START/STOP and start cooking. 6. When cooking is complete, let pressure release naturally for about 10 minutes by turning it into VENT position, then quickly release any remaining pressure. Carefully open the pot. Stir the cashew puree into the chicken mixture, scraping the bottom of the pot. 7. Move the slider towards "AIR FRY/STOVETOP" and Set Ninja Foodi XL Pressure Cooker Steam Fryer with SmartLid to SEAR/SAUTÉ mode. Adjust the temperature to "Hi5" by using up arrow. 8. Press START/STOP to begin cooking, stirring often, until the sauce has thickened and coats the chicken, 4 to 5 minutes. 9. Using potholders, carefully remove the insert from the housing. Let cool for about 5 minutes. Stir in 3 tablespoons of coriander, the lime juice and honey, then taste and season with salt and pepper. 10. Serve sprinkled with the remaining 1 tablespoon coriander.
Per Serving: Calories 411; Fat 28.3g; Sodium 398mg; Carbs 1.9g; Fiber 0.2g; Sugar 0.3g; Protein 36.2g

Hoisin Glazed Drumsticks

Prep Time: 10 minutes | Cook Time: 40 minutes | Serves: 4

2 turkey drumsticks
2 tablespoons balsamic vinegar
2 tablespoons dry white wine
1 tablespoon extra-virgin olive oil
For the Hoisin Glaze:
2 tablespoon hoisin sauce
1 tablespoon honey
1 sprig rosemary, chopped
Salt and black pepper, to taste
2 ½ tablespoon butter, melted

1 tablespoon honey mustard

1. Place the Cook & Crisp Basket in your Pressure Cooker Steam Fryer. 2. In a suitable bowl, coat the turkey drumsticks with the vinegar, wine, olive oil, and rosemary. Allow to marinate for around 3 hours. 3. Sprinkle the turkey drumsticks with salt and black pepper. Cover the surface of each drumstick with the butter. 4. Place the turkey in the basket. Put on the Smart Lid on top of the Ninja Foodi Steam Fryer. Move the Lid Slider to the "Air Fry/Stovetop". Select the "Air Fry" mode for cooking. Air Fry at 175°C for 30 to 35 minutes, flipping it occasionally through the cooking time. Work in batches. 5. In the meantime, make the Hoisin glaze by combining all the glaze ingredients. 6. Pour the glaze over the turkey, and cook for another 5 minutes. 7. Allow the drumsticks to rest for about 10 minutes before carving.
Per Serving: Calories 596; Fat: 24.6g; Sodium 316mg; Carbs: 36.8g; Fiber: 15.6g; Sugars 9.5g; Protein 58.8g

Caprese Chicken

Prep time: 5 minutes | Cook time: 5 minutes | Serves: 4

675g boneless, skinless chicken breasts, cut into 2.5 cm cubes
1 (700g) can diced tomatoes, including juice
1 (200g) ball fresh mozzarella, cubed
1 tablespoon olive oil
½ teaspoon salt
½ teaspoon ground black pepper
15g julienned fresh basil leaves

1. Add chicken and tomatoes with juice to the Ninja Foodi XL Pressure Cooker Steam Fryer with SmartLid cooking pot. 2. Lock lid; move slider towards PRESSURE. Adjust pressure release valve in the SEAL position. Close pressure-release valve. The cooking temperature will default to HIGH, which is accurate. Set time to 5 minutes. Select START/STOP and start cooking. When cooking is complete, let pressure release naturally for about 10 minutes, then quickly release any remaining pressure by turning it into VENT position. 3. Check chicken using a meat thermometer to ensure the internal temperature is at least 75°C. Using a slotted spoon, place chicken and tomatoes to four bowls. 4. Garnish chicken with mozzarella cubes. Drizzle with olive oil. Season with salt, pepper, and basil, and serve.
Per Serving: Calories 387; Fat 32.1g; Sodium 145mg; Carbs 2.3g; Fiber 0.5g; Sugar 0.6g; Protein 21.9g

Herb Roasted Chicken

Prep time: 10 minutes | Cook time: 25 minutes | Serves: 4

1 teaspoon dried thyme leaves
1 teaspoon dried oregano leaves
1 teaspoon dried basil leaves
1 teaspoon garlic powder
1 teaspoon salt
1 teaspoon ground black pepper
1 tablespoon olive oil
1 (2.3kg) whole chicken
1 small red apple, peeled, cored, and quartered
1 medium sweet onion, peeled and roughly chopped, divided
3 cloves garlic, peeled and halved
480ml water

1. In a small bowl, combine thyme, oregano, basil, garlic powder, salt, and pepper. 2. Brush oil on the outside of chicken. Sprinkle mixture from small bowl evenly over chicken. Place apple quarters and half of onion in the cavity of the bird. 3. Add remaining onion and garlic to the Ninja Foodi XL Pressure Cooker Steam Fryer with SmartLid cooking pot. Add water to pot. Insert Deluxe Reversible Rack over vegetables. Place chicken on Deluxe Reversible Rack. 4. Lock lid; move slider towards PRESSURE. Adjust pressure release valve in the SEAL position. Close pressure-release valve. The cooking temperature will default to HIGH, which is accurate. Set time to 25 minutes. Select START/STOP and start cooking. When cooking is complete, let pressure release naturally. Carefully unlock lid. Check chicken using a meat thermometer to ensure the internal temperature is at least 75°C. 5. Transfer chicken to a cutting board and discard apple and onion from the chicken cavity. Let chicken rest for 5 minutes until cool enough to carve. Serve warm.
Per Serving: Calories 396; Fat 28.6g; Sodium 452mg; Carbs 3.8g; Fiber 1g; Sugar 1g; Protein 30.4g

Chicken in Cocotte with White Wine

Prep time: 15 minutes | Cook time: 35 minutes | Serves: 4

1.6kg whole chicken, patted dry, wings tucked
Salt and ground black pepper
5 tablespoons salted butter, cut into 1-tablespoon pieces, divided
1 medium yellow onion, halved and thinly sliced
8 medium garlic cloves, peeled
and halved
240ml dry white wine
2 thyme sprigs or 1 teaspoon dried thyme
3 tablespoons lemon juice
3 tablespoons whole-grain mustard
15g finely chopped fresh tarragon

1. Season the chicken on all sides with salt and pepper. Place the chicken breast side up on the Deluxe Reversible Rack; set aside. 2. Move the slider towards "AIR FRY/STOVETOP" and set Ninja Foodi XL Pressure Cooker Steam Fryer with SmartLid to SEAR/SAUTÉ mode. Adjust the temperature to "Hi5" by using up arrow. Press START/STOP to begin cooking. 3. Add 1 tablespoon of butter and let melt. Add the onion and cook, stirring occasionally, until beginning to brown, about 8 minutes. Add the garlic and cook, stirring, until fragrant, about 30 seconds. Stir in the wine and thyme and bring to a simmer. Press START/STOP, then lower the rack with the chicken into the pot. 4. Lock lid; move slider towards PRESSURE. Adjust pressure release valve in the SEAL position. Close pressure-release valve. The cooking temperature will default to HIGH, which is accurate.

Set time to 16 minutes. Select START/STOP and start cooking. 5. When cooking is complete, let pressure release naturally for 20 minutes by turning it into VENT position, then quick-release any remaining pressure. Carefully open the pot. The center of the thickest part of the breast should register about 70°C and the thickest part of the thighs about 80°C. Using a kitchen towel or 2 pairs of tongs, carefully grab the handles of the rack, lift out the chicken and set the rack on a cutting board. 6. Let rest while you make the sauce. If you used thyme sprigs, remove and discard them. Using a large spoon, skim off and discard the fat from the surface of the cooking liquid. 7. Move the slider towards "AIR FRY/STOVETOP" and set Ninja Foodi XL Pressure Cooker Steam Fryer with SmartLid to SEAR/SAUTÉ mode. Adjust the temperature to "Hi5" by using up arrow. Press START/STOP to begin cooking, bring to a simmer and cook, stirring occasionally, until slightly thickened and reduced to about 1 cup with solids, about 5 minutes. 8. Press START/STOP to turn off the pot. Using potholders, carefully remove the insert from the housing. Whisk in the remaining 4 tablespoons butter, the lemon juice and mustard, then taste and season with salt and pepper. Transfer the chicken from the rack directly to the board. 9. Remove the legs by cutting through the hip joints. Remove and discard the skin from the legs, then separate the thighs from the drumsticks. Remove the breast meat from the bone, remove and discard the skin, then cut each crosswise into thin slices. 10. Arrange the chicken on a platter. Transfer the sauce to a bowl, stir in the tarragon and serve with the chicken.
Per Serving: Calories 151; Fat 7.5g; Sodium 621mg; Carbs 20g; Fiber 5g; Sugar 2g; Protein 5g

chicken in Cocotte with Cherry Tomatoes

Prep time: 15 minutes | Cook time: 40 minutes | Serves: 4

1.6kg whole chicken, patted dry, wings tucked
Salt and ground black pepper
2 tablespoons extra-virgin olive oil
1 medium yellow onion, halved and thinly sliced
1 teaspoon smoked paprika
340g grape or cherry tomatoes
80g pimiento-stuffed green olives, halved
2 teaspoons grated orange zest, plus 240ml orange juice
1 teaspoon dried oregano
2 teaspoons corn flour
10g finely chopped fresh oregano

1. Season the chicken on all sides with salt and pepper. Place the chicken breast side up on the Deluxe Reversible Rack with handles; set aside. 2. Move the slider towards "AIR FRY/STOVETOP" and set Ninja Foodi XL Pressure Cooker Steam Fryer with SmartLid to SEAR/SAUTÉ mode. Adjust the temperature to "Hi5" by using up arrow. Press START/STOP to begin cooking. 3. Add the oil and heat until shimmering. Add the onion and cook, stirring occasionally, until beginning to brown, about 8 minutes. Add the paprika and cook, stirring, until fragrant, about 30 seconds. Stir in the tomatoes, olives, orange juice and dried oregano, then bring to a simmer. 4. Lock lid; move slider towards PRESSURE. Adjust pressure release valve in the SEAL position. Close pressure-release valve. The cooking temperature will default to HIGH, which is accurate. Set time to 16 minutes. Select START/STOP and start cooking. 5. When cooking is complete, let pressure release quickly by turning it into VENT position. Carefully open the pot. The center of the thickest part of the breast should register about 70°C and the thickest part of the thighs about 80°C. 6. Using a kitchen towel or two pairs of tongs, carefully grab the handles of the rack, lift out the chicken and set the rack on a cutting board. Let rest while you make the sauce. Using a large spoon, skim off and discard the fat from the surface of the cooking liquid. 7. Move the slider towards "AIR FRY/STOVETOP" and set Ninja Foodi XL Pressure Cooker Steam Fryer with SmartLid to SEAR/SAUTÉ mode. Adjust the temperature to "Hi5" by using up arrow. 8. Press START/STOP to begin cooking and bring to a simmer. Cook, stirring occasionally, until the tomatoes burst, about 5 minutes. In a small bowl, stir together the corn flour and 2 tablespoons water, then stir into the tomato-olive mixture. Cook, stirring constantly, until the sauce is slightly thickened, about 1 minute. Press START/STOP to turn off the pot. 9. Using potholders, carefully remove the insert from the housing, then stir in the orange zest and the fresh oregano. Taste and season with salt and pepper. Transfer the chicken from the rack directly to the cutting board. Remove the legs from the chicken by cutting through the hip joints. 10. Remove and discard the skin from the legs, then separate the thighs from the drumsticks. Remove the breast meat from the bone, remove and discard the skin, then cut each crosswise into thin slices. 11. Arrange the chicken on a platter. Transfer the sauce to a bowl and serve with the chicken.
Per Serving: Calories 217; Fat 21.8g; Sodium 207mg; Carbs 7g; Fiber 4g; Sugar 3g; Protein 2g

chicken in Cocotte with Shallots

Prep time: 5 minutes | Cook time:40 minutes | Serves: 4

2 crisp, red-skinned apples, unpeeled, quartered lengthwise, cored and thinly sliced
2 tablespoons cider vinegar
Salt and ground black pepper
1.6kg whole chicken, patted dry, wings tucked
2 tablespoons salted butter
3 large shallots, halved and thinly

sliced
240ml unfiltered apple juice or apple cider
2 sprigs thyme or 1 teaspoon dried thyme
2 teaspoons corn flour
10g finely chopped fresh flat-leaf parsley

1. In a small bowl, stir together the apples, vinegar and ½ teaspoon salt; set aside. Season the chicken on all sides with salt and pepper. Place the chicken breast side up on a Deluxe Reversible Rack; set aside. 2. Move the slider towards "AIR FRY/STOVETOP" and set Ninja Foodi XL Pressure Cooker Steam Fryer with SmartLid to SEAR/SAUTÉ mode. Adjust the temperature to "Hi5" by using up arrow. Press START/STOP to begin cooking. 3. Add the butter and let melt. Add the shallots and cook, stirring occasionally, until beginning to brown, about 8 minutes. Stir in the cider and thyme and bring to a simmer. Press START/STOP, then lower the rack with the chicken into the pot. 4. Lock lid; move slider towards PRESSURE. Adjust pressure release valve in the SEAL position. Close pressure-release valve. The cooking temperature will default to HIGH, which is accurate. Set time to 16 minutes. Select START/STOP and start cooking. 5. When cooking is complete, let pressure release naturally for 20 minutes by turning it into VENT position, then quick-release any remaining pressure. Press START/STOP, then carefully open the pot. The center of the thickest part of the breast should register about 70°C and the thickest part of the thighs about 80°C. 6. Using a kitchen towel or two pairs of tongs, carefully grab the handles of the rack, lift out the chicken and set the rack on a cutting board. Let rest while you make the sauce. If you used thyme sprigs, remove and discard them. Using a large spoon, skim off and discard the fat from the surface of the cooking liquid. 7. Move the slider towards "AIR FRY/STOVETOP" and Set Ninja Foodi XL Pressure Cooker Steam Fryer with SmartLid to SEAR/SAUTÉ mode. Adjust the temperature to "Hi5" by using up arrow. 8. Press START/STOP to begin cooking and bring to a simmer. Stir in the apples along with their liquid and cook, stirring occasionally, until tender, about 5 minutes. 9. In a small bowl, stir together the corn flour and 2 tablespoons water, then stir into the apple mixture. Cook, stirring constantly, until the sauce is lightly thickened, about 1 minute. Press START/STOP to turn off the pot. 10. Using potholders, carefully remove the insert from the housing. Taste and season with salt and pepper. Transfer the chicken from the rack directly to the cutting board. 11. Remove the legs from the chicken by cutting through the hip joints. Remove and discard the skin from the legs, then separate the thighs from the drumsticks. 12. Remove the breast meat from the bone, remove and discard the skin, then cut each crosswise into thin slices. Arrange the chicken on a platter. 13. Transfer the sauce to a bowl, stir in the parsley and serve with the chicken.

Per Serving: Calories 268; Fat 13.6g; Sodium 348mg; Carbs 1.2g; Fiber 0.2g; Sugar 0.6g; Protein 35.2g

Pulled Chicken with Chipotle

Prep time: 5 minutes | Cook time: 30 minutes | Serves: 4

3 or 4 chipotle chilies in adobo sauce, minced, plus 2 tablespoons adobo sauce
Salt and ground black pepper
1.1kg boneless, skinless chicken thighs, patted dry and halved crosswise
1 tablespoon extra-virgin olive oil
1 large white onion, halved and

thinly sliced
6 medium garlic cloves, finely chopped
1 tablespoon ground cumin
Two 15cm corn tortillas, torn into rough 5cm pieces
700g can crushed tomatoes
15g finely chopped fresh coriander

1. In a large bowl, combine the adobo sauce and 1 teaspoon salt, then add the chicken and stir to coat. Move the slider towards "AIR FRY/ STOVETOP" and Set Ninja Foodi XL Pressure Cooker Steam Fryer with SmartLid to SEAR/SAUTÉ mode. Adjust the temperature to "Hi5" by using up arrow. Press START/STOP to begin cooking. 2. Add the oil and heat until shimmering. Add the onion and cook, stirring occasionally, until softened, about 5 minutes. Stir in the garlic, cumin and chipotle chilies, then cook, stirring, until fragrant, about 1 minute. Add 120 ml water, scraping up any browned bits. Add the chicken,

stir to combine, then distribute in an even layer. Scatter the tortilla pieces evenly over the chicken. Pour the tomatoes over the top but do not stir. 3. Lock lid; move slider towards PRESSURE. Adjust pressure release valve in the SEAL position. Close pressure-release valve. The cooking temperature will default to HIGH, which is accurate. Set time to 8 minutes. Select START/STOP and start cooking. 4. When cooking is complete, let pressure release naturally for 15 minutes by turning it into VENT position, then quick-release any remaining pressure. Carefully open the pot. 5. Using a slotted spoon, transfer the chicken to a large bowl and let cool for about 5 minutes. Using two forks, shred the meat. 6. Move the slider towards "AIR FRY/STOVETOP" and set Ninja Foodi XL Pressure Cooker Steam Fryer with SmartLid to SEAR/SAUTÉ mode. Adjust the temperature to "Hi5" by using up arrow. Press START/STOP to begin cooking and bring the sauce to a simmer. 7. Cook, stirring often and scraping the bottom of the pot, until slightly thickened, 5 to 8 minutes. Press START/STOP to turn off the pot. 8. Return the chicken to the pot, add the coriander and stir to combine. Taste and season with salt and pepper.

Per Serving: Calories 326; Fat 19.6g; Sodium 458mg; Carbs 1.9g; Fiber 0.4g; Sugar 0.6g; Protein 35.6g

Lemon Garlic Chicken

Prep Time: 10 minutes | Cook Time: 15 minutes | Serves: 1

1 chicken breast
1 teaspoon garlic, minced
1 tablespoon chicken seasoning

1 lemon juice
Handful black peppercorns
Pepper and salt to taste

1. Place the Cook & Crisp Basket in your Pressure Cooker Steam Fryer. 2. Sprinkle the chicken with pepper and salt. Massage the chicken seasoning into the chicken breast, coating it well, and lay the seasoned chicken on a sheet of aluminum foil. 3. Top the chicken with the garlic, lemon juice, and black peppercorns. Wrap the foil to seal the chicken tightly. 4. Put on the Smart Lid on top of the Ninja Foodi Steam Fryer. 5. Move the Lid Slider to the "Air Fry/Stovetop". Select the "Air Fry" mode for cooking. 6. Adjust the cooking temperature to 175°C. 7. Cook the chicken for around 15 minutes.

Per Serving: Calories 347; Fat: 15.7g; Sodium 999mg; Carbs: 11.8g; Fiber: 1.1g; Sugars 7g; Protein 39.6g

Cajun Chicken

Prep Time: 10 minutes | Cook Time: 10 minutes | Serves: 2

2 boneless chicken breasts

3 tablespoon Cajun spice

1. Place the Cook & Crisp Basket in your Pressure Cooker Steam Fryer. 2. Coat both sides of the chicken breasts with Cajun spice. 3. Put the seasoned chicken in "cook & crisp basket". 4. Put on the Smart Lid on top of the Ninja Foodi Steam Fryer. 5. Move the Lid Slider to the "Air Fry/Stovetop". Select the "Air Fry" mode for cooking. 6. Air fry at 175°C for 10 minutes, ensuring they are cooked through before slicing up and serving.

Per Serving: Calories 236; Fat: 10.4g; Sodium 713mg; Carbs: 9.8g; Fiber: 0.5g; Sugars 0.1g; Protein 25.7g

Italian Chicken Fillets

Prep Time: 10 minutes | Cook Time: 6 minutes | Serves: 3

8 pieces of chicken fillet
1 egg
25g salted butter, melted
100g friendly bread crumbs

1 teaspoon garlic powder
50g parmesan cheese
1 teaspoon Italian herbs

1. Place the Cook & Crisp Basket in your Pressure Cooker Steam Fryer. 2. Cover the chicken pieces in the whisked egg, melted butter, garlic powder, and Italian herbs. Allow to marinate for about 10 minutes. 3. In a suitable bowl, mix the bread crumbs and parmesan. Use this mixture to coat the marinated chicken. 4. Put the aluminum foil in your Ninja Foodi Pressure Steam Fryer basket. 5. Place 4 pieces of the chicken in the basket. 6. Put on the Smart Lid on top of the Ninja Foodi Steam Fryer. 7. Move the Lid Slider to the "Air Fry/Stovetop". Select the "Air Fry" mode for cooking. 8. Cook at 200°C for around 6 minutes until golden brown. Don't turn the chicken over. 9. Repeat with the rest of the chicken pieces. 10. Serve the chicken fillets hot.

Per Serving: Calories 427; Fat: 18.1g; Sodium 676mg; Carbs: 13.7g; Fiber: 7.5g; Sugars 1.7g; Protein 51.2g

Spicy Sichuan Chicken

Prep time: 5 minutes | Cook time: 20 minutes | Serves: 4

60ml chili oil
2.5 cm piece fresh ginger, peeled and thinly sliced
1 bunch coriander, stems minced, leaves chopped, reserved separately
2 teaspoons Sichuan peppercorns
3 tablespoons soy sauce
2 tablespoons unseasoned rice vinegar
2 teaspoons white sugar
3 bone-in, skin-on chicken breasts (250g), skin removed and discarded
1 tablespoon corn flour
35g roasted peanuts, chopped

1. Move the slider towards "AIR FRY/STOVETOP" and set Ninja Foodi XL Pressure Cooker Steam Fryer with SmartLid to SEAR/SAUTÉ mode. Adjust the temperature to "Hi5" by using up arrow. Press START/STOP to begin cooking. 2. Add the chili oil, ginger, coriander stems and Sichuan peppercorns. Cook, stirring, until sizzling and fragrant, 2 to 3 minutes. Press START/STOP and let the mixture cool until the sizzling stops, about 5 minutes. Whisk in the soy sauce, vinegar, sugar and 60 ml water. Place the chicken breasts flesh side down in the liquid. 3. Lock lid; move slider towards PRESSURE. Adjust pressure release valve in the SEAL position. Close pressure-release valve. The cooking temperature will default to HIGH, which is accurate. Set time to 8 minutes. Select START/STOP and start cooking. 4. When cooking is complete, let pressure release naturally, then quick-release any remaining pressure by turning it into VENT position. Carefully open the pot. 5. Transfer the chicken to a deep serving platter. Set a fine mesh strainer over a medium bowl. Using potholders, carefully remove the insert from the housing and pour the cooking liquid through the strainer; return the insert to the housing. Press on the solids in the strainer to remove as much liquid as possible; discard the solids. 6. Add the corn flour to the strained liquid and whisk to combine. Return the liquid to the insert and add the peanuts, move the slider towards "AIR FRY/STOVETOP" and set Ninja Foodi XL Pressure Cooker Steam Fryer with SmartLid to SEAR/SAUTÉ mode. Adjust the temperature to "Hi5" by using up arrow. Press START/STOP to begin cooking. 7. Bring to a simmer, stirring constantly, until lightly thickened, 2 to 3 minutes. Press START/STOP to turn off the pot. Carve the chicken off the bones, slicing the breasts crosswise into ½cm slices, and return to the platter. 8. Sprinkle with the coriander leaves, then pour the sauce over. Let stand for about 10 minutes before serving.
Per Serving: Calories 150; Fat 6.7g; Sodium 336mg; Carbs 1.9g; Fiber 0.2g; Sugar 0.1g; Protein 19.6g

Fajita Chicken Bowl

Prep time: 15 minutes | Cook time: 5 minutes | Serves: 4

2 tablespoons olive oil
Zest of 1 lime
Juice of 1 lime
1 teaspoon salt
½ teaspoon ground black pepper
1 tablespoon chili powder
1 tablespoon ground cumin
⅛ teaspoon red pepper flakes
455g boneless, skinless chicken breasts, cut into 2.5 cm cubes
Bowl Ingredients
1 avocado, peeled, pitted, and diced
2 Roma tomatoes, seeded and
1 small green pepper, seeded and sliced
1 small red pepper, seeded and sliced
1 small yellow pepper, seeded, sliced
1 small sweet onion, peeled and sliced
120ml water

diced
120g sour cream
100g shredded cheddar cheese

1. In a medium bowl, whisk together olive oil, lime zest, lime juice, salt, pepper, chili powder, cumin, and red pepper flakes. Add chicken, pepper slices, and onion. Toss and refrigerate at least 30 minutes or up to overnight. 2. Add water and chicken mixture to the Ninja Foodi XL Pressure Cooker Steam Fryer with SmartLid cooking pot. 3. Lock lid; move slider towards PRESSURE. Adjust pressure release valve in the SEAL position. Close pressure-release valve. The cooking temperature will default to HIGH, which is accurate. Set time to 5 minutes. Select START/STOP and start cooking. 4. When cooking is complete, let pressure release naturally for about 10 minutes, then quickly release any remaining pressure by turning it into VENT position. Carefully unlock lid. Check chicken using a meat thermometer to ensure the internal temperature is at least 75°C. 5. Using a slotted spoon, transfer chicken and veggie mixture to four bowls. 5. Garnish with avocado, tomatoes, sour cream, and Cheddar cheese. Serve warm.
Per Serving: Calories 106; Fat 8.7g; Sodium 332mg; Carbs 1.5g;

Fiber 0.3g; Sugar 0.1g; Protein 5.9g

Crusted Chicken Schnitzel

Prep Time: 10 minutes | Cook Time: 20 minutes | Serves: 3

3 chicken legs, boneless and skinless
2 tablespoons olive oil
1 teaspoon dried basil
1 teaspoon dried oregano
1 teaspoon dried sage
Sea salt and freshly cracked black pepper
50g breadcrumbs

1. Place the Cook & Crisp Basket in your Pressure Cooker Steam Fryer. 2. Pat the chicken dry with paper towels. Toss the chicken legs with the remaining recipe ingredients. 3. Put on the Smart Lid on top of the Ninja Foodi Steam Fryer. 4. Move the Lid Slider to the "Air Fry/Stovetop". Select the "Air Fry" mode for cooking. 5. Cook the chicken at 185°C for around 20 minutes, turning them over halfway through the cooking time. 6. Serve.
Per Serving: Calories: 477; Fat:21.2g; Carbs: 14.8g; Proteins: 53.3g; Sugars: 1.9g; Fiber: 1.4g

Cheese Stuffed Chicken

Prep Time: 10 minutes | Cook Time: 20 minutes | Serves: 4

455g chicken breasts, boneless, skinless, cut into four pieces
2 tablespoons sundried tomatoes, chopped
1 garlic clove, minced
50g mozzarella cheese, crumbled
Sea salt and black pepper, to taste
1 tablespoon olive oil

1. Place the Cook & Crisp Basket in your Pressure Cooker Steam Fryer. 2. Flatten the chicken breasts with a mallet. 3. Stuff each piece of chicken with the sundried tomatoes, garlic, and cheese. Roll them up and secure with toothpicks. 4. Season the chicken with the black pepper and salt and drizzle the olive oil over them. 5. Place the stuffed chicken in the Cook and crisp basket. 6. Put on the Smart Lid on top of the Ninja Foodi Steam Fryer. 7. Move the Lid Slider to the "Air Fry/Stovetop". Select the "Air Fry" mode for cooking. 8. Cook the chicken at 200°C for about 20 minutes, turning them over halfway through the cooking time. 9. Serve.
Per Serving: Calories: 257; Fat:13.9g; Carbs: 2.7g; Proteins: 28.3g; Sugars: 1.4g; Fiber: 0.6g

Balsamic Wings

Prep Time: 10 minutes | Cook Time: 22 minutes | Serves: 4

675g chicken wings
2 tablespoons olive oil
2 tablespoons balsamic vinegar
Salt and black pepper, to taste

1. Place the Cook & Crisp Basket in your Pressure Cooker Steam Fryer. 2. Toss the chicken wings with the remaining ingredients. 3. Put on the Smart Lid on top of the Ninja Foodi Steam Fryer. 4. Move the Lid Slider to the "Air Fry/Stovetop". Select the "Air Fry" mode for cooking. 5. Cook the chicken wings at 195°C for around 22 minutes, turning them over halfway through the cooking time. 6. Serve.
Per Serving: Calories: 265; Fat:4g; Carbs: 2.4g; Proteins: 34.4g; Sugars: 1.7g; Fiber: 0.2g

Turkey Sandwiches

Prep Time: 10 minutes | Cook Time: 20 minutes | Serves: 4

140g leftover turkey, cut into bite-sized chunks
2 peppers, deveined and chopped
1 Serrano pepper, deveined and chopped
1 leek, sliced
120g sour cream
1 teaspoon hot paprika
¾ teaspoon salt
½ teaspoon black pepper
1 heaping tablespoon fresh coriander, chopped
Dash of Tabasco sauce
4 hamburger buns

1. Place the Cook & Crisp Basket in your Pressure Cooker Steam Fryer. 2. Mix all of the recipe ingredients except for the hamburger buns, ensuring to coat the turkey well. 3. Place in the Cook & Crisp Basket. 4. Put on the Smart Lid on top of the Ninja Foodi Steam Fryer. 5. Move the Lid Slider to the "Air Fry/Stovetop". Select the "Air Fry" mode for cooking. 6. cook for around 20 minutes at 195°C. 7. Top the hamburger buns with the turkey, and serve with mustard or sour cream as desired.
Per Serving: Calories 334; Fat: 19g; Sodium: 354mg; Carbs: 15g; Fiber: 5.1g; Sugar 8.2g; Protein 12g

Chicken Wings with Piri Piri Sauce

Prep Time: 10 minutes | Cook Time: 1 hr. 30 minutes | Serves: 6

12 chicken wings
35g butter, melted
1 teaspoon onion powder
½ teaspoon cumin powder
1 teaspoon garlic paste
For the Sauce:
50g Piri Piri peppers, stemmed and chopped

1 tablespoon pimiento, deveined and minced
1 garlic clove, chopped
2 tablespoons fresh lemon juice
⅓ teaspoon sea salt
½ teaspoon tarragon
¾ teaspoon sugar

1. Place the Cook & Crisp Basket in your Pressure Cooker Steam Fryer. 2. Place the chicken wings in a steamer basket over a suitable saucepan of boiling water. Lower the temperature and steam the chicken for around 10 minutes over a medium heat. 3. Coat the wings with the butter, onion powder, cumin powder, and garlic paste. 4. Allow the chicken wings to cool slightly. Place them in the refrigerator for around 45 to 50 minutes. Then transfer the chicken wings to the Cook & Crisp Basket. 5. Put on the Smart Lid on top of the Ninja Foodi Steam Fryer. 6. Move the Lid Slider to the "Air Fry/Stovetop". Select the "Air Fry" mode for cooking. 7. Adjust the cooking temperature to 165°C. 8. Cook the chicken wings for around 25 to 30 minutes, turning them once halfway through the cooking time. 9. In the meantime, make the Piri Piri sauce. Blend all of the sauce ingredients in a food processor. 10. Coat the chicken wings in the sauce before serving.
Per Serving: Calories 382; Fat: 12.9g; Sodium: 414mg; Carbs: 11g; Fiber: 5g; Sugar 9g; Protein 31g

Spicy Turkey Wings

Prep Time: 10 minutes | Cook Time: 40 minutes | Serves: 4

340g turkey wings, cut into pieces
1 teaspoon ginger powder
1 teaspoon garlic powder
¾ teaspoon paprika
2 tablespoon soy sauce
1 handful minced lemongrass

Sea salt flakes and black pepper to taste
2 tablespoon rice wine vinegar
65g peanut butter
1 tablespoon sesame oil
120g Thai sweet chili sauce

1. Place the Cook & Crisp Basket in your Pressure Cooker Steam Fryer. 2. Boil the turkey wings in a suitable saucepan full of water for around 20 minutes. 3. Put the turkey wings in a large bowl and cover them with the remaining ingredients, minus the Thai sweet chili sauce. 4. Transfer to the Ninja Foodi Pressure Steam Fryer. 5. Put on the Smart Lid on top of the Ninja Foodi Steam Fryer. 6. Move the Lid Slider to the "Air Fry/Stovetop". Select the "Air Fry" mode for cooking. 7. Cook for around 20 minutes at 175°C, turning once halfway through the cooking time. Ensure they are cooked through before serving with the Thai sweet chili sauce, as well as some lemon wedges if desired.
Per Serving: Calories 416; Fat: 23.6g; Sodium 934mg; Carbs: 6g; Fiber: 2g; Sugars 0.6g; Protein 37.9g

Breaded Chicken

Prep Time: 10 minutes | Cook Time: 52 minutes | Serves: 2

2 chicken breasts, boneless and skinless
2 large eggs
120ml skimmed milk
6 tablespoon soy sauce
125g flour

1 teaspoon smoked paprika
1 teaspoon salt
¼ teaspoon black pepper
½ teaspoon garlic powder
1 tablespoon olive oil
4 hamburger buns

1. Place the Cook & Crisp Basket in your Pressure Cooker Steam Fryer. 2. Slice the chicken breast into 2 to 3 pieces. 3. Place in a large bowl and drizzle with the soy sauce. Sprinkle on the smoked paprika, black pepper, salt, and garlic powder and mix well. 4. Allow to marinate for around 30 to 40 minutes. 5. In the meantime, mix the eggs with the milk in a bowl. Put the flour in a separate bowl. 6. Dip the marinated chicken into the egg mixture before coating it with the flour. Cover each piece of chicken evenly. 7. Drizzle on the olive oil and put chicken pieces in the Cook & Crisp Basket. 8. Put on the Smart Lid on top of the Ninja Foodi Steam Fryer. 9. Move the Lid Slider to the "Air Fry/Stovetop". Select the "Air Fry" mode

for cooking. 10. Adjust the cooking temperature to 195°C. 11. Cook for around 10 to 12 minutes. Flip the chicken once throughout the cooking process. 12. Toast the hamburger buns and put each slice of chicken between two buns to make a sandwich. Serve with ketchup or any other sauce of your choice.
Per Serving: Calories 408; Fat: 23.1g; Sodium: 412mg; Carbs: 27.7g; Fiber: 7.2g; Sugars 19.2g; Protein 24.4g

Roasted Turkey

Prep Time: 10 minutes | Cook Time: 45 minute | Serves: 4

1 red onion, cut into wedges
1 carrot, trimmed and sliced
1 celery stalk, trimmed and sliced
90g Brussels sprouts, trimmed and halved
240ml roasted vegetable stock
1 tablespoon apple cider vinegar
1 teaspoon maple syrup

2 turkey thighs
½ teaspoon mixed peppercorns, freshly cracked
1 teaspoon fine sea salt
1 teaspoon cayenne pepper
1 teaspoon onion powder
½ teaspoon garlic powder
⅓ teaspoon mustard seeds

1. Place the Cook & Crisp Basket in your Pressure Cooker Steam Fryer. 2. Put the vegetables into the Cook & Crisp Basket and add in the roasted vegetable stock. 3. In a large bowl, pour in the rest of the ingredients, and set aside for around 30 minutes. 4. Put on the Smart Lid on top of the Ninja Foodi Steam Fryer. 5. Move the Lid Slider to the "Air Fry/Stovetop". Select the "Air Fry" mode for cooking. 6. Place them on the top of the vegetables. 7. Cook at 165°C for around 40 to 45 minutes.
Per Serving: Calories 289; Fat: 14g; Sodium: 791mg; Carbs: 18.9g; Fiber: 4.6g; Sugar 8g; Protein 6g

Italian Turkey Sausage

Prep Time: 10 minutes | Cook Time: 37 minutes | Serves: 4

1 onion, cut into wedges
2 carrots, trimmed and sliced
1 parsnip, trimmed and sliced
2 potatoes, peeled and diced
1 teaspoon dried thyme
½ teaspoon dried marjoram

1 teaspoon dried basil
½ teaspoon celery seeds
Sea salt and black pepper to taste
1 tablespoon melted butter
340g sweet Italian turkey sausage

1. Place the Cook & Crisp Basket in your Pressure Cooker Steam Fryer. 2. Cover the vegetables with all of the seasonings and the melted butter. 3. Place the vegetables in the Ninja Foodi Pressure Steam Fryer basket. 4. Add the sausage on top. 5. Put on the Smart Lid on top of the Ninja Foodi Steam Fryer. 6. Move the Lid Slider to the "Air Fry/Stovetop". Select the "Air Fry" mode for cooking. 7. Cook at 180°C for around 33 to 37 minutes, ensuring the sausages are no longer pink, giving the "cook & crisp basket" a good shake halfway through the cooking time. You may need to cook everything in batches.
Per Serving: Calories 584; Fat: 15g; Sodium: 441mg; Carbs: 17g; Fiber: 4.6g; Sugar 5g; Protein 29g

Ricotta Chicken Wraps

Prep Time: 10 minutes | Cook Time: 10 minutes | Serves: 12

2 large-sized chicken breasts, cooked and shredded
⅓ teaspoon sea salt
¼ teaspoon black pepper, or more to taste
2 spring onions, chopped
60ml soy sauce

1 tablespoon molasses
1 tablespoon rice vinegar
250g Ricotta cheese
1 teaspoon grated fresh ginger
50 wonton wrappers
Cooking spray

1. Place the Cook & Crisp Basket in your Pressure Cooker Steam Fryer. 2. In a suitable bowl, mix all of the ingredients, minus the wonton wrappers. 3. Unroll the wrappers and spritz with cooking spray. 4. Fill each of the wonton wrappers with equal amounts of the mixture. 5. Dampen the edges with a little water as an adhesive and roll up the wrappers, fully enclosing the filling. 6. Put on the Smart Lid on top of the Ninja Foodi Steam Fryer. 7. Move the Lid Slider to the "Air Fry/Stovetop". Select the "Air Fry" mode for cooking. 8. Cook the rolls in the Ninja Foodi Pressure Steam Fryer for around 5 minutes at 190°C. You will need to do this step in batches. 9. Serve with your preferred sauce.
Per Serving: Calories 334; Fat: 7.9g; Sodium: 704mg; Carbs: 6g; Fiber: 3.6g; Sugar 6g; Protein 18g

Turkey Pepper Meatballs

Prep Time: 10 minutes | Cook Time: 7 minutes | Serves: 6

455g turkey
1 tablespoon fresh mint leaves, finely chopped
1 teaspoon onion powder
1½ teaspoons garlic paste
1 teaspoon crushed red pepper flakes
55g melted butter
¾ teaspoon fine sea salt
25g grated Pecorino Romano

1. Place the Cook & Crisp Basket in your Pressure Cooker Steam Fryer. 2. In a suitable bowl, mix all of the recipe ingredients well. Using an ice cream scoop, mold the meat into balls. 3. Put on the Smart Lid on top of the Ninja Foodi Steam Fryer. 4. Move the Lid Slider to the "Air Fry/Stovetop". Select the "Air Fry" mode for cooking. 5. Air fry the meatballs at 195°C for about 7 minutes, in batches if necessary. Shake the "cook & crisp basket" frequently throughout the cooking time for even results. 6. Serve with basil leaves and tomato sauce if desired.
Per Serving: Calories 372; Fat: 20g; Sodium: 891mg; Carbs: 29g; Fiber: 3g; Sugar 8g; Protein 27g

Chicken Omelet

Prep Time: 10 minutes | Cook Time: 13 minutes | Serves: 2

4 eggs, whisked
100g chicken
80g spring onions, finely chopped
2 cloves garlic, finely minced
½ teaspoon salt
½ teaspoon black pepper
½ teaspoon paprika
1 teaspoon dried thyme
Dash of hot sauce

1. Place the Cook & Crisp Basket in your Pressure Cooker Steam Fryer. 2. Mix all the recipe ingredients in a bowl, ensuring to incorporate everything well. 3. Grease the Cook & Crisp Basket with vegetable oil. 4. Transfer the mixture to the Ninja Foodi Pressure Steam Fryer. Put on the Smart Lid on top of the Ninja Foodi Steam Fryer. Move the Lid Slider to the "Air Fry/Stovetop". Select the "Air Fry" mode for cooking. Air Fry at 175°C for 13 minutes. 5. Ensure they are cooked through and serve immediately.
Per Serving: Calories 489; Fat: 11g; Sodium: 501mg; Carbs: 8.9g; Fiber: 4.6g; Sugar 8g; Protein 26g

Cajun- Turkey Fingers

Prep Time: 10 minutes | Cook Time: 15 minutes | Serves: 4

80g polenta mix
60g flour
1½ tablespoon Cajun seasoning
1½ tablespoon whole-grain mustard
360ml buttermilk
1 teaspoon soy sauce
340g turkey tenderloins, cut into finger-sized strips
Salt and black pepper to taste

1. Place the Cook & Crisp Basket in your Pressure Cooker Steam Fryer. 2. In a suitable bowl, mix the polenta, flour, and Cajun seasoning. 3. In a separate bowl, mix the whole-grain mustard, buttermilk and soy sauce. 4. Sprinkle some black pepper and salt on the turkey fingers. 5. Dredge each finger in the buttermilk mixture, before coating them completely with the polenta mixture. 6. Place the prepared turkey fingers in the Ninja Foodi Pressure Steam Fryer basket. Put on the Smart Lid on top of the Ninja Foodi Steam Fryer. Move the Lid Slider to the "Air Fry/Stovetop". Select the "Air Fry" mode for cooking. Cook for around 15 minutes at 180°C. 7. Serve immediately, with ketchup if desired.
Per Serving: Calories 472; Fat: 10.9g; Sodium: 354mg; Carbs: 10.5g; Fiber: 4.1g; Sugar 8.2g; Protein 26g

Honey Turkey Breast

Prep Time: 10 minutes | Cook Time: 28 minutes | Serves: 6

2 teaspoon butter, softened
1 teaspoon dried sage
2 sprigs rosemary, chopped
1 teaspoon salt
¼ teaspoon black pepper, or more if desired
1 whole turkey breast
2 tablespoon turkey stock
85g honey
2 tablespoon whole-grain mustard
1 tablespoon butter

1. Place the Cook & Crisp Basket in your Pressure Cooker Steam Fryer. 2. Mix the 2 tablespoon of butter, sage, rosemary, salt, and pepper. 3. Rub the turkey breast with this mixture. 4. Place the turkey in your fryer's cooking "cook & crisp basket". Put on the Smart Lid on top of the Ninja Foodi Steam Fryer. Move the Lid Slider to the "Air Fry/Stovetop". Select the "Air Fry" mode for cooking. Adjust the cooking temperature to 180°C and cook for around 20 minutes. 5. Turn the turkey breast over and allow to cook for another 15 to 16 minutes. 6. Finally turn it once more and cook for another 12 minutes. 7. In the meantime, mix the remaining recipe ingredients in a saucepan using a whisk. 8. Coat the turkey breast with the glaze. 9. Cook for an additional 5 minutes. Remove it from the Pressure Cooker Steam Fryer, let it rest, and carve before serving.
Per Serving: Calories 521; Fat: 7.9g; Sodium: 704mg; Carbs: 6g; Fiber: 3.6g; Sugar 6g; Protein 18g

Chicken Turnip Curry

Prep Time: 10 minutes | Cook Time: 30 minutes | Serves: 2

2 chicken thighs
1 small courgette
2 cloves garlic
6 dried apricots
90g long turnip
6 basil leaves
1 tablespoon whole pistachios
1 tablespoon raisin soup
1 tablespoon olive oil
1 large pinch salt
Pinch of pepper
1 teaspoon curry powder

1. Place the Cook & Crisp Basket in your Pressure Cooker Steam Fryer. 2. Cut the chicken into 2 thin slices and chop up the vegetables into bite-sized pieces. 3. In a dish, mix all of the ingredients, incorporating everything well. 4. Place in the basket. Put on the Smart Lid on top of the Ninja Foodi Steam Fryer. Move the Lid Slider to the "Air Fry/Stovetop". Select the "Air Fry" mode for cooking. 5. Adjust the cooking temperature to 160°C. 6. Cook for a minimum of 30 minutes. 7. Serve with rice if desired.
Per Serving: Calories 219; Fat: 10g; Sodium: 891mg; Carbs: 22.9g; Fiber: 4g; Sugar 4g; Protein 13g

Buttered Marjoram Chicken

Prep Time: 10 minutes | Cook Time: 20 minutes | Serves: 2

2 skinless, boneless small chicken breasts
2 tablespoon butter
1 teaspoon sea salt
½ teaspoon red pepper flakes, crushed
2 teaspoon marjoram
¼ teaspoon lemon pepper

1. Place the Cook & Crisp Basket in your Pressure Cooker Steam Fryer. 2. In a suitable bowl, coat the chicken breasts with all of the other ingredients. Set aside to marinate for around 30 to 60 minutes. 3. Put on the Smart Lid on top of the Ninja Foodi Steam Fryer. 4. Move the Lid Slider to the "Air Fry/Stovetop". Select the "Air Fry" mode for cooking. 5. Adjust the cooking temperature to 200°C. 6. Cook for around 20 minutes, turning halfway through cooking time. 7. Check for doneness using an instant-read thermometer. Serve over jasmine rice.
Per Serving: Calories 585; Fat: 39.5g; Sodium 1687mg; Carbs: 10.4g; Fiber: 2.7g; Sugars 3.1g; Protein 43.2g

Stuffed Roulade

Prep Time: 10 minutes | Cook Time: 50 minutes | Serves: 4

1 turkey fillet
Salt and garlic pepper to taste
⅓ teaspoon onion powder
½ teaspoon dried basil
⅓ teaspoon red chipotle pepper
1½ tablespoon mustard seeds
½ teaspoon fennel seeds
2 tablespoon melted butter
3 tablespoon coriander, finely chopped
80g spring onions, finely chopped
2 cloves garlic, finely minced

1. Place the Cook & Crisp Basket in your Pressure Cooker Steam Fryer. 2. Flatten out the turkey fillets with a mallet, until they are about a 1 cm thick. 3. Season each one with salt, garlic pepper, and onion powder. 4. In a suitable bowl, mix the basil, chipotle pepper, mustard seeds, fennel seeds and butter. 5. Use a pallet knife to spread the mixture over the fillets, leaving the edges uncovered. 6. Add the coriander, spring onions and garlic on top. 7. Roll up the fillets into a log and wrap a piece of twine around them to hold them in place. 8. Place them in the Cook and crisp basket. 9. Put on the Smart Lid on top of the Ninja Foodi Steam Fryer. 10. Move the Lid Slider to the "Air Fry/Stovetop". Select the "Air Fry" mode for cooking. 11. Cook at 175°C for about 50 minutes, flipping it at the halfway point. Cook for longer if necessary. Serve warm.
Per Serving: Calories 372; Fat: 16.3g; Sodium 742mg; Carbs: 6.8g; Fiber: 0.8g; Sugars 1.8g; Protein 42.3g

Chicken Nuggets

Prep Time: 10 minutes | Cook Time: 10 minutes | Serves: 4

2 slices friendly breadcrumbs
225g chicken breast, chopped
1 teaspoon garlic, minced
1 teaspoon tomato ketchup
2 medium egg

1 tablespoon olive oil
1 teaspoon paprika
1 teaspoon parsley
Black pepper and salt to taste

1. Place the Cook & Crisp Basket in your Pressure Cooker Steam Fryer. 2. Mix the breadcrumbs, paprika, salt, pepper and oil into a thick batter. 3. Coat the chopped chicken with the parsley, one egg and ketchup. 4. Shape the mixture into several nuggets and dredge each one in the other egg. Roll the nuggets into the breadcrumbs. 5. Put on the Smart Lid on top of the Ninja Foodi Steam Fryer. 6. Move the Lid Slider to the "Air Fry/Stovetop". Select the "Air Fry" mode for cooking. 7. Air Fry at 200°C for 10 minutes in the Ninja Foodi Pressure Steam Fryer. 8. Serve the nuggets with a side of mayo dip if desired.
Per Serving: Calories 326; Fat: 12g; Sodium 779mg; Carbs: 8.3g; Fiber: 2.9g; Sugars 1.3g; Protein 46.9g

Turkey Meatloaf

Prep Time: 10 minutes | Cook Time: 50 minutes | Serves: 6

455g turkey mince
80g spring onions, finely chopped
2 garlic cloves, finely minced
1 teaspoon dried thyme
½ teaspoon dried basil
75g cheddar cheese, shredded
55g crushed crackers

1 tablespoon tamari sauce
Salt and black pepper, to taste
60g roasted red pepper tomato sauce
1 teaspoon sugar
¾ tablespoon olive oil
1 medium egg, well beaten

1. Place the Cook & Crisp Basket in your Pressure Cooker Steam Fryer. 2. Over a suitable heat, fry up the turkey mince, spring onions, garlic, thyme, and basil until soft and fragrant. 3. Mix the mixture with the cheese, crackers and tamari sauce, before shaping it into a loaf. 4. Stir the remaining items and top the meatloaf with them. 5. Place in the Ninja Foodi Pressure Steam Fryer basket. 6. Put on the Smart Lid on top of the Ninja Foodi Steam Fryer. 7. Move the Lid Slider to the "Air Fry/Stovetop". Select the "Air Fry" mode for cooking. 8. Adjust the cooking temperature to 180°C. 9. Allow to cook for around 45 to 47 minutes.
Per Serving: Calories 618; Fat: 13.5g; Sodium 96mg; Carbs: 98.7g; Fiber: 5.3g; Sugars 0.5g; Protein 24.4g

Crusted Chicken Drumsticks

Prep Time: 10 minutes | Cook Time: 35 minutes | Serves: 4

8 chicken drumsticks
1 teaspoon cayenne pepper
2 tablespoon mustard powder
2 tablespoon oregano
2 tablespoon thyme

3 tablespoon coconut milk
1 large egg, beaten
35g cauliflower
25g oats
Pepper and salt to taste

1. Place the Cook & Crisp Basket in your Pressure Cooker Steam Fryer. 2. Sprinkle black pepper and salt over the chicken drumsticks and massage the coconut milk into them. 3. Put all the recipe ingredients except the egg into the food processor and pulse to create a bread crumb-like mixture. 4. Transfer to a suitable bowl. 5. In a separate bowl, put the beaten egg. Coat each chicken drumstick in the bread crumb mixture before dredging it in the egg. Roll it in the bread crumbs once more. 6. Put the coated chicken drumsticks in "cook & crisp basket". Put on the Smart Lid on top of the Ninja Foodi Steam Fryer. Move the Lid Slider to the "Air Fry/Stovetop". Select the "Air Fry" mode for cooking. 7. Adjust the cooking temperature to 175°C. 8. Cook for around 20 minutes. Serve hot.
Per Serving: Calories 412; Fat: 23.6g; Sodium 1495mg; Carbs: 4.8g; Fiber: 1.3g; Sugars 1.7g; Protein 37.9g

Bacon Chicken

Prep Time: 10 minutes | Cook Time: 20 minutes | Serves: 6

1 chicken breast, cut into 6 pieces
6 rashers back bacon

1 tablespoon soft cheese

1. Place the Cook & Crisp Basket in your Pressure Cooker Steam Fryer. 2. Put the bacon rashers on a flat surface and cover one side with the soft cheese. 3. Lay the chicken pieces on each bacon rasher. Wrap the bacon around the chicken and use a toothpick stick to hold each one in place. Put them in "cook & crisp basket". 4. Put on the Smart Lid on top of the Ninja Foodi Steam Fryer. 5. Move the Lid Slider to the "Air Fry/Stovetop". Select the "Air Fry" mode for cooking. 6. Air fry at 175°C for 15 minutes.
Per Serving: Calories 413; Fat: 24.5g; Sodium 962mg; Carbs: 6.9g; Fiber: 1.1g; Sugars 2.9g; Protein 39.1g

Holiday Chicken Wings

Prep Time: 10 minutes | Cook Time: 20 minutes | Serves: 6

6 chicken wings
1 tablespoon honey
2 cloves garlic, chopped
1 teaspoon red chili flakes

2 tablespoon Worcestershire sauce
Pepper and salt to taste
Cooking spray

1. Place the Cook & Crisp Basket in your Pressure Cooker Steam Fryer. 2. Place all the recipe ingredients, except for the chicken wings, in a suitable bowl and mix well. 3. Coat the chicken with the mixture and refrigerate for around 1 hour. 4. Put the marinated chicken wings in the Ninja Foodi Pressure Steam Fryer basket and spritz with cooking spray. 5. Put on the Smart Lid on top of the Ninja Foodi Steam Fryer. 6. Move the Lid Slider to the "Air Fry/Stovetop". Select the "Air Fry" mode for cooking. 7. Air fry the chicken wings at 160°C for around 8 minutes. Raise the temperature to 175°C. Cook for an additional 4 minutes. Serve hot.
Per Serving: Calories 612; Fat: 38.2g; Sodium 76mg; Carbs: 39.1g; Fiber: 5.8g; Sugars 1.6g; Protein 30.6g

Chicken Parsley Nuggets

Prep Time: 10 minutes | Cook Time: 10 minutes | Serves: 4

225g chicken breast, cut into pieces
1 teaspoon parsley
1 teaspoon paprika
1 tablespoon olive oil

2 eggs, beaten
1 teaspoon tomato ketchup
1 teaspoon garlic, minced
50g bread crumbs
Pepper and salt to taste

1. Place the Cook & Crisp Basket in your Pressure Cooker Steam Fryer. 2. In a bowl, mix the bread crumbs, olive oil, paprika, pepper, and salt. 3. Place the chicken, ketchup, one egg, garlic, and parsley in a food processor and pulse together. 4. Put the other egg in a suitable bowl. 5. Shape equal amounts of the pureed chicken into nuggets. Dredge each one in the egg before coating it in bread crumbs. 6. Put the coated chicken nuggets in the Ninja Foodi Pressure Steam Fryer basket. Put on the Smart Lid on top of the Ninja Foodi Steam Fryer. Move the Lid Slider to the "Air Fry/Stovetop". Select the "Air Fry" mode for cooking. Air Fry at 200°C for 10 minutes. 7. Serve the nuggets hot.
Per Serving: Calories 227; Fat: 8.8g; Sodium 302mg; Carbs: 8.9g; Fiber: 2.1g; Sugars 3.3g; Protein 28.5g

Crusted Chicken Tenders

Prep Time: 10 minutes | Cook Time: 15 minutes | Serves: 4

900g skinless and boneless chicken tenders
3 large eggs
6 tablespoon skimmed milk
60g flour

100g bread crumbs
¼ teaspoon black pepper
1 teaspoon salt
2 tablespoons olive oil

1. Place the Cook & Crisp Basket in your Pressure Cooker Steam Fryer. 2. In a suitable bowl, mix the bread crumbs and olive oil. 3. In a separate bowl, stir the eggs and milk using a whisk. Sprinkle in the salt and black pepper. 4. Put the flour in a third bowl. 5. Slice up the chicken tenders into 2.5 cm strips. Coat each piece of chicken in the flour, before dipping it into the egg mixture, followed by the bread crumbs. 6. Put on the Smart Lid on top of the Ninja Foodi Steam Fryer. 7. Move the Lid Slider to the "Air Fry/Stovetop". Select the "Air Fry" mode for cooking. 8. Adjust the cooking temperature to 195°C. 9. Cook the coated chicken tenders for about 13 to 15 minutes, shaking the basket a few times to ensure they turn crispy. Serve hot, with mashed potatoes and a dipping sauce if desired.
Per Serving: Calories 232; Fat: 8.4g; Sodium 300mg; Carbs: 8.6g; Fiber: 0.9g; Sugars 0.1g; Protein 30.1g

Roasted Chicken

Prep Time: 10 minutes | Cook Time: 55 minutes | Serves: 4

2.2-3kg whole chicken with skin
1 teaspoon garlic powder
1 teaspoon onion powder
½ teaspoon dried thyme
½ teaspoon dried basil
½ teaspoon dried rosemary
½ teaspoon black pepper
2 teaspoon salt
2 tablespoons olive oil

1. Place the Cook & Crisp Basket in your Pressure Cooker Steam Fryer. 2. Massage the salt, pepper, herbs, and olive oil into the chicken. Allow to marinade for a minimum of 20 to 30 minutes. 3. Place the chicken in the basket. Put on the Smart Lid on top of the Ninja Foodi Steam Fryer. Move the Lid Slider to the "Air Fry/Stovetop". Select the "Air Fry" mode for cooking. Cook at 170°C for around 18 to 20 minutes. 4. Flip the chicken over. 5. Cook for an additional 20 minutes. 6. Leave the chicken to rest for about 10 minutes before carving and serving.
Per Serving: Calories 314; Fat: 8.7g; Sodium 337mg; Carbs: 21.2g; Fiber: 4.1g; Sugars 16g; Protein 37.9g

Herbed Chicken Wings

Prep Time: 10 minutes | Cook Time: 15 minutes | Serves: 6

1.8kg chicken wings
6 tablespoons red wine vinegar
6 tablespoon lime juice
1 teaspoon fresh ginger, minced
1 tablespoon sugar
1 teaspoon thyme, chopped
½ teaspoon white pepper
¼ teaspoon cinnamon
1 habanero pepper, chopped
6 garlic cloves, chopped
2 tablespoon soy sauce
2 ½ tablespoon olive oil
¼ teaspoon salt

1. Place the Cook & Crisp Basket in your Pressure Cooker Steam Fryer. 2. Place all of the recipe ingredients in a suitable bowl and mix well, ensuring to coat the chicken entirely. 3. Put the chicken in the refrigerator to marinate for around 1 hour. 4. Put half of the marinated chicken in the "cook & crisp basket". Put on the Smart Lid on top of the Ninja Foodi Steam Fryer. Move the Lid Slider to the "Air Fry/Stovetop". Select the "Air Fry" mode for cooking. 5. Adjust the cooking temperature to 200°C. 6. Cook for around 15 minutes, shaking the basket once throughout the cooking process. 7. Repeat with the other half of the chicken. 8. Serve hot.
Per Serving: Calories 347; Fat: 18.8g; Sodium 137mg; Carbs: 13.4g; Fiber: 8.5g; Sugars 1g; Protein 36.3g

Rosemary Spiced Chicken

Prep Time: 10 minutes | Cook Time: 20 minutes | Serves: 2

340g chicken
½ tablespoon olive oil
1 tablespoon soy sauce
1 teaspoon fresh ginger, minced
1 tablespoon oyster sauce
3 tablespoon sugar
1 tablespoon fresh rosemary, chopped
½ fresh lemon, cut into wedges

1. Place the Cook & Crisp Basket in your Pressure Cooker Steam Fryer. 2. In a suitable bowl, mix the chicken, oil, soy sauce, and ginger, coating the chicken well. 3. Refrigerate for around 30 minutes. 4. Place the chicken in the Cook & Crisp Basket, transfer to the Pressure Cooker Steam Fryer. Put on the Smart Lid on top of the Ninja Foodi Steam Fryer. Move the Lid Slider to the "Air Fry/Stovetop". Select the "Air Fry" mode for cooking. 5. Adjust the cooking temperature to 200°C. 6. Cook for around 6 minutes. 7. In the meantime, put the rosemary, sugar, and oyster sauce in a suitable bowl and mix together. 8. Add the rosemary mixture in the Pressure Cooker Steam Fryer over the chicken and top the chicken with the lemon wedges. 9. Resume cooking for another 13 minutes, turning the chicken halfway through.
Per Serving: Calories 344; Fat: 10g; Sodium 251mg; Carbs: 4.7g; Fiber: 0.5g; Sugars 2.2g; Protein 55.7g

Chapter 4 Meat Mains Recipes

Beef Brisket with BBQ Sauce

Prep Time: 10 minutes | Cook Time: 1 hour 10 minutes | Serves: 4

675g beef brisket
60g barbecue sauce
2 tablespoons soy sauce

1. Place the Cook & Crisp Basket in your Pressure Cooker Steam Fryer. 2. Toss the beef with the remaining ingredients; place the beef in the Cook & Crisp Basket. 3. Put on the Smart Lid on top of the Ninja Foodi Steam Fryer. 4. Move the Lid Slider to the "Air Fry/Stovetop". Select the "Air Fry" mode for cooking. 5. Cook the beef at 200°C for around 15 minutes, turn the beef over and turn the temperature to 180°C. 6. Continue to cook the beef for around 55 minutes more. Serve.
Per Serving: Calories 319; Fat: 15.6g; Sodium 99mg; Carbs: 4.8g; Fiber: 0.7g; Sugars 2.9g; Protein 38.5g

Beef with Carrots

Prep Time: 10 minutes | Cook Time: 55 minutes | Serves: 5

900g top sirloin roast
2 tablespoons olive oil
Sea salt and black pepper, to taste
2 carrots, sliced
1 tablespoon fresh coriander
1 tablespoon fresh thyme
1 tablespoon fresh rosemary

1. Place the Cook & Crisp Basket in your Pressure Cooker Steam Fryer. 2. Toss the beef with the olive oil, salt, and black pepper; place the beef in the Cook & Crisp Basket Put on the Smart Lid on top of the Ninja Foodi Steam Fryer. 3. Move the Lid Slider to the "Air Fry/Stovetop". Select the "Air Fry" mode for cooking. 4. Cook the beef eye round cook at 200°C for around 45 minutes, turning it over halfway through the cooking time. 5. Top the beef with the carrots and herbs. Continue to cook an additional 10 minutes. 6. Enjoy!
Per Serving: Calories 349; Fat: 15.1g; Sodium 157mg; Carbs: 25.6g; Fiber: 2.6g; Sugars 22.5g; Protein 29.7g

BBQ Cheeseburgers

Prep Time: 10 minutes | Cook Time: 15 minutes | Serves: 3

340g chuck
1 teaspoon garlic, minced
2 tablespoons BBQ sauce
Sea salt and black pepper, to taste
3 slices cheese
3 hamburger buns

1. Place the Cook & Crisp Basket in your Pressure Cooker Steam Fryer. 2. Mix the chuck, garlic, BBQ sauce, salt, and black pepper until everything is well mixed. Form the mixture into four patties. 3. Put on the Smart Lid on top of the Ninja Foodi Steam Fryer. 4. Move the Lid Slider to the "Air Fry/Stovetop". Select the "Air Fry" mode for cooking. 5. Cook the burgers at 195°C for about 15 minutes or until cooked through; make sure to turn them over halfway through the cooking time. 6. Top each burger with cheese. Serve your burgers on the prepared buns and enjoy!
Per Serving: Calories 182; Fat: 14.1g; Sodium 18mg; Carbs: 8.9g; Fiber: 4.1g; Sugars 4g; Protein 7.2g

Sweet Tangy Ham

Prep time: 5 minutes | Cook time: 20 minutes | Serves: 6

240ml orange juice
120ml water
2 tablespoons butter
1 (1.2–1.5kg) spiral-cut ham
105g packed light brown sugar
1 teaspoon ground cinnamon
1 teaspoon ground cloves
1 teaspoon ground nutmeg
1 tablespoon corn flour

1. In the cooking pot, combine the orange juice, water, and butter. 2. Rub the ham all over with the brown sugar, cinnamon, cloves, and nutmeg. 3. Place the Deluxe reversible rack in the Ninja Foodi XL Pressure Cooker Steam Fryer cooking pot and set the ham on the Deluxe reversible rack. 4. Lock lid; move slider to PRESSURE. Make sure the pressure release valve is in the SEAL position. The cooking temperature will default to HIGH, which is accurate. Set time to 15 minutes. Press START/STOP to cooking. When cooking is complete, let pressure release naturally. 5. Remove the lid and carefully lift out the ham and Deluxe reversible rack. Move the slider towards "AIR FRY/STOVETOP" and set Ninja Foodi XL Pressure Cooker Steam Fryer with SmartLid to SEAR/SAUTÉ mode. Adjust the temperature to "Hi5" by using up arrow. Press START/STOP to begin cooking. Whisk the corn flour into the pot and whisk for about 5 minutes to thicken the sauce. 6. Serve the ham drizzled with the sauce.

Per Serving: Calories 218; Fat 2.4g; Sodium 641mg; Carbs 14g; Fiber 6g; Sugar 2g; Protein 19g

Garlic London Broil

Prep Time: 10 minutes | Cook Time: 28 minutes | Serves: 4

675g London broil
Salt and black pepper, to taste
¼ teaspoon bay leaf
3 tablespoons butter, cold
1 tablespoon Dijon mustard
1 teaspoon garlic, pressed
1 tablespoon fresh parsley, chopped

1. Place the Cook & Crisp Basket in your Pressure Cooker Steam Fryer. 2. Toss the beef with the salt and black pepper; brush the basket with oil and place the beef in it. 3. Put on the Smart Lid on top of the Ninja Foodi Steam Fryer. 4. Move the Lid Slider to the "Air Fry/Stovetop". Select the "Air Fry" mode for cooking. 5. Cook the beef at 200°C for around 28 minutes, turning over halfway through the cooking time. 6. In the meantime, mix the butter with the remaining recipe ingredients and place it in the refrigerator until well-chilled. 7. Serve warm beef with the chilled garlic butter on the side. Serve.
Per Serving: Calories: 394; Fat:17.5g; Carbs: 26.5g; Fiber: 1.3g; Sugars: 6.4g; Proteins: 32.5g

Mexican Carnitas

Prep Time: 10 minutes | Cook Time: 1 hour 10 minutes | Serves: 4

675g beef brisket
2 tablespoons olive oil
Sea salt and black pepper, to taste
1 teaspoon chili powder
4 medium-sized flour tortillas

1. Place the Cook & Crisp Basket in your Pressure Cooker Steam Fryer. 2. Toss the beef brisket with the olive oil, salt, black pepper, and chili powder; now, place the beef brisket in the Cook & Crisp Basket. 3. Put on the Smart Lid on top of the Ninja Foodi Steam Fryer. 4. Move the Lid Slider to the "Air Fry/Stovetop". Select the "Air Fry" mode for cooking. 5. Cook the beef brisket at 200°C for around 15 minutes, turn the beef over and reduce the temperature to 180°C. 6. Continue to cook the beef brisket for approximately 55 minutes or until cooked through. 7. Shred the beef with two forks and serve with tortillas and toppings of choice. Serve.
Per Serving: Calories: 542; Fat:34.2g; Carbs: 25.6g; Fiber: 1.6g; Sugars: 2.1g Proteins: 29.1g

Flank Steak

Prep Time: 10 minutes | Cook Time: 12 minutes | Serves: 5

900g flank steak
2 tablespoons olive oil
1 teaspoon paprika
Sea salt and black pepper, to taste

1. Place the Cook & Crisp Basket in your Pressure Cooker Steam Fryer. 2. Toss the steak with the remaining ingredients; place the steak in the Cook & Crisp Basket. 3. Put on the Smart Lid on top of the Ninja Foodi Steam Fryer. 4. Move the Lid Slider to the "Air Fry/Stovetop". Select the "Air Fry" mode for cooking. 5. Cook the steak at 200°C for around 12 minutes, turning over halfway through the cooking time. 6. Serve.
Per Serving: Calories: 299; Fat:14.5g; Carbs: 0.3g; Fiber: 0.2g; Sugars: 0g; Proteins: 38.5g

Mexican Meatloaf

Prep Time: 10 minutes | Cook Time: 25 minutes | Serves: 4

675g chuck
½ onion, chopped
1 teaspoon habanero pepper, minced
10g tortilla chips, crushed
1 teaspoon garlic, minced
Sea salt and black pepper, to taste
2 tablespoons olive oil
1 egg, whisked

1. Place the Cook & Crisp Basket in your Pressure Cooker Steam Fryer. 2. Mix all the recipe ingredients until everything is well mixed. 3. Brush the Cook & Crisp Basket with oil and scrape the beef mixture into the Cook & Crisp Basket. 4. Put on the Smart Lid on top of the Ninja Foodi Steam Fryer. 5. Move the Lid Slider to the "Air Fry/Stovetop". Select the "Air Fry" mode for cooking. 6. Cook your meatloaf at 200°C for around 25 minutes. Serve.
Per Serving: Calories: 368; Fat:22.4g; Carbs: 5.4g; Fiber: 0.7g; Sugars: 2g; Proteins: 36.5g

Herbed Filet Mignon

Prep Time: 10 minutes | Cook Time: 14 minutes | Serves: 4

675g filet mignon	1 teaspoon dried thyme
Sea salt and black pepper, to taste	1 teaspoon dried basil
2 tablespoons olive oil	2 cloves garlic, minced
1 teaspoon dried rosemary	

1. Place the Cook & Crisp Basket in your Pressure Cooker Steam Fryer. 2. Toss the beef with the remaining ingredients; place the beef in the Cook & Crisp Basket. 3. Put on the Smart Lid on top of the Ninja Foodi Steam Fryer. 4. Move the Lid Slider to the "Air Fry/ Stovetop". Select the "Air Fry" mode for cooking. 5. Cook the beef at 200°C for around 14 minutes, turning it over halfway through the cooking time. 6. Enjoy!
Per Serving: Calories: 385; Fat:26g; Carbs: 2.2g; Fiber: 0.3g; Sugars: 0.5g; Proteins: 36.2g

Beef Meatloaf Cups

Prep Time: 10 minutes | Cook Time: 25 minutes | Serves: 4

Meatloaves:

455g beef	2 garlic cloves, pressed
25g seasoned breadcrumbs	1 egg, beaten
25g parmesan cheese, grated	Sea salt and black pepper, to taste
1 small onion, minced	

Glaze:

4 tablespoons tomato sauce	1 tablespoon Dijon mustard
1 tablespoon brown sugar	

1. Place the Cook & Crisp Basket in your Pressure Cooker Steam Fryer. 2. Mix all the recipe ingredients for the meatloaves until everything is well mixed. 3. Scrape the beef mixture into oiled silicone cups and transfer them to the Cook & Crisp Basket. 4. Put on the Smart Lid on top of the Ninja Foodi Steam Fryer. 5. Move the Lid Slider to the "Air Fry/Stovetop". Select the "Air Fry" mode for cooking. 6. Cook the beef cups at 195°C for around 20 minutes. 7. In the meantime, mix the remaining recipe ingredients for the glaze. Then, spread the glaze on top of each muffin; continue to cook for another 5 minutes. 8. Serve.
Per Serving: Calories: 355; Fat:18.6g; Carbs: 14.2g; Fiber: 2.3g; Sugars: 6.2g; Proteins: 27.5g

Cheese Ribeye Steak

Prep Time: 10 minutes | Cook Time: 15 minutes | Serves: 4

455g ribeye steak, bone-in	½ teaspoon onion powder
Sea salt and black pepper, to taste	1 teaspoon garlic powder
2 tablespoons olive oil	245g blue cheese, crumbled

1. Place the Cook & Crisp Basket in your Pressure Cooker Steam Fryer. 2. Toss the ribeye steak with the salt, black pepper, olive oil, onion powder, and garlic powder; place the ribeye steak in the Cook & Crisp Basket. 3. Put on the Smart Lid on top of the Ninja Foodi Steam Fryer. 4. Move the Lid Slider to the "Air Fry/Stovetop". Select the "Air Fry" mode for cooking. 5. Cook the ribeye steak at 200°C for around 15 minutes, turning it over halfway through the cooking time. 6. Top the ribeye steak with the cheese and serve warm. Serve.
Per Serving: Calories: 399; Fat:29.4g; Carbs: 4.6g; Fiber: 0.3g; Sugars: 0.7g; Proteins: 29.2g

Rump Roast

Prep Time: 10 minutes | Cook Time: 50 minutes | Serves: 4

675g rump roast	2 tablespoons olive oil
Black pepper and salt, to taste	60ml brandy
1 teaspoon paprika	2 tablespoons cold butter

1. Place the Cook & Crisp Basket in your Pressure Cooker Steam Fryer. 2. Brush the basket with oil. 3. Toss the rump roast with the black pepper, salt, paprika, olive oil, and brandy; place the rump roast in Cook & Crisp Basket. 4. Put on the Smart Lid on top of the Ninja Foodi Steam Fryer. 5. Move the Lid Slider to the "Air Fry/Stovetop". Select the "Air Fry" mode for cooking. 6. Cook the rump roast at 200°C for around 50 minutes, turning it over halfway through the cooking time. 7. Serve with the cold butter and enjoy!
Per Serving: Calories: 390; Fat:22.4g; Carbs: 1.4g; Fiber: 0.4g; Sugars: 0.6g; Proteins: 35.2g;

Coulotte Roast

Prep Time: 10 minutes | Cook Time: 55 minutes | Serves: 5

900g Coulotte roast	1 tablespoon fresh coriander,
2 tablespoons olive oil	finely chopped
1 tablespoon fresh parsley, finely	2 garlic cloves, minced
chopped	Salt and black pepper, to taste

1. Place the Cook & Crisp Basket in your Pressure Cooker Steam Fryer. 2. Toss the roast beef with the remaining ingredients; place the roast beef in the Cook & Crisp Basket Put on the Smart Lid on top of the Ninja Foodi Steam Fryer. 3. Move the Lid Slider to the "Air Fry/ Stovetop". Select the "Air Fry" mode for cooking. 4. Cook the roast beef at 200°C for around 55 minutes, turning over halfway through the cooking time. 5. Enjoy!
Per Serving: Calories: 306; Fat:16.7g; Carbs: 1.3g; Fiber: 0.2g; Sugars: 0.4g; Proteins: 37.7g

Soy Dipped Beef Tenderloin

Prep Time: 10 minutes | Cook Time: 20 minutes | Serves: 4

675g beef tenderloin, sliced	1 teaspoon fresh ginger, peeled
2 tablespoons sesame oil	and grated
1 teaspoon Five-spice powder	2 tablespoons soy sauce
2 garlic cloves, minced	

1. Place the Cook & Crisp Basket in your Pressure Cooker Steam Fryer. 2. Toss the beef tenderloin with the remaining ingredients; place the beef tenderloin in the Cook & Crisp Basket Put on the Smart Lid on top of the Ninja Foodi Steam Fryer. 3. Move the Lid Slider to the "Air Fry/Stovetop". Select the "Air Fry" mode for cooking. 4. Cook the beef tenderloin at 200°C for around 20 minutes, turning it over halfway through the cooking time. 5. Enjoy!
Per Serving: Calories: 326; Fat:18.7g; Carbs: 3g; Fiber: 0.3g; Sugars: 1.6g; Proteins: 35.7g

Peppery Beef

Prep Time: 10 minutes | Cook Time: 14 minutes | Serves: 4

675g Tomahawk steaks	2 teaspoons steak seasoning
2 peppers, sliced	2 tablespoons fish sauce
2 tablespoons butter, melted	Sea salt and black pepper, to taste

1. Place the Cook & Crisp Basket in your Pressure Cooker Steam Fryer. 2. Toss all the recipe ingredients in the Cook & Crisp Basket. 3. Put on the Smart Lid on top of the Ninja Foodi Steam Fryer. 4. Move the Lid Slider to the "Air Fry/Stovetop". Select the "Air Fry" mode for cooking. 5. Cook the steak and peppers at 200°C for about 14 minutes, turning it over halfway through the cooking time. 6. Serve.
Per Serving: Calories: 299; Fat:15.6g; Carbs: 4.3g; Fiber: 0.7g; Sugars: 2.2g; Proteins: 33.1g

Sausage with Peppers

Prep time: 10 minutes | Cook time: 20 minutes | Serves: 4

1 (700g) can crushed tomatoes	1 onion, sliced
120ml water	2 garlic cloves, minced
5 links sweet Italian sausage,	1 tablespoon Italian seasoning
halved	4 peppers, any color, cut into strips

1. In the cooking pot, combine the crushed tomatoes, water, sausages, onion, garlic, and Italian seasoning. 2. Place the peppers in a vegetable Cook & Crisp Basket and add it to the pot on top of the sausage mixture. 3. Lock lid; move slider to PRESSURE. Make sure the pressure release valve is in the SEAL position. The cooking temperature will default to HIGH, which is accurate. Set time to 15 minutes. Press START/STOP to cooking. When cooking is complete, let pressure release quickly by turning it into VENT position. 4. Remove the Cook & Crisp Basket of peppers from the pot. 5. Move the slider towards "AIR FRY/STOVETOP" and set Ninja Foodi XL Pressure Cooker Steam Fryer with SmartLid to SEAR/SAUTÉ mode. Adjust the temperature to "Hi5" by using up arrow. Press START/STOP to begin cooking. Cook for about 5 minutes to thicken the sauce. 6. Return the peppers to the pot, stir them into the sauce, and serve.
Per Serving: Calories 605; Fat 31g; Sodium 833mg; Carbs 51g; Fiber 6g; Sugar 5g; Protein 74g

Mushroom Beef Patties

Prep Time: 10 minutes | Cook Time: 15 minutes | Serves: 4

455g chuck
2 garlic cloves, minced
1 small onion, chopped
100g mushrooms, chopped

1 teaspoon cayenne pepper
Sea salt and black pepper, to taste
4 brioche rolls

1. Place the Cook & Crisp Basket in your Pressure Cooker Steam Fryer. 2. Mix the chuck, garlic, onion, mushrooms, cayenne pepper, salt, and black pepper until everything is well mixed. Form the mixture into four patties. 3. Put on the Smart Lid on top of the Ninja Foodi Steam Fryer. 4. Move the Lid Slider to the "Air Fry/Stovetop". Select the "Air Fry" mode for cooking. 5. Cook the patties at 195°C for about 15 minutes or until cooked through; make sure to turn them over halfway through the cooking time. 6. Serve your patties on the prepared brioche rolls and enjoy!
Per Serving: Calories: 305; Fat:10.4g; Carbs: 25.3g; Fiber: 1.7g; Sugars: 4.5g; Proteins: 27.7g

Steak Salad

Prep Time: 10 minutes | Cook Time: 12 minutes | Serves: 5

900g T-bone steak
1 teaspoon garlic powder
Sea salt and black pepper, to taste
2 tablespoons lime juice

60ml extra-virgin olive oil
1 pepper, seeded and sliced
1 red onion, sliced
1 tomato, diced

1. Place the Cook & Crisp Basket in your Pressure Cooker Steam Fryer. 2. Toss the steak with the garlic powder, salt, and black pepper; place the steak in the Cook & Crisp Basket. Put on the Smart Lid on top of the Ninja Foodi Steam Fryer. 3. Move the Lid Slider to the "Air Fry/Stovetop". Select the "Air Fry" mode for cooking. 4. Cook the steak at 200°C for around 12 minutes, turning it over halfway through the cooking time. 5. Cut the steak into slices and add in the remaining ingredients. Serve at room temperature or well-chilled. 6. Serve.
Per Serving: Calories: 316; Fat:16g; Carbs: 3.7g; Fiber: 0.7g; Sugars: 1.7g; Proteins: 38.2g

Beef Dinner Rolls

Prep Time: 10 minutes | Cook Time: 15 minutes | Serves: 4

455g beef
½ teaspoon garlic powder
½ teaspoon onion powder

1 teaspoon paprika
Sea salt and black pepper, to taste
8 dinner rolls

1. Place the Cook & Crisp Basket in your Pressure Cooker Steam Fryer. 2. Mix all the recipe ingredients, except for the dinner rolls. Shape the mixture into four patties. 3. Put on the Smart Lid on top of the Ninja Foodi Steam Fryer. 4. Move the Lid Slider to the "Air Fry/Stovetop". Select the "Air Fry" mode for cooking. 5. Cook the burgers at 195°C for about 15 minutes or until cooked through; make sure to turn them over halfway through the cooking time. 6. Serve your burgers on the prepared dinner rolls and enjoy!
Per Serving: Calories: 406; Fat:16.2g; Carbs: 27g; Fiber: 2.6g; Sugars: 1.5g; Proteins: 35.2g

Smoky Ribs

Prep time: 10 minutes | Cook time: 30 minutes | Serves: 6

2 tablespoons light brown sugar
2 tablespoons smoked paprika
1 teaspoon cayenne pepper
1 (1.3kg) rack pork back ribs, shiny membrane removed
240ml water

240g Sweet and Smoky Barbecue Sauce or store-bought
1 onion, chopped
3 garlic cloves, minced
1 tablespoon Worcestershire sauce

1. In a small bowl, mix together the brown sugar, smoked paprika, and cayenne and rub the spice mixture all over the ribs. 2. In the cooking pot, combine the water, barbecue sauce, onion, garlic, and Worcestershire sauce. Fold the ribs into the pot. You can also cut them up if you like. 3. Lock lid; move slider to PRESSURE. Make sure the pressure release valve is in the SEAL position. The cooking temperature will default to HIGH, which is accurate. Set time to 25 minutes. Press START/STOP to cooking. When pressure cooking is complete, let the pressure release naturally. 4. Remove the lid and transfer the ribs to a serving platter. 5. Move the slider towards "AIR FRY/STOVETOP" and set Ninja Foodi XL Pressure Cooker Steam Fryer with SmartLid

to SEAR/SAUTÉ mode. Adjust the temperature to "Hi5" by using up arrow. Press START/STOP to begin cooking. 6. Cook the sauce for 5 minutes to thicken. Brush the sauce on the ribs and serve.
Per Serving: Calories 300; Fat 24g; Sodium 117mg; Carbs 3g; Fiber 3g; Sugar 2g; Protein 18g

Mustard Tender Filet Mignon

Prep Time: 10 minutes | Cook Time: 14 minutes | Serves: 4

675g filet mignon
2 tablespoons soy sauce
2 tablespoons butter, melted

1 teaspoon mustard powder
1 teaspoon garlic powder
Sea salt and black pepper, to taste

1. Place the Cook & Crisp Basket in your Pressure Cooker Steam Fryer. 2. Toss the filet mignon with the remaining ingredients; place the filet mignon in the Cook & Crisp Basket. 3. Put on the Smart Lid on top of the Ninja Foodi Steam Fryer. 4. Move the Lid Slider to the "Air Fry/Stovetop". Select the "Air Fry" mode for cooking. 5. Cook the filet mignon at 200°C for around 14 minutes, turning it over halfway through the cooking time. 6. Enjoy!
Per Serving: Calories: 393; Fat:26.2g; Carbs: 2.7g; Fiber: 0.2g; Sugars: 1.5g; Proteins: 36.2g

Beef Shoulder

Prep Time: 10 minutes | Cook Time: 55 minutes | Serves: 4

675g beef shoulder
Sea salt and black pepper, to taste
1 teaspoon cayenne pepper
½ teaspoon cumin

2 tablespoons olive oil
2 cloves garlic, minced
1 teaspoon Dijon mustard
1 onion, cut into slices

1. Place the Cook & Crisp Basket in your Pressure Cooker Steam Fryer. 2. Toss the beef with the spices, garlic, mustard, and olive oil; brush the Cook & Crisp Basket with oil and place the beef in it. 3. Put on the Smart Lid on top of the Ninja Foodi Steam Fryer. 4. Move the Lid Slider to the "Air Fry/Stovetop". Select the "Air Fry" mode for cooking. 5. Cook the beef at 200°C for around 45 minutes, turning it over halfway through the cooking time. 6. Add in the onion and continue to cook an additional 10 minutes. 7. Serve.
Per Serving: Calories: 309; Fat:16.2g; Carbs: 2.2g; Fiber: 0.4g; Sugars: 0.7g; Proteins: 36.2g

BBQ Ribs

Prep Time: 10 minutes | Cook Time: 35 minutes | Serves: 4

675g baby back ribs
2 tablespoons olive oil
1 teaspoon smoked paprika
1 teaspoon garlic powder
1 teaspoon onion powder

½ teaspoon cumin
1 teaspoon mustard powder
1 teaspoon dried thyme
Coarse sea salt and freshly cracked black pepper, to season

1. Toss all the recipe ingredients in a greased Cook & Crisp Basket. 2. Place the Cook & Crisp Basket in your Pressure Cooker Steam Fryer. 3. Put on the Smart Lid on top of the Ninja Foodi Steam Fryer. 4. Move the Lid Slider to the "Air Fry/Stovetop". Select the "Air Fry" mode for cooking. 5. Cook the pork ribs at 175°C for around 35 minutes, turning them over halfway through the cooking time. 6. Serve.
Per Serving: Calories: 440; Fat:33.3g; Carbs: 1.8g; Fiber: 0.4g; Sugars: 0.1g; Proteins: 33.7g

Pork Skewers

Prep Time: 10 minutes | Cook Time: 15 minutes | Serves: 4

455g pork tenderloin, cubed
455g peppers, diced
455g aubergine, diced
1 tablespoon olive oil

1 tablespoon parsley, chopped
1 tablespoon coriander, chopped
Sea salt and black pepper, to taste

1. Place the Cook & Crisp Basket in your Pressure Cooker Steam Fryer. 2. Toss all the recipe ingredients in a suitable mixing bowl until well coated on all sides. 3. Thread the ingredients onto skewers and place them in the Cook & Crisp Basket. 4. Put on the Smart Lid on top of the Ninja Foodi Steam Fryer. 5. Move the Lid Slider to the "Air Fry/Stovetop". Select the "Air Fry" mode for cooking. 6. Then, cook the skewers at 200°C for approximately 15 minutes, turning them over halfway through the cooking time. 7. Serve.
Per Serving: Calories: 344; Fat:16.3g; Carbs: 18g; Fiber: 5.3g; Sugars: 10.1g; Proteins: 32.6g

Italian Pork Cut

Prep Time: 10 minutes | Cook Time: 55 minutes | Serves: 5

900g pork center cut
2 tablespoons olive oil
1 tablespoon Italian herb mix

1 teaspoon red pepper flakes, crushed
Sea salt and black pepper, to taste

1. Toss all the recipe ingredients in a greased Cook & Crisp Basket. 2. Place the Cook & Crisp Basket in your Pressure Cooker Steam Fryer. 3. Put on the Smart Lid on top of the Ninja Foodi Steam Fryer. 4. Move the Lid Slider to the "Air Fry/Stovetop". Select the "Air Fry" mode for cooking. 5. Cook the pork at 180°C for around 55 minutes, turning it over halfway through the cooking time. 6. Serve warm and enjoy!
Per Serving: Calories: 356; Fat:21.7g; Carbs: 0.1g; Fiber: 0.1g; Sugars: 0.1g Proteins: 37.5g

Sausage with Fennel

Prep Time: 10 minutes | Cook Time: 15 minutes | Serves: 4

455g pork sausage
455g fennel, quartered
1 teaspoon garlic powder

½ teaspoon onion powder
2 teaspoons mustard

1. Place all the recipe ingredients in a greased Cook & Crisp Basket. 2. Place the Cook & Crisp Basket in your Pressure Cooker Steam Fryer. 3. Put on the Smart Lid on top of the Ninja Foodi Steam Fryer. 4. Move the Lid Slider to the "Air Fry/Stovetop". Select the "Air Fry" mode for cooking. 5. Air fry the sausage and fennel at 185°C for approximately 15 minutes, tossing the basket halfway through the cooking time. 6. Serve.
Per Serving: Calories: 433; Fat:35.7g; Carbs: 9.9g; Fiber: 3.7g; Sugars: 1g; Proteins: 17.8g

Pork Burgers

Prep Time: 10 minutes | Cook Time: 15 minutes | Serves: 4

455g pork
1 small onion, chopped
1 garlic clove, minced
4 tablespoons tortilla chips, crushed
1 teaspoon fresh sage, minced

1 teaspoon fresh coriander, minced
1 tablespoon fresh parsley, minced
1 egg, beaten
½ teaspoon smoked paprika
Sea salt and black pepper, to taste

1. Place the Cook & Crisp Basket in your Pressure Cooker Steam Fryer. 2. In a suitable mixing bowl, mix all the recipe ingredients. Form the mixture into four patties. 3. Put on the Smart Lid on top of the Ninja Foodi Steam Fryer. 4. Move the Lid Slider to the "Air Fry/Stovetop". Select the "Air Fry" mode for cooking. 5. Cook the burgers at 195°C for about 15 minutes or until cooked through; make sure to turn them over halfway through the cooking time. 6. Serve.
Per Serving: Calories: 386; Fat:28.7g; Carbs: 9.2g; Fiber: 1.1g; Sugars: 1g; Proteins: 22.3g

Spicy Beef Stew with Olives

Prep time: 5 minutes | Cook time: 25 minutes | Serves: 4

1.1kg boneless beef short ribs, trimmed, cut into 2.5cm chunks
80ml Worcestershire sauce
Salt and ground black pepper
2 tablespoons salted butter
2 medium yellow onions, chopped
4 medium garlic cloves, smashed and peeled
3 or 4 Fresno or serrano chilies,

stemmed, seeded and thinly sliced, divided
120ml brandy
4 bay leaves
70g pitted Kalamata olives, halved lengthwise
3 tablespoons plain flour
Chopped fresh flat-leaf parsley, to serve

1. In a large bowl, stir together the beef, Worcestershire sauce, 1½ teaspoons salt and 1 teaspoon pepper. Set aside. Move the slider towards "AIR FRY/STOVETOP" and set Ninja Foodi XL Pressure Cooker Steam Fryer with SmartLid to SEAR/SAUTÉ mode. Adjust the temperature to "Hi5" by using up arrow. Press START/STOP to begin cooking. 2. Add butter and let melt, then add the onions and garlic. Cook, stirring often, until the onions are browned, about 8 to 10 minutes. Add half of the chilies and cook, stirring, until fragrant, for about 1 minute. Pour in the brandy and cook, scraping up any browned bits. Then add the bay and beef with its marinade; stir to mix, then distribute in an even layer. 3. Lock lid; move slider to PRESSURE. Make sure the pressure release valve is in the SEAL position. The

cooking temperature will default to HIGH, which is accurate. Set time to 25 minutes. Press START/STOP to cooking. 4. When pressure cooking is complete, let the pressure release naturally for 15 minutes, then quickly release the remaining steam by turning it into VENT position. Then carefully open the lid. 5. Using a large spoon, skim off and discard any fat from the surface of the cooking liquid. Remove and discard the bay, then stir in the olives and remaining chilies. 6. In a small bowl, whisk the flour with 6 tablespoons of the cooking liquid until smooth, then stir into the pot. Select SEAR/SAUTÉ mode again. Bring the stew to a simmer, stirring often, and cook until lightly thickened, 2 to 3 minutes. Press START/STOP to turn off the pot. 7. Taste and season with salt and pepper. Serve sprinkled with parsley.
Per Serving: Calories 153; Fat 2.8g; Sodium 28mg; Carbs 26g; Fiber 1g; Sugar 1g; Protein 6g

Pork Roast with Applesauce

Prep Time: 10 minutes | Cook Time: 1 hour | Serves: 5

1 tablespoon olive oil
2 tablespoons soy sauce
900g pork shoulder
Salt and black pepper, to taste

2 cloves garlic, smashed
2 sprigs fresh sage, chopped
245g applesauce

1. Toss all the recipe ingredients, except for the applesauce, in a greased Cook & Crisp Basket. 2. Place the Cook & Crisp Basket in your Pressure Cooker Steam Fryer. 3. Put on the Smart Lid on top of the Ninja Foodi Steam Fryer. 4. Move the Lid Slider to the "Air Fry/Stovetop". Select the "Air Fry" mode for cooking. 5. Cook the pork shoulder at 180°C for around 45 minutes, turning it over halfway through the cooking time. 6. Top the pork butt with the applesauce and continue cooking for a further 10 minutes. 7. Let it rest for a few minutes before slicing and serving.
Per Serving: Calories: 402; Fat:26.2g; Carbs: 7.4g; Fiber: 0.7g; Sugars: 5.8g; Proteins: 32.3g

Apple Cider Pulled Pork

Prep time: 5 minutes | Cook time: 45 minutes | Serves: 6

900g boneless pork loin roast
Sea salt
Freshly ground black pepper
1 tablespoon vegetable oil
480ml apple cider
2 Honeycrisp apples, peeled and

sliced
1 small onion, chopped
1 tablespoon light brown sugar
1 teaspoon chili powder
1 teaspoon smoked paprika

1. Season the pork with salt and pepper. 2. In the Ninja Foodi XL Pressure Cooker Steam Fryer with SmartLid cooking pot, combine the vegetable oil, pork, apple cider, apples, onion, brown sugar, chili powder, and smoked paprika. 3. Lock lid; move slider to PRESSURE. Make sure the pressure release valve is in the SEAL position. The cooking temperature will default to HIGH, which is accurate. Set time to 45 minutes. Press START/STOP to cooking. When pressure cooking is complete, let the pressure release naturally for at least 10 minutes. 4. Remove the lid, transfer the pork to a medium bowl, and shred it using two forks. Return the pork to the juices and serve.
Per Serving: Calories 543; Fat 38.1g; Sodium 134mg; Carbs 27g; Fiber 1g; Sugar 0g; Protein 23g

Glazed Ham

Prep Time: 10 minutes | Cook Time: 1 hour | Serves: 4

675g ham
60ml sherry wine
2 tablespoons dark brown sugar
2 tablespoons freshly squeezed lime juice

1 tablespoon stone-mustard
A pinch of grated nutmeg
½ teaspoon cloves
¼ teaspoon cardamom
½ teaspoon black pepper, to taste

1. Place the Cook & Crisp Basket in your Pressure Cooker Steam Fryer. 2. In a suitable mixing bowl, mix all the remaining recipe ingredients to make the glaze. 3. Wrap the ham in a piece of aluminum foil and lower it into the Cook & Crisp Basket Put on the Smart Lid on top of the Ninja Foodi Steam Fryer. Move the Lid Slider to the "Air Fry/Stovetop". Select the "Air Fry" mode for cooking. Cook for the ham at 190°C for about 30 minutes. 4. Remove the foil, turn the temperature to 200°C, and continue to cook an additional 15 minutes, coating the ham with the glaze every 5 minutes. 5. Serve.
Per Serving: Calories: 470; Fat:30.3g; Carbs: 1.6g; Fiber: 0.4g; Sugars: 0.4g; Proteins:45.7g

Sausage Patties

Prep Time: 10 minutes | Cook Time: 15 minutes | Serves: 4

455g sausage patties	1 teaspoon jalapeno pepper,
1 tablespoon mustard	minced
1 teaspoon cayenne pepper	

1. Place all the recipe ingredients in a greased Cook & Crisp Basket. 2. Place the Cook & Crisp Basket in your Pressure Cooker Steam Fryer. 3. Put on the Smart Lid on top of the Ninja Foodi Steam Fryer. 4. Move the Lid Slider to the "Air Fry/Stovetop". Select the "Air Fry" mode for cooking. 5. Air fry the sausage at 185°C for approximately 15 minutes, tossing the basket halfway through the cooking time. 6. Serve.
Per Serving: Calories: 392; Fat:35.7g; Carbs: 1.5g; Fiber: 0.4g; Sugars: 0.2g; Proteins: 16.3g

Pork Chops with Peppers

Prep Time: 10 minutes | Cook Time: 15 minutes | Serves: 4

675g center-cut rib chops	Salt and black pepper, to taste
2 peppers, seeded and sliced	1 teaspoon fresh rosemary,
2 tablespoons olive oil	chopped
½ teaspoon mustard powder	1 teaspoon fresh basil, chopped

1. Toss all the recipe ingredients in a greased Cook & Crisp Basket. 2. Place the Cook & Crisp Basket in your Pressure Cooker Steam Fryer. 3. Put on the Smart Lid on top of the Ninja Foodi Steam Fryer. 4. Move the Lid Slider to the "Air Fry/Stovetop". Select the "Air Fry" mode for cooking. 5. Cook the pork chops and peppers at 200°C for around 15 minutes, turning them over halfway through the cooking time. 6. Serve.
Per Serving: Calories: 359; Fat:22.2g; Carbs: 2.3g; Fiber: 0.5g; Sugars: 1.1g; Proteins: 35.7g

Country Style Ribs

Prep Time: 10 minutes | Cook Time: 35 minutes | Serves: 5

900g Country-style ribs	1 teaspoon mustard powder
Coarse sea salt and black pepper,	1 tablespoon butter, melted
to taste	1 teaspoon chili sauce
1 teaspoon smoked paprika	4 tablespoons dry red wine

1. Toss all the recipe ingredients in a greased Cook & Crisp Basket. 2. Place the Cook & Crisp Basket in your Pressure Cooker Steam Fryer. 3. Put on the Smart Lid on top of the Ninja Foodi Steam Fryer. 4. Move the Lid Slider to the "Air Fry/Stovetop". Select the "Air Fry" mode for cooking. 5. Cook the pork ribs at 175°C for around 35 minutes, turning them over halfway through the cooking time. 6. Serve.
Per Serving: Calories: 374; Fat:23.8g; Carbs: 1.4g; Fiber: 0.4g; Sugars: 0.6g; Proteins: 35.4g

Crackled Pork Loin

Prep Time: 10 minutes | Cook Time: 55 minutes | Serves: 5

4 tablespoons beer	Sea salt and black pepper, to taste
1 tablespoon garlic, crushed	900g pork loin
1 teaspoon paprika	

1. Toss all the recipe ingredients in a greased Cook & Crisp Basket. 2. Place the Cook & Crisp Basket in your Pressure Cooker Steam Fryer. 3. Put on the Smart Lid on top of the Ninja Foodi Steam Fryer. 4. Move the Lid Slider to the "Air Fry/Stovetop". Select the "Air Fry" mode for cooking. 5. Cook the pork at 180°C for around 55 minutes, turning it over halfway through the cooking time. 6. Serve warm and enjoy!
Per Serving: Calories: 315; Fat:15.2g; Carbs: 2.1g; Fiber: 0.3g; Sugars: 0.5g; Proteins: 39.1g

Crispy Pork Bites

Prep Time: 10 minutes | Cook Time: 17 minutes | Serves: 5

455g pork belly, cut into cubes	1 tablespoon granulated sugar
1 teaspoon coarse sea salt	1 teaspoon onion powder
Black pepper, to taste	½ teaspoon garlic powder

1. Place the Cook & Crisp Basket in your Pressure Cooker Steam Fryer. 2. Toss all the recipe ingredients in your Cook and crisp basket.

3. Put on the Smart Lid on top of the Ninja Foodi Steam Fryer. 4. Move the Lid Slider to the "Air Fry/Stovetop". Select the "Air Fry" mode for cooking. 5. Cook the pork belly at 200°C for about 17 minutes, shaking the basket halfway through the cooking time. 6. Serve.
Per Serving: Calories: 479; Fat:48.1g; Carbs: 2.3g; Fiber: 0.1g; Sugars: 1.6g; Proteins: 8.6g

Beef, Red Pepper and Paprika Stew

Prep time: 5 minutes | Cook time: 25 minutes | Serves: 4

1 tablespoon extra-virgin olive oil	chopped
10 medium garlic cloves, smashed	4 teaspoons finely chopped fresh
and peeled	rosemary, divided
1 large shallot, halved and thickly	1 tablespoon sweet paprika
sliced	1.3kg boneless beef chuck roast,
1 plum tomato, cored, seeded and	trimmed, cut into 5cm chunks
chopped	2 tablespoons plain flour
75g jarred roasted red peppers,	1 teaspoon lemon juice
patted dry, finely chopped	Salt and ground black pepper
100g prosciutto or pancetta,	

1. Move the slider towards "AIR FRY/STOVETOP" and set Ninja Foodi XL Pressure Cooker Steam Fryer with SmartLid to SEAR/SAUTÉ mode. Adjust the temperature to "Hi5" by using up arrow. Press START/STOP to begin cooking. 2. Add the oil and pancetta and cook, stirring occasionally, until the pancetta is depleted of fat but not yet crisp, 3 to 5 minutes. Stir in the mushrooms and ½ teaspoon of salt and pepper. Cook, stirring occasionally, until the liquid released from the mushrooms has evaporated and the mushrooms begin to brown, 6 to 8 minutes. Add the garlic and cook, stirring, until fragrant, 1 to 2 minutes. 3. Using a slotted spoon, transfer the mixture to a bowl and set aside. To the remaining fat in the pan, add the tomato paste and cook, stirring occasionally, until browned, 1 to 2 minutes. Add the wine and 60 ml water, scraping up any brown bits. 4. Lock lid; move slider to PRESSURE. Make sure the pressure release valve is in the SEAL position. The cooking temperature will default to HIGH, which is accurate. Set time to 35 minutes. Press START/STOP to cooking. 5. When pressure cooking is complete, let the pressure release naturally for 15 minutes, then quickly release the remaining steam by turning it into VENT position. Then carefully open the lid. 6. Using a large spoon, skim and discard the fat from the surface of the cooking liquid. In a small bowl, whisk the flour with 6 tablespoons of the cooking liquid until smooth, then stir the mixture into the pot along with the remaining 1 teaspoon rosemary. 7. Select SEAR/SAUTÉ mode again. Bring the stew to a simmer and cook, stirring often, until thickened, 2 to 3 minutes. Press START/STOP to turn off the pot. Stir in the lemon juice, then taste and sprinkle with salt and pepper.
Per Serving: Calories 134; Fat 2.8g; Sodium 64mg; Carbs 26g; Fiber 4g; Sugar 8g; Protein 3g

Cinnamon Applesauce Chops

Prep time: 10 minutes | Cook time: 12 minutes | Serves: 6

6 (150-200g) boneless pork chops	385g applesauce, store-bought or
(2.5cm thick)	homemade
Sea salt	240ml water
Freshly ground black pepper	1 teaspoon dried sage
1 tablespoon vegetable oil	1 cinnamon stick
1 small onion, chopped	

1. Season the pork chops with salt and pepper. 2. Move the slider towards "AIR FRY/STOVETOP" and set Ninja Foodi XL Pressure Cooker Steam Fryer with SmartLid to SEAR/SAUTÉ mode. Adjust the temperature to "Hi5" by using up arrow. Press START/STOP to begin cooking and let the pot heat up for 2 minutes. 3. Pour the oil into the pot, then add the onion and sauté for about 2 minutes, or until the onion is translucent. Add the pork chops and sear for 1 minute on each side. 4. Add the applesauce, water, sage, and cinnamon stick. 5. Lock lid; move slider to PRESSURE. Make sure the pressure release valve is in the SEAL position. The cooking temperature will default to HIGH, which is accurate. Set time to 10 minutes. Press START/STOP to cooking. When pressure cooking is complete, let the pressure release natural. 6. Remove the lid and transfer the pork chops to a serving dish. Discard the cinnamon stick, scoop the applesauce on top of the pork, and serve.
Per Serving: Calories 205; Fat 5.8g; Sodium 1481mg; Carbs 1g; Fiber 0g; Sugar 0g; Protein 35g

Bacon with Cauliflower

Prep Time: 10 minutes	Cook Time: 12 minutes	Serves: 4

455g bacon, cut into thick slices
455g cauliflower, cut into florets
1 tablespoon maple syrup
1 teaspoon paprika
Salt and black pepper, to taste
2 cloves garlic, minced

1. Place the Cook & Crisp Basket in your Pressure Cooker Steam Fryer. 2. Toss all the recipe ingredients in the Cook & Crisp Basket. 3. Put on the Smart Lid on top of the Ninja Foodi Steam Fryer. 4. Move the Lid Slider to the "Air Fry/Stovetop". Select the "Air Fry" mode for cooking. 5. Then, cook the bacon and cauliflower at 200°C for approximately 12 minutes, turning them over halfway through the cooking time. 6. Serve immediately.
Per Serving: Calories: 512; Fat:44.9g; Carbs: 8g; Fiber: 2.7g; Sugars: 6.7g; Proteins: 16.7g

Spicy Beef Stew with Caraway

Prep time: 5 minutes	Cook time: 25 minutes	Serves: 6

2kg boneless beef chuck roast, trimmed and cut into 4 cm chunks
6 tablespoons sweet paprika, divided
4 tablespoons salted butter
1 large yellow onion, finely chopped
Salt and ground black pepper
2 tablespoons caraway seeds, lightly crushed
1 tablespoon hot paprika
480ml low-sodium beef stock
60g tomato paste
3 bay leaves
6 tablespoons plain flour
10g finely chopped fresh dill, plus dill sprigs to serve
1 tablespoon cider vinegar
Sour cream, to serve

1. In a large bowl, toss the beef with 2 tablespoons sweet paprika until evenly coated. 2. Move the slider towards "AIR FRY/STOVETOP" and set Ninja Foodi XL Pressure Cooker Steam Fryer with SmartLid to SEAR/SAUTÉ mode. Adjust the temperature to "Hi5" by using up arrow. Press START/STOP to begin cooking. 3. Add the butter and let melt. Add the onion and 1 teaspoon salt, then cook, stirring occasionally, until the onion is lightly browned, about 8 minutes. Add the caraway and cook, stirring, until fragrant, about 30 seconds. 4. Add the remaining 4 tablespoons sweet paprika and the hot paprika, then cook, stirring, until fragrant, about 30 seconds. Whisk in the stock and tomato paste, scraping up any browned bits. Add the bay and beef; stir to combine, then distribute in an even layer. 5. Lock lid; move slider to PRESSURE. Make sure the pressure release valve is in the SEAL position. The cooking temperature will default to HIGH, which is accurate. Set time to 25 minutes. Press START/STOP to cooking. 6. When the cooking is complete, let the pressure release naturally for 15 minutes, then release quickly the remaining steam by turning it into VENT position. Then carefully open the lid. Using a large spoon, skim and discard the fat from the surface of cooking liquid. 7. In a medium bowl, whisk the flour with 240ml of the cooking liquid until smooth, then whisk the mixture into the pot. 8. Select SEAR/SAUTÉ mode again. Bring the stew to a simmer and cook, stirring often, until thickened, about 2 minutes. Press START/STOP to turn off the pot. 9. Stir in the dill and vinegar, then taste and sprinkle with salt and pepper. Serve garnished with dill sprigs and with sour cream on the side.
Per Serving: Calories 292; Fat 24.3g; Sodium 660mg; Carbs 5g; Fiber 0g; Sugar 3g; Protein 14g

Beef and Bean Stew with Tomatoes and Dill

Prep time: 5 minutes	Cook time: 25 minutes	Serves: 6

2 tablespoons extra-virgin olive oil, plus more to serve
8 medium garlic cloves, smashed and peeled
3 tablespoons tomato paste
1 tablespoon sweet paprika
1 teaspoon red pepper flakes
1 large yellow onion, chopped
1L low-sodium chicken stock
Salt and ground black pepper
1.3kg beef shanks (each about 2.5 cm thick), trimmed
455g dried navy beans
360g can diced tomatoes, drained
10g finely chopped fresh dill, plus more to serve
2 tablespoons pomegranate molasses, plus more to serve

1. Move the slider towards "AIR FRY/STOVETOP" and set Ninja Foodi XL Pressure Cooker Steam Fryer with SmartLid to SEAR/SAUTÉ mode. Adjust the temperature to "Hi5" by using up arrow. Press START/STOP to begin cooking. 2. Add the oil, heat until shimmering. Add the onion and cook, stirring, until lightly browned, about 8 minutes. Stir in the garlic, tomato paste, paprika and pepper flakes, then cook until fragrant, about 30 seconds. 3. Add the stock and 1 tablespoon salt, then stir in the beans and distribute in an even layer. Place the shanks in the pot in a single layer, submerging them in the liquid. 4. Lock lid; move slider to PRESSURE. Make sure the pressure release valve is in the SEAL position. The cooking temperature will default to HIGH, which is accurate. Set time to 45 minutes. Press START/STOP to cooking. 5. When pressure cooking is complete, let the pressure release naturally for 40 minutes, then quickly release the remaining steam by turning it into VENT position. 6. Then carefully open the lid. Remove and discard the shank bones; the meat should easily fall away from the bones. Stir in the tomatoes, dill and pomegranate molasses, breaking the meat into large bite-size pieces. 7. Taste and sprinkle with salt and black pepper. Serve sprinkled with additional dill and drizzled with additional oil and pomegranate molasses.
Per Serving: Calories 193; Fat 8.9g; Sodium 93mg; Carbs 2g; Fiber 1g; Sugar 0g; Protein 25g

beef and Chickpea Stew with Coriander

Prep time: 5 minutes	Cook time: 25 minutes	Serves: 6

Salt and ground black pepper
2 tablespoons salted butter
1 large yellow onion, chopped
2 medium carrots (about 200g), peeled and shredded
8 medium garlic cloves, smashed and peeled
90g tomato paste
1 tablespoon sweet paprika
1 tablespoon ground cumin
1 teaspoon ground cardamom
1 teaspoon ground cinnamon
900g boneless beef chuck roast, trimmed and cut into 3cm chunks
Two 390g cans chickpeas, rinsed and drained
50g lightly packed fresh coriander, chopped
3 tablespoons lemon juice

1. Move the slider towards "AIR FRY/STOVETOP" and set Ninja Foodi XL Pressure Cooker Steam Fryer with SmartLid to SEAR/SAUTÉ mode. Adjust the temperature to "Hi5" by using up arrow. Press START/STOP to begin cooking. 2. Add the butter and melt. Add the onion and carrots, then cook, stirring occasionally, until the vegetables are softened, for about 5 minutes. Stir in the garlic, tomato paste, paprika, cumin, cardamom, cinnamon and 1 teaspoon salt, then cook, stirring, until fragrant, about 1 minute. Add 1 L water and scrape up any browned bits. Stir in the beef, then distribute in an even layer. 3. Lock lid; move slider to PRESSURE. Make sure the pressure release valve is in the SEAL position. The cooking temperature will default to HIGH, which is accurate. Set time to 30 minutes. Press START/STOP to cooking. 4. When pressure cooking is complete, let the pressure release naturally for 15 minutes, then quickly release the remaining steam by turning it into VENT position. Then carefully open the lid. 5. Stir in the chickpeas, coriander and lemon juice, then taste and season with salt and pepper.
Per Serving: Calories 101; Fat 5.4g; Sodium 106mg; Carbs 8g; Fiber 3g; Sugar 3g; Protein 7g

Sesame-Ginger Tenderloin

Prep time: 10 minutes	Cook time: 23 minutes	Serves: 6

2 tablespoons light brown sugar
1 tablespoon sesame oil
1 tablespoon soy sauce
1 tablespoon rice vinegar
2 teaspoons ground ginger
2 garlic cloves, minced
675g pork tenderloin
Sea salt
Freshly ground black pepper
240ml water
1 tablespoon corn flour

1. Move the slider towards "AIR FRY/STOVETOP" and set Ninja Foodi XL Pressure Cooker Steam Fryer with SmartLid to SEAR/SAUTÉ mode. Adjust the temperature to "Hi5" by using up arrow. Press START/STOP to begin cooking. Add the hoisin sauce, brown sugar, sesame oil, soy sauce, rice vinegar, ground ginger, and garlic. Whisk for about 3 minutes, until a sauce forms. 2. Season the pork tenderloin with salt and pepper. Add the pork tenderloin and water. 3. Lock lid; move slider to PRESSURE. Make sure the pressure release valve is in the SEAL position. The cooking temperature will default to HIGH, which is accurate. Set time to 15 minutes. Press START/STOP to cooking. When pressure cooking is complete, let the pressure release naturally for at least 10 minutes. 4. Remove the lid and transfer the pork to a cutting board. 5. Select SEAR/SAUTÉ. Whisk the corn flour into the pot and whisk for about 5 minutes to thicken the sauce. 6. Slice the pork and serve with the sauce poured over it.
Per Serving: Calories 722; Fat 39g; Sodium 140mg; Carbs 7g; Fiber 2g; Sugar 4g; Protein 18g

Cola Pulled Pork

Prep time: 5 minutes | Cook time: 45 minutes | Serves: 6

900g boneless pork loin roast	1 (300g) can cola
Sea salt	1 onion, chopped
Freshly ground black pepper	2 garlic cloves, minced
240g Sweet and Smoky Barbecue Sauce	2 tablespoons Worcestershire sauce

1. Season the pork with salt and pepper. 2. In the Ninja Foodi XL Pressure Cooker Steam Fryer with SmartLid cooking pot, combine the pork, barbecue sauce, cola, onion, garlic, and Worcestershire sauce. 3. Lock lid; move slider to PRESSURE. Make sure the pressure release valve is in the SEAL position. The cooking temperature will default to HIGH, which is accurate. Set time to 45 minutes. Press START/STOP to cooking. When pressure cooking is complete, let the pressure release naturally for at least 10 minutes. 4. Remove the lid, transfer the pork to a medium bowl, and shred it using two forks. Return the pork to the juices and serve.
Per Serving: Calories 295; Fat 21.2g; Sodium 94mg; Carbs 3g; Fiber 1g; Sugar 1g; Protein 23g

Greek Beef Stew with Tomatoes

Prep time: 5 minutes | Cook time: 15 minutes | Serves: 4

2 tablespoons extra-virgin olive oil, plus more to serve	trimmed and cut into 4 cm chunks
2 medium tomatoes (about 250g), cored and chopped	200g peeled pearl onions
2 cinnamon sticks	Salt and ground black pepper
1 teaspoon ground allspice	1 tablespoon red wine vinegar, plus more to serve
1 teaspoon white sugar	Feta cheese, crumbled, to serve
120g dry red wine	Chopped fresh flat-leaf parsley, to serve
900g boneless beef short ribs,	

1. Move the slider towards "AIR FRY/STOVETOP" and set Ninja Foodi XL Pressure Cooker Steam Fryer with SmartLid to SEAR/SAUTÉ mode. Adjust the temperature to "Hi5" by using up arrow. Press START/STOP to begin cooking. 2. Add the oil and heat until shimmering. Add the tomatoes and their juices, the cinnamon, allspice and sugar, then cook, stirring occasionally, until the juices evaporate and the tomatoes begin to brown, about 5 minutes. Add the wine and scrape up any browned bits. Add the beef, onions, 2 teaspoons salt and 1 teaspoon pepper; stir to combine, then distribute in an even layer. 3. Lock lid; move slider to PRESSURE. Make sure the pressure release valve is in the SEAL position. The cooking temperature will default to HIGH, which is accurate. Set time to 30 minutes. Press START/STOP to cooking. 4. When pressure cooking is complete, let the pressure release naturally for 15 minutes, then quickly release the remaining steam by turning it into VENT position. 5. Then carefully open the lid. Using a large spoon, skim off and discard the fat from the surface of the cooking liquid. Remove and discard the cinnamon sticks. 6. Select SEAR/SAUTÉ mode again. Bring the stew to a simmer, stir in the vinegar and cook, stirring occasionally, until slightly thickened, about 5 minutes. Press START/STOP to turn off the pot. 7. Taste and season with salt and pepper. Serve sprinkled with feta cheese and parsley and drizzled with oil; offer additional vinegar at the table.
Per Serving: Calories 162; Fat 9.4g; Sodium 68mg; Carbs 21g; Fiber 4g; Sugar 16g; Protein 1g

Meatballs in Spicy Tomato Sauce

Prep time: 5 minutes | Cook time: 15 minutes | Serves: 4

50g fine dry breadcrumbs	Salt and ground black pepper
Two 700g cans whole peeled tomatoes, drained, juices reserved	4 tablespoons salted butter
2 teaspoons dried oregano	¾ teaspoon red pepper flakes
2 teaspoons fennel seeds, finely ground	3 tablespoons tomato paste
	3 tablespoons finely chopped fresh basil
1 teaspoon granulated garlic	Grated Parmesan or pecorino
455g 85 percent lean beef mince	Romano cheese, to serve

1. In a large bowl, mix together the breadcrumbs, 120 ml tomato juices, the oregano, fennel seeds and garlic. Add the beef, 1½ teaspoons salt and 1 teaspoon black pepper. 2. Mix with your hands until no streaks of breadcrumbs remain. Divide into 10 portions and form each into a compact ball about 5 cm in diameter, placing the meatballs on a large plate. Refrigerate for 15 minutes. 3. Move the slider towards "AIR FRY/STOVETOP" and set Ninja Foodi XL Pressure Cooker Steam Fryer with SmartLid to SEAR/SAUTÉ mode. Adjust the temperature to "Hi5" by using up arrow. Press START/STOP to begin cooking. Add the tomatoes and their remaining juices, the butter and pepper flakes, then bring to a boil, stirring. Set the meatballs on top of the tomatoes in an even layer, gently pressing to submerge them. 4. Lock lid; move slider to PRESSURE. Make sure the pressure release valve is in the SEAL position. The cooking temperature will default to HIGH, which is accurate. Set time to 3 minutes. Press START/STOP to cooking. 5. When pressure cooking is complete, let the pressure release naturally for 10 minutes, then release the remaining steam by turning it into VENT position. Then carefully open the lid. 6. Using a slotted spoon, transfer the meatballs to a clean plate. Select SEAR/SAUTÉ mode again. Bring the tomato mixture to a boil, mashing with a potato masher to break up the tomatoes. Whisk in the tomato paste and cook, stirring occasionally, until slightly thickened, about 8 minutes. 7. Taste and season with salt and black pepper. Add the basil and return the meatballs to the pot, then gently stir. Press STOP to turn off the pot. 8. Let stand until the meatballs are heated through, about 10 minutes. Serve sprinkled with Parmesan.
Per Serving: Calories 271; Fat 9.3g; Sodium 15mg; Carbs 43g; Fiber 6g; Sugar 2g; Protein 5g

Salsa Pulled Pork

Prep time: 5 minutes | Cook time: 45 minutes | Serves: 6

1 tablespoon vegetable oil	960g Garden Salsa
900g boneless pork loin roast	1 (25g) packet taco seasoning

1. In the Ninja Foodi XL Pressure Cooker Steam Fryer with SmartLid cooking pot, combine the vegetable oil, pork, salsa, and taco seasoning. 2. Lock lid; move slider to PRESSURE. Make sure the pressure release valve is in the SEAL position. The cooking temperature will default to HIGH, which is accurate. Set time to 45 minutes. Press START/STOP to cooking. When pressure cooking is complete, let the pressure release naturally for at least 10 minutes. 3. Remove the lid, transfer the pork to a medium bowl, and shred it using two forks. Return the pork to the juices and serve.
Per Serving: Calories 314; Fat 27.2g; Sodium 182mg; Carbs 0g; Fiber 0g; Sugar 0g; Protein 17g

French Meat and Vegetable Stew with Tarragon

Prep time: 5 minutes | Cook time: 30 minutes | Serves: 4

2 tablespoons salted butter	cut into 4 cm chunks
200g peeled pearl onions	150g green beans, trimmed and cut into 2.5 cm pieces
8 medium garlic cloves, peeled and smashed	150g cherry or grape tomatoes, halved
1 tablespoon fennel seeds	
240ml dry white wine	2 tablespoons lemon juice
Salt and ground black pepper	40g lightly packed fresh tarragon, roughly chopped
1.1kg boneless lamb shoulder or boneless beef chuck, trimmed and	

1. Move the slider towards "AIR FRY/STOVETOP" and set Ninja Foodi XL Pressure Cooker Steam Fryer with SmartLid to SEAR/SAUTÉ mode. Adjust the temperature to "Hi5" by using up arrow. Press START/STOP to begin cooking. 2. Add the butter and melt. Add the onions, garlic and fennel seeds, then cook, stirring occasionally, until the onions are lightly browned, 3 to 4 minutes. Add the wine, 120ml water, 2 teaspoons salt and ½ teaspoon pepper, then bring to a simmer. Add the lamb or beef and stir to combine, then distribute in an even layer. 3. Lock lid; move slider to PRESSURE. Make sure the pressure release valve is in the SEAL position. The cooking temperature will default to HIGH, which is accurate. Set time to 25 minutes. Press START/STOP to cooking. 4. When pressure cooking is complete, let the pressure release naturally for 15 minutes, then quickly release the remaining steam by turning it into VENT position. Then carefully open the lid. 5. Using a large spoon, skim off and discard the fat from the surface of the cooking liquid. Select SEAR/SAUTÉ mode again and bring to a simmer. Add the green beans and tomatoes, then cook, stirring occasionally, until the beans are tender, 7 to 10 minutes. Press START/STOP to turn off the pot. 6. Stir in the lemon juice, then taste and season with salt and pepper. Serve sprinkled with the tarragon.
Per Serving: Calories 147; Fat 7.3g; Sodium 56mg; Carbs 20g; Fiber 5g; Sugar 11g; Protein 4g

Delicious Chili Con Carne

Prep time: 5 minutes | Cook time: 35 minutes | Serves: 6

3 tablespoons ancho chili powder
2 tablespoons chili powder
2 tablespoons packed light or dark brown sugar
2 tablespoons ground cumin
1 tablespoon dried oregano
Salt
1.8kg boneless beef chuck roast, trimmed and cut into 2.5 cm chunks
3 tablespoons grapeseed or other neutral oil

1 large yellow onion, finely chopped
6 medium garlic cloves, finely chopped
3 tablespoons tomato paste
360g can diced fire-roasted tomatoes
4 chipotle chilies in adobo sauce, finely chopped, plus 3 tablespoons adobo sauce
75g tortilla chips, finely crushed

1. In a large bowl, stir together both chili powders, the sugar, cumin, oregano and 2 teaspoons salt. Add the beef and toss until evenly coated; set aside. 2. Move the slider towards "AIR FRY/STOVETOP" and set Ninja Foodi XL Pressure Cooker Steam Fryer with SmartLid to SEAR/SAUTÉ mode. Adjust the temperature to "Hi5" by using up arrow. Press START/STOP to begin cooking. Add the oil and heat until shimmering. 3. Add the onion and cook, stirring occasionally, until lightly browned, about 5 minutes. Add the garlic and cook, stirring, until fragrant, about 30 seconds. Stir in the tomato paste and cook, stirring, until the tomato paste is well browned, about 3 minutes. Stir in the tomatoes with their juice, the chipotle chilies and adobo sauce and 240ml water, scraping up any browned bits. Add the beef; stir to combine, then distribute in an even layer. 4. Lock lid; move slider to PRESSURE. Make sure the pressure release valve is in the SEAL position. The cooking temperature will default to HIGH, which is accurate. Set time to 50 minutes. Press START/STOP to cooking. 5. When pressure cooking is complete, let the pressure release naturally for 15 minutes, then quickly release the remaining steam by turning it into VENT position. Then carefully open the lid. 6. Using a large spoon, skim off and discard the fat from the surface of the cooking liquid. Stir the crushed tortilla chips into the chili. 7. Select SEAR/SAUTÉ mode again and cook, stirring occasionally, until the chili is lightly thickened, about 5 minutes. Press START/STOP to turn off the pot. 8. Let stand for 10 minutes, then taste and sprinkle with salt.
Per Serving: Calories 409; Fat 18.9g; Sodium 214mg; Carbs 10g; Fiber 1g; Sugar 9g; Protein 48g

Indonesian Nutty Beef

Prep time: 5 minutes | Cook time: 25 minutes | Serves: 4

45g unsweetened shredded coconut
3 Fresno or serrano chilies, stemmed, seeded and roughly chopped, plus 1 chili, stemmed and thinly sliced
3 medium garlic cloves, smashed and peeled
1 lemon grass stalk, tough outer layers removed, trimmed to lower 15 cm and thinly sliced
2.5 cm piece fresh ginger, peeled and roughly chopped

1 medium shallot, roughly chopped
½ teaspoon ground turmeric
⅛ teaspoon ground cinnamon
1-star anise pod
1 tablespoon grated lime zest, plus 1 tablespoon juice
Salt and ground black pepper
180ml coconut milk
2½ to 1.3kg boneless beef chuck roast, trimmed and cut into 5 cm chunks
Fresh coriander, to serve

1. Move the slider towards "AIR FRY/STOVETOP" and set Ninja Foodi XL Pressure Cooker Steam Fryer with SmartLid to SEAR/SAUTÉ mode. Adjust the temperature to "Hi5" by using up arrow. Press START/STOP to begin cooking. 2. Add the shredded coconut. Cook, stirring frequently, until the coconut is golden brown, about 5 minutes. Press START/STOP, then add the chopped chilies, garlic, lemon grass, ginger, shallot, turmeric, cinnamon, star anise, lime zest and 1½ teaspoons each salt and pepper. Using the pot's residual heat, cook the mixture, stirring, until fragrant, about 1 minute. Stir in the coconut milk and beef, scraping up any bits stuck to the bottom, then distribute in an even layer. 3. Lock lid; move slider to PRESSURE. Make sure the pressure release valve is in the SEAL position. The cooking temperature will default to HIGH, which is accurate. Set time to 25 minutes. Press START/STOP to cooking. 4. When pressure cooking is complete, let the pressure release naturally for 15 minutes, then quickly release the remaining steam by turning it into VENT position. Then carefully open the lid. 5. Using tongs, place the meat to a small bowl and set aside. Pour the cooking liquid into a fine mesh strainer set over a bowl. Add the solids in the strainer to a blender,

then pour in 60ml of the strained liquid; discard the remaining liquid or reserve for another use. 6. Blend on high until very smooth, 1 to 2 minutes, scraping the sides as needed. Pour the puree back into the pot, then stir in the beef and lime juice. 7. Select SEAR/SAUTÉ mode again and cook, stirring often, until the sauce clinging to the bottom of the pot is golden brown, 3 to 5 minutes. Press START/STOP to turn off the pot. Taste and sprinkle with salt and pepper. 8. Serve garnished with sliced chilies and coriander.
Per Serving: Calories 716; Fat 62.6g; Sodium 302mg; Carbs 18g; Fiber 8g; Sugar 2g; Protein 34g

Herbes de Provence Chops

Prep time: 10 minutes | Cook time: 14 minutes | Serves: 6

60ml freshly squeezed lemon juice
3 tablespoons Dijon mustard
2 tablespoons herbes de Provence
2 tablespoons olive oil
1 small onion, chopped
1 tablespoon minced garlic

4 to 6 (100g) boneless pork chops (1.5 cm thick)
Sea salt
Freshly ground black pepper
240ml water
1 tablespoon corn flour

1. Move the slider towards "AIR FRY/STOVETOP" and set Ninja Foodi XL Pressure Cooker Steam Fryer with SmartLid to SEAR/SAUTÉ mode. Adjust the temperature to "Hi5" by using up arrow. Press START/STOP to begin cooking. Add the lemon juice, mustard, herbes de Provence, olive oil, onion, and garlic. Whisk for 1 minute, until well blended. 2. Season the pork chops with salt and pepper and add to the pot along with the water. 3. Lock lid; move slider to PRESSURE. Make sure the pressure release valve is in the SEAL position. The cooking temperature will default to HIGH, which is accurate. Set time to 8 minutes. Press START/STOP to cooking. When pressure cooking is complete, let the pressure release naturally. 4. Remove the lid and transfer the pork chops to a serving dish. 5. Select SEAR/SAUTÉ. Whisk the corn flour into the pot and whisk for about 5 minutes to thicken the sauce. 6. Pour the sauce on top of the pork chops and serve.
Per Serving: Calories 365; Fat 12.4g; Sodium 717mg; Carbs 29g; Fiber 3g; Sugar 10g; Protein 19g

Korean Braised Ribs

Prep time: 5 minutes | Cook time: 35 minutes | Serves: 6

1.3kg bone-in beef short ribs
120ml soy sauce
120ml sake
8 medium garlic cloves, peeled
10 cm piece fresh ginger (about 75g), peeled and roughly chopped
3 tablespoons packed light brown sugar
2 tablespoons sesame seeds, toasted, plus more to serve
1 ripe pear (about 200g), cored

and roughly chopped
1 dried shiitake mushrooms (about 1 ounce), broken in half
1 medium carrot, peeled and cut into 2.5 cm chunks
1 small daikon radish (about 8 ounces), peeled and cut into 2.5 cm chunks
455g spring onions, thinly sliced on the diagonal

1. In a large bowl, cover the short ribs with cool water. Set aside at room temperature for at least 10 minutes or up to 1 hour. 2. In a blender, combine the soy sauce, sake, garlic, ginger, sugar, sesame seeds and pear, then puree until smooth, scraping down the sides as needed, about 1 minute. Pour the mixture into a Ninja Foodi XL Pressure Cooker Steam Fryer. 3. Drain the short ribs and briefly rinse under running water, then arrange them in an even layer in the pot and add the mushrooms. 4. Lock lid; move slider to PRESSURE. Make sure the pressure release valve is in the SEAL position. The cooking temperature will default to HIGH, which is accurate. Set time to 55 minutes. Press START/STOP to cooking. 5. When pressure cooking is complete, let the pressure release naturally for 15 minutes, then quickly release the remaining steam by turning it into VENT position. Then carefully open the lid. 6. Using a large spoon, skim off and discard the fat from the surface of the cooking liquid. Select SEAR/SAUTÉ mode again, then add the carrot and daikon. Cook, stirring occasionally, until the vegetables are tender and the cooking liquid thickens to a light glaze, about 15 minutes. 7. Press START/STOP to turn off the pot. Remove and discard the beef bones, then stir in half of the spring onions. 8. Serve sprinkled with the remaining spring onions and additional sesame seeds.
Per Serving: Calories 427; Fat 18.3g; Sodium 603mg; Carbs 44g; Fiber 6g; Sugar 3g; Protein 23g

Mexican Brisket Salad

Prep time: 5 minutes | Cook time: 25 minutes | Serves: 4

6 tablespoons extra-virgin olive oil, divided	120ml lime juice, plus lime wedges to serve
1 medium yellow onion, halved and thinly sliced	65g pitted green olives, chopped
5 medium garlic cloves, smashed and peeled	1 medium head romaine lettuce, roughly chopped
Salt and ground black pepper	6 radishes, halved and thinly sliced
3 bay leaves	20g lightly packed fresh coriander, roughly chopped
2 teaspoons dried oregano, divided	1 ripe avocado, halved, pitted, peeled and diced
900g beef brisket, trimmed and cut into 6 cm pieces	

1. Move the slider towards "AIR FRY/STOVETOP" and set Ninja Foodi XL Pressure Cooker Steam Fryer with SmartLid to SEAR/SAUTÉ mode. Adjust the temperature to "Hi5" by using up arrow. Press START/STOP to begin cooking. 2. Add 1 tablespoon oil and heat until shimmering, then add the onion and cook, stirring occasionally, until softened, about 5 minutes. Add the garlic and cook, stirring often, until the onion is golden brown, another 2 to 3 minutes. 3. Stir in 1½ teaspoons salt, 1 teaspoon pepper, the bay, 1 teaspoon oregano and 240ml water, scraping up any browned bits. Add the beef in an even layer, slightly overlapping the pieces if needed. 4. Lock lid; move slider to PRESSURE. Make sure the pressure release valve is in the SEAL position. The cooking temperature will default to HIGH, which is accurate. Set time to 45 minutes. Press START/STOP to cooking. 5. When pressure cooking is complete, let the pressure release naturally for 15 minutes, then quickly release the remaining steam by turning it into VENT position. Then carefully open the lid and let the contents cool for 5 to 10 minutes. 6. While the beef is cooking, in a large bowl whisk together the lime juice, the remaining 5 tablespoons oil, the remaining 1 teaspoon dried oregano and 1 teaspoon each salt and pepper. Set aside. 7. Once the meat is done, use a slotted spoon to transfer the meat and onion to a medium bowl; do not discard the liquid remaining in the pot. With two forks, shred the beef into bite-size pieces. Whisk the dressing to recombine. Add 120ml of the dressing, the olives and 60ml of the reserved cooking liquid to the shredded meat, then toss to coat. Let cool to room temperature. 8. Whisk the remaining dressing once again. Add the lettuce, radishes and coriander to it, then toss to coat. Transfer to a platter and top with the beef and the avocado. Serve with lime wedges.

Per Serving: Calories 162; Fat 5.3g; Sodium 1006mg; Carbs 3g; Fiber 2g; Sugar 0g; Protein 25g

Delicious Beef Picadillo

Prep time: 5 minutes | Cook time: 15 minutes | Serves: 4

2 tablespoons salted butter	3 tablespoons tomato paste
1 large red onion, halved and thinly sliced	675g 85 percent lean beef mince
Salt and ground black pepper	240ml low-sodium beef stock
1 tablespoon ground cumin	110g golden raisins, divided
2 teaspoons dried oregano	100g pimiento-stuffed green olives, chopped
2 medium garlic cloves, finely chopped	10g chopped fresh coriander

1. Move the slider towards "AIR FRY/STOVETOP" and set Ninja Foodi XL Pressure Cooker Steam Fryer with SmartLid to SEAR/SAUTÉ mode. Adjust the temperature to "Hi5" by using up arrow. Press START/STOP to begin cooking. 2. Add the butter and let melt. Add the onion and 1 teaspoon salt, then cook, stirring often, until golden brown at the edges, 5 to 7 minutes. Stir in the cumin, oregano and garlic, then cook until fragrant, about 30 seconds. Stir in the tomato paste and cook until the paste begins to brown, about 1 minute. 3. Stir in the beef and stock, scraping up any browned bits and breaking the meat into smaller pieces. Stir in 35 g of raisins, then distribute the mixture in an even layer. 4. Lock lid; move slider to PRESSURE. Make sure the pressure release valve is in the SEAL position. The cooking temperature will default to HIGH, which is accurate. Set time to 12 minutes. Press START/STOP to cooking. 5. When pressure cooking is complete, let the pressure release naturally for 10 minutes, then quickly release the remaining steam by turning it into VENT position. 6. Then carefully open the lid. Using a large spoon, skim off and discard the fat from the surface. Select SEAR/SAUTÉ mode again. Stir in the olives and the remaining raisins, then cook, breaking up large clumps of beef with a wooden spoon, until most of the liquid has evaporated and the mixture begins to sizzle, 5 to

7 minutes. 7. Press START/STOP to turn off the pot. Taste and season with salt and pepper, then stir in the coriander.

Per Serving: Calories 139; Fat 3.2g; Sodium 45mg; Carbs 26g; Fiber 4g; Sugar 8g; Protein 3g

Braised Beef with Pancettaand Red Wine

Prep time: 5 minutes | Cook time: 35 minutes | Serves: 6

2–2.5kg boneless beef chuck roast, pulled apart at the natural seams into 3 pieces, trimmed, each piece tied with twine at 2.5 cm intervals	trimmed and quartered
	3 medium garlic cloves, thinly sliced
1 teaspoon grated nutmeg	2 tablespoons tomato paste
Salt and ground black pepper	60ml dry red wine
1 teaspoon extra-virgin olive oil	3 tablespoons plain flour
150g pancetta, chopped	20g roughly chopped fresh flat-leaf parsley
200g cremini mushrooms,	5g chopped fresh tarragon

1. In a small bowl, mix together the nutmeg, 2 teaspoons salt and 1 teaspoon pepper. 2. Use to season the beef on all sides. Move the slider towards "AIR FRY/STOVETOP" and set Ninja Foodi XL Pressure Cooker Steam Fryer with SmartLid to SEAR/SAUTÉ mode. Adjust the temperature to "Hi5" by using up arrow. Press START/STOP to begin cooking. 3. Add the oil and pancetta, then cook, stirring occasionally, until the pancetta has rendered its fat but is not yet crisp, 3 to 5 minutes. Stir in the mushrooms and ½ teaspoon each salt and pepper. Cook, stirring occasionally, until the liquid released by the mushrooms has evaporated and the mushrooms begin to brown, 6 to 8 minutes. 4. Add the garlic and cook, stirring, until fragrant, 1 to 2 minutes. Using a slotted spoon, transfer the mixture to a bowl and set aside. To the fat remaining in the pot, add the tomato paste and cook, stirring occasionally, until browned, 1 to 2 minutes. Add the wine and 60ml water, scraping up any browned bits. Nestle the beef in the pot. 5. Lock lid; move slider to PRESSURE. Make sure the pressure release valve is in the SEAL position. The cooking temperature will default to HIGH, which is accurate. Set time to 60 minutes. Press START/STOP to cooking. 6. When pressure cooking is complete, let the pressure release naturally for 25 minutes, then quickly release the remaining steam by turning it into VENT position. Then carefully open the lid. 7. Transfer the beef to a cutting board and tent with foil. Using a large spoon, skim off and discard the fat from the surface of the cooking liquid. In a small bowl, whisk the flour with about 60ml of the cooking liquid until smooth, then stir into the pot along with the mushroom mixture. 8. Select SEAR/SAUTÉ mode again. Bring the mixture to a simmer and cook, stirring often, until lightly thickened, 3 to 5 minutes. Press START/STOP to turn off the pot. 9. Stir in the parsley and tarragon, then taste and season with salt and pepper. Cut the beef into 2 cm slices against the grain, removing the twine as you go. Arrange the slices on a platter, then pour the sauce over the top.

Per Serving: Calories 203; Fat 10.9g; Sodium 402mg; Carbs 2g; Fiber 0g; Sugar 1g; Protein 23g

Pork Tenderloin with Pepper Glaze

Prep time: 10 minutes | Cook time: 20 minutes | Serves: 6

120ml apple juice	Sea salt
120g hot pepper jelly	Freshly ground black pepper
2 tablespoons apple cider vinegar	120ml water
675g pork tenderloin	1½ teaspoons corn flour

1. In the cooking pot, combine the apple juice, hot pepper jelly, and vinegar. Whisk together until a sauce forms. 2. Season the pork with salt and pepper and add the pork tenderloin and water to the pot. 3. Lock lid; move slider to PRESSURE. Make sure the pressure release valve is in the SEAL position. The cooking temperature will default to HIGH, which is accurate. Set time to 15 minutes. Press START/STOP to cooking. When pressure cooking is complete, let the pressure release naturally. 4. Remove the lid and transfer the pork to a cutting board. 5. Move the slider towards "AIR FRY/STOVETOP" and set Ninja Foodi XL Pressure Cooker Steam Fryer with SmartLid to SEAR/SAUTÉ mode. Adjust the temperature to "Hi5" by using up arrow. Press START/STOP to begin cooking. Add the corn flour and whisk until the sauce thickens, about 5 minutes. 6. Slice the pork and serve with the sauce on top.

Per Serving: Calories 153; Fat 39g; Sodium 108mg; Carbs 25g; Fiber 6g; Sugar 2g; Protein 37g

Rib Ragu with Pappardelle

Prep time: 5 minutes | Cook time: 35 minutes | Serves: 4

1 tablespoon extra-virgin olive oil
1 large yellow onion, finely chopped
1 large fennel bulb, trimmed, halved, cored and roughly chopped, divided
Salt and ground black pepper
8 medium garlic cloves, smashed and peeled
2 tablespoons tomato paste
240ml dry red wine
700g can whole peeled tomatoes, crushed by hand
5 cm piece Parmesan cheese rind,
plus finely grated Parmesan, to serve
1.1kg boneless beef short ribs, trimmed and cut into 2.5 cm chunks
3 medium carrots, peeled and finely chopped
120g heavy cream
3 tablespoons finely chopped fresh flat-leaf parsley
300g dried pappardelle pasta, cooked until al dente and drained
1.2L of the ragu

1. Move the slider towards "AIR FRY/STOVETOP" and set Ninja Foodi XL Pressure Cooker Steam Fryer with SmartLid to SEAR/SAUTÉ mode. Adjust the temperature to "Hi5" by using up arrow. Press START/STOP to begin cooking. 2. Add the oil and heat until shimmering, then add the onion, half of the fennel and ½ teaspoon salt. Cook, stirring occasionally, until softened, about 5 minutes. Stir in the garlic and tomato paste and cook until fragrant, about 30 seconds. 3. Add the wine and cook, stirring occasionally, until the liquid has almost fully evaporated, about 4 minutes. Stir in the tomatoes with their juice, add the Parmesan rind and the beef, then distribute in an even layer. 4. Lock lid; move slider to PRESSURE. Make sure the pressure release valve is in the SEAL position. The cooking temperature will default to HIGH, which is accurate. Set time to 30 minutes. Press START/STOP to cooking. 5. When pressure cooking is complete, let the pressure reduce quickly by turning it into VENT position. Then carefully open the lid. Remove and discard the Parmesan rind. (Using a potato masher, mash the beef until shredded. Stir in the carrots, the remaining fennel and the cream. 6. Select SEAR/SAUTÉ mode again and cook, stirring occasionally, until the sauce thickens slightly and the carrots are tender, 10 to 15 minutes. Stir in the parsley, then taste and season with salt and pepper. 7. In a large warmed bowl or the pot used to cook the pasta, toss the pasta with about 1.2L of the ragu. Serve sprinkled with Parmesan and pass the remaining sauce at the table.
Per Serving: Calories 463; Fat 15.5g; Sodium 553mg; Carbs 366g; Fiber 3g; Sugar 3g; Protein 41g

Austrian Beef with Root Vegetables

Prep time: 10 minutes | Cook time: 25 minutes | Serves: 6

2 tablespoons grapeseed or other neutral oil
1 large yellow onion, cut into 6 wedges
6 medium carrots, peeled and cut into 8 cm lengths, thicker pieces halved lengthwise
6 medium parsnips, peeled and cut into 15 cm lengths, thicker pieces halved lengthwise
2L boneless beef chuck roast, pulled apart at the natural seams into 3 pieces, trimmed, each piece
tied at 2.5 cm intervals
720ml low-sodium beef stock
5 bay leaves
2 tablespoons caraway seeds
2 tablespoons allspice berries
2 thyme sprigs
Salt and ground black pepper
900g red potatoes (about 5 cm in diameter), halved
3 dill sprigs, plus 5 cm chopped fresh dill
Prepared horseradish and/or Dijon mustard, to serve

1. Move the slider towards "AIR FRY/STOVETOP" and set Ninja Foodi XL Pressure Cooker Steam Fryer with SmartLid to SEAR/SAUTÉ mode. Adjust the temperature to "Hi5" by using up arrow. Press START/STOP to begin cooking. 2. Add the oil and heat until shimmering, then stir in the onion and cook, stirring, until softened and golden brown at the edges, 5 to 7 minutes. Add 4 pieces each of carrot and parsnip, then nestle in the beef. Add the stock, bay, caraway, allspice, thyme and 1 tablespoon pepper. 3. Lock lid; move slider to PRESSURE. Make sure the pressure release valve is in the SEAL position. The cooking temperature will default to HIGH, which is accurate. Set time to 60 minutes. Press START/STOP to cooking. 4. When pressure cooking is complete, let the pressure release naturally for 25 minutes, then quickly release the remaining steam by turning it into VENT position. Then carefully open the lid. 5. Place the beef to a cutting board and tent with foil. Using potholders, carefully remove the insert from the housing and pour the stock into a fine mesh strainer set over a medium bowl; discard the solids in the strainer. Use a wide

spoon to skim off and discard the fat from the surface of the cooking liquid, then return the liquid to the pot. Add the remaining carrots, the remaining parsnips and the potatoes, distributing them evenly. 6. Lock the lid, move slider to PRESSURE. Make sure the pressure release valve is in the SEAL position. The cooking temperature will default to HIGH, which is accurate. Set time to 7 minutes. Press START/STOP to cooking. 7. When pressure cooking is complete, let the pressure reduce quickly by turning it into VENT position. Then carefully open the lid. Using a slotted spoon, transfer the vegetables to a large platter and tent with foil. 8. Add the dill sprigs to the cooking liquid. Cut the meat against the grain into 1.5 cm slices, removing the twine as you go. Place the slices on the platter with the vegetables. Taste the stock and season with salt and pepper. 9. Remove and discard the dill sprigs, then ladle about 240 ml of the stock over the meat and sprinkle with the chopped dill. 10. Serve with the remaining stock on the side and with horseradish and/or mustard.
Per Serving: Calories 494; Fat 36g; Sodium 690mg; Carbs 17g; Fiber 11g; Sugar 2g; Protein 28g

Pork Ragu

Prep time: 5 minutes | Cook time: 45 minutes | Serves: 6

1 tablespoon olive oil
675g pork tenderloin, cut into 8 cm chunks
1 (700g) can crushed tomatoes
120ml water
3 carrots, cut into 1.5 cm chunks
3 shallots or 1 small onion, chopped
3 garlic cloves, minced
1 tablespoon Italian seasoning

1. In the Ninja Foodi XL Pressure Cooker Steam Fryer with SmartLid cooking pot, combine the olive oil, pork, crushed tomatoes, water, carrots, shallots, garlic, and Italian seasoning. 2. Lock lid; move slider to PRESSURE. Make sure the pressure release valve is in the SEAL position. The cooking temperature will default to HIGH, which is accurate. Set time to 45 minutes. Press START/STOP to cooking. When pressure cooking is complete, let the pressure release naturally for at least 10 minutes. 3. Remove the lid, transfer the pork to a medium bowl, and shred it using two forks. Return the pork to the juices and serve.
Per Serving: Calories 144; Fat 6.6g; Sodium 171mg; Carbs 2g; Fiber 0g; Sugar 1g; Protein 19g

Smoky Barbecue Pork Chop Sandwiches

Prep time: 5 minutes | Cook time: 25 minutes | Serves: 10

For the pork
1 tablespoon butter
1 small onion, chopped
2 garlic cloves, minced
10 (200g) boneless pork chops (2.5 cm thick)
240g Sweet and Smoky Barbecue
For the sandwiches
10 hamburger buns
1 head lettuce, separated into large lettuce leaves
Sauce or store-bought
240ml water
105g packed light brown sugar
1 tablespoon Worcestershire sauce
1 tablespoon apple cider vinegar

3 tomatoes, sliced
125g yellow mustard
Sliced pickles

1. To make the pork: Move the slider towards "AIR FRY/STOVETOP" and set Ninja Foodi XL Pressure Cooker Steam Fryer with SmartLid to SEAR/SAUTÉ mode. Adjust the temperature to "Hi5" by using up arrow. Press START/STOP to begin cooking and let the pot heat up for 2 minutes. 2. Add the butter, onion, and garlic and sauté for 2 minutes, or until the onion is translucent. 3. Add the pork chops, barbecue sauce, water, brown sugar, Worcestershire sauce, and vinegar. 4. Lock lid; move slider to PRESSURE. Make sure the pressure release valve is in the SEAL position. The cooking temperature will default to HIGH, which is accurate. Set time to 20 minutes. Press START/STOP to cooking. 5. When pressure cooking is complete, let the pressure release naturally for at least 10 minutes. 6. To make the sandwiches: Set out the buns and all the fixings and let people assemble their own sandwiches.
Per Serving: Calories 143; Fat 7.5g; Sodium 5mg; Carbs 19g; Fiber 3g; Sugar 3g; Protein 3g

Delicious Ropa Vieja

Prep time: 5 minutes | Cook time: 35 minutes | Serves: 8

2 tablespoons extra-virgin olive oil
2 medium white onions, halved and thinly sliced
2 medium red peppers, stemmed, seeded and sliced ½ cm thick
2 jalapeño chilies, stemmed and sliced into thin rounds
10 medium garlic cloves, smashed and peeled
Salt and ground black pepper
2½ tablespoons ground cumin
2½ tablespoons ground coriander
700g can whole peeled tomatoes, drained, 60ml juices reserved, tomatoes crushed by hand
1.3kg flank steak, halved lengthwise with the grain, then cut across the grain into 4 cm-wide strips
135g pimiento-stuffed green olives, roughly chopped
3 tablespoons lime juice, plus lime wedges to serve

1. Move the slider towards "AIR FRY/STOVETOP" and set Ninja Foodi XL Pressure Cooker Steam Fryer with SmartLid to SEAR/SAUTÉ mode. Adjust the temperature to "Hi5" by using up arrow. Press START/STOP to begin cooking. 2. Add the oil and heat until shimmering. Add the onions, peppers, jalapeños, garlic and 2 teaspoons salt, then cook, stirring occasionally, until the vegetables are softened and beginning to brown, about 10 minutes. Stir in the cumin and coriander, then cook until fragrant, about 30 seconds. 3. Add the tomatoes and reserved juices, scraping up any browned bits. Add the meat and stir to combine, then distribute in an even layer. 4. Lock lid; move slider to PRESSURE. Make sure the pressure release valve is in the SEAL position. The cooking temperature will default to HIGH, which is accurate. Set time to 20 minutes. Press START/STOP to cooking. 5. When pressure cooking is complete, let the pressure release naturally for 25 minutes, then quickly release the remaining steam by turning it into VENT position. Then carefully open the lid. 6. Using a slotted spoon, place the beef and peppers to a large bowl. Select SEAR/SAUTÉ mode again. Bring the cooking liquid to a simmer and cook, stirring often, until reduced and slightly thickened, about 15 minutes. Press START/STOP to turn off the pot. 7. Pour off and discard any accumulated liquid in the bowl with the beef. Using 2 forks or your fingers, shred the meat. Stir the meat, olives and lime juice into the reduced cooking liquid in the pot. 8. Taste and sprinkle with salt and pepper. Serve with lime wedges.
Per Serving: Calories 387; Fat 26.3g; Sodium 602mg; Carbs 12g; Fiber 8g; Sugar 1g; Protein 26g

Savory-Sweet Braised Beef

Prep time: 5 minutes | Cook time: 40 minutes | Serves: 6

2L boneless beef chuck roast, pulled apart at the natural seams into 3 pieces, trimmed, each piece tied at 2.5 cm intervals
Salt and ground black pepper
2 tablespoons grapeseed or other neutral oil
1 large yellow onion, chopped
10 medium garlic cloves, smashed and peeled
2 tablespoons tomato paste
105g packed dark brown sugar
2 cinnamon sticks
1 tablespoon allspice berries
240ml dry red wine
60ml Worcestershire sauce
250g pitted prunes, roughly chopped
1½ tablespoons corn flour
3 to 4 tablespoons red wine vinegar

1. Season the beef on all sides with salt and pepper. 2. Move the slider towards "AIR FRY/STOVETOP" and set Ninja Foodi XL Pressure Cooker Steam Fryer with SmartLid to SEAR/SAUTÉ mode. Adjust the temperature to "Hi5" by using up arrow. Press START/STOP to begin cooking. 3. Add the oil and heat until shimmering. Add the onion and ½ teaspoon salt, then cook, stirring occasionally, until the onion is well browned, about 9 minutes. Add the garlic and cook, stirring, until fragrant, about 30 seconds. 4. Add the tomato paste and cook, stirring constantly, until it begins to brown, about 1 minute. Stir in the sugar, cinnamon, allspice and 1 teaspoon pepper, then add the wine, scraping up any browned bits. Bring to a simmer and cook, stirring occasionally, until thick and syrupy, 3 to 5 minutes. Stir in the Worcestershire sauce, prunes and 240ml water. Nestle the beef in the pot. 5. Lock lid; move slider to PRESSURE. Make sure the pressure release valve is in the SEAL position. The cooking temperature will default to HIGH, which is accurate. Set time to 60 minutes. Press START/STOP to cooking. 6. When pressure cooking is complete, let the pressure release naturally for 25 minutes, then quickly release the remaining steam by turning it into VENT position. Then carefully open the lid. 7. Place the beef to a cutting board and tent with foil. Set a fine mesh strainer over a medium bowl. Using potholders, carefully remove the insert from the housing and pour the contents of the pot into the strainer. 8. Press on the solids with a silicone spatula to extract as much liquid and pulp as possible; scrape the underside of the strainer to collect the pulp. Discard the solids. Let the liquid and pulp settle for about 5 minutes, then use a large spoon to skim off and discard the fat on the surface; you should have about 600ml defatted liquid. Return the liquid to the pot. 9. Select SEAR/SAUTÉ mode again. Bring to a simmer and cook, stirring occasionally, until slightly reduced, about 10 minutes. In a small bowl, stir together the corn flour and 3 tablespoons water. 10. Whisk into the simmering liquid and cook, stirring constantly, until lightly thickened, about 2 minutes. Press START/STOP to turn off the pot. Stir in the vinegar, then taste and season with salt and pepper. Cut the beef into 1.5 cm slices against the grain, removing the twine as you go. 11. Arrange the slices on a platter, then pour about 240ml of the sauce over the top. Serve with the remaining sauce on the side.
Per Serving: Calories 184; Fat 7.4g; Sodium 103mg; Carbs 7g; Fiber 1g; Sugar 1g; Protein 22g

Chapter 5 Soup, Stew, and Chili Recipes

Mexican-Style Chicken Noodle Soup

Prep time: 5 minutes | Cook time: 15 minutes | Serves: 8

2 tablespoons (28g) grass-fed butter, ghee or avocado oil	1 tablespoon (8g) chili powder
1 large yellow onion, thickly sliced	1½ teaspoon (9g) sea salt
5 cloves garlic, finely minced	1½ teaspoon (4g) ground cumin
90g crushed tomatoes or diced fresh tomatoes	½ teaspoon ground coriander
½ small green cabbage, thickly sliced	½ teaspoon dried oregano
	½ teaspoon dried thyme
1 large celery rib, thickly sliced	80ml fresh lime juice
1.kg organic skinless, boneless chicken breast or thighs	210g gluten-free dried pasta; e.g., fusilli, macaroni, penne, egg noodles or broken-up tagliatelle
1.4L chicken stock	Fresh coriander, for garnish
355ml filtered water	Lime wedges, for garnish

1. Move the slider towards "AIR FRY/STOVETOP" and set Ninja Foodi XL Pressure Cooker Steam Fryer with SmartLid to SEAR/SAUTÉ mode. Adjust the temperature to "Hi5" by using up arrow. Press START/STOP to begin cooking. 2. Place your healthy fat of choice in it. Once the fat has melted, add the onion and sauté for 7 minutes, stirring occasionally, then add the garlic and continue to sauté for 1 minute, stirring occasionally. Add the tomatoes, cabbage, celery, chicken, stock, water, chili powder, salt, cumin, coriander, oregano, thyme and lime juice, then give the mixture a stir. Press START/STOP. 3. Lock lid; move slider towards PRESSURE. Adjust pressure release valve in the SEAL position. Close pressure-release valve. The cooking temperature will default to HIGH, which is accurate. Set time to 12 minutes. Select START/STOP and start cooking. 4. When cooking is complete, let pressure release quickly by turning it into VENT position. Transfer the chicken to a large plate and shred the meat, using the tines of two forks. Set aside. Move the slider towards "AIR FRY/STOVETOP" and set Ninja Foodi XL Pressure Cooker Steam Fryer with SmartLid to SEAR/SAUTÉ mode. Adjust the temperature to "Hi5" by using up arrow. 5. As soon as the soup comes to a boil, add the pasta. Cook your pasta al dente according to the package directions—usually this is anywhere from 4 to 8 minutes. Return the shredded chicken to the pot and give it a stir. 6. Serve immediately, garnished with chopped fresh coriander and lime wedges.

Per Serving: Calories 265; Fat 11.3g; Sodium 188mg; Carbs 9.2g; Fiber 1g; Sugar 1g; Protein 12.4g

Beef Spicy Pho

Prep time: 5 minutes | Cook time: 15 minutes | Serves: 4

455g boneless beef eye round	2 whole cloves
1 tablespoon (18g) salt, plus more to season the beef	1 bay leaf
Freshly ground black pepper	4 peppercorns
1 tablespoon rapeseed oil	2-star anise
2 small yellow onions, cut in half, skin on	30g dried shiitake mushrooms
	1.2L water
2 cloves garlic, smashed	710ml beef stock
1 cinnamon stick	270g ramen or udon noodles

Toppings:

shredded red cabbage, thinly sliced red onion, hot sauce, fresh	coriander, lime wedges, sliced jalapeño and sesame seeds

1. Season all sides of the beef with salt and pepper. Place the oil in the cooking pot. Move the slider towards "AIR FRY/STOVETOP" and set Ninja Foodi XL Pressure Cooker Steam Fryer with SmartLid to SEAR/SAUTÉ mode. Adjust the temperature to "Hi5" by using up arrow. Press START/STOP to begin cooking. 2. Once the oil is shimmering, add the beef. Sear each side of the beef for about 5 minutes. Add the onions, garlic, cinnamon stick, cloves, bay leaf, peppercorns, star anise and dried mushrooms to the pot as well. 3. Continue to sear the beef for 5 more minutes while stirring the vegetables and herbs around. Press START/STOP and then remove the beef, transferring it to a nearby plate. Tent with foil and let rest. Pour the water and stock into the pot and add the salt. Stir to combine. 4. Lock lid; move slider towards PRESSURE. Adjust pressure release valve in the SEAL position. Close pressure-release valve. The cooking temperature will default to HIGH, which is accurate. Set time to 20 minutes. Select START/STOP and start cooking. 5. When cooking is complete, let pressure release quickly by turning it into VENT position. Remove the lid. Use a fine-mesh strainer with a handle to remove the onions, garlic, mushrooms and spices from the stock. Discard the onions, garlic and spices, reserving the mushrooms. Add

the mushrooms back to the pot. 6. Move the slider towards "AIR FRY/STOVETOP" and set Ninja Foodi XL Pressure Cooker Steam Fryer with SmartLid to SEAR/SAUTÉ mode. Adjust the temperature to "Hi5" by using up arrow. Press START/STOP to begin cooking and wait a minute or two until the stock starts to bubble. Add the noodles and cook for 5 minutes, or until tender. Ladle the stock into bowls. 7. Use tongs to transfer the noodles to the bowls. Top with red cabbage, sliced red onion, hot sauce, fresh coriander, lime wedges, sliced jalapeño and sesame seeds.

Per Serving: Calories 275; Fat 11.3g; Sodium 511mg; Carbs 8.6g; Fiber 2g; Sugar 1g; Protein 9.5g

Spicy Beef with Broccoli Zoodle Soup

Prep time: 10 minutes | Cook time: 15 minutes | Serves: 5

2 tablespoons (30ml) avocado oil	1.4L beef stock
3 tablespoons (18g) minced fresh ginger	60ml rice vinegar
	60ml coconut aminos or soy sauce
2 cloves garlic, minced	60ml buffalo hot sauce or sriracha
680g top sirloin steak tips, about 2.5 cm pieces	1 large courgette, spiralized into noodles
270g fresh broccoli florets	35g chopped fresh green onion
22g sliced cremini mushrooms	

1. Move the slider towards "AIR FRY/STOVETOP" and set Ninja Foodi XL Pressure Cooker Steam Fryer with SmartLid to SEAR/SAUTÉ mode. Adjust the temperature to "Hi5" by using up arrow. Press START/STOP to begin cooking. 2. Once hot, add the oil, ginger, garlic and steak tips. Cook for a few minutes, until the beef is lightly browned on each side and the garlic and ginger are fragrant. Select START/STOP. Add the broccoli, mushrooms, beef stock, vinegar, coconut aminos and hot sauce and stir. At this point, you can remove and set aside the broccoli and add with the noodles after the soup has cooked, if you want the broccoli to be crisper. 3. Lock lid; move slider towards PRESSURE. Adjust pressure release valve in the SEAL position. Close pressure-release valve. The cooking temperature will default to HIGH, which is accurate. Set time to 8 minutes. Select START/STOP and start cooking. 4. When cooking is complete, let pressure release quickly by turning it into VENT position. Open the lid and add more hot sauce if you desire a spicier stock. 5. Add the spiralized courgette, top with fresh green onion and serve hot.

Per Serving: Calories 262; Fat 11.3g; Sodium 369mg; Carbs 10.4g; Fiber 2g; Sugar 1g; Protein 7.2g

Italian Tuscan Soup

Prep time: 5 minutes | Cook time: 15 minutes | Serves: 4

2 tablespoons (30ml) olive or avocado oil	1 teaspoon dried fennel
	1 teaspoon sea salt, plus more to taste
1 medium yellow onion, chopped	
3 cloves garlic, minced	135g chopped large-leaf curly kale
455g Italian sausage	120ml full-fat coconut milk or heavy cream
1.2L chicken stock	
3 large russet potatoes, peel on, cut into 2.5 cm chunks	1 to 2 teaspoon (1 to 2 g) crushed red pepper flakes
2 teaspoons (3g) dried basil	Freshly ground black pepper

1. Move the slider towards "AIR FRY/STOVETOP" and set Ninja Foodi XL Pressure Cooker Steam Fryer with SmartLid to SEAR/SAUTÉ mode. Adjust the temperature to "Hi5" by using up arrow. Press START/STOP to begin cooking. Once hot, coat the bottom of the pot with the oil. Add the onion and sauté for 2 to 3 minutes, then toss in the garlic and sausage. Brown the sausage until cooked, about 5 minutes. Select START/STOP. Pour the chicken stock over the sausage, then add the potatoes, basil, fennel and salt. 2. Lock lid; move slider towards PRESSURE. Adjust pressure release valve in the SEAL position. Close pressure-release valve. The cooking temperature will default to HIGH, which is accurate. Set time to 7 minutes. Select START/STOP and start cooking. 3. When cooking is complete, let pressure release quickly by turning it into VENT position. 4. Remove the lid and move the slider towards "AIR FRY/STOVETOP" and set Ninja Foodi XL Pressure Cooker Steam Fryer with SmartLid to SEAR/SAUTÉ mode. Adjust the temperature to "Hi5" by using up arrow. Press START/STOP to begin cooking. Add the kale. 5. Stir for a few minutes until the kale begins to wilt. Add the coconut milk. Season with red pepper flakes, and additional salt and pepper to taste.

Per Serving: Calories 246; Fat 12.3g; Sodium 114mg; Carbs 9.2g; Fiber 4g; Sugar 2g; Protein 10.3g

Cheesy Creamy Spinach Soup

Prep time: 10 minutes | Cook time: 15 minutes | Serves: 6

2 tablespoons (28g) grass-fed butter, ghee or avocado oil	1 teaspoon sea salt
1 yellow onion, peeled and diced	1 teaspoon dried thyme
5 fresh cloves garlic, finely minced	1 teaspoon dried dill
2 large celery ribs, thickly sliced	¼ teaspoon ground allspice
455g frozen organic spinach, thawed and moisture squeezed out	950ml chicken or vegetable stock
2 organic russet potatoes, peeled and cubed	225g sour cream, plus more for garnish
	115g shredded cheddar cheese
	Extra-virgin olive oil, for garnish

1. Move the slider towards "AIR FRY/STOVETOP" and set Ninja Foodi XL Pressure Cooker Steam Fryer with SmartLid to SEAR/SAUTÉ mode. Adjust the temperature to "Hi5" by using up arrow. Press START/STOP to begin cooking. Place your healthy fat of choice in the pot. 2. Once the fat has melted, add the onion and sauté for 7 minutes, stirring occasionally, then add the garlic and continue to sauté for 1 minute, stirring occasionally. Add the celery, spinach, potatoes, salt, thyme, dill, allspice and stock, then give the mixture a stir. Press START/STOP. 3. Lock lid; move slider towards PRESSURE. Adjust pressure release valve in the SEAL position. Close pressure-release valve. The cooking temperature will default to HIGH, which is accurate. Set NATURAL RELEASE and time to 9 minutes. Select START/STOP and start cooking. 4. When cooking is complete, let pressure release quickly by turning it into VENT position. In batches, ladle the soup into a blender, taking care to fill the blender only about halfway. Blend on a low setting just until pureed and combined. 5. Return the pureed soup to the pot and Move the slider towards "AIR FRY/STOVETOP" and set Ninja Foodi XL Pressure Cooker Steam Fryer with SmartLid to SEAR/SAUTÉ mode. Adjust the temperature to "Hi5" by using up arrow. Press START/STOP to begin cooking, bring to a boil and give it a few stirs. 6. Add the sour cream and cheese and stir until fully combined. Press START/STOP. 7. Serve immediately. Garnish with a dollop of sour cream or a drizzle of quality extra-virgin olive oil.

Per Serving: Calories 261; Fat 9.2g; Sodium 784mg; Carbs 7.3g; Fiber 1g; Sugar 2g; Protein 6.2g

Creamy Lasagna Soup

Prep time: 10 minutes | Cook time: 15 minutes | Serves: 8

3 tablespoons (45g) grass-fed butter, ghee or avocado oil	1.4L chicken or vegetable stock
455g grass-fed beef mince	210g gluten-free dried pasta; e.g. broken-up lasagna or tagliatelle
1 medium yellow onion, peeled and diced	2 large bunches fresh spinach, leaves only, cleaned well
225g cleaned white button or cremini mushrooms, thinly sliced	5g fresh basil leaves
5 cloves garlic, finely minced	120ml heavy cream
180g crushed tomatoes or diced fresh tomatoes	60g mascarpone or cream cheese
1 teaspoon sea salt	30g shredded mozzarella cheese, for garnish
1 teaspoon dried thyme	20g shredded Parmesan or Asiago cheese, for garnish
½ teaspoon dried oregano	Quality extra-virgin olive oil, for garnish
½ teaspoon finely chopped fresh rosemary leaves	

1. Move the slider towards "AIR FRY/STOVETOP" and set Ninja Foodi XL Pressure Cooker Steam Fryer with SmartLid to SEAR/SAUTÉ mode. Adjust the temperature to "Hi5" by using up arrow. Press START/STOP to begin cooking. 2. And place your healthy fat of choice in the pot. Once the fat has melted, add the beef mince and sauté for 7 minutes, stirring often, allowing the meat to brown, then place the cooked beef to a plate, set aside. Add the onion and mushrooms to the pot and sauté for 5 minutes, stirring occasionally, then add the garlic and continue to sauté for 1 minute, stirring occasionally. Add the cooked meat, tomatoes, salt, thyme, oregano, rosemary and stock, then give the mixture a stir. Press START/STOP. 3. Lock lid; move slider towards PRESSURE. Adjust pressure release valve in the SEAL position. Close pressure-release valve. The cooking temperature will default to HIGH, which is accurate. Set time to 5 minutes. Select START/STOP and start cooking. 4. When cooking is complete, let pressure release quickly by turning it into VENT position. Carefully open the lid. 5. Move the slider towards "AIR FRY/STOVETOP" and set Ninja Foodi XL Pressure Cooker Steam Fryer with SmartLid to SEAR/SAUTÉ mode. Adjust the temperature to "Hi5" by using up arrow. Press START/STOP to begin cooking.

As soon as the soup comes to a boil, add the pasta. Cook your pasta al dente usually this is anywhere from 4 to 8 minutes. Then, add the spinach and basil, stirring until the spinach has fully wilted. Press START/STOP. 6. Add the cream and mascarpone cheese, stirring until incorporated. Taste for seasoning and adjust the salt to taste. 7. Serve immediately. Garnish with the shredded cheeses and a drizzle of quality extra-virgin olive oil.

Per Serving: Calories 252; Fat 11.2g; Sodium 310mg; Carbs 10.3g; Fiber 3g; Sugar 1.5g; Protein 7.3g

Dropped Egg Soup

Prep time: 5 minutes | Cook time: 15 minutes | Serves: 6

950ml water	½ teaspoon black peppercorns
1 carrot, cut in half widthwise	1-star anise
2 celery ribs, cut in half widthwise	1 (2.5 cm) piece fresh ginger
1 yellow onion, cut in half	4 large eggs
1 clove garlic, peeled and smashed	4 teaspoons corn flour
1 teaspoon soy sauce	Freshly ground black pepper
½ teaspoon salt, plus a pinch	4 green onions, sliced

1. In the Ninja Foodi XL Pressure Cooker Steam Fryer with SmartLid cooking pot, combine the water, carrot, celery, onion, garlic, soy sauce, ½ teaspoon of salt, and the peppercorns, star anise and ginger. 2. Lock lid; move slider towards PRESSURE. Adjust pressure release valve in the SEAL position. Close pressure-release valve. The cooking temperature will default to HIGH, which is accurate. Set time to 10 minutes. Select START/STOP and start cooking. 3. When cooking is complete, let pressure release quickly by turning it into VENT position. Remove the lid. Insert a mesh strainer into a large bowl or stockpot. Pour the stock through the strainer into the bowl. Discard the vegetables and spices. Return the stock to the pot. 4. Move the slider towards "AIR FRY/STOVETOP" and set Ninja Foodi XL Pressure Cooker Steam Fryer with SmartLid to SEAR/SAUTÉ mode. Adjust the temperature to "Hi5" by using up arrow. Press START/STOP to begin cooking. 5. After 3 to 4 minutes, the stock should start to bubble up a bit. In small bowl, whisk together the eggs, corn flour and a pinch each of salt and pepper. Slowly pour the eggs into the stock while whisking the whole time. The eggs should start to form fine ribbons as they cook. 6. Press START/STOP and adjust the salt and pepper to taste. Top with the green onions.

Per Serving: Calories 354; Fat 7.9g; Sodium 704mg; Carbs 6g; Fiber 3.6g; Sugar 6g; Protein 18g

Thai Chicken Curry Soup with Veggies "Ramen"

Prep time: 5 minutes | Cook time: 15 minutes | Serves: 6

2 tablespoons (30ml) coconut oil	taste
½ large white onion, diced	1 yellow pepper, seeded and diced
1 tablespoon chopped fresh ginger	3 carrots, peeled and diced
3 cloves garlic, minced	680g chicken breast
710ml chicken stock	1 (400ml) can full-fat coconut milk
1 (410g) can fire-roasted diced tomatoes	Juice of 1 lime
2 tablespoons (30g) Thai red curry paste	2 large courgettes, spiralized into noodles
1 teaspoon sea salt, plus more to	10g chopped fresh coriander

1. Move the slider towards "AIR FRY/STOVETOP" and set Ninja Foodi XL Pressure Cooker Steam Fryer with SmartLid to SEAR/SAUTÉ mode. Adjust the temperature to "Hi5" by using up arrow. Press START/STOP to begin cooking. Coat the bottom of the pot with the oil, and once hot, add the onion. Cook for 2 to 3 minutes, then toss in the ginger and garlic. Once the vegetables are gently browned, about another 3 minutes, select START/STOP. 2. Add the chicken stock, fire-roasted tomatoes, Thai curry paste, salt, pepper, carrots and chicken. 3. Lock lid; move slider towards PRESSURE. Adjust pressure release valve in the SEAL position. Close pressure-release valve. The cooking temperature will default to HIGH, which is accurate. Set time to 8 minutes. Select START/STOP and start cooking. 4. When cooking is complete, let pressure release quickly by turning it into VENT position. 5. Remove the chicken breast and then shred with a fork and knife, then place the chicken back in the pot. Stir in the coconut milk, lime juice and spiralized courgette. Let stand for about 10 minutes before serving. 6. Pour into individual bowls and add additional salt to taste. Garnish with fresh coriander.

Per Serving: Calories 246; Fat 9.3g; Sodium 489mg; Carbs 8.1g; Fiber 2g; Sugar 3g; Protein 7.4g

Ham with Split Pea Soup

Prep time: 10 minutes | Cook time: 20 minutes | Serves: 6

2 teaspoons (10ml) olive oil	1 ham bone
1 medium onion, chopped	455g dried split peas
2 celery ribs, chopped	1 bay leaf
3 carrots, chopped	Coarse salt
1.4L chicken stock	Freshly ground black pepper

1. Move the slider towards "AIR FRY/STOVETOP" and set Ninja Foodi XL Pressure Cooker Steam Fryer with SmartLid to SEAR/SAUTÉ mode. Adjust the temperature to "Hi5" by using up arrow. Press START/STOP to begin cooking. Add the olive oil, then the onion, celery and carrots. Cook, stirring occasionally, until the onion is soft, about 5 minutes. Press START/STOP. 2. Add the chicken stock, taking care to scrape up any browned bits from the bottom of the pot. Add the ham bone, split peas and bay leaf. 3. Lock lid; move slider towards PRESSURE. Adjust pressure release valve in the SEAL position. Close pressure-release valve. The cooking temperature will default to HIGH, which is accurate. Set time to 20 minutes. Select START/STOP and start cooking. 4. When cooking is complete, let pressure release naturally for 10 minutes, then quick-release any remaining pressure by turning it into VENT position. 5. Carefully remove the lid. Remove the ham bone, and any meat that fell from the ham bone, from the pot. Remove and discard the bay leaf. 6. Using an immersion blender, puree the soup until smooth. Remove the meat from the ham bone and add it and any other meat that was removed back to the pot. 7. Season well with salt and pepper, then serve.
Per Serving: Calories 253; Fat 11.2g; Sodium 333mg; Carbs 8.4g; Fiber 2g; Sugar 1g; Protein 6.5g

Tomatoes Stuffed Pepper Soup

Prep time: 15 minutes | Cook time: 15 minutes | Serves: 5

2 tablespoons (30ml) extra-virgin olive oil	475 ml beef stock
1 yellow onion, diced	2 tablespoons (30ml) red wine vinegar
3 cloves garlic, minced	2 teaspoons (5g) Italian seasoning
455g beef mince	2 teaspoons (10g) sea salt
2 green peppers, seeded and diced	340g cooked rice or 220g cauliflower rice
1 red pepper, seeded and diced	20g shredded Parmesan cheese, for garnish
2 (410g) cans fire-roasted diced tomatoes	Fresh basil, for garnish
1 (425g) can tomato sauce	

1. Move the slider towards "AIR FRY/STOVETOP" and set Ninja Foodi XL Pressure Cooker Steam Fryer with SmartLid to SEAR/SAUTÉ mode. Adjust the temperature to "Hi5" by using up arrow. Press START/STOP to begin cooking. 2. Coat the bottom of the pot with oil, then add the onion and garlic. Sauté for 3 to 4 minutes, then add the beef mince. Continue to cook until the beef is no longer pink, about 3 to 4 minutes. Select START/STOP. Top the beef mixture with the peppers, diced tomatoes, tomato sauce, beef stock, red wine vinegar, Italian seasoning and salt. 3. Lock lid; move slider towards PRESSURE. Adjust pressure release valve in the SEAL position. Close pressure-release valve. The cooking temperature will default to HIGH, which is accurate. Set time to 6 minutes. Select START/STOP and start cooking. 4. When cooking is complete, let pressure release quickly by turning it into VENT position. Stir in the rice or cauliflower rice. 5. Serve hot and garnish with Parmesan cheese and fresh basil.
Per Serving: Calories 263; Fat 11.2g; Sodium 218mg; Carbs 8.6g; Fiber 1.6g; Sugar 2.3g; Protein 8.2g

Delicious Zuppa Toscana

Prep time: 10 minutes | Cook time: 20 minutes | Serves: 6

455g hot Italian sausage, casings removed	stock
	200g chopped kale
1 small onion, chopped	240ml heavy cream
4 to 5 cloves garlic, minced	Coarse salt
450g diced red potatoes	Freshly ground black pepper
945ml to 1.2L low-sodium chicken	

1. Move the slider towards "AIR FRY/STOVETOP" and set Ninja Foodi XL Pressure Cooker Steam Fryer with SmartLid to SEAR/SAUTÉ mode. Adjust the temperature to "Hi5" by using up arrow. Press START/STOP to begin cooking. 2. Add the sausage. Cook until the sausage is browned, about 5 minutes. Add the onion and cook until the onion is soft, about 5 minutes, stirring frequently. Add the garlic and cook for 1 more minute, stirring frequently. Add the potatoes and chicken stock, taking care to scrape any browned bits from the bottom. 3. Lock lid; move slider towards PRESSURE. Adjust pressure release valve in the SEAL position. Close pressure-release valve. The cooking temperature will default to HIGH, which is accurate. Set time to 12 minutes. Select START/STOP and start cooking. 4. When cooking is complete, let pressure release quickly by turning it into VENT position. Carefully remove the lid. Add the kale and cream, stirring until the kale is wilted. 5. Season generously with salt and pepper.
Per Serving: Calories 253; Fat 12.2g; Sodium 245mg; Carbs 11.4g; Fiber 3g; Sugar 1g; Protein 7.6g

Spicy Buffalo Chicken Chowder

Prep time: 10 minutes | Cook time: 15 minutes | Serves: 4

2 tablespoons (30ml) olive oil	1.2L chicken stock
1 white or yellow onion, chopped	175ml buffalo hot sauce
600g chicken breast	160ml full-fat canned coconut milk
120g diced celery	
130g diced carrot	10g fresh coriander, for garnish
225g diced Yukon gold potato	

1. Move the slider towards "AIR FRY/STOVETOP" and set Ninja Foodi XL Pressure Cooker Steam Fryer with SmartLid to SEAR/SAUTÉ mode. Adjust the temperature to "Hi5" by using up arrow. Press START/STOP to begin cooking. 2. Coat the bottom of the pot with the oil once hot, add the onion and sauté for 2 to 3 minutes. Select START/STOP. Place the chicken in the Ninja Foodi XL Pressure Cooker Steam Fryer with SmartLid cooking pot first. Then add the celery, carrot, potato, chicken stock and buffalo sauce on top of the chicken. 3. Lock lid; move slider towards PRESSURE. Adjust pressure release valve in the SEAL position. Close pressure-release valve. The cooking temperature will default to HIGH, which is accurate. Set time to 12 minutes. Select START/STOP and start cooking. 4. When cooking is complete, let pressure release quickly by turning it into VENT position. Once the steam is completely released, remove the lid. Add the coconut milk. 5. Top with the fresh coriander and serve.
Per Serving: Calories 243; Fat 8.4g; Sodium 404mg; Carbs 6.3g; Fiber 2g; Sugar 1.5g; Protein 6.2g

Thai Tropical Red Soup

Prep time: 5 minutes | Cook time: 19 minutes | Serves: 6

1 tablespoon extra-virgin olive oil	840ml water
½ yellow onion, chopped	2 teaspoons fine sea salt
455g carrots	840ml full-fat coconut milk
455g sweet potatoes	6 tablespoons dried cranberries
2 cloves garlic, minced	6 tablespoons hulled pumpkin seeds
2 teaspoons curry powder	
1 tablespoon minced fresh ginger (about 2.5 cm knob)	6 tablespoons chopped fresh coriander

1. Move the slider towards "AIR FRY/STOVETOP" and Set Ninja Foodi XL Pressure Cooker Steam Fryer with SmartLid to SEAR/SAUTÉ mode. Adjust the temperature to "Hi5" by using up arrow. Press START/STOP to begin cooking and add the olive oil to the pot. 2. Once the oil is hot but not smoking, add the onion and sauté until tender, about 8 minutes, stirring occasionally so it doesn't stick. Meanwhile, peel and chop the carrots and sweet potatoes into 2.5 cm chunks. 3. Once the onion is tender, add the garlic, curry powder, and ginger and stir with a wooden spoon or spatula just until fragrant, about 1 minute. Add the carrots, sweet potatoes, water, and salt and use the spoon to scrape the bottom of the cooking pot to make sure nothing has stuck. 4. Lock lid; move slider towards PRESSURE. Adjust pressure release valve in the SEAL position. Close pressure-release valve. The cooking temperature will default to HIGH, which is accurate. Set time to 10 minutes. Select START/STOP and start cooking. 5. When cooking is complete, let pressure release naturally. Remove the lid and use an immersion blender to blend the soup directly in the pot until very smooth. Stir in the coconut milk and adjust the seasonings to taste. 6. Serve warm with 1 tablespoon each dried cranberries, pumpkin seeds, and coriander sprinkled over each serving. Store leftovers in an airtight container in the fridge for 5 days.
Per Serving: Calories 256; Fat 9.4g; Sodium 347mg; Carbs 8.6g; Fiber 5g; Sugar 2g; Protein 7.4g

Delicious Colombian Chicken Soup

Prep time: 5 minutes | Cook time: 25 minutes | Serves: 6

2 teaspoons (10ml) olive oil	bite-size pieces
1 medium onion, chopped	195g frozen corn kernels
1 celery rib, chopped	1 tablespoon (15ml) fresh lime
3 cloves garlic, minced	juice
½ teaspoon dried oregano	1g chopped fresh coriander
945ml chicken stock	Coarse salt
905g boneless, skinless chicken	Freshly ground black pepper
breast, cut into bite-size pieces	1 avocado, peeled, pitted and
455g baby red potatoes, cut into	chopped

1. Move the slider towards "AIR FRY/STOVETOP" and set Ninja Foodi XL Pressure Cooker Steam Fryer with SmartLid to SEAR/SAUTÉ mode. Adjust the temperature to "Hi5" by using up arrow. Press START/STOP to begin cooking. 2. Add the onion and celery to the pot. Cook, stirring frequently, until the onion is soft, about 5 minutes. Add the garlic, oregano and cook for 1 more minute. Press START/STOP to turn off the pot. 3. Add the chicken stock, taking care to scrape up any browned bits from the bottom of the pot. Add the chicken, potatoes and corn. 4. Lock lid; move slider towards PRESSURE. Make sure the pressure release valve is in the SEAL position. The cooking temperature will default to HIGH, which is accurate. And set time to 20 minutes. Press START/STOP to cooking. 5. When cooking is complete, let pressure release quickly by turning it into VENT position. Carefully remove the lid. Stir in the lime juice and coriander. Season well with salt and pepper. 6. Serve in bowls, topped with avocado.
Per Serving: Calories 253; Fat 11.3g; Sodium 411mg; Carbs 8.6g; Fiber 1g; Sugar 2g; Protein 7.2g

Bean Tuscan Soup

Prep time: 10 minutes | Cook time: 25 minutes | Serves: 6

2 teaspoons (10ml) olive oil	tomatoes
1 medium onion, chopped	2 (425g) cans white beans
2 celery ribs, chopped	1 bay leaf
2 carrots, chopped	340g fresh spinach leaves
3 cloves garlic, minced	Coarse salt
½ teaspoon Italian seasoning	Freshly ground black pepper
945 ml chicken stock	50g grated Parmesan cheese
2 (410g) cans fire-roasted diced	

1. Move the slider towards "AIR FRY/STOVETOP" and set Ninja Foodi XL Pressure Cooker Steam Fryer with SmartLid to SEAR/SAUTÉ mode. Adjust the temperature to "Hi5" by using up arrow. Press START/STOP to begin cooking. Add the olive oil, then the onion, celery and carrots to the pot. Cook, stirring frequently, until the onion is soft, about 5 minutes. 2. Add the garlic, Italian seasoning. Then cook for 1 minute more. Press START/STOP to turn off the pot. Add the chicken stock to the pot, taking care to scrape up any browned bits from the bottom of the pot. Add the fire-roasted tomatoes, beans and bay leaf. 3. Lock lid; move slider towards PRESSURE. Adjust pressure release valve in the SEAL position. Close pressure-release valve. The cooking temperature will default to HIGH, which is accurate. Set time to 20 minutes. Select START/STOP and start cooking. 4. When cooking is complete, let pressure release quickly by turning it into VENT position. Remove the bay leaf. Add the spinach leaves and then stir until wilted. 5. Season well with salt and pepper. Top each bowl with some grated Parmesan.
Per Serving: Calories 246; Fat 10.4g; Sodium 368mg; Carbs 8.6g; Fiber 4g; Sugar 4g; Protein 8.4g

Five-Ingredient Bean Soup

Prep time: 5 minutes | Cook time: 5 minutes | Serves: 2

475ml chicken or vegetable stock	½ yellow onion, diced
195g jarred salsa	Salt
1 (850g) can black beans, drained	Freshly ground black pepper
and rinsed	Fresh coriander, lime, sour cream
1 jalapeño, seeded and diced	and avocado, for garnish

1. In the Ninja Foodi XL Pressure Cooker Steam Fryer with SmartLid cooking pot, combine all the ingredients except for the garnishes, including salt and pepper to taste. 2. Lock lid; move slider towards PRESSURE. Adjust pressure release valve in the SEAL position. Close pressure-release valve. The cooking temperature will default to HIGH, which is accurate. Set time to 5 minutes. Select START/STOP and start cooking. 3. When cooking is complete, let pressure release quickly by turning it into VENT position. Remove the lid and use an immersion blender to puree about half of the soup. 4. You still want to see a few beans in the soup. Adjust the salt and pepper to taste and top with coriander, lime, sour cream and avocado.
Per Serving: Calories 252; Fat 10.3g; Sodium 277mg; Carbs 7.6g; Fiber 3g; Sugar 4g; Protein 8.7g

Garlicky Green Chickpea Soup

Prep time: 5 minutes | Cook time: 10 minutes | Serves: 8

2 tablespoons (30g) grass-fed	1 teaspoon sea salt
butter, ghee or avocado oil	½ teaspoon dried thyme
1 yellow onion, peeled and diced	½ teaspoon ground allspice
225g cleaned white button or	1.4L chicken or vegetable stock
cremini mushrooms, thinly sliced	2 large bunches fresh spinach
7 cloves garlic, finely minced	(680g total), leaves only, cleaned
2 large celery ribs, thinly sliced	well
1 organic russet potato, peeled and	480g canned or cooked chickpeas
diced	Sour cream, for garnish
1 tablespoon ground cumin	Quality extra-virgin olive oil, for
1 teaspoon ground coriander	garnish

1. Move the slider towards "AIR FRY/STOVETOP" and set Ninja Foodi XL Pressure Cooker Steam Fryer with SmartLid to SEAR/SAUTÉ mode. Adjust the temperature to "Hi5" by using up arrow. Press START/STOP to begin cooking. Place your healthy fat of choice in the pot. 2. Once the fat has melted, add the onion and mushrooms and sauté for 7 minutes, stirring occasionally, then add the garlic and continue to sauté for 1 minute, stirring occasionally. Add the celery, potato, cumin, coriander, salt, thyme, allspice and stock, then give the mixture a stir. Press START/STOP. 3. Lock lid; move slider towards PRESSURE. Adjust pressure release valve in the SEAL position. Close pressure-release valve. The cooking temperature will default to HIGH, which is accurate. Set time to 7 minutes. Select START/STOP and start cooking. 4. When cooking is complete, let pressure release quickly by turning it into VENT position. Carefully open the lid. 5. Move the slider towards "AIR FRY/STOVETOP" and set Ninja Foodi XL Pressure Cooker Steam Fryer with SmartLid to SEAR/SAUTÉ mode. Adjust the temperature to "Hi5" by using up arrow. Press START/STOP to begin cooking and add the spinach and chickpeas. Allow the soup to come to a simmer, stirring until the spinach has fully wilted. Press START/STOP. 6. Taste for seasoning and adjust the salt to taste. Serve immediately. Garnish with a dollop of sour cream or a drizzle of quality extra-virgin olive oil.
Per Serving: Calories 246; Fat 8.4g; Sodium 298mg; Carbs 7.2g; Fiber 1g; Sugar 2g; Protein 6.3g

Creamy Tomato Soup with Basil

Prep time: 5 minutes | Cook time: 10 minutes | Serves: 4

2 tablespoons (30ml) extra-virgin	2 teaspoons Italian seasoning
olive oil	1 teaspoon sea salt, plus more to
1 yellow onion, diced	taste
4 cloves garlic, minced	240ml heavy cream
2 large carrots, peeled and diced	20g fresh basil leaves, chopped,
15g arrowroot starch	divided
710ml vegetable or chicken stock	35g freshly grated Parmesan
1 (800g) can San Marzano whole	cheese
tomatoes, with juice	

1. Move the slider towards "AIR FRY/STOVETOP" and set Ninja Foodi XL Pressure Cooker Steam Fryer with SmartLid to SEAR/SAUTÉ mode. Adjust the temperature to "Hi5" by using up arrow. Press START/STOP to begin cooking. 2. Once the pot is hot, coat the bottom of the pot with the oil. Add the onion, garlic and carrots. Cook until the vegetables are softened, about 5 minutes. Select START/STOP. Sprinkle the mixture with the arrowroot starch. Add the stock, tomatoes, Italian seasoning and salt. Give the mixture a stir. 3. Lock lid; move slider towards PRESSURE. Adjust pressure release valve in the SEAL position. Close pressure-release valve. The cooking temperature will default to HIGH, which is accurate. Set time to 6 minutes. Select START/STOP and start cooking. 4. When cooking is complete, let pressure release quickly by turning it into VENT. Stir in the milk and 10g of the basil. Blend the soup, using an immersion blender or high-powered blender, until smooth. 5. Serve hot, adding more salt to taste, garnishing with the remaining basil and topping with the Parmesan cheese.
Per Serving: Calories 243; Fat 8.7g; Sodium 647mg; Carbs 6.4g; Fiber 3g; Sugar 1g; Protein 6.5g

Two-Bean Chili stew

Prep time: 10 minutes | Cook time: 25 minutes | Serves: 6

170g dried black beans, soaked for 8 hours
170g dried red kidney beans, soaked for 8 hours
1 yellow onion, chopped
3 carrots, peeled and chopped
3 celery stalks, chopped
4 cloves garlic, minced
1 tablespoon chili powder
2 teaspoons ground cumin
¼ teaspoon cayenne pepper

480ml water
700g can diced tomatoes
1 sweet potato, peeled and cut into 2.5 cm chunks
Freshly ground black pepper
2 teaspoons fine sea salt
Chopped green onions, tender white and green parts only, for garnish
Chopped fresh coriander, for garnish

1. Drain the soaked beans and rinse well. Combine the beans, onion, carrots, celery, garlic, chili powder, cumin, cayenne, water, tomatoes with their juices, sweet potato, and several grinds of black pepper in the Ninja Foodi XL Pressure Cooker Steam Fryer with SmartLid cooking pot. Stir well to make sure the beans are submerged in the liquid. 2. Lock lid; move slider towards PRESSURE. Adjust pressure release valve in the SEAL position. Close pressure-release valve. The cooking temperature will default to HIGH, which is accurate. Set time to 10 minutes. Select START/STOP and start cooking. 3. When cooking is complete, let pressure release naturally for about 10 minutes, then quickly release any remaining pressure by turning it into VENT position. Remove the lid and add the salt. 4. Stir well, using the back of the spoon to mash some of the sweet potatoes against the side of the pot to thicken the chili. Adjust the seasonings to taste, and serve immediately with green onions and coriander on top. 5. Store leftovers in an airtight container and put in the fridge for 1 week.
Per Serving: Calories 262; Fat 9.4g; Sodium 312mg; Carbs 8.6g; Fiber 1g; Sugar 1g; Protein 9.2g

Cheesy Broccoli Soup

Prep time: 7 minutes | Cook time: 3 minutes | Serves: 4

1 yellow onion, chopped
2 carrots, peeled and chopped
1 small head (200g) cauliflower, cut into florets
455g broccoli, cut into florets
1 tablespoon spicy brown mustard
920ml water

Fine sea salt
50g shredded sharp Cheddar cheese
25g finely grated Parmesan cheese
120ml almond milk, or any milk of your choice
Freshly ground black pepper

1. Combine the water, 2 teaspoons salt, onion, carrots, cauliflower, broccoli and mustard in the Ninja Foodi XL Pressure Cooker Steam Fryer with SmartLid cooking pot. 2. Lock lid; move slider towards PRESSURE. Adjust pressure release valve in the SEAL position. Close pressure-release valve. The cooking temperature will default to HIGH, which is accurate. Set time to 3 minutes. Select START/STOP and start cooking. 3. When cooking is complete, let pressure release quickly by turning it into VENT position. 4. Blend the soup with an immersion blender, leaving as much texture as you like. Then add the cheddar, parmesan and almond milk and blend until combined. 5. Sprinkle with salt and pepper to taste and serve warm. Store leftovers in an airtight container in the refrigerator for up to 5 days.
Per Serving: Calories 257; Fat 11.3g; Sodium 256mg; Carbs 10.6g; Fiber 6g; Sugar 2g; Protein 8.3g

"Noodle" Soup

Prep time: 10 minutes | Cook time: 16 minutes | Serves: 4

1 tablespoon extra-virgin olive oil
1 yellow onion, chopped
3 cloves garlic, minced
1 teaspoon dried thyme, or 2 teaspoons fresh thyme
½ teaspoon dried oregano
455g boneless, skinless chicken thighs

3 carrots, peeled and chopped
3 celery stalks, chopped
Fine sea salt and freshly ground black pepper
1L low-sodium vegetable stock
455g courgette (about 2 medium)
Chopped fresh flat-leaf parsley, for garnish

1. Move the slider towards "AIR FRY/STOVETOP" and set Ninja Foodi XL Pressure Cooker Steam Fryer with SmartLid to SEAR/SAUTÉ mode. Adjust the temperature to "Hi5" by using up arrow. Press START/STOP to begin cooking and add the olive oil to the cooking pot. 2. Once the oil is hot but not smoking, add the onion and sauté until softened, about 3 minutes. Add the garlic, thyme, and oregano and cook until fragrant, about 1 minute more, then press

START/STOP to stop the cooking cycle. Add the chicken, carrots, celery, 2 teaspoons salt, several grinds of pepper, and the stock to the pot. 3. Lock lid; move slider towards PRESSURE. Adjust pressure release valve in the SEAL position. Close pressure-release valve. The cooking temperature will default to HIGH, which is accurate. Set time to 12 minutes. Select START/STOP and start cooking. Meanwhile, use a spiralizer or vegetable peeler to cut noodle like strips from the courgette; set the noodles aside. 4. When cooking is complete, let pressure release quickly by turning it into VENT position. Use tongs to place the cooked chicken to a cutting board, then use two forks to shred the chicken. 5. Add the shredded chicken and courgette noodles to the pot, and stir well. The noodles will soften quickly from the heat. 6. Sprinkle with additional salt and pepper, to taste, and serve immediately with parsley on top.
Per Serving: Calories 263; Fat 9.2g; Sodium 211mg; Carbs 8.6g; Fiber 2g; Sugar 1g; Protein 8.7g

Chapter 6 Fish and Seafood Recipes

Steamed Prawns

Prep time: 5 minutes | Cook time: 0 minutes | Serves: 4

900g large uncooked prawns, peeled and deveined
240ml water

1 lemon, quartered
2 tablespoons Old Bay Seasoning

1. Place prawns in a bowl. Squeeze lemon quarters over prawns. Toss squeezed lemons in bowl with prawns. Sprinkle Old Bay Seasoning over prawns and toss until evenly coated. 2. Add water to the Ninja Foodi XL Pressure Cooker Steam Fryer with SmartLid cooking pot and insert Cook & Crisp Basket. Place prawns in basket. 3. Lock lid; move slider to AIR FRY/STOVETOP. Select STEAM, and set time to 0 minutes. Press START/STOP to begin cooking. Discard lemons. 4. Transfer prawns to serving dish and serve warm or cold.
Per Serving: Calories 238; Fat 10.3g; Sodium 268mg; Carbs 10.3g; Fiber 0.3g; Sugar 9.2g; Protein 23.6g

Nut Crusted Cod

Prep time: 5 minutes | Cook time: 7 minutes | Serves: 2

1 tablespoon Dijon mustard
1 teaspoon fresh lemon juice
2 tablespoons polenta
35g chopped unsalted almonds

½ teaspoon salt
2 (125g) cod fillets
240ml water

1. Preheat oven to grill for 260°C. 2. In a small bowl, combine mustard, lemon juice, polenta, almonds, and salt to form a thick paste. 3. Pat cod fillets dry with a paper towel. Rub paste on the top of each fillet. 4. Add water to the Ninja Foodi XL Pressure Cooker Steam Fryer with SmartLid cooking pot. Place fillets in Cook & Crisp Basket and insert into pot. 5. Lock lid; move slider towards PRESSURE. Adjust pressure release valve in the SEAL position. Close pressure-release valve. The cooking temperature will default to HIGH, which is accurate. Set time to 5 minutes. Select START/STOP and start cooking. When cooking is complete, let pressure release quickly by turning it into VENT position. 6. Transfer fillets to a baking sheet lined with parchment paper. Grill fillets at 260°C for 2 minutes until tops are browned. 7. Remove fillets from oven and serve warm.
Per Serving: Calories 311; Fat 16.3g; Sodium 257mg; Carbs 8.3g; Fiber 0.6g; Sugar 0.7g; Protein 31.3g

Buttery Cod

Prep time: 5 minutes | Cook time: 7 minutes | Serves: 4

4 (125g) cod fillets
1 teaspoon salt
½ teaspoon ground black pepper
240ml water

4 tablespoons unsalted butter, divided into 8 pats
4 teaspoons capers, drained

1. Preheat oven to broiler for 260°C. 2. Pat cod fillets dry with a paper towel. Season with salt and pepper. 3. Add water to the Ninja Foodi XL Pressure Cooker Steam Fryer with SmartLid cooking pot. Place fillets in Cook & Crisp Basket and insert into pot. 4. Lock lid; move slider towards PRESSURE. Adjust pressure release valve in the SEAL position. Close pressure-release valve. The cooking temperature will default to HIGH, which is accurate. Set time to 5 minutes. Select START/STOP and start cooking. When cooking is complete, let pressure release quickly by turning it into VENT position. 5. Transfer fillets to a baking sheet lined with parchment paper. Add two pats butter to each fillet. Grill fillets 2 minutes until tops are browned. 6. Transfer fish to four plates, garnish with capers, and serve warm.
Per Serving: Calories 397; Fat 5.5g; Sodium 256mg; Carbs 55.5g; Fiber 2g; Sugar 0.7g; Protein 24.8g

Monkfish with Lemon-Caper Sauce

Prep time: 5 minutes | Cook time: 6 minutes | Serves: 2

2 (150g, 2.5 cm thick) monkfish fillets
2 tablespoons fresh lemon juice
2 tablespoons capers
1 teaspoon salt

1 teaspoon lemon zest
2 tablespoons unsalted butter, cut into 4 pats
240ml water
1 tablespoon chopped fresh parsley

1. Place a piece of aluminum foil in the Cook & Crisp Basket. Place fillets on foil. Create a "boat" with the foil by bringing up the edges about 5 cm. 2. Pour lemon juice on fish. Add capers to fish. Season fish with salt and lemon zest. Add two pats butter to each fillet. 3. Add water to the Ninja Foodi XL Pressure Cooker Steam Fryer with SmartLid cooking pot. Insert Deluxe Reversible Rack into the pot, place fillets in the it. 4. Lock lid; move slider towards PRESSURE. Adjust pressure release valve in the SEAL position. Close pressure-release valve. The cooking temperature will default to HIGH, which is accurate. Set time to 6 minutes. Select START/STOP and start cooking. When cooking is complete, let pressure release quickly by turning it into VENT position. 5. Transfer fish to two plates. Garnish each fillet with chopped parsley and serve warm.
Per Serving: Calories 358; Fat 9.8g; Sodium 561mg; Carbs 31.5g; Fiber 5g; Sugar 3.7g; Protein 29.1g

Coconut Halibut

Prep time: 5 minutes | Cook time: 3 minutes | Serves: 2

1 (13.125g) can coconut milk
Juice of 1 lime
Zest of 1 lime
2 teaspoons red curry paste
2 teaspoons honey

⅛ teaspoon red pepper flakes
455g halibut fillets, cubed
15g julienned fresh basil leaves, divided

1. Whisk together milk, lime juice, lime zest, red curry paste, honey, and pepper flakes in the Ninja Foodi XL Pressure Cooker Steam Fryer with SmartLid cooking pot. Add halibut and 5g basil. 2. Lock lid; move slider towards PRESSURE. Adjust pressure release valve in the SEAL position. Close pressure-release valve. The cooking temperature will default to HIGH, which is accurate. Set time to 3 minutes. Select START/STOP and start cooking. When cooking is complete, let pressure release quickly by turning it into VENT position. 3. Ladle mixture into two bowls and garnish with remaining basil. Serve warm.
Per Serving: Calories 308; Fat 10.2g; Sodium 456mg; Carbs 23.5g; Fiber 1.5g; Sugar 3.3g; Protein 27.3g

Sea Bass with fruity Salsa

Prep time: 5 minutes | Cook time: 3 minutes | Serves: 2

Peach Salsa
155g peeled and diced peaches
1 Roma tomato, seeded and diced
60g peeled and diced cucumbers
10g chopped fresh parsley
Fish
2 (125g) sea bass fillets
1 teaspoon salt

1 shallot, peeled and minced
1 tablespoon lime juice
2 tablespoons olive oil
½ teaspoon salt

½ teaspoon ground black pepper
240ml water

1. In a small bowl, combine salsa ingredients and refrigerate covered until ready to use. 2. Season fillets with salt and pepper. 3. Add water to the Ninja Foodi XL Pressure Cooker Steam Fryer with SmartLid cooking pot. Place sea bass in Cook & Crisp Basket and insert basket into pot. 4. Lock lid; move slider towards PRESSURE. Adjust pressure release valve in the SEAL position. Close pressure-release valve. The cooking temperature will default to HIGH, which is accurate. Set time to 3 minutes. Select START/STOP and start cooking. When cooking is complete, let pressure release quickly by turning it into VENT position. 5. Transfer fish and toppings to two plates. Garnish with salsa and serve warm.
Per Serving: Calories 168; Fat 8.9g; Sodium 269mg; Carbs 2.2g; Fiber 0.2g; Sugar 0.7g; Protein 18.2g

Lobster Tails

Prep time: 2 minutes | Cook time: 4 minutes | Serves: 4

240ml water
1 tablespoon Old Bay Seasoning
4 (150g) uncooked lobster tails,

thawed
55g unsalted butter, melted

1. Add water and Old Bay Seasoning to the Ninja Foodi XL Pressure Cooker Steam Fryer with SmartLid cooking pot and insert Cook & Crisp Basket. Add lobster tails to basket. 2. Lock lid; move slider to AIR FRY/STOVETOP. Select STEAM, and set time to 4 minutes. Press START/STOP to begin cooking. 3. Transfer tails to an ice bath to stop the lobster from overcooking, then remove meat from shells. Serve with melted butter.
Per Serving: Calories 255; Fat 13g; Sodium 1453mg; Carbs 2g; Fiber 0g; Sugar 0g; Protein 32g

Crab-Stuffed Sole

Prep time: 5 minutes | Cook time: 3 minutes | Serves: 4

135g lump crabmeat, picked over for shells	1 teaspoon salt
4 teaspoons mayonnaise	½ teaspoon ground black pepper
1 teaspoon prepared horseradish	240ml water
1 teaspoon lemon juice	4 tablespoons gluten-free bread crumbs
1 teaspoon chopped fresh dill	2 tablespoons unsalted butter, melted
4 (125g) sole fillets	

1. Lightly grease a 7-cup glass dish with either oil or cooking spray. 2. In a medium bowl, combine crab, mayonnaise, horseradish, lemon juice, and chopped dill. Set aside. 3. Season fillets with salt and pepper. Spread ¼ crab mixture on the darker side of each fillet. Roll up fillets and place seam-side down in greased glass dish. 4. Add water to the Ninja Foodi XL Pressure Cooker Steam Fryer with SmartLid cooking pot. Insert Deluxe Reversible Rack and place glass dish on Rack. 5. Lock lid; move slider towards PRESSURE. Adjust pressure release valve in the SEAL position. Close pressure-release valve. The cooking temperature will default to HIGH, which is accurate. Set time to 7 minutes. Select START/STOP and start cooking. When cooking is complete, let pressure release quickly by turning it into VENT position. 6. Preheat oven to grill for 260°C. 7. In a small bowl, combine bread crumbs and butter. Evenly distribute mixture to tops of each rolled fillet. 8. Transfer dish with fillets to oven. Grill 2 minutes until browned. Serve warm.

Per Serving: Calories 182; Fat 1.6g; Sodium 258mg; Carbs 1.6g; Fiber 0.3g; Sugar 0.7g; Protein 34.5g

Salmon with Citrus Aioli

Prep time: 5 minutes | Cook time: 5 minutes | Serves: 2

Aioli

60g mayonnaise	2 teaspoons Dijon mustard
1 tablespoon lemon juice	2 teaspoons prepared horseradish
1 teaspoon lemon zest	1 clove garlic, peeled and minced

Salmon

2 (125g) salmon fillets	240ml water
½ teaspoon salt	1 tablespoon chopped fresh dill

1. In a small bowl, combine aioli ingredients. Refrigerate covered until ready to serve. 2. Pat salmon fillets dry with a paper towel and place in Cook & Crisp Basket. Season fillets with salt. 3. Add water to the Ninja Foodi XL Pressure Cooker Steam Fryer with SmartLid cooking pot. Insert Deluxe Reversible Rack. 4. Lock lid; move slider towards PRESSURE. Adjust pressure release valve in the SEAL position. Close pressure-release valve. The cooking temperature will default to HIGH, which is accurate. Set time to 3 minutes. Select START/STOP and start cooking. When cooking is complete, let pressure release quickly by turning it into VENT position. 5. Transfer fish to two plates and drizzle sauce over each fillet. Garnish with dill and serve immediately.

Per Serving: Calories 420; Fat 23g; Sodium 369mg; Carbs 31g; Fiber 1g; Sugar 4g; Protein 20g

Catfish Bites with Slaw

Prep time: 5 minutes | Cook time: 3 minutes | Serves: 4

Creamy Slaw

1 (350g) bag coleslaw mix (shredded cabbage and carrots)	2 teaspoons dill pickle juice, from the jar
120g mayonnaise	2 teaspoons Dijon mustard
80g sour cream	½ teaspoon salt
2 teaspoons granulated sugar	¼ teaspoon ground black pepper

Catfish

240ml water	1 teaspoon salt
900g catfish fillets, rinsed and cut into 2.5 cm pieces	¼ teaspoon ground black pepper

1. In a small bowl, combine slaw ingredients and refrigerate covered until ready to serve. 2. Add water to the Ninja Foodi XL Pressure Cooker Steam Fryer with SmartLid cooking pot. Season catfish with salt and pepper. Place fish in Cook & Crisp Basket and insert into pot. 3. Lock lid; move slider towards PRESSURE. Adjust pressure release valve in the SEAL position. Close pressure-release valve. The cooking temperature will default to HIGH, which is accurate. Set time to 3 minutes. Select START/STOP and start cooking. When cooking is complete, let pressure release quickly by turning it into VENT

position. 4. Transfer catfish to four plates. Serve warm with chilled slaw.

Per Serving: Calories 180; Fat 13.7g; Sodium 147mg; Carbs 9.6g; Fiber 3g; Sugar 6g; Protein 5.8g

Fresh Fish Taco Lettuce Wraps

Prep time: 15 minutes | Cook time: 3 minutes | Serves: 8

Sauce

240g mayonnaise	Juice of ½ lime
1 tablespoon capers	⅛ teaspoon hot sauce

Slaw

35g grated cabbage	Juice of ½ lime
1 large carrot, peeled and grated	1 tablespoon olive oil
2 small radishes, peeled and julienned	⅛ teaspoon hot sauce
5g chopped fresh coriander	
½ teaspoon salt	

Fish

455g cod, cubed	¼ teaspoon cayenne pepper
3 tablespoons lime juice	1 tablespoon olive oil
1 teaspoon garlic salt	240ml water

Extras

1 avocado, peeled, pitted, and diced	with ⅛ teaspoon salt
110g diced tomatoes, seasoned	10 large lettuce leaves

1. Blend sauce ingredients until smooth. Refrigerate covered at least 30 minutes or up to overnight. 2. In a medium bowl, combine slaw ingredients. Refrigerate covered at least 30 minutes or up to overnight. 3. In a large bowl, combine fish, lime juice, garlic salt, cayenne pepper, and olive oil, and refrigerate covered for 15 minutes. 4. Add water to the Ninja Foodi XL Pressure Cooker Steam Fryer with SmartLid cooking pot. Place cod in an even row in Cook & Crisp Basket. Pour in additional marinade from large bowl for steaming aromatics. 5. Lock lid; move slider towards PRESSURE. Adjust pressure release valve in the SEAL position. Close pressure-release valve. The cooking temperature will default to HIGH, which is accurate. Set time to 3 minutes. Select START/STOP and start cooking. When cooking is complete, let pressure release quickly by turning it into VENT position. 6. Transfer fish to a serving bowl. Assemble fish taco wraps by adding equal amounts fish, slaw, avocado, and tomatoes to each lettuce leaf. Drizzle with sauce.

Per Serving: Calories 194; Fat 4.3g; Sodium 369mg; Carbs 11.2g; Fiber 2.6g; Sugar 2.4g; Protein 22.6g

Salmon Salad

Prep time: 5 minutes | Cook time: 5 minutes | Serves: 2

Dressing

85g honey	2 tablespoons olive oil
60g Dijon mustard	1 clove garlic, peeled and minced
60ml apple cider vinegar	

Salmon

2 (125g) salmon fillets	4 tablespoons peeled and diced red onion
½ teaspoon salt	
240ml water	4 tablespoons crumbled feta cheese
Salad	
80g rocket	2 tablespoons chopped pecans
1 Roma tomato, diced	2 tablespoons salted sunflower seeds
40g fresh blueberries	

1. In a small bowl, whisk together dressing ingredients. Refrigerate covered until ready to serve. 2. Pat salmon fillets dry with a paper towel and place in Cook & Crisp Basket. Season fillets with salt. 3. Add water to the Ninja Foodi XL Pressure Cooker Steam Fryer with SmartLid cooking pot. Insert Deluxe Reversible Rack. 4. Lock lid; move slider towards PRESSURE. Adjust pressure release valve in the SEAL position. Close pressure-release valve. The cooking temperature will default to HIGH, which is accurate. Set time to 5 minutes. Select START/STOP and start cooking. When cooking is complete, let pressure release quickly by turning it into VENT position. 5. While salmon is cooking, prepare two salads by dividing salad ingredients between two bowls. Toss with dressing. Place cooked salmon fillets on top of each salad and serve.

Per Serving: Calories 334; Fat 29.1g; Sodium 177mg; Carbs 10.8g; Fiber 5.2g; Sugar 5g; Protein 13.4g

Steamed Mussels with Tomato Sauce

Prep time: 10 minutes | Cook time: 8 minutes | Serves: 4

2 tablespoons unsalted butter	1 teaspoon salt
1 medium yellow onion, peeled and diced	1 teaspoon smoked paprika
4 cloves garlic, peeled and minced	Juice of 1 lemon
240ml dry white wine	900g fresh mussels, cleaned and debearded
1 (360g) can diced tomatoes, including juice	10g chopped fresh basil leaves

1. Move the slider towards "AIR FRY/STOVETOP" and set Ninja Foodi XL Pressure Cooker Steam Fryer with SmartLid to SEAR/SAUTÉ mode. Adjust the temperature to "Hi5" by using up arrow. Press START/STOP to begin cooking. Add butter to pot and heat 30 seconds. Add onion and sauté 5 minutes until translucent. Add garlic and cook for an additional minute. Stir in white wine and cook 2 minutes. 2. Add tomatoes with juice, salt, smoked paprika, and lemon juice. Insert Cook & Crisp Basket. Place mussels in basket. 3. Lock lid; move slider towards PRESSURE. Adjust pressure release valve in the SEAL position. Close pressure-release valve. The cooking temperature will default to HIGH, which is accurate. Set time to 0 minutes. Select START/STOP and start cooking. When cooking is complete, let pressure release quickly by turning it into VENT position. 4. Remove mussels and discard any that haven't opened. Transfer mussels to four bowls and distribute liquid from pot equally among bowls. Garnish with basil. Serve immediately.

Per Serving: Calories 180; Fat 4g; Sodium 321mg; Carbs 5g; Fiber 2g; Sugar 3g; Protein 7g

Gingery-Glazed Mahi-Mahi

Prep time: 5 minutes | Cook time: 5 minutes | Serves: 2

2 tablespoons tamari	ginger
2 tablespoons rice wine vinegar	⅛ teaspoon cayenne pepper
2 teaspoons sesame oil	2 (150g) mahi-mahi fillets, 2.5 cm thick
2 tablespoons honey	
1 teaspoon peeled and grated	240ml water

1. Whisk together tamari, rice wine vinegar, sesame oil, honey, ginger, and cayenne pepper. Brush half of glaze on mahi-mahi fillets. 2. Add water to the Ninja Foodi XL Pressure Cooker Steam Fryer with SmartLid cooking pot. Insert Cook & Crisp Basket. Add fillets to basket. 3. Lock lid; move slider towards PRESSURE. Adjust pressure release valve in the SEAL position. Close pressure-release valve. The cooking temperature will default to HIGH, which is accurate. Set time to 5 minutes. Select START/STOP and start cooking. 4. When cooking is complete, let pressure release naturally for 5 minutes, then quick-release any remaining pressure by turning it into VENT position. 5. Transfer fish to two plates and brush with remaining glaze. Serve warm.

Per Serving: Calories 221; Fat 4g; Sodium 159mg; Carbs 3g; Fiber 1g; Sugar 2g; Protein 3g

Blue Cheese Mussels

Prep time: 10 minutes | Cook time: 8 minutes | Serves: 4

2 tablespoons unsalted butter	900g fresh mussels, cleaned and debearded
100g pancetta or thick-sliced bacon, diced	1 teaspoon salt
1 medium red onion, peeled and diced	1 teaspoon smoked paprika
4 cloves garlic, peeled and minced	110g crumbled blue cheese
2 cans gluten-free beer	10g chopped fresh basil leaves

1. Move the slider towards "AIR FRY/STOVETOP" and set Ninja Foodi XL Pressure Cooker Steam Fryer with SmartLid to SEAR/SAUTÉ mode. Adjust the temperature to "Hi5" by using up arrow. Press START/STOP to begin cooking. Add butter to pot and heat 30 seconds. Add pancetta and onion and cook 5 minutes until onions are translucent. Add garlic and cook for an additional minute. Stir in beer and cook 2 minutes. 2. Insert Cook & Crisp Basket into pot. Place mussels in basket. Sprinkle mussels with salt and smoked paprika. 3. Lock lid; move slider towards PRESSURE. Adjust pressure release valve in the SEAL position. Close pressure-release valve. The cooking temperature will default to HIGH, which is accurate. Set time to 0 minutes. Select START/STOP and start cooking. When cooking is complete, let pressure release quickly by turning it into VENT position. 4. Remove mussels and discard any that haven't opened. Transfer mussels to four bowls and distribute liquid, veggies, and pancetta from pot equally among bowls. Garnish each bowl with blue cheese and basil. 5. Serve immediately.

Per Serving: Calories 224; Fat 16.8g; Sodium 211mg; Carbs 7.7g; Fiber 2.3g; Sugar 5g; Protein 11.4g

Lobster Rolls

Prep time: 2 minutes | Cook time: 6 minutes | Serves: 4

240ml water	1 teaspoon lemon zest
1 tablespoon Old Bay Seasoning	½ teaspoon smoked paprika
4 (150g) uncooked lobster tails, thawed	½ teaspoon salt
60g mayonnaise	¼ teaspoon ground black pepper
1 stalk celery, diced	55g unsalted butter, melted
1 tablespoon lemon juice	4 gluten-free top-split buns
	20g shredded lettuce

1. Add water and Old Bay Seasoning to the Ninja Foodi XL Pressure Cooker Steam Fryer with SmartLid cooking pot and insert Cook & Crisp Basket. Add lobster tails to basket. 2. Lock lid; move slider to AIR FRY/STOVETOP. Select STEAM, and set time to 4 minutes. Press START/STOP to begin cooking. Carefully unlock lid. Transfer tails to an ice bath to stop the lobster from overcooking. 3. Remove lobster meat from shells. Roughly chop meat and transfer to a medium bowl. Combine lobster with mayonnaise, celery, lemon juice, lemon zest, smoked paprika, salt, and pepper. 4. Brush butter on each side of buns. Brown buns in a frying pan over medium heat 2 minutes. Distribute lobster and lettuce among buns and serve.

Per Serving: Calories 192; Fat 4g; Sodium 322mg; Carbs 5g; Fiber 2g; Sugar 3g; Protein 7g

Chili Crispy Haddock

Prep Time: 10 minutes | Cook Time: 8 minutes | Serves: 4

150g haddock fillet	½ teaspoon salt
1 egg, beaten	1 tablespoon flax meal
1 teaspoon cream cheese	Cooking spray
1 teaspoon chili flakes	

1. Place the Cook & Crisp Basket in your Pressure Cooker Steam Fryer. 2. Cut the haddock on 4 pieces and sprinkle with chili flakes and salt. After this, in the small bowl mix up egg and cream cheese. Dip the haddock pieces in the egg mixture and generously sprinkle with flax meal. 3. Spray the Cook & Crisp Basket with cooking spray. Put the prepared haddock pieces in the Cook & Crisp Basket in one layer. 4. Put on the Smart Lid on top of the Ninja Foodi Steam Fryer. Move the Lid Slider to the "Air Fry/Stovetop". Select the "Air Fry" mode for cooking. Adjust the cooking temperature to 200°C. 5. Cook them for around 4 minutes from each side or until they are golden brown.

Per Serving: Calories 596; Fat: 24.6g; Sodium 316mg; Carbs: 36.8g; Fiber: 15.6g; Sugars 9.5g; Protein 58.8g

Sea Scallops with tangy Cherry Sauce

Prep time: 5 minutes | Cook time: 1 minutes | Serves: 2

80g cherry preserves	455g fresh sea scallops
1 teaspoon lemon juice	½ teaspoon salt
1 teaspoon tamari	240ml water
1 tablespoon unsalted butter	

1. In a small bowl, whisk together preserves, lemon juice, and tamari. Set aside. 2. Move the slider towards "AIR FRY/STOVETOP" and set Ninja Foodi XL Pressure Cooker Steam Fryer with SmartLid to SEAR/SAUTÉ mode. Adjust the temperature to "Hi5" by using up arrow. Press START/STOP to begin cooking. Add butter to pot and heat 30 seconds. Season scallops with salt, add to pot, and sear 30 seconds per side. Transfer to Cook & Crisp Basket. Top scallops with preserve mixture. 3. Add water to the Ninja Foodi XL Pressure Cooker Steam Fryer with SmartLid cooking pot. Insert Cook & Crisp Basket. 4. Lock lid; move slider towards PRESSURE. Adjust pressure release valve in the SEAL position. Close pressure-release valve. The cooking temperature will default to HIGH, which is accurate. Set time to 0 minutes. Select START/STOP and start cooking. When cooking is complete, let pressure release quickly by turning it into VENT position. 5. Transfer scallops to two plates. Serve warm.

Per Serving: Calories 311; Fat 17g; Sodium 1110mg; Carbs 3g; Fiber 0g; Sugar 0g; Protein 34g

Delicious Crawfish Étouffée

Prep time: 15 minutes | Cook time: 15 minutes | Serves: 4

6 tablespoons unsalted butter	60ml chicken stock
30g gluten-free plain flour	455g crawfish tails, peeled
1 medium sweet onion, peeled and diced	1 tablespoon Creole seasoning
2 stalks celery, diced	½ teaspoon salt
1 medium green pepper, seeded and diced	½ teaspoon ground black pepper
4 cloves garlic, peeled and minced	⅛ teaspoon hot sauce
1 (360g) can diced tomatoes, including juice	1 tablespoon cooking sherry
	750g cooked long-grain white rice
	40g sliced green onions
	10g chopped fresh parsley

1. Move the slider towards "AIR FRY/STOVETOP" and set Ninja Foodi XL Pressure Cooker Steam Fryer with SmartLid to SEAR/SAUTÉ mode. Adjust the temperature to "Hi5" by using up arrow. Press START/STOP to begin cooking. Add butter to pot and heat 30 seconds. Slowly whisk in flour and cook 5 minutes until browned. Add onion, celery, green pepper, and garlic to pot and heat while stirring for an additional 2 minutes. 2. Add diced tomatoes with juice and stir, scraping any bits on the bottom and sides of pot. Add stock, crawfish, Creole seasoning, salt, pepper, hot sauce, and cooking sherry. 3. Lock lid; move slider towards PRESSURE. Adjust pressure release valve in the SEAL position. Close pressure-release valve. The cooking temperature will default to HIGH, which is accurate. Set time to 8 minutes. Select START/STOP and start cooking. When cooking is complete, let pressure release quickly by turning it into VENT position. 4. Ladle étouffée into four bowls. Garnish each bowl with 200 g rice, green onions, and parsley. Serve warm.
Per Serving: Calories 286; Fat 16g; Sodium 1868mg; Carbs 1g; Fiber 0g; Sugar 0g; Protein 37g

Prawns with Smoked Sausage, and Peppers

Prep time: 5 minutes | Cook time: 5 minutes | Serves: 4

1 tablespoon olive oil	including juice
1 small yellow onion, peeled and diced	900g large uncooked prawns, peeled and deveined
½ green pepper, seeded and thinly sliced	300g smoked sausage, sliced into ½" sections
½ red pepper, seeded and thinly sliced	2 teaspoons Old Bay Seasoning
½ yellow pepper, seeded and thinly sliced	½ teaspoon salt
1 (360g) can diced tomatoes,	½ teaspoon ground black pepper
	240ml water

1. Move the slider towards "AIR FRY/STOVETOP" and set Ninja Foodi XL Pressure Cooker Steam Fryer with SmartLid to SEAR/SAUTÉ mode. Adjust the temperature to "Hi5" by using up arrow. Press START/STOP to begin cooking. 2. Add oil to pot and heat 30 seconds. Add onion and peppers and sauté 5 minutes until onions are translucent. Add tomatoes with juice, prawns, sausage, Old Bay Seasoning, salt, pepper, and water. 3. Lock lid; move slider to AIR FRY/STOVETOP. Select STEAM, and set time to 0 minutes. Press START/STOP to begin cooking. 4. Using a slotted spoon, transfer mixture to four bowls and serve warm.
Per Serving: Calories 294; Fat 11g; Sodium 1766mg; Carbs 20g; Fiber 1g; Sugar 3g; Protein 27g

Nut-Crusted Halibut

Prep time: 5 minutes | Cook time: 7 minutes | Serves: 2

1 tablespoon Dijon mustard	½ teaspoon salt
1 teaspoon fresh lemon juice	2 (125g) halibut fillets
2 tablespoons panko bread crumbs	240ml water
35g chopped unsalted pistachios	

1. Preheat the oven to grill for 260°C. 2. In a small bowl, combine mustard, lemon juice, bread crumbs, pistachios, and salt to form a thick paste. 3. Pat the halibut fillets dry with a paper towel. Rub the paste on the top of each fillet and place in Cook & Crisp Basket. 4. Pour 240 ml water in the Ninja Foodi XL Pressure Cooker Steam Fryer with SmartLid cooking pot. Insert Deluxe reversible rack. Place Cook & Crisp Basket on Deluxe reversible rack. 5. Lock lid; move slider towards PRESSURE. Adjust pressure release valve in the SEAL position. Close pressure-release valve. The cooking temperature will default to HIGH, which is accurate. Set time to 5 minutes. Select START/STOP and start cooking. 6. When cooking is complete,

let pressure release quickly by turning it into VENT position. Transfer fillets to a parchment-paper-lined baking sheet. 7. Grill for approximately 1–2 minutes until tops are browned. Remove from heat and serve hot.
Per Serving: Calories 283; Fat 14g; Sodium 1460mg; Carbs 0g; Fiber 0g; Sugar 0g; Protein 40g

Trout with Herb Sauce

Prep time: 5 minutes | Cook time: 5 minutes | Serves: 4

Trout

4 (225g) fresh river trout	1 teaspoon white wine vinegar
1 teaspoon sea salt	120ml water
80g torn lettuce leaves, divided	

Herb Sauce

15g minced fresh flat-leaf parsley	¼ teaspoon sugar
2 teaspoons Italian seasoning	Pinch of salt
1 small shallot, peeled and minced	2 tablespoons sliced almonds, toasted
2 tablespoons mayonnaise	
½ teaspoon fresh lemon juice	

1. For Trout: Rinse the trout inside and out; pat dry. Sprinkle with salt inside and out. Put 60 g lettuce leaves in the bottom of the Ninja Foodi XL Pressure Cooker Steam Fryer with SmartLid cooking pot. Arrange the trout over the top of the lettuce and top fish with the remaining lettuce. 2. Pour vinegar and water into pot. 3. Lock lid; move slider towards PRESSURE. Adjust pressure release valve in the SEAL position. Close pressure-release valve. The cooking temperature will default to HIGH, which is accurate. Set time to 3 minutes. Select START/STOP and start cooking. When cooking is complete, let pressure release quickly by turning it into VENT position. 4. Transfer fish to a serving plate. Peel and discard the skin from the fish. Remove and discard the heads if desired. 5. For Herb Sauce: In a small bowl, mix together the parsley, Italian seasoning, shallot, mayonnaise, lemon juice, sugar, and salt. Evenly divide among the fish, spreading it over them. 6. Sprinkle toasted almonds over the top of the sauce. Serve.
Per Serving: Calories 239; Fat 9g; Sodium 901mg; Carbs 11g; Fiber 1g; Sugar 1g; Protein 27g

Delicious Fish Tacos

Prep time: 15 minutes | Cook time: 3 minutes | Serves: 8

Slaw

45g grated cabbage	1 tablespoon olive oil
1 large carrot, peeled and grated	2 dashes hot sauce
1 small jicama, peeled and julienned	10g chopped fresh coriander
Juice of ½ lime	½ teaspoon sea salt

Fish

455g cod, cubed	1 teaspoon ground cumin
Juice from ½ lime	1 tablespoon olive oil
2 tablespoons fresh orange juice	240ml water
1 teaspoon garlic salt	

To Serve

75g guacamole	8 (15cm) soft corn tortillas
110g diced tomatoes	

1. For Slaw: Combine slaw ingredients in a medium bowl. Refrigerate covered for 30 minutes up to overnight. 2. For Fish: In a large bowl, combine fish, lime juice, orange juice, garlic salt, cumin, and olive oil and refrigerate for 15 minutes. 3. Add 240 ml water to Ninja Foodi XL Pressure Cooker Steam Fryer with SmartLid cooking pot. Insert Deluxe reversible rack. Place Cook & Crisp Basket on top of Deluxe reversible rack. Add cod in an even row onto Cook & Crisp Basket. Pour in additional marinade for the steaming aromatics. 4. Lock lid; move slider towards PRESSURE. Adjust pressure release valve in the SEAL position. Close pressure-release valve. The cooking temperature will default to HIGH, which is accurate. Set time to 3 minutes. Select START/STOP and start cooking. When cooking is complete, let pressure release quickly by turning it into VENT position. Transfer fish to a serving bowl. 5. To Serve: Assemble fish tacos by adding equal amounts of fish, slaw, guacamole, and tomatoes to each corn tortilla.
Per Serving: Calories 346; Fat 22g; Sodium 1300mg; Carbs 1g; Fiber 0g; Sugar 0g; Protein 32g

Garlic Prawns

Prep Time: 10 minutes | Cook Time: 5 minutes | Serves: 3

455g prawns, peeled
½ teaspoon garlic powder
¼ teaspoon minced garlic
1 teaspoon cumin
¼ teaspoon lemon zest, grated
½ tablespoon avocado oil
½ teaspoon dried parsley

1. Place the Cook & Crisp Basket in your Pressure Cooker Steam Fryer. 2. In the mixing bowl mix up prawns, garlic powder, minced garlic, cumin, lemon zest, and dried parsley. 3. Then add avocado oil and mix up the prawns well. Put the prawns in the "cook & crisp basket". 4. Put on the Smart Lid on top of the Ninja Foodi Steam Fryer. Move the Lid Slider to the "Air Fry/Stovetop". Select the "Air Fry" mode for cooking. Adjust the cooking temperature to 200°C. Cook for around 5 minutes.
Per Serving: Calories 681; Fat: 30.7g; Sodium 1245mg; Carbs: 54.9g; Fiber: 9.9g; Sugars 5g; Protein 42.5g

Tilapia with Tomato Salsa

Prep Time: 5 minutes | Cook Time: 15 minutes | Serves: 4

4 tilapia fillets, boneless
1 tablespoon olive oil
A pinch of salt and black pepper
150g tomatoes, chopped
2 tablespoons green onions,
chopped
2 tablespoons sweet red pepper, chopped
1 tablespoon balsamic vinegar

1. Place the Cook & Crisp Basket in your Pressure Cooker Steam Fryer. 2. Arrange the tilapia in the Cook & Crisp Basket and season with black pepper and salt. In a suitable bowl, mix all the other ingredients, toss and spread over the fish. 3. Put on the Smart Lid on top of the Ninja Foodi Steam Fryer. Move the Lid Slider to the "Air Fry/Stovetop". Select the "Air Fry" mode for cooking. Air Fry at 175°C for around 15 minutes. 4. Divide the mix between plates and serve.
Per Serving: Calories 397; Fat: 19.1g; Sodium 431mg; Carbs: 16.8g; Fiber: 5.3g; Sugars 6.4g; Protein 39.4g

Crusted Salmon

Prep Time: 15 minutes | Cook Time: 8 minutes | Serves: 4

150g salmon fillet
30g pistachios, grinded
1 teaspoon cream cheese
½ teaspoon nutmeg
2 tablespoons coconut flour
½ teaspoon turmeric
¼ teaspoon sage
½ teaspoon salt
1 tablespoon heavy cream
Cooking spray

1. Place the Cook & Crisp Basket in your Pressure Cooker Steam Fryer. 2. Cut the salmon fillet into 4 parts. In the mixing bowl mix up cream cheese, turmeric, sage, salt, and heavy cream. 3. Then in the separated bowl mix up coconut flour and pistachios. Dip the salmon fillets in the cream cheese mixture and then coat in the pistachio mixture. 4. Place the coated salmon fillets in the basket and grease them with the cooking spray. Put on the Smart Lid on top of the Ninja Foodi Steam Fryer. 5. Move the Lid Slider to the "Air Fry/Stovetop". Select the "Air Fry" mode for cooking. Adjust the cooking temperature to 195°C. Cook the fish for around 8 minutes.
Per Serving: Calories 348; Fat: 11.1g; Sodium 139mg; Carbs: 7.9g; Fiber: 3g; Sugars 1.6g; Protein 52.8g

Catfish with Avocado

Prep Time: 5 minutes | Cook Time: 15 minutes | Serves: 4

2 teaspoons oregano, dried
2 teaspoons cumin,
2 teaspoons sweet paprika
A pinch of salt and black pepper
4 catfish fillets
1 avocado, peeled and cubed
80g spring onions, chopped
2 tablespoons coriander, chopped
2 teaspoons olive oil
2 tablespoons lemon juice

1. In a suitable bowl, mix all the recipe ingredients except the fish and toss. 2. Arrange them in the Cook & Crisp Basket, top with the fish. Place the Cook & Crisp Basket in your Pressure Cooker Steam Fryer. 3. Put on the Smart Lid on top of the Ninja Foodi Steam Fryer. Move the Lid Slider to the "Air Fry/Stovetop". Select the "Air Fry" mode for cooking. Air Fry at 180°C for around 15 minutes, flipping the fish halfway. 4. Divide between plates and serve.
Per Serving: Calories 396; Fat: 11.4g; Sodium 448mg; Carbs: 30.7g; Fiber: 3.7g; Sugars 0.8g; Protein 40.2g

Gingered Cod

Prep Time: 10 minutes | Cook Time: 8 minutes | Serves: 2

250g cod fillet
½ teaspoon cayenne pepper
¼ teaspoon coriander
½ teaspoon ginger
½ teaspoon black pepper
1 tablespoon sunflower oil
½ teaspoon salt
½ teaspoon dried rosemary
½ teaspoon paprika

1. Place the Cook & Crisp Basket in your Pressure Cooker Steam Fryer. 2. In the shallow bowl mix up cayenne pepper, coriander, ginger, black pepper, salt, dried rosemary, and paprika. 3. Then rub the cod fillet with the spice mixture. After this, sprinkle it with sunflower oil. Place the cod fillet in the basket. 4. Put on the Smart Lid on top of the Ninja Foodi Steam Fryer. Move the Lid Slider to the "Air Fry/Stovetop". Select the "Air Fry" mode for cooking. Adjust the cooking temperature to 200°C. Cook it for around 4 minutes. 5. Then carefully flip the fish on another side. Cook for around 4 minutes more.
Per Serving: Calories 565; Fat: 14.5g; Sodium 938mg; Carbs: 47g; Fiber: 3.8g; Sugars 5g; Protein 58g

Paprika Tilapia with Capers

Prep Time: 5 minutes | Cook Time: 20 minutes | Serves: 4

4 tilapia fillets, boneless
3 tablespoons ghee, melted
A pinch of salt and black pepper
2 tablespoons capers
1 teaspoon garlic powder
½ teaspoon smoked paprika
½ teaspoon oregano, dried
2 tablespoons lemon juice

1. Place the Cook & Crisp Basket in your Pressure Cooker Steam Fryer. 2. In a suitable bowl, mix all the recipe ingredients except the fish and toss. Arrange the fish in the Cook & Crisp Basket, pour the capers mix all over. 3. Put on the Smart Lid on top of the Ninja Foodi Steam Fryer. Move the Lid Slider to the "Air Fry/Stovetop". Select the "Air Fry" mode for cooking. Cook for 180°C for around 20 minutes, shaking halfway. 4. Divide between plates and serve hot.
Per Serving: Calories 402; Fat: 19.9g; Sodium 1387mg; Carbs: 24g; Fiber: 8g; Sugars 12.7g; Protein 32.1g

Paprika Catfish with Tarragon

Prep time: 5 minutes | Cook time: 3 minutes | Serves: 2

1 (360g) can diced tomatoes, including juice
2 teaspoons dried minced onion
¼ teaspoon onion powder
1 teaspoon dried minced garlic
¼ teaspoon garlic powder
2 teaspoons smoked paprika
1 tablespoon chopped fresh
tarragon
1 medium green pepper, seeded and diced
1 stalk celery, finely diced
1 teaspoon salt
¼ teaspoon ground black pepper
455g catfish fillets, rinsed and cut into bite-sized pieces

1. Add all ingredients except fish to the Ninja Foodi XL Pressure Cooker Steam Fryer with SmartLid cooking pot and stir to mix. Once mixed, add the fish on top. 2. Lock lid; move slider towards PRESSURE. Adjust pressure release valve in the SEAL position. Close pressure-release valve. The cooking temperature will default to HIGH, which is accurate. Set time to 3 minutes. Select START/STOP and start cooking. When cooking is complete, let pressure release quickly by turning it into VENT position. 3. Transfer all ingredients to a serving bowl. Serve warm.
Per Serving: Calories 355; Fat 16g; Sodium 750mg; Carbs 25g; Fiber 1g; Sugar 13g; Protein 25g

Air-Fried Cod

Prep Time: 5 minutes | Cook Time: 14 minutes | Serves: 4

15g stevia
2 tablespoons coconut aminos
4 cod fillets, boneless
A pinch of salt and black pepper

1. In the Cook & Crisp Basket, mix all the recipe ingredients and toss gently. Place the Cook & Crisp Basket in your Pressure Cooker Steam Fryer. 2. Put on the Smart Lid on top of the Ninja Foodi Steam Fryer. Move the Lid Slider to the "Air Fry/Stovetop". Select the "Air Fry" mode for cooking. Air Fry at 175°C for around 14 minutes, flipping the fish halfway. 3. Divide everything between plates and serve.
Per Serving: Calories 375; Fat: 19.8g; Sodium 2105mg; Carbs: 29g; Fiber: 0.7g; Sugars 24.8g; Protein 24.3g

Tropical Sea Bass

Prep time: 5 minutes | Cook time: 3 minutes | Serves: 3

1 (360g) can coconut milk	1 teaspoon ground turmeric
Juice of 1 lime	1 teaspoon ground ginger
1 tablespoon red curry paste	½ teaspoon sea salt
1 teaspoon fish sauce	½ teaspoon white pepper
1 teaspoon coconut aminos	455g sea bass, cut into 2.5 cm
1 teaspoon honey	cubes
2 teaspoons sriracha	10g chopped fresh coriander
2 cloves garlic, minced	3 lime wedges

1. In a large bowl, whisk together coconut milk, lime juice, red curry paste, fish sauce, coconut aminos, honey, sriracha, garlic, turmeric, ginger, sea salt, and white pepper. 2. Place sea bass in the bottom of Ninja Foodi XL Pressure Cooker Steam Fryer with SmartLid cooking pot. Pour coconut milk mixture over the fish. 3. Lock lid; move slider towards PRESSURE. Adjust pressure release valve in the SEAL position. Close pressure-release valve. The cooking temperature will default to HIGH, which is accurate. Set time to 3 minutes. Select START/STOP and start cooking. When cooking is complete, let pressure release quickly by turning it into VENT position. 4. Transfer fish and stock into three bowls. Garnish each with equal amounts of chopped coriander and a lime wedge. Serve.
Per Serving: Calories 262; Fat 11g; Sodium 482mg; Carbs 26g; Fiber 1.5g; Sugar 1g; Protein 13g

Herbed Prawns Skewers

Prep Time: 10 minutes | Cook Time: 5 minutes | Serves: 5

1.8kg prawns, peeled	1 teaspoon coriander
2 tablespoons fresh coriander, chopped	1 tablespoon avocado oil
2 tablespoons apple cider vinegar	Cooking spray

1. Place the Cook & Crisp Basket in your Pressure Cooker Steam Fryer. 2. In the shallow bowl mix up avocado oil, coriander, apple cider vinegar, and fresh coriander. Then put the prawns in the big bowl and sprinkle with avocado oil mixture. Mix them well and leave for around 10 minutes to marinate. 3. After this, string the prawns on the skewers. Arrange the prawn's skewers in the Cook & Crisp Basket. 4. Put on the Smart Lid on top of the Ninja Foodi Steam Fryer. Move the Lid Slider to the "Air Fry/Stovetop". Select the "Air Fry" mode for cooking. Adjust the cooking temperature to 200°C. Cook for them for around 5 minutes.
Per Serving: Calories 654; Fat: 46.8g; Sodium 845mg; Carbs: 9.9g; Fiber: 3.5g; Sugars 3.5g; Protein 56.9g

Crab Muffins

Prep Time: 15 minutes | Cook Time: 20 minutes | Serves: 2

125g crab meat, chopped	½ teaspoon apple cider vinegar
2 eggs, beaten	½ teaspoon paprika
2 tablespoons almond flour	1 tablespoon butter, softened
¼ teaspoon baking powder	Cooking spray

1. Place the Cook & Crisp Basket in your Pressure Cooker Steam Fryer. 2. Grind the chopped crab meat and put it in the bowl. Add eggs, almond flour, baking powder, apple cider vinegar, paprika, and butter. Stir the mixture until homogenous. 3.Grease the muffin molds with cooking spray. Then pour the crab meat batter in the muffin molds and place them in the Cook & Crisp Basket. 4. Put on the Smart Lid on top of the Ninja Foodi Steam Fryer. Move the Lid Slider to the "Air Fry/Stovetop". Select the "Air Fry" mode for cooking. Adjust the cooking temperature to 185°C. Cook the crab muffins for around 20 minutes or until they are light brown. 5. Cool the cooked muffins to the room temperature and remove from the muffin mold.
Per Serving: Calories 388; Fat: 21.8g; Sodium 787mg; Carbs: 5.4g; Fiber: 1.5g; Sugars 1.4g; Protein 49.3g

Tilapia with Kale

Prep Time: 5 minutes | Cook Time: 20 minutes | Serves: 4

4 tilapia fillets, boneless	½ teaspoon red pepper flakes, crushed
Salt and black pepper to the taste	
2 garlic cloves, minced	1 bunch kale, chopped
1 teaspoon fennel seeds	3 tablespoons olive oil

1. In the Cook & Crisp Basket, mix all the recipe ingredients. 2. Place

the Cook & Crisp Basket in your Pressure Cooker Steam Fryer. 3. Put on the Smart Lid on top of the Ninja Foodi Steam Fryer. Move the Lid Slider to the "Air Fry/Stovetop". Select the "Air Fry" mode for cooking. Air Fry at 180°C for around 20 minutes. 4. Divide everything between plates and serve.
Per Serving: Calories 585; Fat: 39.5g; Sodium 1687mg; Carbs: 10.4g; Fiber: 2.7g; Sugars 3.1g; Protein 43.2g

Lime paprika Cod

Prep Time: 5 minutes | Cook Time: 14 minutes | Serves: 4

4 cod fillets, boneless	2 teaspoons sweet paprika
1 tablespoon olive oil	Juice of 1 lime
Salt and black pepper to the taste	

1. Place the Cook & Crisp Basket in your Pressure Cooker Steam Fryer. 2. In a suitable bowl, mix all the recipe ingredients, transfer the fish to the Cook & Crisp Basket. 3. Put on the Smart Lid on top of the Ninja Foodi Steam Fryer. Move the Lid Slider to the "Air Fry/Stovetop". Select the "Air Fry" mode for cooking. Cook for 175°C for around 7 minutes on each side. 4. Divide the fish between plates and serve with a side salad.
Per Serving: Calories 343; Fat: 20.1g; Sodium 903mg; Carbs: 0.2g; Fiber: 0.1g; Sugars 0.2g; Protein 37.1g

Mackerel with Peppers

Prep Time: 15 minutes | Cook Time: 20 minutes | Serves: 5

455g mackerel, trimmed	1 tablespoon avocado oil
1 tablespoon paprika	1 teaspoon apple cider vinegar
1 green pepper	½ teaspoon salt
80g spring onions, chopped	

1. Place the Cook & Crisp Basket in your Pressure Cooker Steam Fryer. 2. Wash the mackerel if needed and sprinkle with paprika. Chop the green pepper. 3. Then fill the mackerel with pepper and spring onion. After this, sprinkle the fish with avocado oil, apple cider vinegar, and salt. 4. Place the mackerel in the Ninja Foodi Pressure Steam Fryer basket. Put on the Smart Lid on top of the Ninja Foodi Steam Fryer. Move the Lid Slider to the "Air Fry/Stovetop". Select the "Air Fry" mode for cooking. 5. Adjust the cooking temperature to 190°C. Cook for it for around 20 minutes.
Per Serving: Calories 416; Fat: 23.6g; Sodium 934mg; Carbs: 6g; Fiber: 2g; Sugars 0.6g; Protein 37.9g

Ginger Lime Salmon

Prep Time: 5 minutes | Cook Time: 12 minutes | Serves: 4

2 tablespoons lime juice	4 teaspoons olive oil
455g salmon fillets, boneless, skinless and cubed	1 tablespoon coconut aminos
	1 tablespoon sesame seeds, toasted
1 tablespoon ginger, grated	1 tablespoon chives, chopped

1. In the Cook & Crisp Basket, mix all the recipe ingredients and toss. 2. Place the Cook & Crisp Basket in your Pressure Cooker Steam Fryer. Put on the Smart Lid on top of the Ninja Foodi Steam Fryer. Move the Lid Slider to the "Air Fry/Stovetop". Select the "Air Fry" mode for cooking. Air Fry at 180°C for around 12 minutes. 3. Divide into bowls and serve.
Per Serving: Calories 372; Fat: 16.3g; Sodium 742mg; Carbs: 6.8g; Fiber: 0.8g; Sugars 1.8g; Protein 42.3g

Peppered Tuna Skewers

Prep Time: 5 minutes | Cook Time: 12 minutes | Serves: 4

455g tuna steaks, boneless and cubed	2 tablespoons lime juice
	A drizzle of olive oil
1 chili pepper, minced	Salt and black pepper to the taste
4 green onions, chopped	

1. Place the Cook & Crisp Basket in your Pressure Cooker Steam Fryer. 2. In a suitable bowl mix all the recipe ingredients and toss them. Thread the tuna cubes on skewers, arrange them in the Cook & Crisp Basket. 3. Put on the Smart Lid on top of the Ninja Foodi Steam Fryer. Move the Lid Slider to the "Air Fry/Stovetop". Select the "Air Fry" mode for cooking. 4. Air Fry at 190°C for around 12 minutes. Divide between plates and serve with a side salad.
Per Serving: Calories 344; Fat: 10g; Sodium 251mg; Carbs: 4.7g; Fiber: 0.5g; Sugars 2.2g; Protein 55.7g

Crusted Cheesy Prawns

Prep Time: 15 minutes | Cook Time: 5 minutes | Serves: 4

100g prawns, peeled
2 eggs, beaten
60g heavy cream
1 teaspoon salt
1 teaspoon black pepper

100g Monterey jack cheese, shredded
5 tablespoons coconut flour
1 tablespoon lemon juice, for garnish

1. Place the Cook & Crisp Basket in your Pressure Cooker Steam Fryer. 2. In the mixing bowl mix up heavy cream, salt, and black pepper. Add eggs and mix the mixture until homogenous. 3. After this, mix up coconut flour and Monterey jack cheese. Dip the prawns in the heavy cream mixture and coat in the coconut flour mixture. 4. Then dip the prawnss in the egg mixture again and coat in the coconut flour. Arrange the prawnss in the Cook & Crisp Basket in one layer. 5. Put on the Smart Lid on top of the Ninja Foodi Steam Fryer. Move the Lid Slider to the "Air Fry/Stovetop". Select the "Air Fry" mode for cooking. Adjust the cooking temperature to 200°C. Cook for them for around 5 minutes. 6. Repeat the same step with remaining prawnss. Sprinkle the prawnss with lemon juice.
Per Serving: Calories 612; Fat: 38.2g; Sodium 76mg; Carbs: 39.1g; Fiber: 5.8g; Sugars 1.6g; Protein 30.6g

Salmon with Lime Sauce

Prep Time: 5 minutes | Cook Time: 20 minutes | Serves: 4

4 salmon fillets, boneless
60g coconut cream
1 teaspoon lime zest, grated
80g heavy cream

60ml lime juice
40g coconut, shredded
A pinch of salt and black pepper

1. In a suitable bowl, mix all the recipe ingredients except the salmon and whisk. Arrange the fish in the Cook & Crisp Basket, drizzle the coconut sauce all over. Place the Cook & Crisp Basket in your Pressure Cooker Steam Fryer. 2. Put on the Smart Lid on top of the Ninja Foodi Steam Fryer. Move the Lid Slider to the "Air Fry/Stovetop". Select the "Air Fry" mode for cooking. Air Fry at 180°C for around 20 minutes. 3. Divide between plates and serve.
Per Serving: Calories 408; Fat: 23.1g; Sodium 412mg; Carbs: 27.7g; Fiber: 7.2g; Sugars 19.2g; Protein 24.4g

Catfish Fillet Bites

Prep Time: 10 minutes | Cook Time: 10 minutes | Serves: 4

40g coconut flakes
3 tablespoons coconut flour
1 teaspoon salt

3 eggs, beaten
250g catfish fillet
Cooking spray

1. Place the Cook & Crisp Basket in your Pressure Cooker Steam Fryer. 2. Cut the catfish fillet on the small pieces (nuggets) and sprinkle with salt. After this, dip the catfish pieces in the egg and coat in the coconut flour. Then dip the fish pieces in the egg again and coat in the coconut flakes. 3. Spray the Cook & Crisp Basket with cooking spray. Place the catfish nuggets in the Ninja Foodi Pressure Steam Fryer basket. 4. Put on the Smart Lid on top of the Ninja Foodi Steam Fryer. Move the Lid Slider to the "Air Fry/Stovetop". Select the "Air Fry" mode for cooking. Adjust the cooking temperature to 195°C. 5. Cook them for around 6 minutes. Then flip the nuggets on another side. Cook for them for around 4 minutes more.
Per Serving: Calories 347; Fat: 15.7g; Sodium 999mg; Carbs: 11.8g; Fiber: 1.1g; Sugars 7g; Protein 39.6g

Mustard Parmesan Cod

Prep Time: 10 minutes | Cook Time: 14 minutes | Serves: 4

100g parmesan, grated
4 cod fillets, boneless

Salt and black pepper to the taste
1 tablespoon mustard

1. Place the Cook & Crisp Basket in your Pressure Cooker Steam Fryer. 2. In a suitable bowl, mix the parmesan with salt, pepper and the mustard and stir. Spread them over the cod, arrange the fish in the Cook & Crisp Basket. 3. Put on the Smart Lid on top of the Ninja Foodi Steam Fryer. Move the Lid Slider to the "Air Fry/Stovetop". Select the "Air Fry" mode for cooking. Air Fry at 190°C for around 7 minutes on each side. 4. Divide between plates and serve with a side salad.
Per Serving: Calories 236; Fat: 10.4g; Sodium 713mg; Carbs: 9.8g; Fiber: 0.5g; Sugars 0.1g; Protein 25.7g

Turmeric Salmon with Cream

Prep Time: 10 minutes | Cook Time: 7 minutes | Serves: 2

200g salmon fillet
2 tablespoons coconut flakes
1 tablespoon coconut cream
½ teaspoon salt

½ teaspoon turmeric
½ teaspoon onion powder
1 teaspoon nut oil

1. Place the Cook & Crisp Basket in your Pressure Cooker Steam Fryer. 2. Cut the salmon fillet into halves and sprinkle with salt, turmeric, and onion powder. After this, dip the fish fillets in the coconut cream and coat in the coconut flakes. 3. Sprinkle the salmon fillets with nut oil. Arrange the salmon fillets in the Ninja Foodi Pressure Steam Fryer basket. 4. Put on the Smart Lid on top of the Ninja Foodi Steam Fryer. Move the Lid Slider to the "Air Fry/Stovetop". Select the "Air Fry" mode for cooking. Adjust the cooking temperature to 195°C. Cook for around 7 minutes.
Per Serving: Calories 427; Fat: 18.1g; Sodium 676mg; Carbs: 13.7g; Fiber: 7.5g; Sugars 1.7g; Protein 51.2g

Air-Fried Tilapia

Prep Time: 15 minutes | Cook Time: 9 minutes | Serves: 2

1 chili pepper, chopped
1 teaspoon chili flakes
1 tablespoon sesame oil

½ teaspoon salt
250g tilapia fillet
¼ teaspoon onion powder

1. Place the Cook & Crisp Basket in your Pressure Cooker Steam Fryer. 2. In the shallow bowl mix up chili pepper, chili flakes, salt, and onion powder. Gently churn the mixture and add sesame oil. 3. After this, slice the tilapia fillet and sprinkle with chili mixture. Massage the fish with the help of the fingertips gently and leave for around 10 minutes to marinate. 4. Put the tilapia fillets in the Ninja Foodi Pressure Steam Fryer basket. Put on the Smart Lid on top of the Ninja Foodi Steam Fryer. Move the Lid Slider to the "Air Fry/Stovetop". Select the "Air Fry" mode for cooking. Adjust the cooking temperature to 200°C. 5. Cook for around 5 minutes. Then flip the fish on another side. Cook for around 4 minutes more.
Per Serving: Calories 232; Fat: 8.4g; Sodium 300mg; Carbs: 8.6g; Fiber: 0.9g; Sugars 0.1g; Protein 30.1g

Paprika Cod with Chicory

Prep Time: 5 minutes | Cook Time: 20 minutes | Serves: 4

2 chicories, shredded
2 tablespoons olive oil
Salt and black pepper to the taste

4 salmon fillets, boneless
½ teaspoon sweet paprika

1. In the Cook & Crisp Basket, mix the fish with the rest of the ingredients and toss. 2. Place the Cook & Crisp Basket in your Pressure Cooker Steam Fryer. Put on the Smart Lid on top of the Ninja Foodi Steam Fryer. Move the Lid Slider to the "Air Fry/Stovetop". Select the "Air Fry" mode for cooking. 3. Air Fry at 175°C for around 20 minutes, flipping the fish halfway. Divide between plates and serve right away.
Per Serving: Calories 314; Fat: 8.7g; Sodium 337mg; Carbs: 21.2g; Fiber: 4.1g; Sugars 16g; Protein 37.9g

Sesame Crusted Salmon

Prep Time: 10 minutes | Cook Time: 9 minutes | Serves: 6

200g salmon fillet
2 tablespoons swerve
1 tablespoon apple cider vinegar
6 teaspoons liquid aminos
1 teaspoon minced ginger

1 tablespoon sesame seeds
2 tablespoons lemon juice
½ teaspoon minced garlic
1 tablespoon avocado oil

1. Place the Cook & Crisp Basket in your Pressure Cooker Steam Fryer. 2. Cut the salmon fillet into 8 portions and sprinkle with apple cider vinegar, minced ginger, lemon juice, minced garlic, and liquid aminos. Leave the fish for around 10 to 15 minutes to marinate. 3. After this, sprinkle the fish with avocado oil and put in the Cook & Crisp Basket in one layer. Cook the fish fillets for around 7 minutes. Then sprinkle them with swerve and sesame seeds. 4. Put on the Smart Lid on top of the Ninja Foodi Steam Fryer. Move the Lid Slider to the "Air Fry/Stovetop". Select the "Air Fry" mode for cooking. 5. Cook for around 2 minutes more at 200°C.
Per Serving: Calories 347; Fat: 18.8g; Sodium 137mg; Carbs: 13.4g; Fiber: 8.5g; Sugars 1g; Protein 36.3g

Crusted Sardine Cakes

Prep Time: 15 minutes | Cook Time: 10 minutes | Serves: 5

150g sardines, trimmed, cleaned
30g coconut flour
1 egg, beaten
2 tablespoons flax meal
1 teaspoon black pepper
1 teaspoon salt
Cooking spray

1. Place the Cook & Crisp Basket in your Pressure Cooker Steam Fryer. 2. Chop the sardines and put them in the bowl. Add coconut flour, egg, flax meal, black pepper, and salt. Mix up the mixture with the help of the fork. Then make 5 cakes from the sardine mixture. Grease the Ninja Foodi Pressure Steam Fryer basket with cooking spray and place the cakes inside. Put on the Smart Lid on top of the Ninja Foodi Steam Fryer. 3. Move the Lid Slider to the "Air Fry/Stovetop". Select the "Air Fry" mode for cooking. Adjust the cooking temperature to 200°C. Cook them for around 5 minutes from each side.
Per Serving: Calories 326; Fat: 12g; Sodium 779mg; Carbs: 8.3g; Fiber: 2.9g; Sugars 1.3g; Protein 46.9g

Parsley Coconut Prawns

Prep Time: 5 minutes | Cook Time: 12 minutes | Serves: 4

1 tablespoon ghee, melted
455g prawns, peeled and deveined
60g coconut cream
A pinch of red pepper flakes
A pinch of salt and black pepper
1 tablespoon parsley, chopped
1 tablespoon chives, chopped

1. Place the Cook & Crisp Basket in your Pressure Cooker Steam Fryer. 2. In the Cook & Crisp Basket, mix all the recipe ingredients except the parsley. Place the Cook & Crisp Basket in your Pressure Cooker Steam Fryer. 3. Put on the Smart Lid on top of the Ninja Foodi Steam Fryer. Move the Lid Slider to the "Air Fry/Stovetop". Select the "Air Fry" mode for cooking. Air Fry at 180°C for around 12 minutes. 4. Divide the mix into bowls, sprinkle the parsley on top and serve.
 Per Serving: Calories 618; Fat: 13.5g; Sodium 96mg; Carbs: 98.7g; Fiber: 5.3g; Sugars 0.5g; Protein 24.4g

Bacon Halibut Steaks

Prep Time: 15 minutes | Cook Time: 10 minutes | Serves: 4

2 halibut steaks (150g each fillet)
½ teaspoon salt
½ teaspoon black pepper
100g bacon, sliced
1 tablespoon sunflower oil

1. Place the Cook & Crisp Basket in your Pressure Cooker Steam Fryer. 2. Cut every halibut fillet on 2 parts and sprinkle with salt and black pepper. Then wrap the fish fillets in the sliced bacon. Sprinkle the halibut bites with sunflower oil and put in the "cook & crisp basket". 3. Put on the Smart Lid on top of the Ninja Foodi Steam Fryer. Move the Lid Slider to the "Air Fry/Stovetop". Select the "Air Fry" mode for cooking. Adjust the cooking temperature to 200°C. Cook the meal for around 5 minutes. 4. Then flip the fish bites on another side. Cook for them for around 5 minutes more.
Per Serving: Calories 412; Fat: 23.6g; Sodium 1495mg; Carbs: 4.8g; Fiber: 1.3g; Sugars 1.7g; Protein 37.9g

Parmesan Salmon

Prep Time: 5 minutes | Cook Time: 15 minutes | Serves: 4

4 salmon fillets, skinless
1 teaspoon mustard
A pinch of salt and black pepper
40g coconut flakes
1 tablespoon parmesan, grated
Cooking spray

1. Place the Cook & Crisp Basket in your Pressure Cooker Steam Fryer. 2. In a suitable bowl, mix the parmesan with the other ingredients except the fish and cooking spray and stir well. 3. Coat the fish in this mixture, grease it with cooking spray and arrange in the Cook & Crisp Basket. 4. Put on the Smart Lid on top of the Ninja Foodi Steam Fryer. Move the Lid Slider to the "Air Fry/Stovetop". Select the "Air Fry" mode for cooking. 5. Air Fry these fillets at 200°C for around 15 minutes, divide between plates and serve with a side salad.
Per Serving: Calories 413; Fat: 24.5g; Sodium 962mg; Carbs: 6.9g; Fiber: 1.1g; Sugars 2.9g; Protein 39.1g

Chapter 7 Snack and Appetizer Recipes

Olive-Stuffed Jalapeños

Prep Time: 10 minutes | Cook Time: 8 minutes | Serves: 5

60g plain cream cheese
25g finely grated Cheddar cheese
2 tablespoons chopped black

olives
5 medium jalapeño peppers, cut
lengthwise, seeded

1. Place the Cook & Crisp Basket in your Pressure Cooker Steam Fryer. 2. In a suitable bowl, cream cheese, Cheddar cheese, and black olives. 3. Press cream cheese mixture into each jalapeño half. 4. Lay stuffed peppers in ungreased "cook & crisp basket". 5. Put on the Smart Lid on top of the Ninja Foodi Steam Fryer. 6. Move the Lid Slider to the "Air Fry/Stovetop". Select the "Air Fry" mode for cooking. 7. Adjust the cooking temperature to 175°C for 8 minutes. 8. Once done, transfer stuffed peppers to a suitable serving plate and serve warm.
Per Serving: Calories 319; Fat: 15.6g; Sodium 99mg; Carbs: 4.8g; Fiber: 0.7g; Sugars 2.9g; Protein 38.5g

Cheese Quesadillas

Prep Time: 10 minutes | Cook Time: 24 minutes | Serves: 4

8 tablespoons Mexican blend
shredded cheese

8 (15cm) soft corn tortillas
2 teaspoons olive oil

1. Place the Cook & Crisp Basket in your Pressure Cooker Steam Fryer. 2. Evenly sprinkle cheese over four tortillas. Top each with a remaining tortilla and brush the tops with oil. 3. Place one quesadilla in ungreased "cook & crisp basket". 4. Put on the Smart Lid on top of the Ninja Foodi Steam Fryer. 5. Move the Lid Slider to the "Air Fry/Stovetop". Select the "Air Fry" mode for cooking. 6. Adjust the cooking temperature to 175°C for 6 minutes. 7. Remove and repeat with remaining quesadillas. 8. Transfer quesadillas to a suitable serving tray and serve warm.
Per Serving: Calories 349; Fat: 15.1g; Sodium 157mg; Carbs: 25.6g; Fiber: 2.6g; Sugars 22.5g; Protein 29.7g

Deviled Eggs

Prep Time: 5 minutes | Cook Time: 15 minutes | Serves: 4

4 large eggs
240g ice cubes
240ml water
2 tablespoons mayonnaise
1 tablespoon Thousand Island
dressing
⅛ teaspoon salt

⅛ teaspoon black pepper
2 tablespoons finely chopped
corned beef
1 teaspoon caraway seeds
2 tablespoons finely chopped
Swiss cheese

1. Place the Cook & Crisp Basket in your Pressure Cooker Steam Fryer. 2. Place eggs in silicone cupcake liners to avoid eggs from moving around or cracking during cooking process. Add silicone cups to "cook & crisp basket". 3. Put on the Smart Lid on top of the Ninja Foodi Steam Fryer. 4. Move the Lid Slider to the "Air Fry/Stovetop". Select the "Air Fry" mode for cooking. Cook at 120°C for 15 minutes. 5. Add ice and water to a suitable bowl. Transfer cooked eggs to water bath immediately to stop cooking process. After 5 minutes, carefully peel eggs. 6. Cut eggs in half lengthwise. Spoon yolks in a suitable bowl. Arrange white halves on a suitable plate. 7. Using a fork, blend egg yolks with mayonnaise, dressing, salt, pepper, corned beef, and caraway seeds. Fold in cheese. Spoon mixture into egg white halves. Serve.
Per Serving: Calories 182; Fat: 14.1g; Sodium 18mg; Carbs: 8.9g; Fiber: 4.1g; Sugars 4g; Protein 7.2g

Hot Wings

Prep Time: 15 minutes | Cook Time: 44 minutes | Serves: 6

900g chicken wings, split at the
joint
1 tablespoon water
1 tablespoon butter, room

temperature
120ml buffalo wing sauce
Cooking oil

1. Place the Cook & Crisp Basket in your Pressure Cooker Steam Fryer. 2. Place water in bottom of the Cook & Crisp Basket to ensure minimum smoke from fat: drippings. 3. Place half of chicken wings in "cook & crisp basket" greased with cooking oil. Put on the Smart Lid on top of the Ninja Foodi Steam Fryer. Move the Lid Slider to the "Air Fry/Stovetop". Select the "Air Fry" mode for cooking. 4. Adjust the

cooking temperature to 120°C. 5. Cook 6 minutes. Flip wings, then cook an additional 6 minutes. 6. While wings are cooking, mix butter and wing sauce in a suitable bowl. 7. Increase temperature on air fryer to 200°C. Flip wings and cook for 5 minutes. 8. Once done, transfer to bowl with sauce and toss. Set aside. 9. Repeat process with remaining wings. Serve warm.
Per Serving: Calories 271; Fat: 19.2g; Sodium 124mg; Carbs: 7.2g; Fiber: 2.9g; Sugars 0.5g; Protein 18.6g

Mustard Wings

Prep Time: 15 minutes | Cook Time: 44 minutes | Serves: 6

90g chicken wings, split at the
joint
1 tablespoon butter, melted
1 tablespoon water
1 tablespoon Dijon mustard

2 tablespoons yellow mustard
85g honey
1 teaspoon apple cider vinegar
⅛ teaspoon salt
Cooking oil

1. Place the Cook & Crisp Basket in your Pressure Cooker Steam Fryer. 2. Place water in bottom of the Cook & Crisp Basket to ensure minimum smoke from fat: drippings. 3. Place half of wings in "cook & crisp basket" greased with cooking oil. Put on the Smart Lid on top of the Ninja Foodi Steam Fryer. Move the Lid Slider to the "Air Fry/Stovetop". Select the "Air Fry" mode for cooking. Adjust the cooking temperature to 120°C. 4. Cook for 6 minutes. Flip wings, then cook an additional 6 minutes. 5. While wings are cooking, mix butter, Dijon mustard, yellow mustard, honey, cider vinegar, and salt in a suitable bowl. 6. Raise temperature to 200°C. Flip wings and cook for 5 minutes. Flip wings once more. Cook for an additional 5 minutes. 7. Transfer cooked wings to bowl with sauce and toss. Repeat process with remaining wings. Serve warm.
Per Serving: Calories 309; Fat: 5.1g; Sodium 245mg; Carbs: 43g; Fiber: 9.6g; Sugars 14.2g; Protein 25.8g

Pizza Bombs with Marinara Sauce

Prep Time: 10 minutes | Cook Time: 12 minutes | Serves: 9 pizza bites

80g gluten-free plain flour
¼ teaspoon salt
¼ teaspoon baking powder
70g small-diced pepperoni
50g cream cheese, room
temperature

30g shredded mozzarella cheese
½ teaspoon Italian seasoning
2 tablespoons whole milk
1 teaspoon olive oil
120g marinara sauce, warmed

1. Place the Cook & Crisp Basket in your Pressure Cooker Steam Fryer. 2. In a suitable bowl, mix flour, salt, and baking powder. 3. In a suitable bowl, mix remaining ingredients, except marinara sauce. Add dry recipe ingredients to bowl and mix until well mixed. 4. Form mixture into nine (2.5 cm) balls and place on the Cook & Crisp Basket. Put on the Smart Lid on top of the Ninja Foodi Steam Fryer. 5. Move the Lid Slider to the "Air Fry/Stovetop". Select the "Air Fry" mode for cooking. Adjust the cooking temperature to 160°C. 6. Cook for 12 minutes. 7. Transfer balls to a suitable plate. Serve warm with marinara sauce.
Per Serving: Calories 217; Fat: 5.1g; Sodium 624mg; Carbs: 6.8g; Fiber: 0.8g; Sugars 1.8g; Protein 31.1g

Cauliflower Pizza Crusts

Prep Time: 10 minutes | Cook Time: 30 minutes | Serves: 2

110g cauliflower rice
1 large egg
55g grated mozzarella cheese
1 tablespoon grated Parmesan
cheese

1 clove garlic, peeled and minced
1 teaspoon Italian seasoning
⅛ teaspoon salt
Cooking oil

1. Place the deluxe reversible rack in your Pressure Cooker Steam Fryer. 2. In a suitable bowl, mix all the recipe ingredients. 3. Divide mixture in half and spread into two pizza suitable pans greased with preferred cooking oil. 4. Place one pan in the deluxe reversible rack. Put on the Smart Lid on top of the Ninja Foodi Steam Fryer. Move the Lid Slider to the "Air Fry/Stovetop". Select the "Air Fry" mode for cooking. 5. Adjust the cooking temperature to 200°C. 6. Cook for 12 minutes. Once done, remove pan and repeat with second pan. 7. Top crusts with your favorite toppings. Cook for an additional 3 minutes.
Per Serving: Calories 309; Fat: 17.4g; Sodium 348mg; Carbs: 4.8g; Fiber: 1.9g; Sugars 0.6g; Protein 33.4g

Air-Fried Pumpkin Seeds

Prep Time: 10 minutes | Cook Time: 13 minutes | Serves: 4

235g fresh pumpkin seeds, rinsed and dried
2 teaspoons olive oil
½ teaspoon, ¼ teaspoon salt, divided

1. Place the Cook & Crisp Basket in your Pressure Cooker Steam Fryer. 2. In a suitable bowl, toss seeds with oil and ½ teaspoon salt. 3. Place seeds in ungreased "cook & crisp basket". 4. Put on the Smart Lid on top of the Ninja Foodi Steam Fryer. 5. Move the Lid Slider to the "Air Fry/Stovetop". Select the "Air Fry" mode for cooking. 6. Adjust the cooking temperature to 160°C. 7. Cook for 7 minutes. Using a spatula, turn seeds, then cook an additional 6 minutes. 8. Transfer seeds to a suitable bowl and let cool 5 minutes before serving.
Per Serving: Calories 481; Fat: 14.6g; Sodium 285mg; Carbs: 57.5g; Fiber: 7.3g; Sugars 1g; Protein 31.1g

Grilled Pimento Croutons

Prep Time: 10 minutes | Cook Time: 24 minutes | Serves: 4

200g shredded sharp Cheddar cheese
1 (100g) jar chopped pimientos, including juice
120g mayonnaise
¼ teaspoon salt
¼ teaspoon black pepper
8 slices gluten-free sandwich bread
4 tablespoons butter, melted

1. Place the Cook & Crisp Basket in your Pressure Cooker Steam Fryer. 2. Mix cheese, pimientos including juice, mayonnaise, salt, and pepper in a suitable bowl. Refrigerate covered 30 minutes. 3. Spread pimento cheese mixture evenly over four slices gluten-free bread. Top each slice with a plain slice and press down just enough to not smoosh cheese out of edges of sandwich. 4. Brush top and bottom of each sandwich with melted butter. Place one sandwich at a time in ungreased "cook & crisp basket". Put on the Smart Lid on top of the Ninja Foodi Steam Fryer. Move the Lid Slider to the "Air Fry/Stovetop". Select the "Air Fry" mode for cooking. 5. Adjust the cooking temperature to 175°C. 6. Cook for 3 minutes. Flip sandwich. Cook for an additional 3 minutes. Repeat with remaining sandwiches. 7. Slice each sandwich into sixteen sections and serve warm.
Per Serving: Calories 384; Fat: 23.6g; Sodium 80mg; Carbs: 20.7g; Fiber: 8.3g; Sugars 3.5g; Protein 24.6g

Aubergine Fries

Prep Time: 10 minutes | Cook Time: 12 minutes | Serves: 2

2 large eggs
2 tablespoons whole milk
50g gluten-free bread crumbs
50g grated Parmesan cheese
1 teaspoon salt
1 medium aubergine, cut into 1 cm rounds, then sliced
120g marinara sauce, warmed

1. Place the Cook & Crisp Basket in your Pressure Cooker Steam Fryer. 2. Mix eggs and milk in a suitable bowl. In a separate shallow dish, mix bread crumbs, Parmesan cheese, and salt. 3. Dip aubergine in egg mixture. Dredge in bread crumb mixture. 4. Place aubergine fries in ungreased "cook & crisp basket". Put on the Smart Lid on top of the Ninja Foodi Steam Fryer. Select the "Air Fry/Stovetop". Select the "Air Fry" mode for cooking. 5. Adjust the cooking temperature to 200°C. 6. Cook for 5 minutes. Flip fries, then cook an additional 5 minutes. Flip once more. Cook for an additional 2 minutes. 7. Transfer fries to a suitable plate and serve with warmed marinara sauce on the side for dipping.
Per Serving: Calories 314; Fat: 8.7g; Sodium 337mg; Carbs: 21.2g; Fiber: 4.1g; Sugars 16g; Protein 37.9g

French Fries

Prep Time: 10 minutes | Cook Time: 15 minutes | Serves: 4

2 russet potatoes, scrubbed and cut into ½ cm fries
3 teaspoons salt

1. Place the Cook & Crisp Basket in your Pressure Cooker Steam Fryer. 2. Place fries in a suitable saucepan. Add water to pan to cover fries. Add 1 teaspoon salt. Bring to a boil over high heat. Boil 3 minutes until fork tender. Drain. 3. Toss fries with 1 teaspoon salt. Place salted fries in ungreased "cook & crisp basket". Put on the Smart Lid on top of the Ninja Foodi Steam Fryer. Move the Lid Slider to the "Air Fry/Stovetop". Select the "Air Fry" mode for cooking.

4. Adjust the cooking temperature to 200°C. 5. Cook for 5 minutes. Shake basket, then cook an additional 5 minutes. Shake basket once more and season with remaining teaspoon salt. Cook an additional 5 minutes. 6. Transfer fries to a suitable plate and serve warm.
Per Serving: Calories 422; Fat: 7.3g; Sodium 1093mg; Carbs: 26.9g; Fiber: 5.9g; Sugars 2.4g; Protein 58.5g

Courgette Fries

Prep Time: 10 minutes | Cook Time: 20 minutes | Serves: 2

1 large courgette, cut into ½ cm fries
1 teaspoon salt
120ml buttermilk
75g gluten-free bread crumbs
2 teaspoons dried thyme

1. Place the Cook & Crisp Basket in your Pressure Cooker Steam Fryer. 2. Scatter courgette fries evenly over a paper towel. Sprinkle with salt. Let sit 10 minutes, then pat with paper towels. 3. Pour buttermilk into a shallow dish. Place bread crumbs in a second shallow dish. Dip courgette in buttermilk, then dredge in bread crumbs. 4. Place half of courgette fries in ungreased "cook & crisp basket". Put on the Smart Lid on top of the Ninja Foodi Steam Fryer. Move the Lid Slider to the "Air Fry/Stovetop". Select the "Air Fry" mode for cooking. 5. Adjust the cooking temperature to 190°C. 6. Cook for 5 minutes. Flip fries, then cook an additional 5 minutes. 7. Transfer fries to a suitable serving dish. Repeat cooking steps with remaining fries. Season with thyme and serve warm.
Per Serving: Calories 393; Fat: 11.7g; Sodium 591mg; Carbs: 16.4g; Fiber: 4.3g; Sugars 6.6g; Protein 56.4g

Avocado Fries

Prep Time: 10 minutes | Cook Time: 10 minutes | Serves: 2

1 large egg
2 tablespoons whole milk
40g crushed chili corn chips
1 medium avocado, halved,
peeled, pitted, and sliced into 12 "fries"
Cooking oil

1. Place the Cook & Crisp Basket in your Pressure Cooker Steam Fryer. 2. Mix egg and milk in a suitable bowl. Add chili corn chip crumbs to a separate shallow dish. 3. Dip avocado slices into egg mixture. Dredge in chip crumbs to coat. 4. Place half of avocado slices in "cook & crisp basket" greased with cooking oil. 5. Put on the Smart Lid on top of the Ninja Foodi Steam Fryer. 6. Move the Lid Slider to the "Air Fry/Stovetop". Select the "Air Fry" mode for cooking. 7. Adjust the cooking temperature to 190°C. 8. Cook for 5 minutes. Transfer to serving plate and repeat with remaining avocado slices. 9. Serve fries warm.
Per Serving: Calories 275; Fat: 2.2g; Sodium 486mg; Carbs: 27.3g; Fiber: 0.4g; Sugars 17.5g; Protein 36.3g

Prawns Sesame Toasts

Prep Time: 10 minutes | Cook Time: 8 minutes | Serves: 6

225g raw prawns, peeled and de-veined
1 egg (or 2 egg whites)
2 spring onions, more for garnish
2 teaspoons grated fresh ginger
1 teaspoon soy sauce
½ teaspoon toasted sesame oil
2 tablespoons chopped fresh
coriander or parsley
1 to 2 teaspoons sriracha sauce
6 slices thinly-sliced white sandwich bread (Pepperidge Farm®)
65g sesame seeds
Thai chili sauce

1. Place the Cook & Crisp Basket in your Pressure Cooker Steam Fryer. 2. Mix the prawns, egg, spring onions, fresh ginger, soy sauce, sesame oil, coriander (or parsley) and sriracha sauce in a food processor and process into a chunky paste, scraping down the sides of the food processor bowl as necessary. 3. Cut the crusts off the sandwich bread and generously spread the prawns paste onto each slice of bread. Place the sesame seeds on a plate and invert each prawns toast into the sesame seeds to coat, pressing down gently. Cut each slice of bread into 4 triangles. 4. Transfer one layer of prawns toast triangles to the Cook & Crisp Basket. 5. Put on the Smart Lid on top of the Ninja Foodi Steam Fryer. 6. Move the Lid Slider to the "Air Fry/Stovetop". Select the "Air Fry" mode for cooking. 7. Cook on the "Air Fry" mode at 200°C for 6 to 8 minutes, or until the sesame seeds are toasted on top. 8. Serve warm with a little Thai chili sauce and some sliced spring onions as garnish.
Per Serving: Calories 223; Fat: 10.6g; Sodium 646mg; Carbs: 4.1g; Fiber: 2.4g; Sugars 1.6g; Protein 29.5g

Ranch Potato Chips

Prep Time: 10 minutes | Cook Time: 16 minutes | Serves: 2

1 teaspoon dry ranch seasoning mix	300g sliced scrubbed fingerling potatoes
½ teaspoon salt	2 teaspoons olive oil
¼ teaspoon black pepper	

1. Place the Cook & Crisp Basket in your Pressure Cooker Steam Fryer. 2. Mix ranch seasoning mix, salt, and pepper in a suitable bowl. Set aside ½ teaspoon for garnish. 3. Toss sliced potatoes with oil in a suitable bowl. Sprinkle with seasoning mix, except reserved ½ teaspoon, to coat. 4. Place chips in ungreased "cook & crisp basket". Put on the Smart Lid on top of the Ninja Foodi Steam Fryer. Move the Lid Slider to the "Air Fry/Stovetop". Select the "Air Fry" mode for cooking. 5. Adjust the cooking temperature to 200°C. 6. Cook for 3 minutes. Shake basket. Cook an additional 3 minutes. 7. basket. Cook for 5 minutes. Shake basket once more. Cook an additional 5 minutes. 8. Transfer chips to a suitable bowl. Garnish with remaining seasoning, then let rest 15 minutes before serving.
Per Serving: Calories 385; Fat: 13.2g; Sodium 929mg; Carbs: 31.6g; Fiber: 4.2g; Sugars 2.6g; Protein 36.4g

Barbecue Chips

Prep Time: 10 minutes | Cook Time: 17 minutes | Serves: 2

½ teaspoon smoked paprika	⅛ teaspoon light brown sugar
¼ teaspoon chili powder	1 teaspoon salt
¼ teaspoon garlic powder	1 medium russet potato, scrubbed
⅛ teaspoon onion powder	and sliced into ¼ cm-thick circles
⅛ teaspoon cayenne pepper	2 teaspoons olive oil

1. Place the Cook & Crisp Basket in your Pressure Cooker Steam Fryer. 2. In a suitable bowl, mix smoked paprika, chili powder, garlic powder, onion powder, cayenne pepper, brown sugar, and ½ teaspoon salt. Set aside. 3. In a separate large bowl, toss chips with olive oil and ½ teaspoon salt. 4. Place chips in ungreased "cook & crisp basket". Put on the Smart Lid on top of the Ninja Foodi Steam Fryer. Move the Lid Slider to the "Air Fry/Stovetop". Select the "Air Fry" mode for cooking. 5. Adjust the cooking temperature to 200°C. 6. Cook for 6 minutes. Shake basket, then cook an additional 5 minutes. Shake basket once more. Cook for an additional 6 minutes. 7. Transfer chips to bowl with seasoning mix and toss. Let rest 15 minutes before serving.
Per Serving: Calories 342; Fat: 13.7g; Sodium 678mg; Carbs: 32.3g; Fiber: 4.5g; Sugars 22.1g; Protein 26.7g

Dill Pickles with Ranch Dip

Prep Time: 10 minutes | Cook Time: 8 minutes | Serves: 4

4 to 6 dill pickles, sliced in half or quartered lengthwise	1 teaspoon salt
	⅛ teaspoon cayenne pepper
60g plain flour	2 tablespoons fresh dill leaves, dried well
2 eggs, beaten	
100g plain breadcrumbs	Vegetable oil, in a spray bottle
Light Ranch Dip	
60ml reduced-fat: mayonnaise	1 tablespoon chopped fresh parsley
55g buttermilk	1 tablespoon lemon juice
60g non-fat: Greek yogurt	salt and black pepper
1 tablespoon chopped fresh chives	

1. Place the Cook & Crisp Basket in your Pressure Cooker Steam Fryer. 2. Set up your dredging station using three shallow dishes. Place the flour in the first shallow dish. Place the eggs into the second dish. Mix the breadcrumbs, salt, cayenne and fresh dill in a food processor and process until everything is mixed and the crumbs are very fine. Place the crumb mixture in the third dish. 3. Coat the pickles pieces by dredging them first in the flour, then the egg, and then the breadcrumbs, pressing the crumbs on gently with your hands. Set the coated pickles on the Cook & Crisp Basket and grease them on all sides with vegetable oil. 4. Put on the Smart Lid on top of the Ninja Foodi Steam Fryer. 5. Move the Lid Slider to the "Air Fry/Stovetop". Select the "Air Fry" mode for cooking. 6. Cook one layer of pickles at a time at 200°C for 8 minutes, turning them over halfway through the cooking process and spraying again. 7. While the pickles are cooking, make the light ranch dip by mixing everything in a suitable bowl. 8. Serve the pickles warm with the dip on the side.
Per Serving: Calories 353; Fat: 18.5g; Sodium 682mg; Carbs: 2.3g; Fiber: 0.8g; Sugars 1g; Protein 45.8g

Avocado Fries with Salsa Fresca

Prep Time: 10 minutes | Cook Time: 6 minutes | Serves: 6

60g flour	¼ teaspoon smoked paprika (optional)
2 teaspoons salt	
2 eggs, beaten	2 large avocados, just ripe
110g panko breadcrumbs	Vegetable oil, in a spray bottle
⅛ teaspoon cayenne pepper	
Quick Salsa Fresca	
150g cherry tomatoes	1 teaspoon chopped fresh coriander or parsley
1 tablespoon-sized chunk of shallot or red onion	
	Salt and black pepper
2 teaspoons fresh lime juice	

1. Place the Cook & Crisp Basket in your Pressure Cooker Steam Fryer. 2. Set up your dredging station with three shallow dishes. Place the flour and salt in the first shallow dish. Place the eggs into the second dish. Mix the breadcrumbs, cayenne pepper and paprika (if using) in the third dish. 3. Cut the avocado in half around the pit and separate the two sides. Slice the avocados into long strips while still in their skin. Run a spoon around the slices, separating them from the avocado skin. Try to keep the slices whole, but don't worry if they break – you can still coat. 4. Coat the avocado slices by dredging them first in the flour, then the egg and then the breadcrumbs, pressing the crumbs on gently with your hands. Set the coated avocado fries on the Cook & Crisp Basket and grease them on all sides with vegetable oil. 5. Put on the Smart Lid on top of the Ninja Foodi Steam Fryer. 6. Move the Lid Slider to the "Air Fry/Stovetop". Select the "Air Fry" mode for cooking. 7. Air-fry the avocado fries, one layer at a time at 200°C for 6 minutes, turning them over halfway through the cooking time and spraying again if necessary. When the fries are nicely browned on all sides, season with salt and remove. 8. While the avocado fries are cooking, make the salsa fresca by combining everything in a food processor. Pulse several times until the salsa is a chunky purée. 9. Serve the fries warm with the salsa on the side for dipping.
Per Serving: Calories 282; Fat: 15.4g; Sodium 646mg; Carbs: 16.4g; Fiber: 7g; Sugars 6.5g; Protein 22.5g

Brie with Tomatoes

Prep Time: 10 minutes | Cook Time: 15 minutes | Serves: 8

1 baguette	1 tablespoon chopped fresh parsley
680g red and yellow cherry tomatoes	1 (200g) wheel of Brie cheese
	Olive oil
1 tablespoon olive oil	½ teaspoon Italian seasoning
Salt and black pepper	1 tablespoon chopped fresh basil
1 teaspoon balsamic vinegar	

1. Place the Cook & Crisp Basket in your Pressure Cooker Steam Fryer. 2. Start by making the crostini. Slice the baguette diagonally into 1 cm slices and brush the slices with olive oil on both sides. Transfer them into the Cook & Crisp Basket. 3. Put on the Smart Lid on top of the Ninja Foodi Steam Fryer. Move the Lid Slider to the "Air Fry/Stovetop". Select the "Air Fry" mode for cooking. 4. Air fry the baguette slices at 175°C in batches for around 6 minutes or until browned on all sides. Set the bread aside on your serving platter. 5. Toss the cherry tomatoes in a suitable bowl with the olive oil, black pepper and salt. Put on the Smart Lid on top of the Ninja Foodi Steam Fryer. Move the Lid Slider to the "Air Fry/Stovetop". Select the "Air Fry" mode for cooking. 6. Air fry the cherry tomatoes at 175°C for around 3 to 5 minutes, shaking the basket a few times during the cooking process. The tomatoes should be soft and some of them will burst open. Toss the warm tomatoes with the balsamic vinegar and fresh parsley and set aside. 7. Cut a circle of parchment paper the same size as your wheel of Brie cheese. Brush both sides of the Brie wheel with olive oil and sprinkle with Italian seasoning, if using. 8. Place the circle of parchment paper on one side of the Brie and transfer the Brie to the Ninja Foodi Pressure Steam Fryer basket, parchment side down. Put on the Smart Lid on top of the Ninja Foodi Steam Fryer. Move the Lid Slider to the "Air Fry/Stovetop". Select the "Air Fry" mode for cooking. 9. Air Fry the brie at 175°C for 10 minutes. Watch carefully and remove the Brie before the rind cracks and the cheese starts to leak out. 10. Transfer the wheel to your serving platter and top with the roasted tomatoes. Sprinkle with basil and serve with the toasted bread slices.
Per Serving: Calories 476; Fat: 37.7g; Sodium 742mg; Carbs: 15.3g; Fiber: 6g; Sugars 5g; Protein 24.8g

Mozzarella with Puttanesca Sauce

Prep Time: 10 minutes | Cook Time: 8 minutes | Serves: 8

8 slices of sliced white bread (Pepperidge Farm®)
200g mozzarella cheese, sliced
60g plain flour
3 eggs, beaten
Puttanesca Sauce
2 teaspoons olive oil
1 anchovy, chopped
2 cloves garlic, minced
1 (350g) can petite diced tomatoes
120ml chicken stock or water
45g Kalamata olives, chopped
2 tablespoons capers

170g seasoned panko breadcrumbs
½ teaspoon garlic powder
½ teaspoon salt
Black pepper
Olive oil, in a spray bottle

½ teaspoon dried oregano
¼ teaspoon crushed red pepper flakes
Salt and black pepper
1 tablespoon fresh parsley, chopped

1. Place the Cook & Crisp Basket in your Pressure Cooker Steam Fryer. 2. Start by making the puttanesca sauce. Heat the olive oil in a suitable saucepan on the stovetop. Stir in anchovies and garlic and sauté for around 3 minutes. Stir in the tomatoes, chicken stock, olives, capers, oregano and crushed red pepper flakes and simmer the sauce for around 20 minutes. Season with salt and black pepper and stir in the parsley. 3. Cut the bread crust. Keep four slices of the bread on a cutting board. Divide the cheese between the four slices of bread. Top the cheese with the remaining four slices of bread to make little sandwiches and cut each sandwich into 4 triangles. 4. Set up your dredging station using three shallow dishes. Place the flour in the first shallow dish, the eggs in the second dish and in the third dish, mix the garlic powder, panko breadcrumbs, salt and black pepper. 5. Dredge each little triangle in the flour first and then dip them into the egg. 6. Let the excess egg drip off and then press the triangles into the breadcrumb mixture, pressing the crumbs on with your hands so they adhere. Place the coated triangles in the freezer for around 2 hours, until the cheese is frozen. 7. Grease all sides of the mozzarella triangles with oil and transfer a single layer of triangles to the Ninja Foodi Pressure Steam Fryer basket. Put on the Smart Lid on top of the Ninja Foodi Steam Fryer. Move the Lid Slider to the "Air Fry/Stovetop". Select the "Air Fry" mode for cooking. Air fry in batches at 200°C for 5 minutes. 8. Serve with the warm puttanesca sauce.
Per Serving: Calories 371; Fat: 4.9g; Sodium 1207mg; Carbs: 57.5g; Fiber: 25g; Sugars 7g; Protein 25.6g

Chicken Bites

Prep Time: 5 minutes | Cook Time: 20 minutes | Serves: 4

2 teaspoons garlic powder
2 eggs
Salt and black pepper to the taste
70g coconut flakes

Cooking spray
455g chicken breasts, skinless, boneless and cubed

1. Place the Cook & Crisp Basket in your Pressure Cooker Steam Fryer. 2. Put the coconut in a suitable bowl and mix the eggs with garlic powder, black pepper and salt in a second one. Dredge the chicken cubes in eggs and then in coconut and arrange them all in Cook & Crisp Basket. Grease with cooking spray. 3. Put on the Smart Lid on top of the Ninja Foodi Steam Fryer. 4. Move the Lid Slider to the "Air Fry/Stovetop". Select the "Air Fry" mode for cooking. 5. Air Fry at 185°C for around 20 minutes. Arrange the chicken bites on a platter and serve as an appetizer.
Per Serving: Calories 339; Fat: 14g; Sodium 556mg; Carbs: 44.6g; Fiber: 6.4g; Sugars 3.8g; Protein 10.5g

Pizza Cheese Bites

Prep Time: 15 minutes | Cook Time: 3 minutes | Serves: 10

10 Mozzarella cheese slices   10 pepperoni slices

1. Place the Cook & Crisp Basket in your Pressure Cooker Steam Fryer. 2. Line the Cook & Crisp Basket with baking paper and put Mozzarella in it in one layer. Put on the Smart Lid on top of the Ninja Foodi Steam Fryer. Move the Lid Slider to the "Air Fry/Stovetop". Select the "Air Fry" mode for cooking. Cook for the cheese at 200°C for around 3 minutes or until it is melted. After this, remove the cheese from the Ninja Foodi Pressure Steam Fryer and cool it to room temperature. 4. Then remove the melted cheese from the baking paper and put the pepperoni slices on it. Fold the cheese in the shape of turnovers.
Per Serving: Calories 373; Fat: 3.1g; Sodium 687mg; Carbs: 69.2g; Fiber: 9.6g; Sugars 3.4g; Protein 17.8g

Mozzarella Bites

Prep Time: 5 minutes | Cook Time: 5 minutes | Serves: 8

225g mozzarella, shredded
85g almond flour

2 teaspoons psyllium husk powder
¼ teaspoon sweet paprika

1. Place the Cook & Crisp Basket in your Pressure Cooker Steam Fryer. 2. Put the mozzarella in a suitable bowl, melt it in the microwave for around 2 minutes, add all the other ingredients quickly and stir really until you obtain a dough. 3. Divide the prepared dough into 2 balls, roll them on 2 baking sheets and cut into triangles. Arrange the tortillas in the Cook & Crisp Basket. 4. Put on the Smart Lid on top of the Ninja Foodi Steam Fryer. Move the Lid Slider to the "Air Fry/Stovetop". Select the "Air Fry" mode for cooking. Air Fry at 190°C for around 5 minutes. 5. Transfer to bowls and serve as a snack.
Per Serving: Calories 283; Fat: 3.6g; Sodium 381mg; Carbs: 55.4g; Fiber: 8.1g; Sugars 3.1g; Protein 8.7g

Mushroom Bites

Prep Time: 10 minutes | Cook Time: 7 minutes | Serves: 6

6 cremini mushroom caps
75g Parmesan, grated
1 tablespoon olive oil
½ tomato, chopped

½ teaspoon dried basil
1 teaspoon ricotta cheese

1. Place the Cook & Crisp Basket in your Pressure Cooker Steam Fryer. 2. Sprinkle the mushroom caps with olive oil and put in the Ninja Foodi Pressure Steam Fryer basket in one layer. Put on the Smart Lid on top of the Ninja Foodi Steam Fryer. 3. Move the Lid Slider to the "Air Fry/Stovetop". Select the "Air Fry" mode for cooking. 4. Cook them at 200°C for around 3 minutes. After this, mix up tomato and ricotta cheese. Fill the mushroom caps with tomato mixture. Then top them with parmesan and sprinkle with dried basil. 5. Put on the Smart Lid on top of the Ninja Foodi Steam Fryer. 6. Move the Lid Slider to the "Air Fry/Stovetop". Select the "Air Fry" mode for cooking. 7. Cook the mushroom pizzas for around 4 minutes at 200°C.
Per Serving: Calories 254; Fat: 2.6g; Sodium 482mg; Carbs: 49.1g; Fiber: 4.8g; Sugars 0.2g; Protein 7.8g

Paprika Cheese Chips

Prep Time: 2 minutes | Cook Time: 5 minutes | Serves: 4

200g cheddar cheese, shredded
1 teaspoon sweet paprika

1. Divide the cheese in small heaps in the Cook & Crisp Basket, sprinkle the paprika on top. Place the Cook & Crisp Basket in your Pressure Cooker Steam Fryer. 2. Put on the Smart Lid on top of the Ninja Foodi Steam Fryer. Move the Lid Slider to the "Air Fry/Stovetop". Select the "Air Fry" mode for cooking. Air Fry at 200°C for around 5 minutes. 3. Cool the chips down and serve them.
Per Serving: Calories 128; Fat: 1.7g; Sodium 771mg; Carbs: 22.1g; Fiber: 4.5g; Sugars 3.9g; Protein 7.1g

Crispy Courgette Crackers

Prep Time: 15 minutes | Cook Time: 20 minutes | Serves: 16

125g courgette, grated
2 tablespoons flax meal
1 teaspoon salt
3 tablespoons almond flour
¼ teaspoon baking powder

¼ teaspoon chili flakes
1 tablespoon xanthan gum
1 tablespoon butter, softened
1 egg, beaten
Cooking spray

1. Place the Cook & Crisp Basket in your Pressure Cooker Steam Fryer. 2. Squeeze the courgette to get rid of vegetable juice and transfer in the big bowl. Add flax meal, salt, almond flour, baking powder, chili flakes, xanthan gum, and stir well. 3. After this, add butter and egg. Knead the non-sticky dough. Place it on the baking paper and cover with the second sheet of baking paper. Roll up the prepared dough into the flat square. 4. After this, remove the baking paper from the prepared dough surface. Cut it on medium size crackers. Line the Ninja Foodi Pressure Steam Fryer basket with baking paper and put the crackers inside in one layer. Grease them with cooking spray. 5. Put on the Smart Lid on top of the Ninja Foodi Steam Fryer. Move the Lid Slider to the "Air Fry/Stovetop". Select the "Air Fry" mode for cooking. 6. Cook them at 180°C for 20 minutes.
Per Serving: Calories 244; Fat: 9.1g; Sodium 1399mg; Carbs: 34.3g; Fiber: 8.7g; Sugars 15.7g; Protein 8.3g

Chapter 8 Dessert Recipes

Toffee Puddings

Prep time: 10 minutes | Cook time: 25 minutes | Serves: 2

1½ tablespoons unsalted butter, at room temperature, plus more for greasing	1 egg
	½ teaspoon baking soda
	Pinch salt
35g medjool dates, pitted and chopped	1 tablespoon molasses
	3 tablespoons packed brown sugar
60ml boiling water	3 tablespoons turbinado sugar
60g plain flour	½ teaspoon vanilla extract

1. Add 240ml water to your Ninja Foodi XL Pressure Cooker Steam Fryer cooking pot and place the Deluxe reversible rack in the bottom. Butter two (1-cup) ramekins and set aside. 2. In a small bowl, combine the dates and boiling water to soften, 5 minutes. Mix and let cool. (Do not discard the water.) 3. Combine the flour, egg, baking soda, salt, molasses, brown sugar, turbinado sugar, and vanilla extract in a food processor or blender and pulse until just combined. Add the softened dates and 60ml of their soaking water and pulse until almost smooth. 4. Divide the batter evenly between the two prepared ramekins. Cover each with a piece of buttered foil, Seal well. Set the ramekins on the Deluxe reversible rack in the pot, placing a third empty ramekin inside with them to ensure they don't jostle during cooking. 5. Lock lid; move slider to PRESSURE. Make sure the pressure release valve is in the SEAL position. The cooking temperature will default to HIGH, which is accurate. Set time to 25 minutes. Press START/STOP to cooking. When cooking is complete, let pressure release quickly by turning it into VENT position. Carefully remove the ramekins from the cooking pot and put them on a cooling rack. 6. Remove the foil, turn the puddings out onto dessert plates, and serve warm with caramel or toffee sauce.

Per Serving: Calories 240; Fat 4.3g; Sodium 278mg; Carbs 47g; Fiber 7g; Sugar 3g; Protein 6g

Nutty Rice Pudding

Prep time: 5 minutes | Cook time: 12 minutes | Serves: 2

1 tablespoon butter	50g sugar
90g Arborio rice	½ teaspoon almond extract
240ml coconut milk, divided	¼ teaspoon ground cinnamon
60ml water	Pinch salt

1. Move the slider towards "AIR FRY/STOVETOP" and set Ninja Foodi XL Pressure Cooker Steam Fryer with SmartLid to SEAR/SAUTÉ mode. Adjust the temperature to "Hi5" by using up arrow. Press START/STOP to begin cooking. When the display reads hot, add the butter to melt. Add the rice and toast for 1 minute, stirring. Add 120 ml of coconut milk, the water, sugar, almond extract, cinnamon, and salt. Simmer for 1 to 2 minutes to dissolve the sugar. 2. Lock lid; move slider to PRESSURE. Make sure the pressure release valve is in the SEAL position. The cooking temperature will default to HIGH, which is accurate. Set time to 12 minutes. Press START/STOP to cooking. When cooking is complete, let pressure release naturally. Remove the lid then select SEAR/SAUTÉ. 3. Stir the pudding and add the remaining coconut milk, stirring until the desired texture is reached. Divide between two bowls and garnish with toasted almonds and shredded coconut.

Per Serving: Calories 232; Fat 8.5g; Sodium 465mg; Carbs 38g; Fiber 1g; Sugar 15g; Protein 2g

Creamy Crème Brûlée

Prep time: 5 minutes | Cook time: 10 minutes | Serves: 2

2 egg yolks, lightly beaten	160g heavy cream
6 tablespoons sugar, divided	1 teaspoon vanilla extract
Pinch salt	

1. Add 240ml water to your Ninja Foodi XL Pressure Cooker Steam Fryer cooking pot and place the Deluxe reversible rack in the bottom. 2. In a medium bowl, whisk together the egg yolks, 4 tablespoons of sugar, and the salt. Add the cream and vanilla and whisk until well blended. 3. Divide the mixture between two (1-cup) ramekins and cover with foil. Set the ramekins on the Deluxe reversible rack, placing a third empty ramekin next to them to ensure they don't jostle during cooking. 4. Lock lid; move slider to PRESSURE. Make sure the pressure release valve is in the SEAL position. The cooking temperature will default to HIGH, which is accurate. Set time to 9 minutes. Press START/STOP to cooking. When cooking is complete, let pressure release naturally for 10 minutes. 5. Using tongs, remove

the ramekins from the pressure cooker, transfer to a heatproof surface, and let cool to room temperature. Cover with plastic wrap and refrigerate for at least 2 hours or up to 2 days. 6. When ready to serve, sprinkle the entire surface of each custard with 1 tablespoon of sugar. Caramelize the sugar with a kitchen torch or grill in the oven for 2 to 3 minutes, watching carefully, until the sugar is melted and browned.

Per Serving: Calories 567; Fat 16.3g; Sodium 478mg; Carbs 19g; Fiber 14g; Sugar 6g; Protein 18g

Basic Flan

Prep time: 15 minutes | Cook time: 9 minutes | Serves: 2

4 tablespoons raw sugar, divided	two pieces for garnish
3 tablespoons orange juice, plus 2 teaspoons	½ teaspoon vanilla extract
	Pinch salt
120g heavy cream	1 egg
1 teaspoon grated orange zest, plus	

1. Add 240ml water to your Ninja Foodi XL Pressure Cooker Steam Fryer cooking pot and place the Deluxe reversible rack in the bottom. 2. In a small saucepan set over medium heat on the stove top, heat 2 tablespoons of sugar and 2 teaspoons of orange juice. Cook, stirring constantly, until reduced and thickened, 3 to 4 minutes. Swirl the pan occasionally until the mixture takes on a dark golden brown color. Carefully pour the caramel liquid evenly into two (1-cup) ramekins, tilting the ramekins to coat the bottoms completely. Set aside. 3. In a clean small saucepan, heat the remaining 3 tablespoons of orange juice, the cream, and grated orange zest over medium heat. Add the remaining 2 tablespoons of sugar, the vanilla, and salt and stir until the sugar has fully dissolved. Remove from the heat. 4. In a medium bowl, beat the egg lightly. Temper it slowly by whisking in a little of the hot cream mixture at a time. Continue to whisk until all of the cream mixture is incorporated with the egg. 5. Pour the egg-cream mixture through a fine-mesh strainer into the caramel-filled ramekins. Cover the ramekins with foil, set them on the Deluxe reversible rack, and place a third empty ramekin next to them to ensure that they don't jostle during cooking. 6. Lock lid; move slider to PRESSURE. Make sure the pressure release valve is in the SEAL position. The cooking temperature will default to HIGH, which is accurate. Set time to 9 minutes. Press START/STOP to cooking. When cooking is complete, let pressure release naturally for 10 minutes. 7. Using tongs, remove the ramekins from the pressure cooker, transfer to a heatproof surface, and let cool to room temperature. Cover with plastic wrap and then refrigerate for at least 4 hours or up to 2 days. 8. When ready to serve, run a small, sharp knife around the edges of the ramekins and invert the flan onto a plate. The melted caramel in the bottom of the ramekins will flow over the flan. Garnish each flan with a twist of orange.

Per Serving: Calories 169; Fat 1.5g; Sodium 629mg; Carbs 36g; Fiber 6g; Sugar 14g; Protein 8g

Stout Pears

Prep time: 5 minutes | Cook time: 9 minutes | Serves: 2

3 peeled (stem on) firm Bartlett pears	1 vanilla bean, split lengthwise and seeds scraped
1 bottle stout beer	105g packed brown sugar

1. Slice a thin layer from the bottom of each pear so they can stand upright. Using a melon baller, scoop out the seeds and core from the bottom. 2. In the pressure cooker pot, stir together the beer, vanilla bean and seeds, and brown sugar. Place the pears upright in the pot. 3. Lock lid; move slider to PRESSURE. Make sure the pressure release valve is in the SEAL position. The cooking temperature will default to HIGH, which is accurate. Set time to 9 minutes. Press START/STOP to cooking. When cooking is complete, let pressure release quickly by turning it into VENT position. 4. Using tongs, carefully remove the pears by their stems and transfer to a plate. Set aside. Move the slider towards "AIR FRY/STOVETOP" and set Ninja Foodi XL Pressure Cooker Steam Fryer with SmartLid to SEAR/SAUTÉ mode. Adjust the temperature to "Hi5" by using up arrow. Press START/STOP to begin cooking. Simmer the liquid in the pot until reduced by half. 5. Strain the liquid into a bowl through a fine-mesh sieve, then pour over the pears. Serve at room temperature or chilled, plain or with whipped cream and a drizzle of chocolate sauce.

Per Serving: Calories 505; Fat 38.1g; Sodium 264mg; Carbs 6g; Fiber 2g; Sugar 3g; Protein 34g

Tangy Lime Pie

Prep time: 15 minutes | Cook time: 15 minutes | Serves: 2

2 tablespoons unsalted butter, melted, plus more for greasing
35g digestive biscuit crumbs
½ teaspoon sugar
2 egg yolks
½ can (175g) sweetened

condensed milk
120ml freshly squeezed Key lime juice
1 tablespoon grated Key lime zest
60g sour cream

1. Add 240ml water to the Ninja Foodi XL Pressure Cooker Steam Fryer with SmartLid cooking pot and place the Deluxe reversible rack in the bottom. Coat the Cook & Crisp Basket with butter. 2. In a medium bowl, combine biscuit crumbs, 2 tablespoons of butter, and the sugar. Press the crumb mixture evenly into the bottom and up the side of the pan. Refrigerate the crust while you make the filling. 3. In a medium bowl, beat the egg yolks until they thicken and turn pale yellow, 2 to 3 minutes. Gradually beat in the condensed milk until thickened. Slowly add the lime juice and zest and beat until smooth. Stir in the sour cream. 4. Pour the batter into the prepared Cook & Crisp Basket. Cover the top of the Cook & Crisp Basket with aluminum foil. For basket, prepare a foil sling, center the basket on it, and lower into the pressure cooker pot. Arrange the sling ends across the basket. 5. Lock lid; move slider to PRESSURE. Make sure the pressure release valve is in the SEAL position. The cooking temperature will default to HIGH, which is accurate. Set time to 15 minutes. Press START/STOP to cooking. 6. When cooking is complete, let pressure release naturally for about 10 minutes. 7. Using the foil sling ends, carefully transfer the Cook & Crisp Basket to a cooling rack. Remove the foil. 8. When the pie is cool, cover with plastic wrap and refrigerate for at least 4 hours until set. Serve with whipped cream, toasted almonds, and Key lime slices.
Per Serving: Calories 281; Fat 17.2g; Sodium 407mg; Carbs 4g; Fiber 2g; Sugar 1g; Protein 28g

Zesty Raspberry Muffins

Prep Time: 10 minutes | Cook Time: 35 minutes | Serves: 10

1 egg
250g frozen raspberries, coated with some flour
185g flour
100g sugar
80ml vegetable oil

2 teaspoon baking powder
Yogurt, as needed
1 teaspoon lemon zest
2 tablespoon lemon juice
Pinch of sea salt

1. Place the Cook & Crisp Basket in your Pressure Cooker Steam Fryer. 2. Place all of the dry recipe ingredients in a bowl and mix well. 3. Beat the egg and pour it into a cup. Mix it with the oil and lemon juice. Add in the yogurt, to taste. 4. Mix the dry and wet recipe ingredients. 5. Add in the lemon zest and raspberries. 6. Coat the insides of 10 muffin tins with a little butter. 7. Spoon an equal amount of the mixture into each muffin tin. 8. Transfer to the Cook & Crisp Basket. Put on the Smart Lid on top of the Ninja Foodi Steam Fryer. Move the Lid Slider to the "Air Fry/Stovetop". Select the "Air Fry" mode for cooking. Adjust the cooking temperature to 175°C. 9. Cook for around 10 minutes, in batches if necessary.
Per Serving: Calories 257; Fat: 16.5g; Sodium 1031mg; Carbs: 23.6g; Fiber: 3.4g; Sugars 6.1g; Protein 4.7g

Chocolate Lava Cakes

Prep time: 10 minutes | Cook time: 9 minutes | Serves: 2

Butter, at room temperature, for greasing
50g bittersweet chocolate, chopped
1 egg
1 egg yolk

2 tablespoons granulated sugar
75g hazelnut spread
3 tablespoons plain flour
Pinch salt

1. Add 240ml water to your Ninja Foodi XL Pressure Cooker Steam Fryer with SmartLid cooking pot and place the Deluxe reversible rack in the bottom. Butter two 1-cup ramekins; set aside. 2. Put the chocolate in a microwave-safe bowl and microwave in 30-second bursts, stirring with a rubber spatula at the end of each one, until melted and smooth. Let cool. 3. In a medium bowl, whisk the egg and egg yolk until smooth. Add the granulated sugar and whisk well. Add the hazelnut spread tand cooled chocolate and mix with a rubber spatula until smooth. Gently fold in the flour and salt until no streaks remain. 4. Spoon the batter into the prepared ramekins, dividing it evenly. Set the ramekins on the Deluxe reversible rack in the pot,

placing a third empty ramekin inside with them to ensure they don't jostle during cooking. 5. Lock lid; move slider towards PRESSURE. Adjust pressure release valve in the SEAL position. Close pressure-release valve. The cooking temperature will default to HIGH, which is accurate. Set time to 9 minutes. Select START/STOP and start cooking. 6. When cooking is complete, let pressure release quickly by turning it into VENT position. Using tongs, carefully remove the ramekins from the pot and transfer to a rack to cool for 5 minutes. 7. When ready to serve turn the cakes out onto individual serving plates and dust with powdered sugar. Serve with a scoop of high-quality vanilla ice cream, whipped cream, toasted hazelnuts, and sliced strawberries.
Per Serving: Calories 145; Fat 7.2g; Sodium 66mg; Carbs 7g; Fiber 2g; Sugar 2g; Protein 15g

Delicious Brown Rice Pudding

Prep time: 5 minutes | Cook time: 22 minutes | Serves: 6

185g long-grain brown rice, like jasmine or basmati, rinsed
480ml water
One 375g can full-fat coconut milk

105g maple syrup
½ teaspoon pure vanilla extract
½ teaspoon ground cinnamon, plus more for serving
Pinch of fine sea salt

1. Combine the rice and water in the Ninja Foodi XL Pressure Cooker Steam Fryer. 2. Lock lid; move slider towards PRESSURE. Adjust pressure release valve in the SEAL position. Close pressure-release valve. The cooking temperature will default to HIGH, which is accurate. Set time to 22 minutes. Select START/STOP and start cooking. 3. When cooking is complete, let pressure release naturally for 10 minutes, then quickly release by turning it into VENT position. Carefully remove the lid. 4. Stir the rice, making sure that it's tender, then add in the coconut milk, maple syrup, vanilla, cinnamon, and salt. Stir well to combine and adjust any seasoning to taste. 5. Use an immersion blender directly in the pot to briefly pulse the pudding until your desired texture has been reached. The more you blend, the creamier it will be. 6. Serve warm, with extra cinnamon on top. If you'd prefer to serve it cold, transfer it to an airtight container and chill for 2 hours. 7. The pudding will thicken and you'll need to add water to thin it to your desired serving consistency again. Store leftovers in an airtight container in the fridge for 4 days.
Per Serving: Calories 350; Fat 16.7g; Sodium 428mg; Carbs 22g; Fiber 1g; Sugar 3g; Protein 28g

Oatmeal Raisin Cookie

Prep time: 10 minutes | Cook time: 25 minutes | Serves: 8

60g 100 percent white whole-wheat flour
100g coconut sugar
¼ teaspoon fine sea salt
¼ teaspoon baking soda
1 teaspoon ground cinnamon

1 egg
55g melted coconut oil or butter
½ teaspoon pure vanilla extract
40g quick-cooking oats
70g raisins

1. Grease an 18cm round pan and line it with parchment paper. In a large bowl, stir together the flour, sugar, salt, baking soda, and cinnamon. 2. Add the egg, coconut oil, and vanilla and stir until a smooth batter forms. Fold in the oats and raisins. The batter will be thick and sticky. Transfer the batter to the prepared pan and use a spatula to smooth the top. 3. Pour 240ml water into the Ninja Foodi XL Pressure Cooker Steam Fryer cooking pot and arrange the handled Deluxe reversible rack on the bottom. Place the pan on top of the Deluxe reversible rack and cover it with an upside-down plate or another piece of parchment to protect the cookie from condensation. 4. Lock lid; move slider towards PRESSURE. Adjust pressure release valve in the SEAL position. Close pressure-release valve. The cooking temperature will default to HIGH, which is accurate. Set time to 25 minutes. Select START/STOP and start cooking. 5. When cooking is complete, let pressure release naturally for 10 minutes, then quickly release by turning it into VENT position. 6. Use oven mitts to lift the Deluxe reversible rack and the pan out of the pot. Let the cookie cool completely, about 1 hour, before cutting and serving. 7. Store leftovers in an airtight container in the fridge for 1 week.
Per Serving: Calories 426; Fat 22.6g; Sodium 357mg; Carbs 36g; Fiber 2g; Sugar 19g; Protein 20g

Delicious Cannoli Cheesecake

Prep time: 15 minutes | Cook time: 25 minutes | Serves: 2

2 tablespoons unsalted butter, melted, plus more at room temperature, for greasing
4 anise biscotti
⅛ teaspoon salt
250g ricotta cheese, at room temperature
100g mascarpone cheese, at room

temperature
100g sugar
2 tablespoons flour
2 teaspoons vanilla extract
½ teaspoon ground cinnamon
2 eggs, at room temperature
85g mini semisweet chocolate chips

1. Add 240ml water to the Ninja Foodi XL Pressure Cooker Steam Fryer with SmartLid cooking pot and place the Deluxe reversible rack in the bottom. Coat the Cook & Crisp Basket with butter. 2. In a food processor or blender, pulse the biscotti to fine crumbs. Add the melted butter and the salt and pulse until the mixture has the texture of wet sand. Press the crumb mixture into the bottom of the Cook & Crisp Basket to form a crust. 3. In a stand mixer fitted with the paddle attachment (or in a tall bowl using a hand mixer), beat the ricotta, mascarpone, sugar, and flour on low speed until smooth, about 3 minutes, scraping down the side of the bowl occasionally with a rubber spatula. Add the vanilla and cinnamon and continue beating on low speed. 4. Add the eggs one at a time, beating on low speed after each addition until well combined. Scrape down the side of the bowl. Fold in the chocolate chips. 5. Pour the batter into the crust in the Cook & Crisp Basket. Gently tap the basket on the counter to release any air bubbles. Cover the Cook & Crisp Basket with a paper towel and then with a piece of aluminum foil. Prepare a foil sling center the basket on it, and lower it into the cooker pot. Arrange the sling ends across the basket. 6. Lock lid; move slider towards PRESSURE. Adjust pressure release valve in the SEAL position. Close pressure-release valve. The cooking temperature will default to HIGH, which is accurate. Set time to 25 minutes. Select START/STOP and start cooking. When cooking is complete, let pressure release naturally for about 10 minutes. 7. Using the sling ends, lift the cheesecake out of the cooker and transfer to a cooling rack. Remove the foil and paper towel. 8. Let cool for about 30 minutes. Refrigerate for 3 to 4 hours before serving. Serve with whipped cream, pistachios, and cherries, if desired.
Per Serving: Calories 170; Fat 7.9g; Sodium 204mg; Carbs 3g; Fiber 0g; Sugar 2g; Protein 19g

Upside-Down Cake

Prep time: 10 minutes | Cook time: 20 minutes | Serves: 2

6 tablespoons butter, at room temperature, divided
70g packed brown sugar
4 slices fresh or canned pineapple
4 pitted maraschino cherries, stems removed
90g plain flour
1 teaspoon baking powder

¼ teaspoon ground cinnamon
Pinch ground nutmeg
Pinch salt
100g granulated sugar
1 egg, at room temperature
½ teaspoon vanilla extract
3 teaspoons dark rum
60ml pineapple juice

1. Add 240 ml water to the Ninja Foodi XL Pressure Cooker Steam Fryer with SmartLid cooking pot and place the Deluxe reversible rack in the bottom. 2. In a small microwave-safe bowl, melt 3 tablespoons of butter in the microwave. Pour into an 18 cm cake pan, tipping it to distribute the butter evenly across the bottom. Sprinkle the brown sugar on top of the butter, then place the pineapple slices on top of the brown sugar, slightly overlapping them if necessary to fit. Place the cherries in the holes in the pineapple slices. Set the cake pan aside. 3. In a medium bowl, whisk together the flour, baking powder, cinnamon, nutmeg, and salt. 4. In another medium bowl, using an electric hand mixer on medium speed, cream the remaining 3 tablespoons of butter and the granulated sugar until light and fluffy. Add the egg, vanilla, and rum, beating just until incorporated; scrape down the sides of the bowl as needed. 5. Add the flour mixture to the butter mixture in two batches, alternating with the pineapple juice. Beat until just blended.6. Pour the batter over the pineapple slices in the pan, spreading it in an even layer. Cover the pan with a paper towel and then with a piece of aluminum foil. Prepare a foil sling, center the pan on it, and lower the pan into the pressure cooker pot. Arrange the sling ends across the pan.7. Lock lid; move slider to PRESSURE. Make sure the pressure release valve is in the SEAL position. The cooking temperature will default to HIGH, which is accurate. Set time to 20 minutes. Press START/STOP to cooking. 8. When cooking is complete, let pressure release naturally for 15 to 20 minutes. Remove the foil and paper towel from the cake and let cool in the cooker for 10 minutes. Using

the sling tails, carefully transfer the cake to a cooling rack. 9. Cut the cake into slices and serve warm or at room temperature.
Per Serving: Calories 354; Fat 7.9g; Sodium 704mg; Carbs 6g; Fiber 3.6g; Sugar 6g; Protein 18g

Flourless Espresso Cake

Prep time: 15 minutes | Cook time: 35 minutes | Serves: 2

230g unsalted butter, cubed, plus more for greasing
455g bittersweet chocolate, finely chopped

8 eggs, whites and yolks separated
2 tablespoons espresso powder
Pinch salt

1. Place a round of parchment paper on the bottom of an 18 cm cake pan. Grease the pan and paper with butter. Set aside. 2. Put the chocolate and butter in a microwave-safe medium bowl and microwave in 30-second bursts, stirring with a rubber spatula at the end of each one, until melted and smooth. 3. When the chocolate is melted, add the egg yolks and espresso powder to the bowl and stir to combine. 4. In another medium bowl, using an electric hand mixer, beat the egg whites on high speed until soft peaks form. 5. Gently fold the egg whites into the chocolate mixture until fully combined. 6. Pour the batter into the prepared pan, then cover it with aluminum foil. 7. Add 240ml water to the Ninja Foodi XL Pressure Cooker Steam Fryer with SmartLid cooking pot and place the Deluxe reversible rack in the bottom. 8. Prepare a foil sling, center the pan on it, and lower it into the pressure cooker. Arrange the sling ends across the cake pan. 9. Lock lid; move slider towards PRESSURE. Adjust pressure release valve in the SEAL position. Close pressure-release valve. The cooking temperature will default to HIGH, which is accurate. Set time to 35 minutes. Select START/STOP and start cooking. 10. When cooking is complete, let pressure release quickly by turning it into VENT position. Carefully remove the lid, then remove the cake from the cooker using the foil sling ends and transfer to a rack and cool completely. 11. Remove the cake from the pan and transfer to a serving plate. Before serving, dust with powdered sugar and drizzle with dulce de leche, then cut into slices.
Per Serving: Calories 629; Fat 61g; Sodium 64mg; Carbs 3g; Fiber 1g; Sugar 1g; Protein 18g

Mini Chocolate–Cherry Bundt Cakes

Prep time: 15 minutes | Cook time: 25 minutes | Serves: 2

5 tablespoons butter, at room temperature, plus more for greasing
60g plain flour, plus 1 tablespoon
½ teaspoon baking powder
⅛ teaspoon baking soda
Pinch salt
65g sugar
1 egg, at room temperature

1 teaspoon vanilla extract
¼ teaspoon almond extract
50g white chocolate, melted and cooled, divided
60g sour cream
25g drained chopped Maraschino cherries, plus a few whole ones for garnish

1. Add 240ml water to your Ninja Foodi XL Pressure Cooker Steam Fryer with SmartLid cooking pot and place the Deluxe reversible rack in the bottom. Butter two mini Bundt cake pans and set aside. 2. In a medium bowl, whisk together 60 g of flour, the baking powder, baking soda, and salt. 3. In another medium bowl, using an electric hand mixer, cream the 5 tablespoons of butter and the sugar on medium speed until light and fluffy, about 2 minutes. Beat in the egg, vanilla, and almond extract just until incorporated. Slowly beat in half of the melted white chocolate, scraping down the side of the bowl with a rubber spatula as needed. 4. Beat the flour mixture into the butter mixture in two batches, alternating with the sour cream, just until combined. Toss the chopped cherries with the remaining 1 tablespoon of flour, then fold gently into the batter. Pour the batter into the two prepared pans and cover with aluminum foil. Place the pans on the Deluxe reversible rack in the pot. 5. Lock lid; move slider towards PRESSURE. Adjust pressure release valve in the SEAL position. Close pressure-release valve. The cooking temperature will default to HIGH, which is accurate. Set time to 25 minutes. Select START/STOP and start cooking. When cooking is complete, let pressure release quickly by turning it into VENT position. Carefully transfer the Bundt pans from the pot to a rack and let cool for 10 minutes. 6. Remove the Bundt cakes from the pans and let cool completely on the rack, 30 to 45 minutes. Serve on dessert plates, drizzled with the remaining melted white chocolate and garnished with whole Maraschino cherries.
Per Serving: Calories 276; Fat 16g; Sodium 70mg; Carbs 1g; Fiber 0g; Sugar 0g; Protein 30g

Mini Bananas Cheesecakes

Prep time: 20 minutes | Cook time: 15 minutes | Serves: 2

2 tablespoons butter, melted, plus more at room temperature for greasing
50g vanilla wafers, crushed
1 (200g) package cream cheese, at room temperature
For the Bananas Foster
55g butter, at room temperature
60ml water
60ml dark rum
105g packed brown sugar

50g granulated sugar
2 tablespoons sour cream
2 teaspoons vanilla extract
Pinch salt
1 egg
40g mashed ripe banana

½ teaspoon ground cinnamon
½ teaspoon vanilla extract
2 slightly green medium bananas, peeled and cut into thick slices

1. Add 240ml water to the Ninja Foodi XL Pressure Cooker Steam Fryer with SmartLid cooking pot and place the Deluxe reversible rack in the bottom. Line two 10 cm springform pans with small circles of parchment paper and butter the pans and the paper. Set aside. 2. In a medium bowl, mix the crushed vanilla wafers and melted butter with a fork until well combined. Divide evenly between the two pans and press firmly into the bottoms and up the sides to make a crust. 3. In a medium bowl, using a hand mixer, beat the cream cheese and granulated sugar together until smooth. Add the sour cream, vanilla, and salt and beat well, then beat in the egg until just combined. Gently stir in the banana. 4. Divide the mixture between the two crusts. Gently tap each pan on the counter to release any air bubbles. Cover each pan with foil and place on top of the Deluxe reversible rack in the pressure cooker. 5. Lock lid; move slider towards PRESSURE. Adjust pressure release valve in the SEAL position. Close pressure-release valve. The cooking temperature will default to HIGH, which is accurate. Set time to 13 minutes. Select START/STOP and start cooking. When cooking is complete, let pressure release naturally. 6. Using tongs, carefully remove the cheesecakes from the pressure cooker, transfer to a cooling rack, and let cool to room temperature, 30 to 40 minutes. 7. Cover with plastic wrap and chill in the refrigerator for at least 4 hours or up to 2 days.

To Make the Bananas Foster

1. Move the slider towards "AIR FRY/STOVETOP" and set Ninja Foodi XL Pressure Cooker Steam Fryer with SmartLid to SEAR/SAUTÉ mode. Adjust the temperature to "Hi5" by using up arrow. Press START/STOP to begin cooking. Once hot, combine the butter, water, rum, brown sugar, cinnamon, and vanilla in the pot, mixing until well combined and the sugar is mostly dissolved. Add the bananas and toss to coat in the sauce. 2. Lock lid; move slider towards PRESSURE. Adjust pressure release valve in the SEAL position. Close pressure-release valve. The cooking temperature will default to HIGH, which is accurate. Set time to 8 minutes. Select START/STOP and start cooking, then quick release the pressure in the pot and remove the lid. Remove the pot from the cooker and pour the bananas foster into a heatproof medium bowl. Cover and refrigerate until ready to serve. 3. When ready to serve, remove the chilled cheesecakes from the springform pans and transfer to serving plates. Reheat the bananas Foster in the microwave just until saucy. 4. Top each cheesecake with your desired amount of the warmed bananas Foster.
Per Serving: Calories 216; Fat 10.4g; Sodium 311mg; Carbs 14g; Fiber 1g; Sugar 2g; Protein 18g

Chocolate Nutty Brownies

Prep time: 10 minutes | Cook time: 25 minutes | Serves: 2

3 tablespoons unsalted butter, plus more for greasing
40g semisweet chocolate chips, divided
100g sugar
20g unsweetened cocoa powder
1 tablespoon water

½ teaspoon vanilla extract
1 egg, lightly beaten
60g plain flour
¼ teaspoon baking powder
Pinch salt
2 to 3 tablespoons natural peanut butter, at room temperature

1. Add 240ml water to your Ninja Foodi XL Pressure Cooker Steam Fryer with SmartLid cooking pot and place the Deluxe reversible rack in the bottom. Coat a small loaf pan or an 18 cm cake pan with butter and set aside. 2. Place 3 tablespoons of butter and 20g of chocolate chips in a microwave-safe bowl and microwave on high for 1 to 2 minutes, stirring every 30 seconds, until the chocolate is smooth. Stir in the sugar and cocoa powder until well combined. Add the water, vanilla, and egg and stir to mix well. Fold in the flour, baking powder, and salt and stir until combined. Spread the batter evenly in the prepared pan. 3. Drop the peanut butter by the spoonful onto the chocolate batter and use a butter knife to swirl it in just a bit. Sprinkle the remaining 20g of chocolate chips on top. Prepare a foil sling center the pan on it, and lower it into the pressure cooker pot. Tuck the sling ends around the outside edges of the brownie pan. 4. Lock lid; move slider towards PRESSURE. Adjust pressure release valve in the SEAL position. Close pressure-release valve. The cooking temperature will default to HIGH, which is accurate. Set time to 25 minutes. Select START/STOP and start cooking. When cooking is complete, let pressure release naturally for about 10 minutes. Using the foil sling ends, remove the brownies from the cooker, transfer to a cooling rack, and let cool completely. 5. To serve, cut the brownies into 4 large squares and, using a wide spatula, transfer 2 squares to dessert bowls. Top with high-quality vanilla ice cream and whipped cream. 6. The remaining two brownies can be wrapped in plastic and kept at room temperature to use for another dessert.
Per Serving: Calories 282; Fat 13.7g; Sodium 50mg; Carbs 4g; Fiber 0g; Sugar 1g; Protein 35g

Basic Apple pie

Prep time: 15 minutes | Cook time: 8 minutes | Serves: 6

5 large apples, cut into 2.5 cm chunks
80ml water
3 tablespoons 100 percent white whole-wheat flour

60g quick-cooking oats
100g coconut sugar
2 teaspoons ground cinnamon
¼ teaspoon fine sea salt
55g melted coconut oil or butter

1. Add the apples and the water to the Ninja Foodi XL Pressure Cooker Steam Fryer with SmartLid cooking pot and stir well to be sure the apples cover the bottom of the pot in an even layer. 2. In a separate bowl, combine the flour, oats, coconut sugar, cinnamon, and salt and stir well. Add the melted coconut oil and stir until thoroughly mixed. Spoon the oat crumble over the apples as a topping. 3. Lock lid; move slider towards PRESSURE. Adjust pressure release valve in the SEAL position. Close pressure-release valve. The cooking temperature will default to HIGH, which is accurate. Set time to 8 minutes. Select START/STOP and start cooking. 4. When cooking is complete, let pressure release naturally for 10 minutes, then quickly release by turning it into VENT position. 5. Use oven mitts to remove the insert from the Ninja Foodi XL Pressure Cooker Steam Fryer and let the crumble cool for 10 minutes before serving warm. 6. This dessert has the best taste and texture when it's served the day it is made, so I don't recommend making it ahead of time for guests. Store leftovers in an airtight container in the fridge for 5 days.
Per Serving: Calories 227; Fat 11.2g; Sodium 412mg; Carbs 1g; Fiber 0g; Sugar 1g; Protein 31g

Flourless Delicious Brownies

Prep time: 10 minutes | Cook time: 15 minutes | Serves: 8

190g almond butter
150g coconut sugar
30g raw cacao powder
1 egg

¼ teaspoon fine sea salt
½ teaspoon baking soda
½ teaspoon pure vanilla extract
90g dark chocolate chips

1. Line an 18 cm round pan with parchment paper. In a large bowl, combine the almond butter, coconut sugar, cacao powder, vanilla, egg, salt, baking soda, and stir well to create a thick batter. 2. Place the batter to the prepared pan and then use your hands to press it evenly in the pan. Sprinkle with the chocolate chips and gently press them into the batter. 3. Pour 240 ml water into the Ninja Foodi XL Pressure Cooker Steam Fryer and arrange the handled Deluxe reversible rack on the bottom. Place the pan on top of the Deluxe reversible rack. 4. Cover it with an upside-down plate or another piece of parchment to protect the brownies from condensation. 5. Lock lid; move slider towards PRESSURE. Adjust pressure release valve in the SEAL position. Close pressure-release valve. The cooking temperature will default to HIGH, which is accurate. Set time to 8 minutes. Select START/STOP and start cooking. 6. When cooking is complete, let pressure release naturally for 10 minutes, then quickly release by turning it into VENT position. 7. Use oven mitts to lift the Deluxe reversible rack and the pan out of the pot. Let the brownies cool completely in the pan before cutting and serving, as they will be very fragile when warm. 8. Store leftovers in an airtight container in the fridge for 2 weeks.
Per Serving: Calories 342; Fat 11.8g; Sodium 683mg; Carbs 24g; Fiber 4g; Sugar 1g; Protein 38g

Nutty Coffee Cake

Prep time: 10 minutes | Cook time: 30 minutes | Serves: 8

180g almond flour or almond meal
150g coconut sugar
½ teaspoon baking soda
¼ teaspoon fine sea salt
1 teaspoon ground cinnamon
3 eggs, at room temperature
2 tablespoons melted coconut oil
55g finely chopped pecans

1. Lightly grease an 18 cm round pan and line it with parchment paper. In a bowl, mix the almond flour, coconut sugar, baking soda, salt, and cinnamon and whisk to break up any lumps. 2. Add the eggs and melted coconut oil and mix with a spatula until smooth. Pour the batter in the pan and smooth the top with spatula. Sprinkle the pecans over the batter. 3. Pour 240ml water into the Ninja Foodi XL Pressure Cooker Steam Fryer cooking pot and arrange the handled Deluxe reversible rack on the bottom. Place the pan on top of the Deluxe reversible rack and cover it with an upside-down plate or another piece of parchment to protect the cake from condensation. 4. Lock lid; move slider towards PRESSURE. Adjust pressure release valve in the SEAL position. Close pressure-release valve. The cooking temperature will default to HIGH, which is accurate. Set time to 30 minutes. Select START/STOP and start cooking. 5. When cooking is complete, release naturally for 10 minutes, then quickly release by turning it into VENT position. 6. Use oven mitts to lift the Deluxe reversible rack and the pan out of the pot. Let the cake cool in pan for 30 minutes before cutting and serving. Store leftovers in an airtight container in the fridge for 1 week.
Per Serving: Calories 433; Fat 37g; Sodium 192mg; Carbs 14g; Fiber 1g; Sugar 4g; Protein 11g

Creamy Pudding

Prep time: 5 minutes | Cook time: 10 minutes | Serves: 4

1 large sweet potato (about 455g), peeled and cut into 2.5 cm pieces
120ml full-fat canned coconut milk
6 tablespoons pure maple syrup
(see this page), plus more as needed
1 teaspoon grated fresh ginger (about 1.5 cm knob), plus more as needed

1. Pour 240ml water into the Ninja Foodi XL Pressure Cooker Steam Fryer cooking pot and arrange the Cook & Crisp Basket. Place the Deluxe Reversible Rack on the bottom. 2. Place the sweet potato pieces in the Cook & Crisp Basket and lock lid; move slider towards PRESSURE. Adjust pressure release valve in the SEAL position. Close pressure-release valve. The cooking temperature will default to HIGH, which is accurate. Set time to 10 minutes. Select START/STOP and start cooking. 3. When cooking is complete, let pressure release naturally for 10 minutes, then quickly release by turning it into VENT position. Use oven mitts to lift the Cook & Crisp Basket and Deluxe Reversible Rack out of the pot and transfer the cooked potatoes to a large bowl. 4. Add the coconut milk, maple syrup, and ginger. Use an immersion blender or potato masher to puree the potatoes into a smooth pudding. Taste and adjust the flavor, adding more ginger or maple syrup as needed. 5. Serve the pudding right away, or chill it in the fridge. Store leftover pudding in an airtight container in the fridge for 1 week.
Per Serving: Calories 291; Fat 15.4g; Sodium 96mg; Carbs 3g; Fiber 1g; Sugar 2g; Protein 33g

Chocolate Cake with Frosting

Prep time: 20 minutes | Cook time: 40 minutes | Serves: 8

Chocolate Frosting
240ml water
½ sweet potato (about 200g), peeled and cut into chunks
3 tablespoons raw cacao powder
6 tablespoons pure maple syrup
1 tablespoon melted coconut oil or butter
½ teaspoon pure vanilla extract
Pinch of fine sea salt
Chocolate Cake
60g 100 percent white whole-wheat flour
5 tablespoons raw cacao powder
200g coconut sugar
½ teaspoon baking soda
¼ teaspoon fine sea salt
2 eggs, at room temperature
55g melted coconut oil or butter
2 tablespoons water

1. To make the frosting, pour the water into the Ninja Foodi XL Pressure Cooker Steam Fryer cooking pot and place the sweet potato chunks in the bottom. 2. Arrange the Deluxe reversible rack over the potatoes. To make the cake, grease an 18 cm round pan with the coconut oil or butter and press a piece of parchment paper into the bottom. 3. In a bowl, whisk together the flour, cacao powder, coconut sugar, baking soda, and salt, breaking up any large clumps. Add the eggs, coconut oil, and water and whisk again, until a uniform batter forms. (If your eggs are cold from the fridge, the batter will be thick and difficult to stir, but the cake will still bake well.) 4. Pour the batter into the pan and use a spatula to smooth the top. Put the cake pan on top of the Deluxe reversible rack and cover it with an upside-down plate or another piece of parchment to protect the cake from condensation. 5. Lock lid; move slider towards PRESSURE. Adjust pressure release valve in the SEAL position. Close pressure-release valve. The cooking temperature will default to HIGH, which is accurate. Set time to 40 minutes. Select START/STOP and start cooking. 6. When cooking is complete, let pressure release naturally for 10 minutes, then quickly release by turning it into VENT position. Use oven mitts to lift the Deluxe reversible rack and the cake pan out of the pot. 7. Let the cake cool completely in the pan, about 1 hour. To finish the frosting, drain the cooked sweet potatoes through a colander and transfer them to a mixing bowl. Use an immersion blender or potato masher to puree the potatoes until smooth. 8. Add the cacao powder, maple syrup, coconut oil, vanilla, and salt and whisk to combine. The frosting will become silky smooth. Taste and adjust the flavor, adding more cacao powder or maple syrup as needed. Chill the frosting in the fridge for 1 hour. It will thicken as it cools. 9. Once the cake and frosting have cooled completely, frost the cake and slice to serve. Store leftovers in an airtight container in the fridge for 1 week.
Per Serving: Calories 253; Fat 13.4g; Sodium 663mg; Carbs 7g; Fiber 3g; Sugar 2g; Protein 26g

Vanilla Pecan Pie

Prep Time: 10 minutes | Cook Time: 1 hour 10 minutes | Serves: 4

1x 20 cm pie dough
½ teaspoon cinnamon
¾ teaspoon vanilla extract
2 eggs
235g maple syrup
⅛ teaspoon nutmeg
2 tablespoon butter
1 tablespoon butter, melted
2 tablespoon sugar
55g chopped pecans
Oil

1. Place the Cook & Crisp Basket in your Pressure Cooker Steam Fryer. 2. In a suitable bowl, coat the pecans in the melted butter. 3. Transfer the pecans to the Cook & Crisp Basket. Put on the Smart Lid on top of the Ninja Foodi Steam Fryer. Move the Lid Slider to the "Air Fry/Stovetop". Select the "Air Fry" mode for cooking. Cook at 185°C for 10 minutes. Then grease the Cook & Crisp Basket with oil. Put the pie dough in it and add the pecans on top. 4. In a suitable bowl, mix the rest of the ingredients. Pour this over the pecans. 5. Put on the Smart Lid on top of the Ninja Foodi Steam Fryer. Move the Lid Slider to the "Air Fry/Stovetop". Select the "Air Fry" mode for cooking. Adjust the cooking temperature to 370°F/190°C. 6. Air Fry for around 25 minutes.
Per Serving: Calories 194; Fat: 13g; Sodium 208mg; Carbs: 30.6g; Fiber: 5.6g; Sugars 20.7g; Protein 9.1g

Easy Butter Cake

Prep Time: 10 minutes | Cook Time: 25 minutes | Serves: 2

1 egg
60g flour
7 tablespoon butter, at room temperature
6 tablespoon milk
6 tablespoon sugar
Pinch of sea salt
Cooking spray
Dusting of sugar to serve

1. Place the Cook & Crisp Basket in your Pressure Cooker Steam Fryer. 2. Spritz the inside of a suitable ring cake tin with cooking spray. 3. In a suitable bowl, mix the butter and sugar using a whisk. 4. Stir in the egg and continue to mix everything until the mixture is smooth and fluffy. 5. Pour the flour through a sieve into the bowl. 6. Pour in the milk, before adding a pinch of salt, and mix once again to incorporate everything well. 7. Pour the prepared batter into the tin and use the back of a spoon to make sure the surface is even. 8. Place in the Cook & Crisp Basket. Put on the Smart Lid on top of the Ninja Foodi Steam Fryer. Move the Lid Slider to the "Air Fry/Stovetop". Select the "Air Fry" mode for cooking. Adjust the cooking temperature to 180°C. 9. Cook for around 15 minutes. 10. Before removing it from Pressure Cooker Steam Fryer, ensure the cake is cooked through by inserting a toothpick into the center and checking that it comes out clean. 11. Allow the cake to cool and serve with dusting of sugar.
Per Serving: Calories 281; Fat: 6.7g; Sodium 187mg; Carbs: 52.7g; Fiber: 6.6g; Sugars 29g; Protein 5.1g

Chocolate Mug Cake

Prep Time: 10 minutes | Cook Time: 15 minutes | Serves: 1

1 tablespoon cocoa powder	3 tablespoons whole milk
3 tablespoon coconut oil	5 tablespoon sugar
30g flour	

1. Place the Cook & Crisp Basket in your Pressure Cooker Steam Fryer. 2. In a suitable bowl, stir all of the recipe ingredients to mix them completely. 3. Take a short, stout mug and pour the mixture into it. 4. Put the mug in your Ninja Foodi Pressure Steam Fryer. Put on the Smart Lid on top of the Ninja Foodi Steam Fryer. Move the Lid Slider to the "Air Fry/Stovetop". Select the "Air Fry" mode for cooking. Cook for around 10 minutes at 200°C.
Per Serving: Calories 361; Fat: 31.3g; Sodium 385mg; Carbs: 13.8g; Fiber: 7.3g; Sugars 2.5g; Protein 9.7g

Dough Dippers with Chocolate Sauce

Prep Time: 10 minutes | Cook Time: 45 minutes | Serves: 5

150g sugar	chocolate chips
455g friendly bread dough	115g butter, melted
240g heavy cream	2 tablespoon extract
150g high quality semi-sweet	

1. Place the Cook & Crisp Basket in your Pressure Cooker Steam Fryer. 2. Coat the inside of the basket with a little melted butter. 3. Halve and roll up the prepared dough to create two 38 cm logs. Slice each log into 20 disks. 4. Halve each disk and twist it 3 or 4 times. 5. Lay out a cookie sheet and lay the twisted dough pieces on top. Brush the pieces with some more melted butter and sprinkle on the sugar. 6. Place the sheet in the Cook & Crisp Basket. Put on the Smart Lid on top of the Ninja Foodi Steam Fryer. Move the Lid Slider to the "Air Fry/Stovetop". Select the "Air Fry" mode for cooking. 7. Adjust the cooking temperature to 175°C. 8. Air Fry for around 5 minutes. Flip the prepared dough twists over, and brush the other side with more butter. Cook for an additional 3 minutes. It may be necessary to complete this step in batches. 9. In the meantime, make the chocolate sauce. Firstly, put the heavy cream into a suitable saucepan over the medium heat and allow it to simmer. 10. Put the chocolate chips into a large bowl and add the simmering cream on top. Mix the chocolate chips everything until a smooth consistency is achieved. Stir in 2 tablespoons of extract. 11. Transfer the fried cookies in a shallow dish, pour over the rest of the melted butter and sprinkle on the sugar. 12. Drizzle on the chocolate sauce before serving.
Per Serving: Calories 469; Fat: 36.5g; Sodium 46mg; Carbs: 31.4g; Fiber: 4.5g; Sugars 17.9g; Protein 9.1g

Honey Chocolate Cookies

Prep Time: 10 minutes | Cook Time: 30 minutes | Serves: 8

75g sugar	150g flour
100g butter	1½ tablespoon milk
1 tablespoon honey	50g chocolate chips

1. Place the Cook & Crisp Basket in your Pressure Cooker Steam Fryer. 2. Mix the sugar and butter using an electric mixer, until a fluffy texture is achieved. 3. Stir in the remaining ingredients, minus the chocolate chips. 4. Gradually fold in the chocolate chips. 5. Spoon equal portions of the mixture onto a lined baking sheet and flatten out each one with a spoon. Ensure the cookies are not touching. 6. Place in the Cook & Crisp Basket. Put on the Smart Lid on top of the Ninja Foodi Steam Fryer. Move the Lid Slider to the "Air Fry/Stovetop". Select the "Air Fry" mode for cooking. Adjust the cooking temperature to 175°C. 7. Cook for around 18 minutes.
Per Serving: Calories 148; Fat: 0.7g; Sodium 3mg; Carbs: 57.4g; Fiber: 5.1g; Sugars 40.4g; Protein 2g

Butter Peach Crumble

Prep Time: 10 minutes | Cook Time: 35 minutes | Serves: 6

675g peaches, peeled and chopped	100g sugar
2 tablespoon lemon juice	5 tablespoons cold butter
125g flour	Pinch of sea salt
1 tablespoon water	

1. Place the Cook & Crisp Basket in your Pressure Cooker Steam Fryer. 2. Mash the peaches a little with a fork to achieve a lumpy consistency. 3. Add in two tablespoons of sugar and the lemon juice. 4. In a bowl, mix the flour, salt, and sugar. Throw in a tablespoon of water before adding in the cold butter, mixing until crumbly. 5. Grease the Cook & Crisp Basket and arrange the berries at the bottom. Top with the crumbs. 6. Put on the Smart Lid on top of the Ninja Foodi Steam Fryer. Move the Lid Slider to the "Air Fry/Stovetop". Select the "Air Fry" mode for cooking. Air Fry for around 20 minutes at 200°C.
Per Serving: Calories 363; Fat: 10.7g; Sodium 253mg; Carbs: 63.7g; Fiber: 3.8g; Sugars 22.9g; Protein 4.9g

Banana Cake

Prep Time: 10 minutes | Cook Time: 55 minutes | Serves: 6

400g bananas, mashed	125g butter
200g flour	2 eggs
150g sugar	¼ teaspoon baking soda
125g walnuts, chopped	Oil

1. Place the Cook & Crisp Basket in your Pressure Cooker Steam Fryer. 2. Coat the Cook & Crisp Basket with a little oil. 3. In a suitable bowl mix the sugar, butter, egg, flour and soda using a whisk. Throw in the bananas and walnuts. 4. Transfer the mixture to the Cook & Crisp Basket. Put on the Smart Lid on top of the Ninja Foodi Steam Fryer. Move the Lid Slider to the "Air Fry/Stovetop". Select the "Air Fry" mode for cooking. Adjust the cooking temperature to 180°C. 5. Cook for around 10 minutes. 6. Reduce its heat to 165°C. Cook for another 15 minutes. Serve hot.
Per Serving: Calories 363; Fat: 10.7g; Sodium 253mg; Carbs: 63.7g; Fiber: 3.8g; Sugars 22.9g; Protein 4.9g

Lemon Cake

Prep Time: 10 minutes | Cook Time: 60 minutes | Serves: 6

125g ricotta cheese	1 lemon, juiced and zested
100g sugar	2 teaspoon vanilla extract
3 eggs	[optional]
3 tablespoon flour	

1. Place the Cook & Crisp Basket in your Pressure Cooker Steam Fryer. 2. Mix all of the recipe ingredients until a creamy consistency is achieved. 3. Place the mixture in a cake tin. 4. Transfer the tin to the Cook & Crisp Basket. Put on the Smart Lid on top of the Ninja Foodi Steam Fryer. Move the Lid Slider to the "Air Fry/Stovetop". Select the "Air Fry" mode for cooking. Adjust the cooking temperature to 160°C. 5. Cook for the cakes for around 25 minutes. 6. Remove the cake from the fryer, allow to cool, and serve.
Per Serving: Calories 420; Fat: 17.1g; Sodium 282mg; Carbs: 65.7g; Fiber: 4.5g; Sugars 35.1g; Protein 7g

Strawberry Shortcake

Prep Time: 10 minutes | Cook Time: 15 minutes | Serves: 4 to 6

165g all-purpose flour	320g heavy cream, chilled
3 tablespoons granulated sugar	Icing sugar for sprinkling
1½ teaspoons baking powder	2 tablespoons icing sugar, more
1 teaspoon salt	for dusting
8 tablespoons butter, cubed and	½ teaspoon vanilla extract
chilled	165g quartered fresh strawberries

1. In a suitable bowl, mix the flour, granulated sugar, baking powder, and salt. Add the butter and use your fingers to break apart the butter pieces while working them into the flour mixture, until pea-size pieces form. Pour 180g of the cream over the flour mixture and, using a rubber spatula, mix the ingredients until just mixed. 2. Transfer the prepared dough to a work surface and form into an 18 cm-wide disk. Brush the top with water, then sprinkle with some turbinado sugar. Using a suitable metal spatula, transfer the prepared dough to the Cook & Crisp Basket. Place the Cook & Crisp Basket in your Pressure Cooker Steam Fryer. 3. Put on the Smart Lid on top of the Ninja Foodi Steam Fryer. Move the Lid Slider to the "Air Fry/Stovetop". Select the "Air Fry" mode for cooking. Air Fry at 175°C until golden brown and fluffy, about 20 minutes. Let cool in the "cook & crisp basket" for around 5 minutes, then turn out onto a wire rack, right-side up, to cool completely. 4. Meanwhile, in a suitable bowl, beat the remaining cream, the icing sugar, and vanilla until stiff peaks form. Split the scone like a hamburger bun and spread the strawberries over the bottom. 5. Top with the whipped cream and cover with the top of the scone. Dust with icing sugar and cut into wedges to serve.
Per Serving: Calories 339; Fat: 14g; Sodium 556mg; Carbs: 44.6g; Fiber: 6.4g; Sugars 3.8g; Protein 10.5g

Pumpkin Pudding

Prep Time: 10 minutes | Cook Time: 25 minutes | Serves: 4

865g pumpkin puree
3 tablespoon honey
1 tablespoon ginger
1 tablespoon cinnamon
1 teaspoon clove
1 teaspoon nutmeg
240g full-fat cream
2 eggs
200g sugar

1. Place the Cook & Crisp Basket in your Pressure Cooker Steam Fryer. 2. In a suitable bowl, stir all of the recipe ingredients to mix. 3. Grease inside of the Cook & Crisp Basket. 4. Pour the mixture into the Cook & Crisp Basket. 5. Put on the Smart Lid on top of the Ninja Foodi Steam Fryer. 6. Move the Lid Slider to the "Air Fry/Stovetop". Select the "Air Fry" mode for cooking. 7. Adjust the cooking temperature to 200°C. 8. Cook for around 15 minutes. Serve with whipped cream if desired.
Per Serving: Calories 360; Fat: 7.8g; Sodium 280mg; Carbs: 74.4g; Fiber: 8g; Sugars 47.4g; Protein 2.7g

Walnut Bread

Prep Time: 10 minutes | Cook Time: 40 minutes | Serves: 1 loaf

175g flour
¼ teaspoon baking powder
125g butter
125g sugar
2 medium eggs
100g bananas, peeled
200g chopped walnuts

1. Place the Cook & Crisp Basket in your Pressure Cooker Steam Fryer. 2. Grease the Cook & Crisp Basket with butter. 3. Mix the flour and the baking powder in a suitable bowl. 4. In a separate bowl, beat the sugar and butter until fluffy and pale. Gradually add in the flour and egg. Stir. 5. Throw in the walnuts and mix again. 6. Mash the bananas using a fork and transfer to the bowl. Mix once more, until everything is incorporated. 7. Pour the mixture into the Cook & Crisp Basket. Put on the Smart Lid on top of the Ninja Foodi Steam Fryer. Move the Lid Slider to the "Air Fry/Stovetop". Select the "Air Fry" mode for cooking. 8. Adjust the cooking temperature to 175°C. 9. Cook for around 10 minutes.
Per Serving: Calories 488; Fat: 34.3g; Sodium 130mg; Carbs: 42.4g; Fiber: 1.7g; Sugars 21.5g; Protein 4.8g

Air-Fried Peach Slices

Prep Time: 10 minutes | Cook Time: 40 minutes | Serves: 4

615g peaches, sliced
2–3 tablespoons sugar
2 tablespoon flour
25g oats
2 tablespoons unsalted butter
¼ teaspoon vanilla extract
1 teaspoon cinnamon

1. Place the Cook & Crisp Basket in your Pressure Cooker Steam Fryer. 2. In a large bowl, mix the peach slices, sugar, vanilla extract, and cinnamon. Pour the prepared mixture into the Cook & Crisp Basket. 3. Put on the Smart Lid on top of the Ninja Foodi Steam Fryer. 4. Move the Lid Slider to the "Air Fry/Stovetop". Select the "Air Fry" mode for cooking. 5. Cook for around 20 minutes on 145°C. 6. In the meantime, mix the oats, flour, and unsalted butter in a separate bowl. 7. Once the peach slices cooked, pour the butter mixture on top of them. 8. Cook for around 10 minutes at 155°C. 9. Remove from the Pressure Cooker Steam Fryer and allow to crisp up for around 5–10 minutes. Serve with ice cream if desired.
Per Serving: Calories 130; Fat: 3.9g; Sodium 3mg; Carbs: 21.6g; Fiber: 1.6g; Sugars 9.8g; Protein 3.6g

Easy Vanilla Soufflé

Prep Time: 10 minutes | Cook Time: 50 minutes | Serves: 6

30g flour
55g butter, softened
240ml whole milk
50g sugar
2 teaspoon vanilla extract
1 vanilla bean
5 egg whites
4 egg yolks
25g sugar
1 teaspoon cream of tartar

1. Mix the flour and butter to create a smooth paste. 2. In a saucepan, heat up the milk. Add the 50g sugar and allow it to dissolve. 3. Put the vanilla bean in the mixture and bring it to a boil. 4. Pour in the flour-butter mixture. Beat the contents of the saucepan with wire whisk, removing all the lumps. 5. Reduce its heat and allow the mixture to simmer and thicken for a number of minutes. 6. Take the saucepan off the heat. Remove the vanilla bean and let the mixture cool for around 10 minutes in an ice bath. 7. In the meantime, grease six 75g ramekins or soufflé dishes with butter and add a sprinkling of sugar to each one. 8. In a separate bowl quickly, rigorously stir the egg yolks and vanilla extract together. Mix with the milk mixture. In another bowl, beat the egg whites,25 g sugar and cream of tartar to form medium stiff peaks. 10. Fold the egg whites into the soufflé base. Transfer everything to the ramekins, smoothing the surfaces with a knife or the back of a spoon. 11. Put the ramekins in the cook and crisp basket. Place the Cook & Crisp Basket in your Pressure Cooker Steam Fryer. 12. Put on the Smart Lid on top of the Ninja Foodi Steam Fryer. Move the Lid Slider to the "Air Fry/Stovetop". Select the "Air Fry" mode for cooking. Adjust the cooking temperature to 165°C. 13. Cook for around 14 to 16 minutes. You may need to complete this step in multiple batches. 14. Serve the soufflés topped with icing sugar and with a side of chocolate sauce.
Per Serving: Calories 182; Fat: 0.7g; Sodium 7mg; Carbs: 46.3g; Fiber: 6.2g; Sugars 40.7g; Protein 1.9g

Marshmallow Fluff Turnover

Prep Time: 10 minutes | Cook Time: 35 minutes | Serves: 4

4 sheets filo pastry, defrosted
4 tablespoons chunky peanut butter
4 teaspoon marshmallow fluff
50g butter, melted
Pinch of sea salt

1. Place the Cook & Crisp Basket in your Pressure Cooker Steam Fryer. 2. Roll out the pastry sheets. Coat one with a light brushing of butter. 3. Lay a second pastry sheet on top of the first one. Brush once again with butter. Repeat until all 4 sheets have been used. 4. Slice the filo layers into four strips, measuring 8 cm x 30 cm. 5. Spread one tablespoon of peanut butter and one teaspoon of marshmallow fluff on the underside of each pastry strip. 6. Take the tip of each sheet and fold it backwards over the filling, forming a triangle. Repeat this action in a zigzag manner until the filling is completely enclosed. 7. Seal the ends of each turnover with a light brushing of butter. 8. Put the turnovers in the Cook & Crisp Basket. Put on the Smart Lid on top of the Ninja Foodi Steam Fryer. Move the Lid Slider to the "Air Fry/Stovetop". Select the "Air Fry" mode for cooking. Adjust the cooking temperature to 180°C. 9. Cook for around 3 to 5 minutes, until they turn golden brown and puffy. 10. Sprinkle a little sea salt over each turnover before serving.
Per Serving: Calories 281; Fat: 6.7g; Sodium 187mg; Carbs: 52.7g; Fiber: 6.6g; Sugars 29g; Protein 5.1g

Pear Crumble

Prep Time: 10 minutes | Cook Time: 15 minutes | Serves: 4

2 ripe d'Anjou pears (455g), peeled, cored, and chopped
55g packed light brown sugar
2 tablespoons corns flour
1 teaspoon salt
50g granulated sugar
3 tablespoons unsalted butter, at
room temperature
40g all-purpose flour
2½ tablespoons cocoa powder
30g chopped blanched hazelnuts
Vanilla ice cream or whipped cream (optional)

1. In the Cook & Crisp Basket, mix the pears, brown sugar, corn flour, and ½ teaspoon salt and toss until the pears are evenly coated in the sugar. 2. In a suitable bowl, mix the remaining ½ teaspoon salt with the granulated sugar, butter, flour, and cocoa powder and pinch and press the butter into the other ingredients with your fingers until a sandy, shaggy crumble dough forms. Stir in the hazelnuts. Sprinkle the crumble topping evenly over the pears. 3. Place the Cook & Crisp Basket in your Pressure Cooker Steam Fryer. Put on the Smart Lid on top of the Ninja Foodi Steam Fryer. Move the Lid Slider to the "Air Fry/Stovetop". Select the "Air Fry" mode for cooking. Air Fry at 160°C until the crumble is crisp and the pears are bubbling in the center, about 30 minutes. 4. Carefully remove the basket from the Ninja Foodi Pressure Steam Fryer and serve the hot crumble in bowls, topped with ice cream or whipped cream, if you like.
Per Serving: Calories 254; Fat: 2.6g; Sodium 482mg; Carbs: 49.1g; Fiber: 4.8g; Sugars 0.2g; Protein 7.8g

Chocolate-Covered Bacon

Prep Time: 10 minutes | Cook Time: 25 minutes | Serves: 4

8 slices bacon	chips
1 tablespoon granular erythritol	1 teaspoon coconut oil
55g low-carb sugar-free chocolate	½ teaspoon maple extract

1. Place the Cook & Crisp Basket in your Pressure Cooker Steam Fryer. 2. Place the bacon in the Cook & Crisp Basket and add the erythritol on top. 3. Put on the Smart Lid on top of the Ninja Foodi Steam Fryer. 4. Move the Lid Slider to the "Air Fry/Stovetop". Select the "Air Fry" mode for cooking. 5. Cook for 6 minutes at 175°C and turn the bacon over. Leave to cook another 6 minutes or until the bacon is sufficiently crispy. 6. Take the bacon out of the fryer and leave it to cool. 7. Microwave the chocolate chips and coconut oil for half a minute. Remove from the microwave and mix before stirring in the maple extract. 8. Set the bacon flat on a piece of parchment paper and pour the mixture over. Allow to harden in the refrigerator for 5 minutes before serving.
Per Serving: Calories 361; Fat: 31.3g; Sodium 385mg; Carbs: 13.8g; Fiber: 7.3g; Sugars 2.5g; Protein 9.7g

Crispy Pork Rinds

Prep Time: 10 minutes | Cook Time: 10 minutes | Serves: 2

50g pork rinds	5g powdered erythritol
2 teaspoons unsalted butter, melted	½ teaspoon cinnamon

1. Place the Cook & Crisp Basket in your Pressure Cooker Steam Fryer. 2. Coat the rinds with the melted butter. 3. In a separate bowl, mix the erythritol and cinnamon and pour over the pork rinds, ensuring the rinds are covered completely and evenly. 4. Transfer the pork rinds into the Cook & Crisp Basket. Put on the Smart Lid on top of the Ninja Foodi Steam Fryer. Move the Lid Slider to the "Air Fry/Stovetop". Select the "Air Fry" mode for cooking. Air Fry at 200°C for 5 minutes.
Per Serving: Calories 469; Fat: 36.5g; Sodium 46mg; Carbs: 31.4g; Fiber: 4.5g; Sugars 17.9g; Protein 9.1g

Toasted Flakes

Prep Time: 10 minutes | Cook Time: 5 minutes | Serves: 1

95g unsweetened coconut flakes	5g granular erythritol
2 teaspoon coconut oil, melted	Salt

1. Place the Cook & Crisp Basket in your Pressure Cooker Steam Fryer. 2. In a suitable bowl, mix the coconut flakes, oil, granular erythritol, and a pinch of salt, ensuring that the flakes are coated completely. 3. Place the coconut flakes in the Cook & Crisp Basket. Put on the Smart Lid on top of the Ninja Foodi Steam Fryer. Move the Lid Slider to the "Air Fry/Stovetop". Select the "Air Fry" mode for cooking. 4. Air Fry at 150°C for 3 minutes, giving the basket a good shake a few times throughout the cooking time. Fry until golden and serve.
Per Serving: Calories 363; Fat: 10.7g; Sodium 253mg; Carbs: 63.7g; Fiber: 3.8g; Sugars 22.9g; Protein 4.9g

Blackberry Granola Crisp

Prep Time: 10 minutes | Cook Time: 18 minutes | Serves: 1

2 tablespoon lemon juice	290g blackberries
10g powdered erythritol	120g crunchy granola
¼ teaspoon xanthan gum	

1. Place the Cook & Crisp Basket in your Pressure Cooker Steam Fryer. 2. In a suitable bowl, mix the lemon juice, erythritol, xanthan gum, and blackberries. Transfer to the Cook & Crisp Basket and seal with aluminum foil. Put on the Smart Lid on top of the Ninja Foodi Steam Fryer. Move the Lid Slider to the "Air Fry/Stovetop". Select the "Air Fry" mode for cooking. 3. Cook for 12 minutes at 175°C. 4. Take care when removing the dish from the Pressure Cooker Steam Fryer. Give the blackberries another stir and top with the granola. 5. Return the dish to the Pressure Cooker Steam Fryer. Put on the Smart Lid on top of the Ninja Foodi Steam Fryer. Move the Lid Slider to the "Air Fry/Stovetop". Select the "Air Fry" mode for cooking. Cook for minutes at 160°C. 6. Serve once the granola has turned brown and enjoy.
Per Serving: Calories 420; Fat: 17.1g; Sodium 282mg; Carbs: 65.7g; Fiber: 4.5g; Sugars 35.1g; Protein 7g

Sugary Churros

Prep Time: 10 minutes | Cook Time: 15 minutes | Serves: 1

120ml water	3 eggs
55g butter	2½ teaspoon sugar
60g flour	

1. Place the Cook & Crisp Basket in your Pressure Cooker Steam Fryer. 2. In a suitable saucepan, bring the water and butter to a boil. Once it is bubbling, add the flour and mix to create a doughy consistency. 3. Remove from the heat, allow to cool, and crack the eggs into the saucepan. Blend with a hand mixer until the prepared dough turns fluffy. 4. Transfer the prepared dough into a piping bag. 5. Pipe the prepared dough into the Cook & Crisp Basket in several 8 cm-long segments. 6. Put on the Smart Lid on top of the Ninja Foodi Steam Fryer. 7. Move the Lid Slider to the "Air Fry/Stovetop". Select the "Air Fry" mode for cooking. 8. Adjust the cooking temperature to 195°C. 9. Cook for 10 minutes before removing from the fryer and coating in the sugar. 10. Serve with the low-carb chocolate sauce of your choice.
Per Serving: Calories 256; Fat: 3.5g; Sodium 7mg; Carbs: 54.2g; Fiber: 10.7g; Sugars 32.2g; Protein 4.9g

Quick Peanut Butter Cookies

Prep Time: 10 minutes | Cook Time: 15 minutes | Serves: 1

¼ teaspoon salt	130g peanut butter
4 tablespoon erythritol	1 egg

1. Place the Cook & Crisp Basket in your Pressure Cooker Steam Fryer. 2. Mix the salt, erythritol, and peanut butter in a suitable bowl, incorporating everything well. Break the egg over the mixture and mix to create a dough. 3. Flatten the prepared dough using a rolling pin and cut into shapes with a knife or cookie cutter. Make a crisscross on the top of each cookie with a fork. 4. Put the cookies inside the Cook & Crisp Basket. Put on the Smart Lid on top of the Ninja Foodi Steam Fryer. 5. Move the Lid Slider to the "Air Fry/Stovetop". Select the "Air Fry" mode for cooking. Adjust the cooking temperature to 180°C. 6. Leave to cook for 10 minutes. Take care when taking them out and allow to cool before enjoying.
Per Serving: Calories 360; Fat: 7.8g; Sodium 280mg; Carbs: 74.4g; Fiber: 8g; Sugars 47.4g; Protein 2.7g

Avocado Cocoa Pudding

Prep Time: 10 minutes | Cook Time: 5 minutes | Serves: 1

1 avocado	4 teaspoons unsweetened milk
3 teaspoon liquid sugar	¼ teaspoon vanilla extract
1 tablespoon cocoa powder	

1. Place the Cook & Crisp Basket in your Pressure Cooker Steam Fryer. 2. Halve the avocado, twist to open, and scoop out the pit. 3. Spoon the flesh into a suitable bowl and mash it with a fork. Throw in the sugar, cocoa powder, milk, and vanilla extract, and mix everything with a hand mixer. 4. Transfer this mixture to the Cook & Crisp Basket. Put on the Smart Lid on top of the Ninja Foodi Steam Fryer. Move the Lid Slider to the "Air Fry/Stovetop". Select the "Air Fry" mode for cooking. Adjust the cooking temperature to 180°C. 5. Cook for 3 minutes.
Per Serving: Calories 488; Fat: 34.3g; Sodium 130mg; Carbs: 42.4g; Fiber: 1.7g; Sugars 21.5g; Protein 4.8g

Chia Coconut Pudding

Prep Time: 10 minutes | Cook Time: 10 minutes | Serves: 1

255g chia seeds	1 tablespoon coconut oil
240ml unsweetened coconut milk	1 teaspoon butter
1 teaspoon liquid sugar	

1. Place the Cook & Crisp Basket in your Pressure Cooker Steam Fryer. 2. In a suitable bowl, gently mix the chia seeds with the milk and sugar, before mixing the coconut oil and butter. Spoon seven equal-sized portions into seven ramekins and set these inside the Cook & Crisp Basket. 3. Put on the Smart Lid on top of the Ninja Foodi Steam Fryer. 4. Move the Lid Slider to the "Air Fry/Stovetop". Select the "Air Fry" mode for cooking. Adjust the cooking temperature to 180°C. 5. Cook for 4 minutes. 5. Take care when removing the ramekins from the fryer and allow to cool for 4 minutes before serving.
Per Serving: Calories 130; Fat: 3.9g; Sodium 3mg; Carbs: 21.6g; Fiber: 1.6g; Sugars 9.8g; Protein 3.6g

Ginger Bacon Bites

Prep Time: 10 minutes | Cook Time: 15 minutes | Serves: 2

¼ teaspoon ginger
⅕ teaspoon baking soda
170g peanut butter

2 tablespoon Swerve
3 slices bacon, cooked and chopped

1. Place the Cook & Crisp Basket in your Pressure Cooker Steam Fryer. 2. In a suitable bowl, mix the ginger, baking soda, peanut butter, and Swerve together, making sure to mix everything well. 3. Stir in the chopped bacon. 4. With clean hands, shape the mixture into a cylinder and cut in six. Press down each slice into a cookie with your palm. 5. Put the cookies inside the Cook & Crisp Basket. Put on the Smart Lid on top of the Ninja Foodi Steam Fryer. Move the Lid Slider to the "Air Fry/Stovetop". Select the "Air Fry" mode for cooking. Adjust the cooking temperature to 175°C. 6. Cook for 7 minutes. Take care when taking them out of the fryer and allow to cool before serving.
Per Serving: Calories 182; Fat: 0.7g; Sodium 7mg; Carbs: 46.3g; Fiber: 6.2g; Sugars 40.7g; Protein 1.9g

Poppy Seed Cake

Prep Time: 10 minutes | Cook Time: 15 minutes | Serves: 8

For the Cake:
185g plain flour
2 teaspoons baking powder
1 teaspoon salt
100g granulated sugar
6 tablespoons unsalted butter,

melted
2 large eggs
120ml whole milk
1 tablespoon poppy seeds
Finely grated zest of 1 lemon

For the Syrup:
3 tablespoons fresh lemon juice

50g granulated sugar

For the Glaze:
125g icing sugar
1 tablespoon 1 teaspoon fresh

lemon juice

1. To make the cake: In a suitable bowl, mix the flour, baking powder, and salt until evenly mixed. In a suitable bowl, mix the granulated sugar, melted butter, and eggs until smooth, then mix in the milk, poppy seeds, and lemon zest. 2. Pour the liquid ingredients over the dry recipe ingredients and mix until just mixed. Pour the prepared batter into a greased the Cook & Crisp Basket and smooth the top. 3. Place the Cook & Crisp Basket in your Pressure Cooker Steam Fryer. Put on the Smart Lid on top of the Ninja Foodi Steam Fryer. Move the Lid Slider to the "Air Fry/Stovetop". Select the "Air Fry" mode for cooking. Air Fry at 155°C until a toothpick inserted into the center of the cake comes out clean, about 30 to 35 minutes. 4. Meanwhile, make the syrup: In a microwave-safe bowl, heat the lemon juice and granulated sugar in the microwave, stirring until the sugar dissolves. 5. Remove the pan from the Ninja Foodi Pressure Steam Fryer and transfer to a wire rack set over a rimmed baking sheet. Let cool for around 5 minutes in the pan, then turn the cake out onto the rack and invert it so it's right-side up. 6. As soon as you unmold it, use a toothpick to stab the top of the warm cake all over, making as many holes as you can. Slowly pour the warm lemon syrup over the top of the cake so that it absorbs as you pour it on. Let the cake cool completely on the rack to allow the syrup to hydrate the cake fully. 7. To make the glaze: In a glass bowl, mix the icing sugar and lemon juice and stir into a thick glaze. Microwave the glaze until loose and pourable, about 30 seconds, then stir until completely smooth. 8. Pour the hot glaze over the top of the cake, still on the rack, letting it drip over the edges. Let the cake stand for at least 10 minutes to allow the glaze to set. 9. Transfer the cake to a plate before serving.
Per Serving: Calories 161; Fat: 12.4g; Sodium 375mg; Carbs: 9.8g; Fiber: 1.5g; Sugars 2.6g; Protein 3.8g

Gooey Brownies

Prep Time: 10 minutes | Cook Time: 15 minutes | Serves: 4 to 6

200g granulated sugar
30g cocoa powder
½ teaspoon salt
8 tablespoons unsalted butter, melted
1 teaspoon vanilla extract

2 large eggs, beaten
30g plain flour
140g chopped bittersweet chocolate
Vanilla ice cream and flaky sea salt, for serving

1. Place the Cook & Crisp Basket in your Pressure Cooker Steam Fryer. 2. In a suitable bowl, mix the sugar, cocoa powder, and salt. Then add the melted butter, vanilla, and eggs and mix until smooth. Stir in the flour and chocolate and pour the prepared batter into the Cook & Crisp Basket. 3. Place the Cook & Crisp Basket in your Pressure Cooker Steam Fryer. 4. Put on the Smart Lid on top of the Ninja Foodi Steam Fryer. Move the Lid Slider to the "Air Fry/Stovetop". Select the "Air Fry" mode for cooking. Air Fry at 155°C until the brownie "pudding" is set at the edges but still jiggly in the middle (it may form a "skin" in the middle, but it doesn't affect the taste), about 30 minutes. 5. Let the brownie cool in the Ninja Foodi Pressure Steam Fryer for around 5 minutes, enough time to grab some bowls and allow the ice cream to soften to the perfect scooping consistency. 6. Divide the gooey brownies among serving bowls and top with a scoop of ice cream and, if you like, a decent pinch of flaky sea salt.
Per Serving: Calories 373; Fat: 3.1g; Sodium 687mg; Carbs: 69.2g; Fiber: 9.6g; Sugars 3.4g; Protein 7.8g

Cinnamon Beignets

Prep Time: 10 minutes | Cook Time: 15 minutes | Serves: 16

3 tablespoons unsalted butter, cut into small cubes
½ teaspoon salt
1 teaspoon vanilla extract
125g 2 tablespoons flour, more for

dusting
2 large eggs
200g granulated sugar
2 teaspoons cinnamon
Vegetable oil, for brushing

1. In a suitable saucepan, mix the butter, salt, vanilla, and 240 ml water and bring to a boil over high heat. Add the flour and cook, with constant stirring with a wooden spoon, until a smooth dough forms, about 30 seconds. 2. Transfer the prepared dough to a suitable bowl, let cool for around 1 minute, then add 1 egg, stirring vigorously until the prepared dough is smooth again. Repeat with the remaining egg. 3. Transfer the prepared dough to a floured work surface and sprinkle the top with more flour. Pat the prepared dough into 23 cm square about ½ cm thick. 4. Flip the prepared dough sheet over from time to time and add more flour if it's sticking to the surface (don't worry about adding too much flour since you will brush it off later). 5. Cut the prepared dough square into 16 smaller squares and transfer them to a foil-lined baking sheet. 6. Using a dry pastry brush, dust off as much of the excess flour as you can on both sides. Chill the beignets on the sheet in the freezer until frozen solid, at least 1 hour. 7. Meanwhile, mix the sugar and cinnamon in a suitable brown paper bag. Using a pastry brush, brush 4 squares all over with enough oil to coat well. Place them in one layer in the Cook & Crisp Basket. 8. Place the Cook & Crisp Basket in your Pressure Cooker Steam Fryer. Put on the Smart Lid on top of the Ninja Foodi Steam Fryer. Move the Lid Slider to the "Air Fry/Stovetop". Select the "Air Fry" mode for cooking. Air Fry at 200°C until golden brown and puffed, about 13 minutes. 9. As soon as the beignets are done, use tongs to immediately transfer them to the paper bag and shake them in the cinnamon-sugar to coat. 10. Repeat with the remaining dough squares and cinnamon-sugar in three more batches. Serve the beignets hot.
Per Serving: Calories 283; Fat: 3.6g; Sodium 381mg; Carbs: 55.4g; Fiber: 8.1g; Sugars 3.1g; Protein 8.7g

Pineapple Galette

Prep Time: 10 minutes | Cook Time: 15 minutes | Serves: 2

¼ medium-size pineapple, peeled, crosswise into 1/2 cm-thick slices
2 tablespoons dark rum
1 teaspoon vanilla extract
½ teaspoon salt
Grated zest of ½ lime

1 sheet puff pastry, cut into a 20 cm round
3 tablespoons granulated sugar
2 tablespoons unsalted butter, cubed and chilled
Coconut ice cream, for serving

1. In a suitable bowl, mix the pineapple slices, rum, vanilla, salt, and lime zest and let stand for at least 10 minutes to allow the pineapple to soak in the rum. 2. Press the puff pastry round into the bottom and up the Cook & Crisp Basket and use the tines of a fork to dock the bottom and sides. 3. Place the pineapple slices on the bottom of the pastry in more or less a single layer, then sprinkle with the sugar and dot with the butter. Drizzle with the leftover juices from the bowl. 4. Place the Cook & Crisp Basket in your Pressure Cooker Steam Fryer. 5. Put on the Smart Lid on top of the Ninja Foodi Steam Fryer. Move the Lid Slider to the "Air Fry/Stovetop". Select the "Air Fry" mode for cooking. Air Fry at 155°C until the pastry is puffed and golden brown and the pineapple is caramelized on top, about 40 minutes. 6. Transfer the basket to a wire rack to cool for around 15 minutes. Serve warm with coconut ice cream.
Per Serving: Calories 128; Fat: 1.7g; Sodium 771mg; Carbs: 22.1g; Fiber: 4.5g; Sugars 3.9g; Protein 7.1g

Apple Butter

Prep Time: 10 minutes | Cook Time: 15 minutes | Serves: 1 ¼ cups

Cooking spray
510g store-bought unsweetened applesauce
125g packed light brown sugar

3 tablespoons fresh lemon juice
½ teaspoon salt
¼ teaspoon cinnamon
⅛ teaspoon allspice

1. Spray the Cook & Crisp Basket with cooking spray. Mix all the recipe ingredients in a suitable bowl until smooth, then pour into the Cook & Crisp Basket. 2. Place the Cook & Crisp Basket in your Pressure Cooker Steam Fryer. 3. Put on the Smart Lid on top of the Ninja Foodi Steam Fryer. Move the Lid Slider to the "Air Fry/Stovetop". Select the "Air Fry" mode for cooking. Air Fry at 170°C until the apple mixture is caramelized, reduced to a thick puree, and fragrant, about 1 hour. 4. Remove the Cook & Crisp Basket in your Pressure Cooker Steam Fryer., stir to mix the caramelized bits at the edge with the rest, then let cool completely to thicken. 5. Scrape the apple butter into a jar and store in the refrigerator for up to 2 weeks.

Espresso Brownies

Prep Time: 10 minutes | Cook Time: 36 minutes | Serves: 8

200g dark chocolate, chopped into chunks
1 teaspoon pure coffee extract
2 tablespoons liquid Stevia
1 tablespoon cocoa powder
2 tablespoons instant espresso powder
130g almond butter

80g almond flour
½ teaspoon lime peel zest
25g almond meal
2 eggs and 1 egg yolk
½ teaspoon baking soda
½ teaspoon baking powder
½ teaspoon cinnamon

1. Melt the chocolate and almond butter in your microwave. Allow the mixture to cool at room temperature. Then, mix the eggs, stevia, cinnamon, espresso powder, coffee extract and lime zest. 2. Next, add the egg mixture to the chocolate butter mixture. Stir in almond flour and almond meal along with baking soda, baking powder, and cocoa powder. 3. Finally, press the prepared batter into a buttered Cook & Crisp Basket. Place the Cook & Crisp Basket in your Pressure Cooker Steam Fryer. 4. Put on the Smart Lid on top of the Ninja Foodi Steam Fryer. Move the Lid Slider to the "Air Fry/Stovetop". Select the "Air Fry" mode for cooking. Air fry for around 35 to minutes at 345°F/175°C.
Per Serving: Calories 244; Fat: 9.1g; Sodium 1399mg; Carbs: 34.3g; Fiber: 8.7g; Sugars 15.7g; Protein 8.3g

Apple Almond Turnovers

Prep Time: 10 minutes | Cook Time: 15 minutes | Serves: 8

3 apples, cored, peeled and diced
45g almonds, chopped
½ tablespoon cinnamon
½ teaspoon vanilla extract
½ teaspoon star anise,

2 tablespoons Truvia for baking
1 tablespoon corn flour
½ pack phyllo pastry sheets
60g butter, melted
1 teaspoon orange peel, grated

1. In a suitable pan, cook the apples, corn flour, Truvia, vanilla and orange peel. Cook for around 5 minutes or until apple filling thickens. Remove from heat and set aside. 2. Brush a piece of phyllo dough with melted butter; use a pastry brush. Cover with another sheet and brush again. Continue with two more sheets of phyllo dough. Then, cut the phyllo dough in half lengthwise. 3. Add 1 tablespoon of the apple filling at the end of the prepared dough; scatter chopped almonds over the top. Fold to create a triangle. It is important that the apple filling is completely enclosed. 4. Continue with remaining phyllo dough. Brush with extra butter. Place into the Cook & Crisp Basket in a single layer. Place the Cook & Crisp Basket in your Pressure Cooker Steam Fryer. 5. Put on the Smart Lid on top of the Ninja Foodi Steam Fryer. Move the Lid Slider to the "Air Fry/Stovetop". Select the "Air Fry" mode for cooking. Air Fry at 175°C for around 15 minutes; cook in batches. 6. Meanwhile, mix Truvia, star anise and cinnamon. When your turnovers are done, brush them with some extra butter. Dust them with the seasoned sweetener and serve.
Per Serving: Calories 541; Fat: 12.4g; Sodium 250mg; Carbs: 85.4g; Fiber: 21.3g; Sugars 6.1g; Protein 6.5g

Prune Muffins

Prep Time: 10 minutes | Cook Time: 13 minutes | Serves: 6

35g walnut meal
40g walnuts, chopped
¼ teaspoon salt
½ teaspoon pure hazelnut extract
⅓ teaspoon cloves
½ teaspoon pure vanilla extract
⅓ teaspoon cinnamon
1 teaspoon baking powder

½ teaspoon baking soda
2 teaspoons fresh apple juice
240g yogurt
2 eggs
85g butter, room temperature
2 tablespoons Truvia for baking
90g almond flour
60g prunes, chopped

1. In a suitable bowl, mix walnut meal, almond flour, baking soda, baking powder, cloves, cinnamon, and Truvia. Take another bowl, mix eggs, yogurt, butter and apple juice; mix to mix well. 2. Next, add your wet mixture to the dry mixture. Fold in the prunes and walnuts. Press the prepared batter mixture into a greased muffin tin. Transfer them to the Cook & Crisp Basket. Place the Cook & Crisp Basket in your Pressure Cooker Steam Fryer. 3. Put on the Smart Lid on top of the Ninja Foodi Steam Fryer. Move the Lid Slider to the "Air Fry/Stovetop". Select the "Air Fry" mode for cooking. Air Fry at 180°C for around 13 minutes.
Per Serving: Calories 669; Fat: 53.8g; Sodium 905mg; Carbs: 41.7g; Fiber: 8.6g; Sugars 12.3g; Protein 14g

Coconut Cake

Prep Time: 10 minutes | Cook Time: 17 minutes | Serves: 6

60g shredded coconut
¼ teaspoon salt
⅓ teaspoon nutmeg, grated
½ teaspoon baking powder
155g almond flour

2 eggs
2 tablespoons Truvia
115g butter
2 tablespoons orange jam
80ml coconut milk

1. Spritz the Cook & Crisp Basket with cooking spray. Then, beat the butter with Truvia until fluffy. 2. Fold in the eggs; continue mixing until smooth. Add nutmeg, salt, and flour; then, slowly pour in the coconut milk. Finally, add the shredded coconut and orange jam; mix to create cake batter. 3. Then, press the prepared batter into the Cook & Crisp Basket. Place the Cook & Crisp Basket in your Pressure Cooker Steam Fryer. 4. Put on the Smart Lid on top of the Ninja Foodi Steam Fryer. Move the Lid Slider to the "Air Fry/Stovetop". Select the "Air Fry" mode for cooking. Adjust the cooking temperature to 180°C. 5. Air Fry cake for around 17 minutes, then transfer the cake to a cooling rack. Serve chilled.
Per Serving: Calories 194; Fat: 2.6g; Sodium 1257mg; Carbs: 35.4g; Fiber: 3.7g; Sugars 3.1g; Protein 9.4g

Chocolate Muffins

Prep Time: 10 minutes | Cook Time: 15 minutes | Serves: 6

3 teaspoons cocoa powder
125g dried apricots, chopped
120g almond flour
1 teaspoon pure rum extract
1½ tablespoons Truvia for baking
2 eggs
115g butter, room temperature

80g maple syrup, sugar-free
240ml rice milk
½ teaspoon baking soda
1 teaspoon baking powder
¼ teaspoon nutmeg, grated
½ teaspoon cinnamon
⅛ teaspoon salt

1. In a suitable bowl, mix Truvia, almond flour, baking soda, baking powder, salt, nutmeg, cinnamon and cocoa powder. 2. In another bowl, add butter and cream it, also add egg, rum extract, rice milk, sugar-free maple syrup; mix to mix. Next, add your wet mixture to the dry mixture and fold in the apricots. 3. Press the prepared batter into a greased muffin tin. Transfer them to the Cook & Crisp Basket. Place the Cook & Crisp Basket in your Pressure Cooker Steam Fryer. 4. Put on the Smart Lid on top of the Ninja Foodi Steam Fryer. Move the Lid Slider to the "Air Fry/Stovetop". Select the "Air Fry" mode for cooking. Air Fry at 175°C for around 15 minutes.
Per Serving: Calories 344; Fat: 3g; Sodium 603mg; Carbs: 73.8g; Fiber: 11.5g; Sugars 8.6g; Protein 9.4g

Mini Crustless Pies

Prep time: 5 minutes | Cook time: 10 minutes | Serves: 2

Butter, at room temperature, for greasing
145g pumpkin purée
3 tablespoons packed brown sugar
1 teaspoon corn flour

Pinch salt
½ teaspoon pumpkin pie spice
1 egg, lightly beaten
60g plus 2 tablespoons heavy cream

1. Add 240ml water to your Ninja Foodi XL Pressure Cooker Steam Fryer with SmartLid cooking pot and place the Deluxe reversible rack in the bottom. Butter two 1-cup ramekins. 2. In a medium bowl, whisk together the pumpkin, brown sugar, corn flour, salt, pumpkin pie spice, and egg. Add the cream and stir to combine. 3. Divide the pumpkin mixture between the prepared ramekins. Set the ramekins on the Deluxe reversible rack, placing a third empty ramekin next to them to ensure that they don't jostle during cooking. 4. Lock lid; move slider to PRESSURE. Make sure the pressure release valve is in the SEAL position. The cooking temperature will default to HIGH, which is accurate. Set time to 10 minutes. Press START/STOP to cooking. 5. When cooking is complete, let pressure release naturally for about 10 minutes. 6. Using tongs, remove the ramekins from the cooker, transfer to a heatproof surface, and let cool for 5 to 10 minutes before serving with a dollop of whipped cream and crumbled gingersnap cookies, if you're looking for some crunch. 7. The pie can also be refrigerated for up to 2 days; let cool completely first and cover with plastic wrap.
Per Serving: Calories 685; Fat 35g; Sodium 239mg; Carbs 4g; Fiber 2g; Sugar 1g; Protein 26g

Conclusion

In this fast-paced world, everything moves quickly, and your lifestyle needs to match that. For this reason, many cooking appliances are made to make it easier and take less time to make a tasty, healthy, and nutritious meal. Ninja Foodi Multi-Cooker is one of the best appliances for today's fast-paced world because it lets you cook quickly, gives you a healthy meal that meets your dietary needs, and doesn't break the bank. With this appliance, you can quickly cook, bake, slow cook, and steam food.

The Ninja Foodi Multi-Cooker cookbook is the perfect guidance that shows you how to use your device like a pro and gives you quick, easy, and healthy recipes. You can spend your time in the kitchen and do other things simultaneously. You and your family can enjoy a fantastic meal when you're done.

This fantastic cookbook has recipes for food from all over the world. Even if you don't cook often or professionally, it's easy to make food. This fantastic cookbook shows you how to prepare and cook your meal like a pro. So, guys, let's start our Ninja Foodi Multi-Cooker journey and enjoy our fast-forward life with delicious food.

Appendix 1 Measurement Conversion Chart

VOLUME EQUIVALENTS (LIQUID)

US STANDARD	US STANDARD (OUNCES)	METRIC (APPROXIMATE)
2 tablespoons	1 fl.oz	30 mL
¼ cup	2 fl.oz	60 mL
½ cup	4 fl.oz	120 mL
1 cup	8 fl.oz	240 mL
1½ cup	12 fl.oz	355 mL
2 cups or 1 pint	16 fl.oz	475 mL
4 cups or 1 quart	32 fl.oz	1 L
1 gallon	128 fl.oz	4 L

VOLUME EQUIVALENTS (DRY)

US STANDARD	METRIC (APPROXIMATE)
⅛ teaspoon	0.5 mL
¼ teaspoon	1 mL
½ teaspoon	2 mL
¾ teaspoon	4 mL
1 teaspoon	5 mL
1 tablespoon	15 mL
¼ cup	59 mL
½ cup	118 mL
¾ cup	177 mL
1 cup	235 mL
2 cups	475 mL
3 cups	700 mL
4 cups	1 L

TEMPERATURES EQUIVALENTS

FAHRENHEIT(F)	CELSIUS（C) (APPROXIMATE)
225 °F	107 °C
250 °F	120 °C
275 °F	135 °C
300 °F	150 °C
325 °F	160 °C
350 °F	180 °C
375 °F	190 °C
400 °F	205 °C
425 °F	220 °C
450 °F	235 °C
475 °F	245 °C
500 °F	260 °C

WEIGHT EQUIVALENTS

US STANDARD	METRIC (APPROXINATE)
1 ounce	28 g
2 ounces	57 g
5 ounces	142 g
10 ounces	284 g
15 ounces	425 g
16 ounces (1 pound)	455 g
1.5pounds	680 g
2pounds	907 g

Appendix 2 Air Fryer Cooking Chart

Vegetables	Temp (°F)	Time (min)
Asparagus	375	4 to 6
Baked Potatoes	400	35 to 45
Broccoli	400	8 to 10
Brussels Sprouts	350	15 to 18
Butternut Squash (cubed)	375	20 to 25
Carrots	375	15 to 25
Cauliflower	400	10 to 12
Corn on the Cob	390	6
Eggplant	400	15
Green Beans	375	16 to 20
Kale	250	12
Mushrooms	400	5
Peppers	375	8 to 10
Sweet Potatoes (whole)	380	30 to 35
Tomatoes (halved, sliced)	350	10
Zucchini (½-inch sticks)	400	12

Frozen Foods	Temp (°F)	Time (min)
Breaded Shrimp	400	9
Chicken Burger	360	11
Chicken Nudgets	400	10
Corn Dogs	400	7
Curly Fries (1 to 2 lbs.)	400	11 to 14
Fish Sticks (10 oz.)	400	10
French Fries	380	15 to 20
Hash Brown	360	15 to 18
Meatballs	380	6 to 8
Mozzarella Sticks	400	8
Onion Rings (8 oz.)	400	8
Pizza	390	5 to 10
Pot Pie	360	25
Pot Sticks (10 oz.)	400	8
Sausage Rolls	400	15
Spring Rolls	400	15 to 20

Meat and Seafood	Temp (°F)	Time (min)
Bacon	400	5 to 10
Beef Eye Round Roast (4 lbs.)	390	45 to 55
Bone to in Pork Chops	400	4 to 5 per side
Brats	400	8 to 10
Burgers	350	8 to 10
Chicken Breast	375	22 to 23
Chicken Tender	400	14 to 16
Chicken Thigh	400	25
Chicken Wings (2 lbs.)	400	10 to 12
Cod	370	8 to 10
Fillet Mignon (8 oz.)	400	14 to 18
Fish Fillet (0.5 lb., 1-inch)	400	10
Flank Steak(1.5 lbs.)	400	10 to 14
Lobster Tails (4 oz.)	380	5 to 7
Meatballs	400	7 to 10
Meat Loaf	325	35 to 45
Pork Chops	375	12 to 15
Salmon	400	5 to 7
Salmon Fillet (6 oz.)	380	12
Sausage Patties	400	8 to 10
Shrimp	375	8
Steak	400	7 to 14
Tilapia	400	8 to 12
Turkey Breast (3 lbs.)	360	40 to 50
Whole Chicken (6.5 lbs.)	360	75

Desserts	Temp (°F)	Time (min)
Apple Pie	320	30
Brownies	350	17
Churros	360	13
Cookies	350	5
Cupcakes	330	11
Doughnuts	360	5
Roasted Bananas	375	8
Peaches	350	5

Appendix 3 Recipes Index